A Comparative Sociology of World Religions

56 - cvy form means the people are organized religiously,
130   not just the clergi; this helps to shape religion 2
                                                           masses -

theme: rel. in US can be seen as either very
      pluralistic or very homogeneous -

236 - cvys develop where religion relies on
              resources of the people

- some interesting observations, but mainly a
disappointing book, with little systematic comparison
or attempts at explaining variation -

A Comparative Sociology of World Religions

Virtuosos, Priests, and Popular Religion

Stephen Sharot

NEW YORK UNIVERSITY PRESS

New York and London

For Tali and Danny

NEW YORK UNIVERSITY PRESS
New York and London

Library of Congress Cataloging-in-Publication Data
Sharot, Stephen.
A comparative sociology of world religions : virtuosos, priests, and
popular religion / Stephen Sharot.
p.   cm.
Includes bibliographical references and index.
ISBN 0-8147-9804-7 (alk. paper) — ISBN 0-8147-9805-5 (pbk. : alk. paper)
1. Religion and sociology. 2. Religions.   I. Title
BL60 .S529 2001
306.6—dc21   2001000737

New York University Press books are printed on acid-free paper,
and their binding materials are chosen for strength and durability.

Manufactured in the United States of America
10 9 8 7 6 5 4 3 2 1

Contents

Acknowledgments

I began this work many years ago. I knew that I was taking on an ambitious and long-term project, but I nevertheless misjudged by some years the time it would take me. It has been with me so long that I find it difficult to let it go. For such a broad comparative work as this, there is no end to the additions and changes one can make.

Apart from a sabbatical at Cambridge University, I have worked on this book at my home department, the Department of Behavioural Sciences in Ben-Gurion University of the Negev. Most of my colleagues, among whom are psychologists as well as sociologists and anthropologists, have interests somewhat distant from the sociology of religion. I thank them, however, along with our administrative staff, for providing a congenial environment for scholarship and teaching. In particular, I thank Alex Weingrod, who recruited me to the department and has given his warm support over the years. I did test out my perspective and material on many classes of students, and I was encouraged by how the enrollment to my course "Religion and Society" grew as I focused more and more on a comparison of the world religions.

This is a work of synthesis, and I have depended on hundreds of scholars, anthropologists, and historians more than sociologists, many of whom will doubtless be displeased by my use of their work within a macrosociological framework with which they may have little sympathy. I wish to convey, therefore, my thanks and my apologies.

I am grateful for the comments of the anonymous reviewers of this book. They were very useful.

My thanks to Tami, who has lived with this work, for the most part patiently, over the years. I was working on this book during my children's teenage years, and since they left for university, they have occasionally asked, "What about the book?" They have given me much *nahat*, and I dedicate it to them.

PART I

Concepts and Theories

1

World Religions, Elites, and Popular Religion

The period of the emergence of the world religions has been termed an *axial age*, an age in which independent but, in some respects, parallel religious breakthroughs took place in China, India, and the Middle East.[1] Beginning 800 to 600 B.C.E., the period is compressed by some to about seven hundred years, ending around 100 B.C.E., and is extended by others to incorporate the beginnings of Christianity and of Islam.[2] The emergences of the world religions are viewed as "massive facts" of religious history,[3] as synonymous with the rise of "higher civilizations,"[4] and as the "most deep cut"[5] or "big divide"[6] in human history.

Most of the religious breakthroughs involved only small numbers in their initial stages, but the extent to which they came to encompass the rural masses of agrarian or preindustrial societies is a subject of some contention. A common assumption has been that the fundamental changes filtered down to envelop the masses after the world religions' missionizing, military conquests, or adoption by political regimes. Entire populations then came to be identified as Buddhists, Christians, and so forth. Many scholars have argued, however, that in the historical agrarian societies and in contemporary societies with large peasant populations, the religious breakthroughs have remained limited to small circles or elites and have had only minor or superficial effects on the masses, who have remained within a magical or animistic world. The possibility remains that certain world religions penetrated into the religions of the masses far more successfully and extensively than others.

A comparative analysis is required to address such questions, but there has been very little comparison of what are variously called the popular, common, folk, unofficial religious forms, or little traditions, and their relationships with the elite, official forms, or great traditions, of the world religions. In this work I present such a comparative analysis by synthesizing an extensive literature on popular religion, drawing on works by sociologists, anthropologists, and historians. The synthesis is organized within an analytical scheme of religious action that builds principally on the writings of Max Weber, but I extend this scheme by incorporating facets of the analytical perspectives established by Emile Durkheim and Karl Marx.

Weber's writings have provided the foundation for a huge literature of commentary and research, particularly around his thesis of the Protestant ethic and the spirit of capitalism and, more generally, around the effects of the ethics of the world religions on practical, especially economic, behavior. I contend, however, that Weber's action scheme has been underutilized as an analytical framework for the comparison of patterns of religious behavior, both within and across the world religions. In particular, the Weberian framework has been underutilized in the study of popular religion, a burgeoning field that has remained undersystematized and undertheorized.

The following quote from Max Weber provides the starting point for the analytical scheme of religious action that I attempt to reconstruct and develop systematically in chapter 2: "All serious reflection about the ultimate elements of meaningful human conduct is oriented primarily in terms of the categories 'end' and 'means'. We desire something concretely either 'for its own sake' or as a means of achieving something else which is more highly desired."[7] In his writings on religion, Weber focused on salvation as the "highly desired" end, but he emphasized that worldly ends were the most common in the religion of the masses. Thus, Weber emphasized two goals of religious action, what I call the "transformative" and the "thaumaturgical." The transformative refers to a pervasive or radical change in nature, society, and the individual. The thaumaturgical refers to special dispensation and release from personal, familial, or other specific ills.

The framework of religious action employed here is extended to include two additional goals, which I call the "nomic" and the "extrinsic." The nomic, a category drawn from Durkheimian analysis, refers to the maintenance of the existing order and religious foundations of nature, society, and individual being. The extrinsic, a notion drawn from utilitarian as well as Marxist analysis, refers to religious action that is performed for ends conceived by the actors to be mundane in nature, such as individual status and the strengthening of a status quo. Thus, Weber's typology of ideal types of religious action is extended by "Weberizing" the Durkheimian and Marxist traditions.

The framework of religious action is used as an analytical tool to compare elite and popular forms of religion, both their similarities and their differences. In chapter 3 a framework of the "environments" of religious action is worked out in order to account for the variations among the world religions with respect to the interrelationships of elite and popular forms of religion. I distinguish three environments of religious action: religious values, religious organizations, and the socioeconomic and political environments. Again, the writings of Max Weber provide the foundation for this explanatory framework, but with respect to the social-structural factors that affect the interrelationships of elite and popular forms of religion, I strengthen the framework by incorporating a number of Marxian analyses.

Before presenting the analytical framework in detail, it is necessary to clarify concepts that are used throughout this work (world religion, elite religion, popular religion), especially since the use of these concepts has come under considerable criticism.

The Notion of World Religions

Max Weber wrote: "By 'world religions' we understand the five religions or religiously determined systems of life-regulation which have known how to gather multitudes and confessors around them."[8] These religions were Confucianism, Hinduism, Buddhism, Christianity, and Islam. Judaism was also included among Weber's comparisons of world religions "because it contains historical preconditions decisive for understanding Christianity and Islam, and because of its historic and autonomous significance for the development of the modern economic ethic of the Occident."[9] Thus, with the exception of Judaism, Weber's list of world religions followed the simple criterion of size.

Most books on world religions cover the six religions listed by Weber, although some include additional religions such as Zoroastrianism, Sikhism, Jainism, and Taoism. The phenomenally complex cultural configurations and internal diversity of these religions have prompted some scholars to question the meaningfulness of using singular terms such as *Hinduism* and *Christianity*. *Hinduism*, in particular, has been rejected by some as a misnomer; the critics point out that the word was manufactured by Catholic missionaries of the sixteenth century, who sought to impose a false conceptual unity on what was and continues to be an extraordinary diversity of beliefs and practices.[10] Some seek to overcome these objections by the use of plural forms, not only with respect to Hinduism (Hinduisms) but with respect to other traditions as well (Judaisms, Islams). This still assumes common or overlapping characteristics that differentiate the "family" of traditions from others, and if this is the case, there seems little point in abandoning the long-established usage of singular forms. My position is that world religions are composed of what are often loosely linked subtraditions, but the world religions are sufficiently differentiated from one another to justify the established terms and to allow for meaningful comparisons. Certain subtraditions with strong syncretistic orientations have contributed to the fuzziness of the boundaries of the world religions, but in most cases it is possible to identify, say, a Hindu tradition from a Buddhist one, or a Christian tradition from a Jewish one.

Apart from the size of their constituencies and their internal differentiations, the world religions have been distinguished from other religions with respect to their rationalization, transcendentalism, and universalism. In Weber's historical-comparative framework, the process of rationalization did not begin with the world religions, but they did represent significant advances; the developments involved various degrees of "demagification" or "disenchantment" and formulations of coherent, unified worldviews and ethical systems. With respect to the intellectual dimension of rationalization, the multiple representations of supramundane beings and processes in magical religions gave way to a unified point of reference, represented in the monotheistic religions as the creator God and in the Eastern religions by a more impersonal notion, such as the cosmic principle or ground of being. With respect to the ethical dimension of rationalization, the magical taboo systems, in which individuals conformed to a heterogeneous variety of prescriptions and proscriptions because they feared the consequences of taboo acts or magical refractions, gave way to coherent systems of religious ethics that were unambiguously oriented to fixed goals of salvation. Weber was inclined to put greater stress on the ethical dimension because he believed it had the greatest implications for practical, this-worldly behavior, and in his comparisons of the world religions, Weber emphasized that this form of rationalization had gone further in the West than in the East. In general, Weber emphasized the differences among the world religions in the nature of their rationalization rather than on any formal similarity.[11]

Contemporary scholars have tended to describe the religious breakthroughs of the world religions in terms of transcendentalism and universalism, and just as Weber argued that rationalization had gone further in some world religions than in others, contemporary scholars assert that some world religions are more transcendental and/or universalistic than others. Some have questioned whether, according to these definitional qualities, all the religions listed by Weber as world religions should be recognized as such. Others have questioned the very notion of "world religion."

One dimension of transcendentalism is a transcendental vision of the supernatural, the divine sphere, or, a preferred term here, the *supramundane*.[12] Robert Bellah contrasts the "primitive" and "archaic" religions, in which gods and humans are seen to inhabit a single world, with the chasm opened up by the "historic" religions between the supramundane and the mundane.[13] Shmuel Eisenstadt makes a similar contrast between the homologous relations of the human and divine orders in "pagan" societies and the qualitative difference and basic tension between the transcendental and mundane orders of the world religions.[14] Peter Berger also distinguishes transcendental religions from the religions of primitive and archaic societies, but he makes a strong contrast between the radical transcendentalism that emerged in Ancient Judaism and continued in the other "monotheistic" religions, on the one hand, and the Eastern religions, which remained in what he calls the "macrocosm-microcosm" scheme. In the macrocosm-microcosm scheme, gods and humans participate in common institutional complexes, such as kinship institutions; and in religious ceremonies to renew the cosmos, humans cooperate with the gods or become identified with the gods. Ancient Judaism broke this scheme by postulating an absolute differentiation between God and the world, but the developments within the Eastern religions, however important in other respects, remained essentially within the scheme: in China, the societal order continued to be conceived as a reflection of the cosmic order of harmony and equilibrium, and in India, both gods and humans were subject to the cosmic principles of reincarnation.[15]

As the source of all things or as grounds of all existence, such notions as the Tao in Confucianism and the Brahman in Hinduism might be viewed as impersonal conceptions of the divine that are no less transcendent than the personal God of the monotheistic faiths. In Theravada Buddhism, however, there is no such ultimate ground of being. Buddhism does not deny the existence of supramundanes, but it does deny the existence of any supramundane, personal or impersonal, outside the conditional universe of space and time (*samsara*). The transcendentalism of Theravada Buddhism takes the form of the goal of nirvana, whose attainment does not require the intervention of supramundanes.[16]

All world religions have been said to have transcendental aims or soteriologies, and it is this dimension, rather than conceptions of transcendental beings or divine sphere, that may be considered as common, if not restricted, to the world religions. *Soteriology* refers to a form of salvation that cannot be attained within the parameters of mundane existence. As an aspiration that goes beyond the here and now, salvation is normally conceived to be accomplished after death (or after many reincarnations and deaths), although a taste of what is to come is sometimes believed to be attainable prior to death. Notions of salvation are to be found in tribal and archaic religions, but in contrast with the world religions, they tend to envisage salvation in terms of physical continuity, and their other worlds or locations of salvation tend to be more closely modeled on the mundane world and human society.[17] The promises held out by world religions are commonly said to be indescribable or ineffable, although their heavens have often been described in some detail and in ways that resemble this-worldly rewards.[18]

In the attempt to formulate the religious transformation represented by the world religions, some scholars have put greater emphasis on the religious behaviors thought appropriate to achieve salvation than on the state of salvation itself. Gananath Obeyesekere writes that, in those primitive religions where there are conceptions of salvation, compensation in the other world is not seen to depend on conformity to a system of moral laws or ethical norms governing behavior in this world. Violations of the moral code in primitive societies are punished by human rather than nonhuman agencies, and in those cases where supramundanes punish the breaking of taboos, they are believed to cause misfortune to the offender in this world rather than the next. In some primitive religions, the breaking of taboos is believed to be punished in the next world, but taboo violation involves offenses against the moral code only coincidentally, and breaches of ethical tenets are, for the most part, independent of religion. The ethicalization of the religious life in the world religions meant that salvation became dependent on ethical behavior in this life, and this involved the emergence of notions of religious merit, sin, and the division of another world (or worlds) into specialized places of reward and punishment.[19]

One aspect of ethical systematization in the world religions is the extension of ethical behavior beyond ascriptive social categories and particularistic social relations; ethical behavior is appropriate not only within the family, the local community, or other particular social units but also outside them. This is related to what may be considered another dimension of transcendentalism of the world religions: the transcendence of social boundaries, whether of groups, communities, nations, or states. It is this "universalism" that many have identified as central to the notion of world religion. Some world religions, however, appear to be more universalistic than others. Buddhism, Christianity, and Islam have generally been considered the most universalistic in their inclusion of different ethnic groups and their accommodation to a wide variety of social structures. Confucianism, in contrast, has been tied to Chinese culture; Judaism has been intricately linked to the Jewish people; and Hinduism has been anchored in a particular social system, the caste system.

Confucianism, Judaism, and Hinduism have not been closed or thoroughly particularistic religions. Confucianism, together with Taoism, was adopted in part by kingdoms on China's borders and by Japan, where the Chinese religions syncretized with other religions including Buddhism and Shinto. Judaism has been a missionary religion in the past, and although it has become identified with an ascriptively defined people, it has remained open to converts, most of whom have assimilated into the Jewish people. The spread of Hinduism through the Hinduization of non-Hindu tribes and other peoples, including former adherents of other world religions, has generally involved incorporation into the all-pervasive caste system, which has traditionally been more important than any personal assent or conversion to a set of beliefs and practices. Only during the nineteenth century did Hinduism begin to proselytize by universalizing its message; missionary activity began among the non-Hindus in India and has since become worldwide.

Doubts about Confucianism, Judaism, and Hinduism as truly world religions have been expressed because of their comparatively limited diffusion over cultural, ethnic, or social-structural boundaries, but the characterization of a world religion as an entity that crosses societal boundaries has led to a questioning of the very notion of world religion. The tendency in religious studies has been to treat the world religions as essential entities that exist independent of the social groups who identify with them. This usage has been questioned by Timothy Fitzgerald, who writes that, although different groups may refer to their religion by a common name (Christianity, Islam, etc.), we are likely to find the groups have very different understandings of the religion's contents.

The sociologist would be the first to agree with Fitzgerald when he writes that a world religion is not an abstraction contained in its texts or an essential entity that is only contingently associated with particular social groups. An analytical distinction between a "societal-bound religion," such as Nuer religion or Dinka religion, and a world religion can be made only in a qualified sense. The difference is not that the world religion is an empirical object of study that transcends social groups but rather that group carriers of a world religion espouse a tradition that they claim is available to people who belong to societies and cultures other than their own.[20]

As has been indicated, the ideology of universalism is a variable among the religions that have been designated as "world religions," but even in the most universalistic of these religions, the question remains of whether universalism has usually been confined to the religions' elites. The question of differences between elites and masses may be asked with respect to all three dimensions of transcendence: To what extent, if at all, have the masses, particularly the peasant masses of agrarian societies, adopted transcendental visions of the supramundane, focused their religious concerns on transcendental aims, and transcended in their religious behavior and identities their primordial social ties and local communities? Many of the scholars who portray the transcendentalism of the world religions as a phenomenal break in history admit that, within the societies encompassed by the world religions, monistic visions continued; religious activities continued to be directed to the achievement of worldly goals; and religious social organization and identities remained embedded in primordial units and local communities. An analysis of the tensions and interrelationships of divergent tendencies within the societies covered by the world religions, between transcendentalism and monism, soteriological and mundane goals, community and transcommunity, requires that the social carriers and institutional contexts of these tendencies be identified. A social distinction relevant to such an analysis is that between religious elites and the lay masses.

Elites and Masses

Two general definitions of elite have been made by sociologists. The first defines an elite as composed of those who are recognized as having reached the highest level in a particular branch of activity. The second defines an elite as composed of those who occupy the highest positions of a social organization that has an internal authority structure.[21] When applied to the field of religion, a distinction can be made between those who are recognized as exemplifying the highest values of the religion and those who occupy the highest positions of formal authority in religious organizations or institutions. As in other branches of activity, there may be an overlap of the people found in the two types of elite, but the overlaps are unlikely to be complete, and the relationships between them constitute an important area of investigation.

The two general definitions of elite parallel Max Weber's distinction between religious virtuosos and hierocracy. Weber contrasted virtuoso and mass religiousness by pointing to the recognition, evident in all world religious contexts, that humans are differently qualified in religious ways and that few are capable of seeking the sacred values in a perfect form.[22] The examples of virtuoso religious observation given by Weber are various, but Weber gave particular attention to monks, who have been the major source of saints in a number of world religions.[23] Virtuosos are distinguished from those who hold high positions of authority in hierocratic organizations that seek to monopolize the distribution of religious benefits within societies.[24] The latter have been termed *clerics* or the *clerisy* by some sociologists.

Weber wrote that hierocratic organizations struggle against the autonomous development of virtuoso religion because it is seen as a challenge to the general accessibility to sacred values provided by the organizations. In the case of hierocratic organizations called churches, in which charisma is separated from the person, the struggle with virtuoso religion is one between office charisma and personal charisma. Rather than deny the legitimacy of all virtuoso religiousness, hierocratic organizations have admitted that full adherence to the religion's highest ideals is an extraordinary achievement that can be channeled for the benefit of the majority, who lack the qualifications or ability to achieve such heights. Thus, virtuoso religion, particularly as organized in monastic organizations, has been transformed into an instrument of hierocratic control, even though tensions often persist between hierocrats and virtuosos.[25]

The societies encompassed by the world religions differ in the degrees of differentiation or overlap between virtuosos and hierocratic elites. They also differ in the degrees of differentiation of the religious elites from other elites, of which the political is the most significant for religious elites, and from the upper class, stratum, or caste. Whatever the level of differentiation and autonomy of a religious elite, a distinction can be made between its patterns of religious action and those of the non-elite, or the masses. Depending on which of the two usages of elite is applied, the masses are either the nonvirtuosos or those who do not occupy high positions in the religious organizations or institutions.

The vast majority of the religious nonelite are likely to be laypeople; there may, however, be lay virtuosos (nonclerics), and clerics occupying low positions in religious organizations who may be categorized as part of the non-elite. There is likely to be considerable differentiation among the masses or non-elite in the extent to which their religious beliefs and practices differ from or are shared with the religious elite. Weber suggests, for example, that the relatively rational economic lifestyle of the European urban bourgeoisie in the Middle Ages predisposed them, to a greater extent than the agrarian strata of feudal nobles and peasants, to support the hierocracy and adopt their religious orientations.[26] Secular feudal powers frequently opposed a hierocracy over political and economic interests, but common social background could bring the religious orientations of the political elite and upper strata closer to the religious elite and distance them from the religion of the peasants.

The popular religions dealt with in this work are primarily those of peasants. The vast majority of the populations of the historical agrarian societies described in following chapters (late imperial China, medieval and early modern Europe) were peasants. The ruling elites of the agrarian or preindustrial societies—the kings, their courts and administrators, and the aristocracies—typically made up less than 2 percent of the population, and the urban trading and artisan stratum rarely brought the non-food-producing strata to more than 10 percent. In the chapters that draw on contemporary anthropological rather than historical studies (Hinduism in India, Theravada Buddhism in Southeast Asia), the focus remains on rural populations, many of whom are peasants. These peasant communities provide the principal examples in our analysis of popular religion, and although the religious differences between peasants and other lay strata may warrant on occasion references to aristocratic and bourgeois (or urban) religion, the emphasis here is on those characteristics of popular religion that are shared by the lay masses. The major comparison, then, is between the religion of religious elites (henceforth *elite religion*) and the religion of lay, primarily peasant masses (henceforth *popular religion*).

Elite Religion and Popular Religion

A comparison of elite and popular religions requires some defense against the criticisms that have been made of the use of these terms, as well as of similar or overlapping concepts such as great and little traditions and official and unofficial religions. One objection to these distinctions has been that they give the impression of the religions of the learned and the masses as fixed and uniform and as divided in a clear-cut fashion into separate compartments, each impervious to the influence of the other. The dichotomization is seen to lead to caricatured portrayals of popular religion as magic, oriented solely to practical and materialistic ends, without any ethical, philosophical, or soteriological concerns. A no-less-caricatured portrayal of the religious elite may be implied, as concerned solely with the spiritual, distant from worldly matters. These depictions distort the complexity of people's religious beliefs and practices and ignore the historically dynamic and complex relationships among social groups and strata that result in religious overlaps and integrations.[27] Where an influence of one group on another is postulated, it is often presumed to be in a downward direction, from the learned to the unlearned, with the laity, especially the peasants, regarded as passive receptacles. In fact, peasants were often highly innovative in their religious practices.[28]

A "two-tier" model that has dynamic aspects and acknowledges the influence of the masses on the religious elite has also been criticized. This model has been traced back to David Hume, who argued that, although theism represented a coherent, rational view of the universe, the intellectual limitations of the human mind made it a precarious vision. Only the enlightened few were able to abstract general principles from their immediate environment and deduce the existence of a Supreme Being from the multiforms of the visible world. It proved difficult for the intellectual elite to preserve the purity of their religion from the superstitious contaminations of the masses, and they capitulated to the demands of the vulgar by allowing pagan practices into Christianity. In criticisms similar to those made of the great and little traditions distinction in discussions on Hinduism and Buddhism, this model is faulted for presenting popular religion as a deviation from a "higher religion," a "pure" Christianity that is assumed to be represented in the expressions of theologians and church leaders. The religion of the masses, who were unable to acquire the understandings and complex formulations of the enlightened elite, is presented as uniform and continuous.[29]

Writers who wish to represent popular religion as a class phenomenon object when the term is used to gloss over class divisions of society.[30] Others argue, however, that popular religion in agrarian societies could be said to encompass almost everyone, kings as well as peasants and clergy as well as laypeople.[31] Karen Louise Jolly writes that, with respect to early medieval England, it is appropriate to use the term *popular religion* to refer to the beliefs and practices shared by almost all the population. She does, however, point to a process of mutual accommodation and assimilation between popular religion and formal religion, which refers to the clerical hierarchy and its councils as well as the doctrines and practices formulated by them.[32] This conflates cultural constructions and social groups, a conflation that is a source of many of the problems that have arisen in the attempts by anthropologists and historians to provide conceptual distinctions to make sense of the complex nature of religious cultures.[33]

The use of the terms *elite religion* and *popular religion* in this work refers to the patterns of religious action of social collectivities (religious elites and lay, especially peasant, masses). Although sociological theories can provide us with hypotheses regarding their differences, no attempt is made to provide an a priori characterization of their religious content. Popular religion is not viewed as an inferior version of an elite archetype, nor is it presumed to be cut off from elite religion or necessarily opposed to it. The extent to which the religion of the elites and the religion of peasants overlap, differ, and conflict, and the extent to which these dimensions vary from society to society, are subject to empirical investigations, comparisons, and explanations.

Overlapping Distinctions

The distinction between elite and popular religion overlaps, but is not identical with, the distinctions that have been made between great and little traditions and between official and unofficial religion. Each distinction has been associated with a particular discipline and the analyses of particular religious cultures. The great/little traditions distinction was developed principally within anthropology and was applied most extensively in studies of Hinduism and Buddhism. After considerable criticism of the usage within anthropology it has lost favor, but when used in a critical way, it has been shown to have heuristic value. The official/unofficial distinction is a common one used by social historians of Christianity, especially in works on the Middle Ages and early modern periods.

Although the elite/popular distinction is the most prominent one in this work, I occasionally draw on the great/little and official/unofficial distinctions for special purposes. By using the three terms *elite religion, great tradition,* and *official religion,* I am able to distinguish religion as practiced, religion as proclaimed, and religion as prescribed.

The great tradition is understood here to refer to those elements of the religious cultural system that religious elites present and interpret as constituting the authentic religious tradition. These are likely to include myths, doctrines, laws, and rituals that, according to the religious elites, are found in the religious texts containing the essence or core of their religious traditions. Religious elites promote great traditions as transcending time and the social divisions within the religious civilizations that they claim to represent, but as a great tradition is constructed by members of the elites in specific places and periods, its content can vary over locations and times. Official religion may be defined as those religious elements that the religious elite allow as justified or legitimate within the boundaries of the religion they claim to represent. These conceptual formulations allow us to envisage possible divergences between a great tradition, which is promoted by the religious elite, an official religion, which is allowed or tolerated by the religious elite, and an elite religion, which includes all the religious components that are believed in and practiced by the religious elite.

By using the three terms *popular religion, little tradition,* and *unofficial religion,* I am able to distinguish the overall complex of religion as practiced by the masses from that part which represents local adaptations of the great tradition and from that part which exists despite of (and perhaps sometimes because of) the proscriptions of the elite. The little tradition may be defined as the interpretations, adaptations, and uses of the great tradition that are made by groups of the religious non-elite in accord with their local and community concerns. There are many little traditions (popular Catholicisms, popular Buddhisms, etc.) in the sense that there are many different local formulations of the themes and symbols of a particular great tradition. The elements of the local tradition exist side by side or are combined with religious elements that have no connection with the relevant great tradition, such as water spirits or fairies in Christian societies. Popular religion, or the religion of the non-elite, is normally constituted of the little tradition formulations together with other elements that appear unrelated to the elites' formulations of the world religion.

An unofficial religion contains all those beliefs and practices of popular religion that are not allowed or recognized as legitimate by the elite. It is likely to include elements in a popular religion that are not part of little tradition adaptations of the great tradition—for instance, supramundanes, such as elves in Christianity, that are not part of the official pantheon—and also certain elements of the little tradition, such as attempts made to coerce supramundanes from the official pantheon. The contents of an unofficial religion are cultural constructs of the non-elite, but the boundary separating the official from the unofficial is a construct of an elite. The boundaries are often shifting and unclear: what was allowed by an elite at one time is condemned at another time, and certain practices disallowed by persons occupying the higher positions of a religious organization may be tolerated by persons occupying lower positions.

Bases of Religious Differences between Elites and Masses

This work addresses the interrelationships as much as the differences between elite and popular forms of religion. The differences, however, in the symbolic and material resources and life contexts of religious elites and peasants would lead us to expect that in all agrarian societies we will find substantial differences between elite religion and popular religion. One symbolic resource that has been an important locus of inequality in agrarian societies is literacy.

The development of literacy was integrally linked to the spread of world religions; in contrast with nonliterate religions, whose boundaries are identical with the boundaries of the societies in which they are embedded, the written word can be said to have created and defined the boundaries of literate religions. Sacred writings provide a common measuring stick of the truth, a common reference for the performance of ritual, and a common foundation for identity across all societal and political boundaries.[34] Yet, although literacy rates in agrarian societies have varied considerably, up to recent times the masses have usually been illiterate, and illiteracy rates remain high today in many of the poorer countries. Even where laypeople have some literacy, they are unlikely to be able to understand the sacred languages (Sanskrit, Pali, Latin) that have been the languages of the canons and official ceremonies.

A number of French historians of medieval and early modern Christianity have emphasized literacy in their portrayal of a gulf between a rationalized ecclesiastical culture and a popular animistic cosmos. Jean-Claude Schmitt, for example, maintained that there were two opposing, mutually hostile cultures in feudal society: the literate, Latinate culture of the clergy and the oral, vernacular culture of laypeople who, even at the highest levels of society, knew no Latin and had therefore no direct access to the scriptures.[35]

Literacy may have played a less important role in accounting for differences within Hinduism and Buddhism, but even with respect to medieval Europe it has been argued that the distinction between a literal and an oral culture has been overdrawn. It should not be assumed that the oral discourse of the illiterate majority was unaffected by the realm of communications governed by texts or that the religious elite lived in a world of books.[36]

Whereas the members of religious elites have used the sacred languages to communicate across vernacular linguistic barriers, the masses have been divided into many linguistic collectivities, often within single countries and regions. Apart from their use of a common language, the development of translocal cultures by elites has been possible because elites have been subject to fewer restrictions than peasants with respect to residence and travel. The peasant masses have commonly been tied by laws and the institution of serfdom to villages and estates, and most of their social contacts have been restricted to the other residents of their villages, which are largely self-sufficient and worlds unto themselves. Peasants in contemporary societies are likely to be influenced by geographically extensive markets, modern forms of communication, and the culture of the wider, including the global, society; but in a great many cases, the village or local rural community remains the major context of social interaction and identity.

In accord with the Durkheimian perspective on religion, we would expect the religion of peasants to be an integral part of their communities, built on local social networks and local customs, celebrating and legitimizing what is held in common. As long as the locus of life is the community, translocal elites might, to some degree, regulate and circumscribe local religion, but they are unlikely to be able to replace it.[37]

Inequality in material conditions is also likely to have produced differences in religion between elites and peasants. Elites could aspire to some level of comfort and security, but poverty and chronic insecurity have been the inevitable conditions of the masses in agrarian societies. Historians of popular religion in Europe during the medieval and early modern periods have argued that popular religion provided compensation or relief from suffering, and that this is to be expected when hunger, disease, plague, attacks from animals and humans, and various kinds of misfortune were all part of everyday life. In the absence of preventive health measures or effective therapies, frequent pain and an early death were the lot of the majority.[38] That such conditions colored religious beliefs can be acknowledged without accepting the more deterministic formulations of the effects of physical deprivation, but such an acknowledgment does not necessarily support the clear division, drawn by many of the historians, between popular religion and elite Christianity. From the perspective of most modern Westerners, the environment of all strata in the medieval and early period was intensely insecure; the higher strata may have been less concerned with food and shelter, but they could hardly have been less fearful of illness, plague, murderous attacks, and an early death.

Religion as compensation for sufferings and deprivation, especially among lower classes and strata, was one facet in the writings on religion of Karl Marx and Max Weber. Marx's often-quoted characterization of religion would appear especially appropriate to the miserable existence of most peasants: religion is "the sigh of the oppressed creature, the heart of a heartless world, [and] the spirit of a spiritless situation."[39] Writing on India, Marx stated that the low level of production and the narrow social relations characteristic of Indian villages produced a primitive worship of nature, the adoration of animals, and animal sacrifice.[40]

Max Weber provided a more comprehensive and systematic analysis than Marx of the characteristic religious features of social categories when he wrote of the "elective affinities" between general religious orientations (especially soteriological modes) and social carriers. He distinguished between two types of social "carriers" of the world religions: carriers such as classes and status groups, whose characteristics had been formed within the stratification system of the society, and carriers who are elites of the religious organizations or hierocracies of the society. The development of intellectualism by priests and monks was important in religious developments in both East and West, but with respect to social strata, Weber emphasized the difference between the aristocratic origin of religious intellectuals in the East and the pariah and petit-bourgeois intellectualism that appeared in the Middle East and West.[41] The one class or status group that, according to Weber, was never a leading carrier of a world religion was the peasantry. Strongly tied to nature and dependent on organic processes, the religion of the peasantry remained one of magic, animism, and ritualism.[42]

One has, therefore, good reasons to expect the religions of elites and masses to differ. There has been a tendency to simplify the differences by presenting them in terms of religion, which displays great variety, and magic, which has a universal sameness. Few scholars would go so far as to suggest that the masses have been uninfluenced by religious elites, and many have assumed that the masses have incorporated, at a less intellectual level, the distinctive notions that are to be found in the literature of each world religion. It should not be assumed, however, that differences among popular religions are simply a reflection of differences among elite religions. The interrelationships of masses and religious elites are likely to be complex, and not only are influences likely to move from masses to elite as well as from elite to masses, but also the processes of diffusion from one to another are likely to involve adaptations, change, and transformations.

Having indicated the reasons elite and popular forms of religion are likely to differ in all class-divided societies with large peasant populations, I now address the analytical framework for comparison of the relationships between elite and popular forms within the different world religious contexts.

2

Religious Action
A Weberian Model

The comparative questions asked in this work require a conceptual framework that will be sensitive to differences across the world religions and between elites and masses within each religion but that will also be sufficiently broad to avoid one becoming lost in a multitude of differences and details. Most works in comparative religion have attempted to make sense of the complexity by breaking up each religion into several dimensions, such as beliefs, doctrines, myths, rituals, mysticism, and institutions. Many sociologists have followed such distinctions, but this has had the disadvantage of conceptualizing religious behavior in terms of dimensions that differ from the dimensions used in the analysis of nonreligious behavior. An alternative is to treat religious behavior as one form of action and to distinguish its dimensions in line with the dimensions of any action: goals, means, and conditions. This was the framework introduced by Max Weber, and considering the enormous influence that Weber's works have had on sociology, it is surprising how few sociologists have adopted religious action as a framework.

Max Weber: The Understanding and Dimensions of Religious Action

Following Max Weber's discussion of action, the aim here is an "interpretative understanding" and "causal explanation"[1] of religious action. As in other forms of social action, actors in religious action attach subjective meanings to their behavior and take into account the behavior of others. There are many schema and theories of action, but their central components are in all important respects identical to those of Weber: the actor, who may be a person or collectivity; ends; means; and conditions. The ends, means, and conditions are understood here from the subjective viewpoint of the actors. The end is the future state of affairs toward which actors understand their action to be oriented. The means are those objects, persons, groups, or processes that actors understand can be used or manipulated in the realization of their ends. The conditions are those objects, persons, groups, or processes that actors understand cannot be used or manipulated but that must be taken into account or addressed.

The first task is to distinguish what is particular to the ends, means, and conditions of religious action that will make the term *religious* appropriate. Weber did not define a special category of "religious action," but his typology of four ideal types of social action provides some clues of the directions to follow in establishing such a category.[2] The first type, *zweckrational*, instrumentally or purposively rational social action, appears to have the least applicability to religious action. No end is sacred; every end competes with others in terms of their relative costs, benefits, and secondary consequences. The ends are of a this-worldly nature, and actions of this type are most likely to be found in the modern economic sphere. A clear distinction can be made between means and ends (this type is sometimes translated as means-ends rationality), and actors will apply what they consider the most efficient means in order to achieve a given end.

The second type, *wertrational*, encompasses important types of religious action, but Weber's formulation presents some ambiguity. In one formulation, no meaningful distinction exists between means and ends; action is performed as a value "for its own sake," without reference to its consequences. A religious commandment or a good deed, for example, might be performed by actors who feel that they could not possibly act in another way. Weber implies, however, that means and ends can also be distinguished in this type as long as the end is regarded as absolute, to be pursued whatever the costs and regardless of the chances of success. Salvation in the world religions provides a clear example of an absolute end. It is typically believed that only certain means will achieve an absolute end, and in the case of salvation, religions stipulate particular paths as the only means of redemption. Some religions present a number of means to salvation that complement each other, and in such cases actors may consider them in terms of their relative importance or believe them to vary in appropriateness according to context.

The third and fourth types of social action, the traditional and affectual, are both on the borderline of action because they are not meaningfully oriented in terms of conscious means and ends. Traditional action in the sense of ingrained habit, which is un-self-conscious and unreflective, encompasses, according to Weber, a large part of everyday action. The type of religious action often characterized in this manner is stereotyped ritualism, performed in an unthinking and automatic fashion. It is often difficult to know whether such ritualism is as unreflective to the actor as it appears to the observer, and it is possible that the actor has a semiconscious or latent awareness of the ends that can become conscious or manifest in particular circumstances. Traditional action is meaningful in the value-rational sense when the maintenance of the tradition becomes an absolute goal. Affectual or emotional action is nonmeaningful when it is an unmediated expression of inner drives or impulses, but affective states or emotional tension can become subject to a means-end schema when consciously expressed or channeled through, for example, religious rituals.

Religious action would appear to be included in at least three types of social action (*wertrational*, traditional, and affectual), but nonreligious action is also encompassed within these categories, and the framework does not provide us with a clear notion of religious action. Weber did not provide a definition of *religion*, but a characterization of religious action in terms of goals, means, and conditions can be gleaned from his writings. It is clear that religious action cannot be delineated by its ends alone; although some ends are particular to religious action, others are shared with non-religious forms of social action.

Weber's discussion of the ends of religious action can be systematized by reference to two dimensions: first, by the degree to which the end or future state of affairs is conceived as transformative of, or a change within, the conditions or states of being. Salvation is the prime example of a general or encompassing transformation. At the other end of the scale are those ends, such as the cure of an illness or the inducement of rain, that are conceived as special dispensations or thaumaturgies within the existing conditions or states of being.

The second dimension is the degree to which the end is conceived as this-worldly or as other-worldly. Most thaumaturgies have a clearly this-worldly character, but salvation can take both other-worldly and this-worldly forms. In this-worldly salvation, people believe they will be redeemed from economic and political oppression and suffering, and they expect to become politically dominant or attain social or religious prestige. Examples include messianic kingdoms and rebirth into a higher state. In other-worldly forms of salvation, people believe they will be freed from the physical, psychological, and social sufferings of terrestrial life, liberated from the transitoriness of life as such, or redeemed from individual imperfections such as sin and earthly ignorance. Examples include a state of nonbeing, union with a divinity, and permanent bliss in a heaven.[3]

Weber wrote extensively on types and paths of salvation, but he emphasized that, even in the most other-worldly religions, most people were predominantly concerned with obtaining advantages and combating evils in this world.[4] The this-worldly, thaumaturgical goals of religious action cannot be placed firmly in either the *zweckrational* or the *wertrational* type of action; the cure of an illness, for example, is not weighed with other goals in terms of relative costs and benefits, but neither is it an absolute goal in the sense that it may be pursued without regard for the chances of success. Such goals are shared with nonreligious forms of action, and the distinctiveness of religious action has to be sought in two other overlapping components of action: (1) the particular categories of actors with whom actors believe they interact and (2) the special means that are used to achieve the goals.

Actors in religious action attribute extraordinary powers to other actors, such as spirits, magicians, demons, and gods, and it is the ordering of relations of "supernatural" powers to men that constitutes the realm of religious behavior.[5] Supramundane forces differ in the extent to which they are conceived naturalistically—as identified with or residing in natural objects, artifacts, animals, or persons—or abstractly—as being symbolized by various phenomena. They differ also in the extent to which they are conceived in an impersonal idiom, such as fate and cosmic order, or in a personal idiom, such as anthropomorphic forms. Other differentiations include the supramundanes' spatial status (specific location or spatially diffuse and infinite), temporal status (mortal or immortal), moral status (ethical or non-ethical), functional range (limited or universal), and social references (household, kin, city, nation, etc.).[6]

Supramundanes may be part of the goal of religious action, such as the goal of self-deification or absolute union with the divinity, and they are integral to the conditions and means of religious action. Weber distinguished three methods by which actors believe they can influence supramundanes in order to achieve their goals: by coercion or manipulation; by supplication and entreaty through gifts, service, and sacrifice; and by obedience to the religious law.[7] This was one way by which Weber distinguished between magic and religion: the first method was magical and the second and third were religious. Weber also distinguished magic and religion according to goals: magic was directed to "rational," this-worldly, dispensational goals, and religion was concerned with "irrational" salvation.[8]

A Defense of the Action Perspective

The schema of religious action adapted from Weber's writings and presented above distinguishes two broad categories of goals, soteriological and thaumaturgical, and a variety of conditions and means considered relevant to their achievement, including the purported characteristics of supramundanes and the relationships that humans enter into with them. The conceptual framework of religious action can be expanded on and made more comprehensive by drawing on the works of other sociologists and anthropologists, but because Weber's writings provide the most important source, it is appropriate at this point to defend the religious action perspective from possible criticisms.

My focus is on actions that people perform because they believe they will achieve a consequence or consequences that they desire. The concern is with subjective meanings of instrumental action rather than intersubjective meanings of communicative action. Of relevance here is the distinction made by Colin Campbell between action theory, which stresses the actor's definition of the situation, and social action theory, which stresses how actors understand the conduct of others. Campbell argues that most contemporary sociologists have attended little to how meanings inform the actions of individuals and have focused instead on how individuals perceive the actions of others as meaningful. The dominant paradigm has become that of communicative action or symbolic, expressive action designed to convey meanings from one individual to another, and this has meant that the fundamental instrumental nature of most actions has been ignored. Campbell acknowledges that most actions include both instrumental and expressive components, but he asserts that the vast majority of human actions are instrumental, designed primarily to achieve a change in the actors' state of being or relationship with their environment.[9]

The instrumental component of action is emphasized in this work, and communicative acts are incorporated into the framework insofar as they serve as means to an end that goes further than the intent of communication or the conveyance of information to another. Of special concern are culturally prescribed patterns of communication with supra-mundanes. Successful communication with supramundanes, which are culturally significant rather than socially significant others, is often understood to require other humans as intermediaries with whom communication becomes another link in the means-end chain.

Expressive and symbolic processes have been central in the interpretation of religion, and people may be disinclined to accept that the instrumental component is no less important in religious action than in other fields of activity. One argument against adopting a means-end schema in the study of religion is that it involves accepting the unsuitable criterion of "rationality" as a standard in analyzing religious action. It is true that Weber emphasized the importance of zweckrational action and that this type is sometimes translated as "means-end rationality," but the *zweckrational* is only one type of action where the means-end schema is appropriate. As already noted, although one formulation of *wertrational* action collapses the distinction between means and ends, another formulation uses it: the end is absolute and there are appropriate means toward it, even though, unlike the *zweckrational*, they are not normally based on the criteria of efficiency and relative costs. The relationship between means and end in *wertrational* action may be regarded as an essential one, making impossible the application of other means, but this does not invalidate the distinction. Nor is the schema invalidated by the observation that, in many cases, the relationship between means and end is not conceived by actors as that of cause and effect but rather as a symbolic one.

Another possible objection to the application of the means-end schema in the analysis of religion is that much of religious behavior is "traditional" in the sense of habit or routine and is carried out without actors having any end in mind. Actors may carry out prescribed rituals while thinking about something quite different, or perhaps without thinking of anything in particular. The "automatic" or "mechanical" performance of ritual has been raised in religious polemics by those who portray their own religion as ethical and other religions as "ritualistic." The framework of religious action does not, however, require that every single religious act be accompanied by subjective meanings that relate conduct to its "appropriate" end. As Campbell notes with respect to habitual action in general, although a particular performance of an action may appear to be unaccompanied by subjective meaning, it is likely to have been so accompanied in past performances, especially when the actor learned the action.[10]

It is not assumed here that the delineation of the goals, conditions, and means of religious actions provide us with explanations in the sense of the motives or causes of the actions. The ends of religious action that are stated by actors or that are conventionally understood as such within a religious community are not necessarily the only motives, the principal motives, or even among the motives of the action. For example, although particular Catholics may say they are participating in the ritual of the mass as part of their endeavors to achieve salvation, their actual motive may be to impress on others their religious piety and thereby gain recognition and status in the community. Actors may perform a religious action simply because other members of the community expect it of them and because failure to perform it may invite sanctions. Of course, religious action motivated by status seeking or simple conformity can still be said to be goal directed, but the relative importance of such motives in any particular group or community is difficult to discover, especially when actors do not wish to acknowledge them or are unaware of them. A motivation such as the desire to conform is so common that it is not likely to help in the delineation or explanation of differences in religious actions among collectivities and societies.

In some cases actors may draw on conventionally understood goals of religious actions in order to justify or legitimize their participation in the action, whereas their motivation is quite different. Reference to a goal as justification does not, however, necessarily mean that it is not a motive; it may be used as justification because it was an important motive. In many cases the stated objects of religious action are believed by actors to be their motives, are actually among the motives, or were among the motives in past performances of the actions. It must be admitted, however, that when a goal is also a motive, this does not establish how the accomplishment of the action was made possible. Campbell emphasizes the importance of emotion, effort, and will in the accomplishment of action and criticizes theorists of social action for their failure to consider such factors. His comment that the problem is not how an actor goes about getting something done, because the means are likely to be as prescribed as the goals,[11] is particularly apposite with respect to religious action.

The problem of how individuals will actions into being even when there is no choice over means or ends is not tackled in this work. The integration of such factors as effort and will into a model of religious action, involving the linking of psychology and sociology, is an ambitious task, but it is a reasonable assumption that an element such as effort will be related to the relative importance of particular goals. For example, a concern to avoid hellfire may induce considerable effort to perform those acts understood to have the effect of avoiding such an afterlife.

Whether or not the reasons actors give for their religious actions are among their motivations, it is of interest to investigate why some actors and collectivities give certain reasons and other actors and collectivities report different ones. The concern of this work is to distinguish collective actors and collectivities, not so much in terms of different motives but in terms of the ends they pursue, the relative importance they put on those ends, and the differences in the envisaged conditions and means undertaken to attain those ends.

Widening the Model of Religious Action

Distinctions similar to the one we have made between transformative and thaumaturgical goals have been made by various scholars. David Mandelbaum, an anthropologist, distinguished between "transcendental" and "pragmatic" complexes that have separate practitioners (priests as distinct from curers, exorcists, and shamans), supramundanes (high gods as distinct from local spirits), and ritual orientations (supplication as distinct from mechanical and coercive techniques). Mandelbaum noted that the complexes often overlap and mutually reinforce each other: learned Brahman priests sometimes give pragmatic services; a local god may gradually be endowed with transcendental attributes; and Buddhist verses may be chanted in the course of exorcising goblins. Nevertheless, many religious cultures differentiate between a pragmatic complex, which deals with the immediate, specific, and personal, and a transcendental complex, which is timeless, general, and societal. We note that Mandelbaum's "transcendental" category includes elements that confirm the social order, such as rites of passage and rites for the long-term welfare of the society, and elements that transcend that order, such as the survival of the soul after death.[12] This collapses two quite different types of goals.

Bryan Wilson, a sociologist, distinguishes between "spiritual" conceptions of salvation, such as nirvana and God's kingdom, and "particularistic" conceptions of salvation, such as temporal well-being and protection from evil spirits. He writes that, although the first concern of the "higher" religions is spiritual salvation, none ignore the more proximate, personal, or local ideas of salvation.[13] Steven Collins states that Wilson's use of the term *salvation* across the whole spectrum obscures the qualitative difference at the "spiritual" end, where salvation is final;[14] and in other writings, Wilson does use the term *thaumaturgical* as an alternative to "particularistic salvation."[15] An important point Wilson makes with respect to spiritual salvation is that, although the monotheistic religions and Buddhism speak to the effort and choices that individuals have to make, people do not conceive of attaining salvation in isolation. The operative conception of salvation has a communal nature; humans "necessarily envisage the condition of salvation as something that might be attained, or which is even contained within, the ideal community life."[16]

Wilson's emphasis on the community is linked more to the sociology of Emile Durkheim than to that of Max Weber, and although Durkheim's work has rarely been considered within an action framework, I believe the Weberian model can usefully be extended by incorporating elements from Durkheim. The goals and paths of salvation to which Weber gave most attention were those formulated in terms of individual, rather than collective, action, and we find little reflection in his work on collective religious action that affirms the social order.[17] Durkheim's work, in contrast, presents an analysis of rituals that have the purpose of affirming or renewing the natural and social order.

Emile Durkheim: Functions and Goals

In his classic work on religion, *The Elementary Forms of the Religious Life*, Durkheim combined what have been come to be called the "symbolist" and the "functionalist" perspectives on religion. The symbolist analysis in the first half of the book was the most removed from the framework of religious action; the focus was on religious symbols as expressions of society as a moral force and unity. The framework of Durkheim's interpretation of rituals in the second half of the book was functionalist rather than employing an action perspective, but his analysis pointed to important patterns of religious action, particularly with respect to goals and patterns of communication with supramundane forces, that complement Weber's writings.

Unlike Weber, Durkheim gave little attention to either the absolute goal of salvation, which involves a transcendence of the natural and social worlds, or the pragmatic goals of dispensation from the natural and social worlds. One reason Durkheim did not discuss salvation was that his empirical data were taken predominantly from studies of tribal societies and not from the world religions. Durkheim paid little attention to the thaumaturgical goals of individuals and small groups because these were related to the exigencies of material life, private interests of a predominantly economic character, that Durkheim categorized as part of the profane side of life. Such goals were pursued in everyday life outside the sacred times and places of the collective assemblies, when the whole clan gathered to celebrate and renew its collective sentiments and identity. If such individual interests came within the purview of the sacred, they did so as magic and not as religion. The important goals of religious action in Durkheim's descriptions are those that confirm, reinforce, strengthen, or renew the natural and social order. These goals, which we will call *nomic*, are in contrast to the transcendence of or dispensation from the natural and social order.

Durkheim made a clear distinction between the participants' stated or recognized aims and the functions of rituals. The manifest goal of the Aborigines' rituals most frequently mentioned by Durkheim was the reproduction of the sacred totemic species, but what were important for a sociological analysis were the functions: "the true justification of religious practices does not lie in the apparent ends which they pursue, but rather in the invisible action which they exercise over the mind and in the way they effect our mental state."[18] The major function of the rituals was to assemble members of the clan together for an occasion during which their thoughts and feelings centered on their common beliefs and sentiments. At the societal level, the rite expressed and rekindled the ties of kinship and renewed the collective representations of the clan. At the individual level, the rite produced in participants feelings of belonging, security, strength, and happiness, a sense of well-being that they were part of the same moral community. These expressive and solidarity functions were an indispensable condition of social and individual life and therefore universal: "There can be no society which does not feel the need of upholding and reaffirming at regular intervals the collective sentiments and the collective ideas which make its unity and its personality."[19]

Durkheim argued that the function of the rituals transcended the purposes of participants and were not determined by them. Participants do not necessarily have to believe the intended consequences will occur, but natives do not doubt the efficacy of their rites, because the "moral efficacy" of the rites appears to confirm the "physical efficacy." The physical efficacy finds apparent confirmation insofar as the totemic species does reproduce regularly, but the "physical efficaciousness assigned to [the rites] by the believer is the product of an interpretation which conceals the essential reason for their existence: it is because they serve to remake individuals and groups morally that they are believed to have a power over things."[20] This emphasis on function did not, however, provide a clear rationale for Durkheim's categorization of three major forms of rites: positive, negative, and "piacular" (rites conducted on the occasion of death, misfortune, or collective crisis). These distinctions made more sense in terms of the participants' goals than in terms of the rituals' functions, although the three types differed in the extent to which Durkheim was able to separate goal and function.

The distinction between purpose and function is perhaps the most opaque in negative rites, which serve to separate and protect the sacred from the profane. The elimination of the profane is a condition of access to the positive cult, as when individuals undergo purification before they can participate in a rite. Many negative rites are no more than a preparation for the positive cult and may therefore be termed a means to a proximate end. When Durkheim discussed negative rites in relationship to initiation rites and asceticism, however, he pointed to other manifest purposes. The goal of the initiation rite is to transform youth into men or to effect the admission of the youth into the society of men. Initiation rites, like all rites of passage, are seen to effect a change in the condition of the actor, and they may be categorized as a subtype of the nomic rituals that reconfirm and renew the natural and social order. The rites of passage move individuals through a life cycle of institutionalized positions and thereby confirm the various positions occupied by actors.

Initiation involves ascetic practices, and with respect to asceticism as a general phenomenon, Durkheim mentions that one conscious aim is to attain religious prestige. When Durkheim writes that by ascetic practices and suffering the self is transformed into an instrument of deliverance, he appears to be indicating a goal of transcendence. Durkheim's argument, however, is that the hidden message of the privations and sufferings of asceticism is that society is possible only at a price; actors are required to do violence to their individual inclinations in order for society to exist. For Durkheim, the object of the religious life is to be understood not in terms of the actors' transcendental goal but rather as one that raises humans above their biological nature and makes them lead lives superior to those that they would otherwise follow in accord with natural impulses or spontaneous desires. It is social life itself that is transcendent.[21]

Durkheim's distinction between function and purpose is clearer in the case of the positive cults. The purpose, the reproduction of the totemic species, is well defined in most of the positive cults, and the three sub-types—sacrificial, imitative, and commemorative—can be understood as means or forms of communication with supramundanes in the pursuit of that goal. In his discussion on sacrificial rites, Durkheim distinguishes two forms of interaction with the totem or god: (1) a communion or identification with the totemic animal by the solemn eating of part of it and (2) an act of oblation or renouncement. The offering expresses the mutual dependence of participants and gods, which, according to Durkheim, is an expression of the mutual dependence between individuals and society. The rites of imitation are also a form of identification with the deity, and since they appear to be based on the assumption that like produces like, they provide the clearest expression of the goal of assuring the reproduction of the totemic species. James Frazer was mistaken to interpret such rites as sympathetic magic; it was the moral efficacy of the rites that produced the belief in their physical efficacy. Only some of the rites of commemoration, in which the mythology was dramatically represented, were considered by the natives as effecting the reproduction of the totemic species. Other rites whose purpose was commemoration for its own sake demonstrated that when physical efficacy was expected, it was an accessory and contingent element. Durkheim writes that when the natives explained that they carried out the rites because their ancestors had arranged them in that manner, they were admitting the authority of tradition and were thereby reinforcing the essential elements of the collective consciousness. In these cases, the purpose reflected the function.[22]

The explicit goals of piacular rites, such as the rituals of mourning, were to meet the wishes of the dead, who wished to be lamented, and to transform hostile spirits into benevolent protectors. Again, for Durkheim, such purposes were not a part of the analysis that was functional. Like other rites, the piacular rites functioned to bring about the assembly of the group, to make individual members feel strong again, and to renew the collective representations and sentiments.[23]

Durkheim's analysis of religion cannot be understood as simply a functionalist analysis, but in the section of his book on rituals, which is the most relevant for religious action, functionalism is central. The criticisms of Durkheim's functionalist approach will not be reiterated here,[24] and it is sufficient to note that an investigator with comparative interests is unlikely to find that the functionalist part of Durkheim's analysis, with its emphasis on the universal functions of religion, will be of aid in explaining religious differences, either among or within societies. Nevertheless, Durkheim's clear distinction between purpose and function and his typology of rituals have pointed to religious goals and patterns of communication with supramundanes that complement those goals and religious paths emphasized by Weber.

Marx and Engels, Functionalism, and the Symbolic Approach

Unlike Durkheim's writings, the work of Karl Marx and Frederick Engels on religion, although interesting in many ways, can contribute little to a model of religious action. Marx and Engels interpreted certain types of religious behavior as having what might be termed *extrinsic* goals; the actual purpose of the religious action, which was very much "this-worldly," was quite different from the declared "other-worldly" or spiritual goal. They wrote, for example, that the aristocracy and bourgeoisie supported the evangelical efforts of the churches among the proletariat in order to prevent the development of a proletarian class consciousness and to strengthen their class domination.[25] The interpretation of religion in terms of manipulation for the purposes of class interests was, however, a relatively minor motif in Marx's writings on religion. The major motif, at least in his early writings, was the relationship of religion to alienation, and in his later writings religion was treated in passing, as peripheral to his analysis of economic and political factors.

Some functionalists have concurred with Marxists that religion has, in some instances, been consciously manipulated to control the masses, or that ideological thinkers, having come to appreciate religion as a means of social control, have supported it despite their doubts about its truth value.[26] These ends, however, are examples of manifest functions of religion, whereas functionalists have generally been more interested in latent functions, those that have gone unrecognized by the religious actors. Following Durkheim, the "classical" anthropologists of tribal societies, Bronislaw Malinowski and A. R. Radcliffe-Brown, emphasized functions of social integration and the reinforcement of tradition. When sociologists of religion have taken a functionalist stance, they have tended to emphasize other functions, particularly functions of legitimation[27] and meaning.[28] But whatever function they emphasized, one outcome of the focus on consequences has been a lack of attention to the components of action.

Like the functionalist approach, the symbolic approach emphasizes the distinction between the goals of actors and a deeper level of understanding or explaining religious action. The symbolists have made a clear distinction between, on the one hand, the instrumentalism of technology and the concern to explain events in science and, on the other hand, the symbolic or expressive aspects of all religious activity, including magic. The symbolists admit that there may be a level at which certain rituals are instrumental, but recording the goals of actors is just the beginning of the analysis. The important level of understanding is to be sought at the non-instrumental, symbolic level, as showing or saying rather than doing.[29]

Symbolists have admitted that not all ritual participants are aware of the meanings of the symbols or of the importance of what they are symbolizing, and like functionalism, the symbolic approach has been criticized for its failure to address the question of why actors perform rites if they are unaware of their true meanings or significance. The reading of meaning into action that is not intentionally meaningful is problematic, and this is especially the case when symbolists point to considerable differences between the literal level of the ritual and what the symbolists believe is the "true" or fundamental message of the ritual. For example, although the literal level of many rituals in tribal societies is cosmocentric, dealing with the relations of gods and nature, the symbolist interpretations tend to be anthropocentric, dealing with the world of humans.[30]

The Symbolic and the Instrumental

Symbolists have conducted a polemic with "intellectualists" over the relative importance of instrumental and symbolic components in tribal or traditional religion. The only avowed goals that have been discussed in these polemics have been of a this-worldly nature, and it remains unclear how the incorporation of transcendental goals into the discussion might affect symbolic analysis. An emphasis on the symbolic component of religious behavior has, however, contributed to an understanding of the relationship between ritual means and this-worldly, dispensatory goals in "magical" action.

An appreciation of the importance of the symbolic link between means and ends in magic is found in the sociological classic *The Structure of Social Action*, the first major work by Talcott Parsons, who subsequently became the foremost proponent of structural functionalism in sociology. Parsons distinguished between the "intrinsic means-end schema," in which means are chosen by the "logico-experimental standard," or according to scientifically understood processes of causation, and the "symbolic means-end relationship," in which means are selected according to their symbolic appropriateness, as "expressions" of normative sentiments or ultimate values. Judgment of the means-end relationship by the logico-experimental method was clearly inappropriate when the end was transcendental and unobservable, but Parsons noted that ritual means, an important subtype of the symbolic means-end relationship, were also applicable where the ends were empirical, as in magic. For example, a sacrifice to a god to insure good weather was symbolic in at least two ways: as a symbol of goodwill that called for reciprocation and as a symbolic expression of a desire for good weather. Thus, in neither religion nor magic was the relationship between means and goals understood as a mechanical one of cause and effect. Magic was employed not in place of but in addition to rational technique, and insofar as sacred things were involved in the action, the means-end relationship was symbolic rather than intrinsic.[31]

The relationship of the instrumental and symbolic components in magic has been taken up by the anthropologist Stanley Tambiah, who begins with a critique of Malinowski's argument that the Trobriand islanders performed more magic in deep-sea fishing than in lagoon fishing to assuage their anxiety over the danger and unpredictability of the open sea. Tambiah notes that Malinowski omitted to point out that deep-sea fishing differed from lagoon fishing in that it produced the shark, which was of high ritual value among the Trobriand islanders, and he adds that Malinowski's theory could not explain why "magical" rites were performed around certain vegetables and fruits and not others.

Tambiah writes that magic both imitates the causal logic of technical action, which seeks to make changes in the natural world, and is rhetorical and performative, indicating the objects and activities that are important to the group or society. He demonstrates this by an example of the rituals of propitiation of the goddess, or female spirit, of rice in the villages of northeast Thailand. At harvesttime the villages use cosmetic articles to beautify the goddess and lead her out to the rice fields. The villagers say that the ceremonies enable a good harvest, but the rites also express the value of rice to the people and situate its production in the larger contexts of their lives. The production of rice cannot be separated from their Buddhism because it enables them to make religious merit by, for example, giving gifts of food to the Buddhist monks. Thus, "magical" ceremonies are "totalities in which instrumental and performative symbols and action, causal logic and communicative logic, are intertwined and fused."[32]

It should be noted that Tambiah's distinction between the instrumental and the performative is not a distinction between goal orientation and non–goal orientation. The intention to increase the rice harvest is a goal, and the expression of the value of rice in the ritual is part of a hierarchy of goals: by giving rice as gifts to Buddhist monks, actors earn merit that contributes to a good rebirth, which in turn is a stage in the long path to ultimate salvation. A single ritual may relate to both mundane and supramundane goals, and the meanings of participants can vary according to the goal that is uppermost in their minds and the kind of relationship that is conceived between means and goals.

In a comparison of two Catholic villages in Sri Lanka, R. L. Stirrat has shown that the relative importance of the instrumental and performative aspects of a particular ritual can vary among different groups. In one village, the saints were believed to have real efficacy in the mundane world, and sorcery was often used to attain benefits. In the other, it was not believed that the saints had a direct effect; appeals to the saints and the priests' blessings of the fishermen's boats to increase their catch were understood by the villagers as action that manifested their inner states, that gave them confidence and made them "feel better." The efficacy was recognized by the actors to be in their minds and not through a direct effect on the natural world.[33]

Stirrat appears confident that whereas in one case the means-end relationship was understood by actors to be one of cause and effect, in the other actors were fully appreciative of the expressive, symbolic nature of the ritual. In most cases of religious action where the ends are mundane, and certainly in most historical cases, however, we simply do not know whether the actors understand the means to be causal, symbolic, or both. We can only surmise that when actors initiate a ritual or invite a magician to undertake a ritual in order to attain an empirical end, it is the instrumental and efficacious elements that are uppermost in their minds.[34]

A Framework

As the examples from the anthropological literature have indicated, a particular religious action may be directed to a number of quite different goals, and no particular act or range of acts is fixed as ends or as means. What is a means in one context or for certain actors can be an end in another context or for other actors. Empirical "messiness," however, is not an excuse for analytical haziness, and there can be little advance in understanding and explanation without the distinctions of analytical categories.

I have formulated a typology of four types of religious goals that represent a partial synthesis of various perspectives in the sociology and anthropology of religion. First is the *nomic*, where the goal is to maintain an existing order of nature and society, which are conceived as anchored in the supramundane. This type includes calendrical rites, with the goals of rebirth or renewal of the cycle of seasons, and rites of passage, with the goals of placing persons within society and its role structure. Second is the *transformative*, where the goal is to produce a pervasive or fundamental change in nature, society, and individual being or nonbeing. Two subtypes can be distinguished: sacralization, where the goal is to infuse worldly activities with sacredness so that the world conforms to divine directives or ethical imperatives, and soteriology, where the goals take the forms of rebirth and a millennial or terrestrial paradise. Third is the *thaumaturgical*, where special dispensation and release are sought from specific ills within a nature and a society whose basic features are not expected to change. In this type, supramundane assistance is sought either for protection from evil supramundanes who wish to do harm to specific persons or for relief from sickness and other woeful conditions affecting particular individuals and families. Fourth is the *extrinsic*, where mundane goals are the object of actions that are purported to be supramundane in their goal and means. Examples are the display of wealth and the assertion or confirmation of social status and political power. It is, perhaps, rare for extrinsic goals to be the sole goals of particular religious actions, but they are often found together with intrinsic goals; the goals of a lavish funeral, for example, can include both a display of wealth and an appeal for salvation.

Goals are only one component of religious action. The conditions and means include such elements as the pantheons of supramundanes, the types of communication with supramundanes, and behaviors in accord with ritual formulas or ethical imperatives. This framework is used to organize the data on elite and popular forms of religion in the world religions discussed in this work.

3

Elites and Masses

Max Weber, Weberian Scholars, and Marxist Analysis

This chapter has two aims. The first is to present Weber's comparisons of the world religions, systematized within the conceptual framework of religious action. The presentation is slanted in accordance with the major themes in this work that diverge from Weber's own major organizing principles and questions. I am concerned far less than Weber with the effects of religious differences on practical behavior (this was, perhaps, his major organizing principle), and I make the differences between the elites and the masses, and the interaction between them, the most important focus.

Weber's analyses lead into the second aim of this chapter: to point to those "environments" of religious action that will contribute to an understanding and explanation of the similarities and differences of elite and popular patterns of religious action. Weber's writings on the principal social carriers and organizations of the world religions are an important contribution to this endeavor, but just as in the previous chapter I drew on non-Weberian theoretical traditions to arrive at a more comprehensive scheme of religious action, so too in this chapter I draw on Marxian analyses of religion to strengthen the account of the social-structural factors that are relevant to explanations of the similarities and differences between elite and popular forms of religion.

Max Weber: Patterns of Action in the World Religions

Religious Goals

The world religions differ in their emphases on and conceptions of salvation. The distinction between a salvational and nonsalvational religion was sometimes confused in Weber's writings with the distinction between ethical and magical religion, but he portrayed Confucianism as a religion with an ethic that knew nothing of salvation. Confucianism was concerned with the cultured person's fate and self-perfection in this world. The ultimate aim of the Confucian was "only long life, health, and wealth in this world and beyond death the retention of his good name."[1] Taoism did include a salvational goal, the achievement of non-existence through union with the divine, but there remained a strong worldly orientation in Taoism, especially in its use of magical techniques and its emphasis on avoiding mortality in this world.[2]

Weber's classification of Islam in this context is unclear: although it had salvational elements, it was primarily a religion of world adjustment that had, like Confucianism, a strong political component. With its emphasis on the holy war and its promises to warriors that they would enjoy paradise if they died in battle, Islam lacked a conception of ethical salvation.[3] Judaism was a salvational religion, but Weber also emphasized its this-worldly character: the this-worldly promises of the Israelite prophets were contrasted with the Hellenic mysteries of the Orphic religion, with their promises of the beyond.[4]

Among those religions with an emphasis on salvation, a distinction can be made between those with a single and universal mode of salvation and those that limit the highest form of salvation to a religious elite. Weber distinguished among three aims of salvation in Hinduism: rebirth on earth or in paradise (as a god or near to one), immortality of the soul in various forms, and cessation of individual existence through unity with the divine. Insofar as the masses were concerned with salvation (and this was rarely the case), the best they could hope for was rebirth in a higher form. A person could be reborn in hell, but this was a temporary condition, for in contrast with Christianity, in Hinduism there was no eternal reward or punishment for deeds and omissions in this ephemeral life. The ultimate form of salvation, possible only for the virtuosos, was to escape from the wheel of meaningless deaths and reincarnations. This escape did not signify a rejection of suffering, sin, or an imperfect world but rather a rejection of the transitory nature of the world (including the world of gods). Despite its opposition to the caste system, Buddhism also made clearly drawn distinctions between the salvation aims of virtuosos and the masses. Whereas the virtuoso monks sought nirvana, the everlasting tranquillity of absolute annihilation, the laity sought rebirth in one of the transitory godly paradises.[5]

The monotheistic religions made no distinction between religious elites and the masses in the nature of the salvation that they might attain, but here also, in most religious contexts, salvation was "a special concern cultivated in narrow conventicles."[6] For most people, sacred values are the solid goods of this world: "With the only partial exception of Christianity and a few other specifically ascetic creeds, [the goals of religion] have consisted of health, a long life and wealth."[7]

In comparing soteriologies, Weber paid special attention to the virtuosos, who were often concerned with their individual salvation rather than that of the collective. The hierocratic elite, in comparison, sought to organize the religious behavior, soteriological and otherwise, of the masses. Weber wrote that the best solution for the tension of virtuosos and hierocracy was found in Buddhism, which was a religion created by and for monks.[8] This was like saying there was no hierocracy in Buddhism apart from monks, but where there were developments of churches, which stood for the universalism of grace and were "democratic" in the sense of making sacred values generally accessible,[9] they have had to compromise with monasticism. The Catholic Church succeeded to integrate monks into its bureaucratic organization and to use them as an instrument of hierocratic influence and control of the laity. Weber pointed to the Jesuit order as one that, without any emphasis on an individual search for salvation, became an important tool of the hierocracy, especially of the Holy See, to whom Jesuits swore an oath of unconditional obedience.[10]

Conditions: Supramundane Forces

Conceptions of salvation were intimately bound up with conceptions of the divine. The soteriological goal of Protestants, highly differentiated from social aims, was wedded to a view of God who was radically transcendent over creation. The nonsoteriological Confucian ideal of adjustment to the traditional social order rested on a cosmocentric vision of correspondence and harmony between the divine and society. In India, the two soteriologically related beliefs shared by all Hindus, transmigration of souls and ethical compensation, were anchored in a cosmology of a rational, hierarchically structured, eternal order.

Rationalization in the sense of a unified supramundane principle was a feature of all the world religions, but the conceptions of this unified principle varied greatly, especially between East and West. The dominant conception that emerged in the Near East and spread to the West was a personalized, historicized, supramundane creator God who rules over creation. Similar notions occasionally surfaced in the East, but the gods of the Eastern religions were, like humans, generally conceived as subject to an eternal, immanent, sacred celestial order.

Weber wrote that, in both the Near East and China, the dominant conceptions emerged out of naturalistic-animistic notions of spirits, but whereas in China the most powerful spirits increasingly assumed an impersonal character, in the Near East personal, supramundane spirits were raised above the semipersonal spirits and local deities. The idea of a single, personal god was held for a short time in Confucianism, but it disappeared without seriously challenging the dominant notion of the impersonal power of Heaven.[11] In Hinduism, the early conception of a personal god-father and creator of the world was displaced by the impersonal Brahman principle. The impersonal Brahman became the classical conception, but its centrality was confined to the esoteric thought of philosophically schooled Brahman intellectuals. Among lower strata, there often reappeared the conception of a supreme, personal creator god who rules over and above the host of local and functional deities.[12]

If the impersonal principle did not take hold among the masses in the Eastern religions, neither was monotheism held consistently among the masses in the Near East and West. Belief in the power of natural or material objects was not confined to tribal societies; it was also found in folk Christianity, where icons or figures of the Madonna were conceived not as symbols but as objects that had extraordinary power in their own right. Weber emphasized that the masses were often opposed to religious changes that increased their distance from the supernatural. In Ancient Judaism, for example, Yahweh was not the God of "popular religion" but the God of the prophets and teachers who sought to impose their conceptions on the people, who frequently resisted them.[13] A general impediment to the development of monotheism was the demand among the masses for tangible and accessible religious objects that could be brought into relationship with concrete life situations and influenced through magic. Not even in the essentially monotheistic faiths of Judaism and Islam were beliefs in spirits and demons permanently eliminated; the decisive consideration was whether the supreme God or the spirits and the demons exerted the stronger influence on the interests of individuals in their everyday lives.[14]

Weber noted that Yahweh of Ancient Israel was, from the beginning, more than a functional or local god; this was a creator god from afar who could not be seen. There were, however, gods of the sky and mountains in neighboring societies, and in almost all the cosmologies of the area, a single god had created the world. Yahweh differed in that Yahweh's mere "word" had produced the creation; there were no images of Yahweh; the mythology around Yahweh was very limited; and unlike other great deities, whose primary field of activity was nature, Yahweh was the guardian primarily of the sociolegal order. Yahweh had originally been a god of nature, and a number of myths, such as the great flood, had been adopted from neighboring cultures, but these elements gradually became subsidiary to the notion of an ethical, law-making God who presided over the historical destinies of his people and, in later developments, of the world.[15]

The Covenant was an important stage in this development because it both signified and promoted the uniqueness of the relation of Israel to its God. It was constituted of mutual promises: the people of Israel promised to obey God's law, and in return, Yahweh, who had already liberated them from slavery in Egypt, would grant them domination over the promised land and protect them from their enemies. As a contractual partner, Yahweh could not be viewed as a mere local god or functional deity, and the rules of society could not be identified with the forces of nature, because Yahweh was not sanctifying an already immutable order of law but had created the law.[16]

The gradual crystallization of the monotheistic idea continued during the periods of the kings and the Babylonian exile and was advanced considerably by the Israelite prophets. An earlier form of ecstatic and war prophecy was like that of other religions, but the new type of prophecy that emerged by the end of the sixth century B.C.E. promoted the majesty and universalism of Yahweh. The prophets built on and extended conceptions of the divine that were, from an early stage, inherent in the conception of Yahweh.[17] Such conceptions had not developed in the Eastern religions, and this is one reason their prophets were different in type; the Eastern prophets were "exemplary" rather than "ethical."

The Israelite prophets provide the classic examples of the ethical prophet who proclaims himself the instrument of a transcendental god, demands obedience to that god as an ethical duty, and promises salvation if the god's ethical code, as revealed to the prophets, is fulfilled. In contrast, the exemplary prophet demonstrates to others, by personal example, the way to salvation. The exemplary prophet appeared principally in

India; the type also appeared less frequently in China and the Near East, but the ethical prophet was found only in the Near East.[18]

Means: Paths to Salvation

The differences in the conceptions of the divine and the related types of prophecies had clear implications for the appropriate religious means or paths to achieve salvation and other religious goals. Certain paths to salvation, if delineated in a general way, are common to both Western and Eastern religions: ritualism, good works, dependence on a savior, and sanctification. The particulars of such common paths, however, vary enormously. For example, the system of rituals is far more comprehensive in Hinduism than it is in Catholicism, a comparatively ritualistic form of Christianity. Saviors descend from higher spheres to earth in most of the world religions, but they differ in many respects: what they save humans from (bad spirits, a sinful world, individual sin); the means they use to do so (intercession with a god, battles with demons, dying in order to atone for the sins of humans); and the number of times they appear (once, several times, or in every generation).

Sanctification, the achievement of a state of sacredness or self-perfection, also took very different forms: the belief in a transcendental god directed humans to achieve self-perfection as instruments of God, whereas the absence of such a notion opened up the possibility of self-deification or absolute unity with the divine. Certain salvation paths were ruled out by the absence of a transcendental god in Eastern religions: an absolute faith in the god, in which the emphasis is on the limitations of the intellect when confronted with the deity, and predestination, in which the emphasis is on salvation as a gift of the god, entirely unaffected by human action in this world.[19]

The this-worldly goals of Confucianism were to be attained by following the Tao, the true way that inheres in the cosmos. A person who had an extensive knowledge of the Confucianist literature and conformed to the codes of ceremonial and social propriety could achieve a oneness with what was conceived as an internally harmonious cosmos. This involved an adaptation to the world rather than a tension between moral ideals and the world. Within a worldview that did not include the notions of radical evil or sin, the only conception of salvation was to be saved from behavioral inadequacies and cultural barbarism. In contrast, the achievement of salvation in Taoism was to be attained by the minimization of action, rendering the self void of worldly interests and desires, thereby making the self a vessel of mystical possession.[20]

The pluralism of the aims of salvation in Hinduism and Buddhism determined, in part, the relativization of holy paths. The path of the masses in Hinduism was to perform the appropriate rituals and social accomplishments of their caste. Worship of and gifts to the virtuosos were included among the ritually good works that could bring credit toward a higher rebirth. This meant the individual alone determined his or her fate after death, but an alternative or additional path to salvation was through enthusiastic faith (*bhakti*), often directed toward a savior such as Krishna. For the virtuosos, freedom from the bonds of karma could be attained through two often interrelated paths: first, contemplation leading to a higher knowledge (gnosis), wisdom, or illumination that dissolved the linkage between spirit and matter; and second, an ascetic flight from the world, involving techniques such as regulated breathing, yoga, and the repetition of certain words that emptied the consciousness of worldly thoughts, freed the self from the senses, and thereby prepared the self for the final state of eternal rest. The Buddhist virtuosos who wished to attain nirvana had to overcome ephemeral life by giving up every desire that linked them to the imperfect world. In contrast to Hinduism, this amounted to the extinction of the soul, but as in Hinduism, the appropriate path was through higher knowledge or mystical gnosis, to be attained by an ascetic, intensive regimen of body and spirit or by strict methodical meditation.[21]

The contemplative-world flight and mystical gnostic paths were rare in Judaism. The path to salvation for most Jews was the study and observance of the religious law, and the difference between virtuosos and the masses was measured by level of scholarship and meticulousness of observance.[22]

Participation in the core rituals or sacraments, such as the Eucharist, was an essential precondition of salvation in Catholicism, although its theologians had emphasized that the ethical purity of participants was also necessary. In accord with institutional grace, salvation could be attained only through the church, which was the institution in control of the mediation and distribution of grace. Other important paths in many Christian streams were faith or unlimited trust in the transcendental God, salvation through Christ, and good works. In the more popular form of the last path, the individual's fate after death was decided by the balance of discrete good and bad actions during a lifetime. According to the more ethically rational version, what was important was not necessarily a particular good or bad action but rather actions conceived as symptoms or expressions of the total personality. Such a conception meant that people were more likely to act methodically, according to general rules. It was, however, the belief that God had made known signs of the predestined that produced the most systematic form of asceticism.[23]

Rationalization, Elites, and Popular Religion

The account above of differences among the world religions with respect to their goals, conditions, and means is primarily synchronic. Weber's comparisons of the world religions have, however, a diachronic thrust that focuses on the processes of rationalization. Divergences in the processes of rationalization influenced the relationships that emerged between the elite and popular forms of religion.

Rationalization in Hinduism produced the most consistent theodicy that ever existed: the doctrine of karma stated that a person's caste and condition, whether high or low, were consequences of the balance of their good and bad actions in their previous lives. What might appear as unjust suffering was the consequence of people's sinful behavior in previous lives, and to improve their situation in the next reincarnation, it was necessary that they accept their condition and conform rigidly to their dharma, the ritual obligations of their caste. This provided an unambiguous and metaphysically satisfying conception of the individual's place in the world, but it could not satisfy the reflective person, who was likely to perceive an eternal repetition of deaths and reincarnations as senseless and unbearable. The question to be addressed, therefore, was how to escape from the wheel of rebirths and deaths. This, however, was a question most likely to be addressed by members of an elite who were able to remove themselves from material concerns.[24]

In addition to the high level of rationalization in the theoretical level of the theodicies, the religions of India also tended to become highly rationalized in their methodical, formal techniques of achieving salvation. Yoga, for example, was a methodical, systematized, rationalized form of ecstatic practice. It was less rational than contemplation in the sense that it sought feeling and not knowledge, but it was more rational in the sense of the systematization of technique.[25] In another sense, all the means of Indian virtuosos were irrational because they resulted in fleeting experiences rather than the application of practical ethics in everyday life, which, for Weber, was the most significant rationalization of means.

The intellectual-theoretical side of rationalization may have been weaker in the religions of the Near East and West (where it was more developed in Greek philosophy), but it was the ethical rationalization in Judaism and Christianity that opened up greater possibilities for the influence of religious elites over the masses. The crucial development in ethical rationalization in Western religion was from ethical ritualism and legalism to an ethic of conviction. Ancient Judaism included "a highly rational religious ethic of social conduct . . . free of magic and all forms of irrational quest for salvation,"[26] but post-exilic Judaism remained a religion of law, centered on concrete, discrete norms rather than on abstract principles.[27]

The break of the Pauline mission from Judaism, replacing a religion of law and knowledge with a religion of faith and spirit, prepared the way for further ethical rationalization.[28] As Wolfgang Schluchter has argued in his interpretation of Weber, however, early Christianity was both a setback in rationalization (promoting an enchanted path to salvation) and an advance (in its more active asceticism). By its emphasis on nonrational holy states and by including a magical quality in its central acts of ritual, early Christianity reversed somewhat the process of disenchantment that had occurred in Judaism.

Remagification was promoted further in the church by its institutionalization of the sacraments. By contrast, early Christianity's anti-intellectual emphasis on faith, its concern with self-perfection, and its promotion of a universal ethic of conviction constituted an important advance in ethical rationalization. The process was carried much further by ascetic Protestantism, which combined the demagification of Judaism with the ethic of conviction of early Christianity, setting them within the framework of a more radical, religious individualism.[29]

Ethical rationalization and demagification were closely interrelated. It was of enormous importance for the divergent tendencies of Western and Eastern civilizations that rationalization in the Near East and West included a far deeper and more extensive demagification than in the East. Monotheism was less congenial to the continuation of magic than religions in which the gods were subordinated to a cosmic and moral order; the omnipotent god could not be coerced through magic.[30] Among the Israelites, miracles had a place comparable to sorcery in the Eastern religions, but whereas in Eastern religions it was the magicians who practiced magic, it was the God of Israel who, sometimes in voluntary response to the people's imploring or requests for intercession, performed miracles.[31] Weber was careful to note, however, that opposition to magic did not necessarily mean the disappearance of or disbelief in magic. In Judaism, magical beliefs in the possibilities of coercing God came to be considered as blasphemous, but magic continued to exist in the coercion of demons, exorcism, and healing through word magic.[32]

The sacraments of Catholicism were believed to have magical properties, and the Catholic priest was, in part, a magician who performed the miracle of transubstantiation. By destroying all intermediary agencies between God and man, Protestantism, especially Calvinism, represented the last phase of disenchantment within religion. Although the existence of magic was admitted by many Protestants, it was considered the work of the devil.[33]

In contrast with the Near East and West, the forms that rationalization took in Chinese and Indian religions did not entail the elimination of magic or consistent opposition to it. Educated Confucianists were skeptical of magic or emphasized its limitations; individuals who lived virtuous lives had no need to fear the spirits. Nevertheless, the Confucian ethic of affirmation of and adjustment to the world presupposed the continuation of magical religion. This was demonstrated by the emperor's responsibility for the weather, good harvests, and the good conduct of spirits, and by the prevalence of ancestor worship, which was equally fundamental for official and popular religious observance.

The Confucian literati scorned and rejected magicians and magical techniques, but they tolerated magic among the masses (who attributed magical qualities to the literati) and allowed it to be cultivated by the Taoists.[34] The Brahmans rejected all popular magicians, cult priests, and holy seekers who did not have a Vedic education, but whereas in China the literati allowed magic to become the province of professional magicians and Taoists, in India the Brahmans were a caste of magicians who rationalized magic in the sense of limiting the emotional and ecstatic elements and developing a system of ritual formulas.[35]

Virtuosos and Masses

Both the hierocratic elite and the virtuosos have had to adapt their religious orientations in order to influence and secure support from the masses. Struggles between virtuosos and priests for lay support have been between the appeal of personal charisma and "heroic" religiousness of the virtuosos and the priests' mediation of sacred values available to all, regardless of the priests' personal religious qualifications.[36] Priests have sought to secure their position and counter alternative lay interpretations by producing canonical writings, which at some time were declared closed by the priesthood, and dogmas, which are the priestly interpretations of the canon. The exceptional development of dogma in Christianity was a consequence of its mode of organization of religious congregations and the relative independence achieved by the church from political authorities.[37]

It was, however, the differentiation between virtuosos and masses rather than between priests and laypeople that interested Weber. He wrote that different religious qualifications stand at the beginning of the history of religion, and that the masses have remained religiously "unmusical" (a term Weber also used to refer to his own lack of religiousness). The most important sacred values could not be attained by everyone, and in most of the world's religions, only the religious virtuosos strove to attain them. To gain and maintain support, material and ideational, from the masses, the virtuosos have often taken into consideration the constraints of everyday life with which the majority have to cope. It was with respect to these concessions that Weber made a clear contrast between the Eastern religions on the one hand and Judaism and Christianity on the other.[38]

Ascetic Protestantism shared with Judaism the characteristic of having a religious ethic that penetrated the masses. Even the doctrine of predestination was a popular one and not just a dogma of theologians, although for the broad mass of believers it became of utmost importance to recognize their state of grace.[39] This lack of opposition between virtuoso and mass religiosity was, however, an exception, and a clear division between virtuosos and the masses had normally been prevalent in Christianity.

Sacramental grace had remained open to all within the Catholic Church, but by the institution of monasticism and the religious orders, the church had catered to the inclination of religious virtuosos to set themselves apart from the rest. Weber did not enter into any detail on the extent to which Christianity, prior to Protestantism, penetrated popular religious behavior, but it is possible to infer from his writings that he believed the nature of the salvational goals and techniques of the Eastern religions created a wider gulf than in the Near East and the West between the virtuosos and the masses.[40]

The rationalization of popular religion was perhaps the least developed in China, where the literati tended to ignore folk religion as long as it did not constitute a challenge to the state. The term *virtuoso* did not apply to the literati, who were not interested in other-worldly salvation and were likely to oppose soteriological tendencies among the rest of the population. Weber presented Confucianism as the religion of state bureaucrats who were socially, educationally, and culturally distant from the masses and whose interests did not incline them to attempt to diffuse their religion among the masses. The nature of orthodox Confucianism, which lacked emotional elements and came to equate ritual with social convention, meant that the typical religious needs of the masses were ignored by the literati.

The masses in China were blocked from participating in the state cult, and their worship in households of the "Lord of Heaven" was ignored by the representatives of the official cult. The official religion did, however, have some influence on the masses, especially through negative effects: the literati blocked the emergence of salvational or prophetic religion and eradicated the orgiastic components in animism. As a consequence of the sober nature of the bureaucratic cult, Chinese religion lacked a Dionysian element, but Weber did not infer from this that mass religious behavior was rationalized. The single systematic cult in popular religion, which the masses shared to some extent with the literati, was the ancestral cult, but otherwise popular religion remained an unsystematic pluralism of magical, animistic, and heroistic cults.[41]

The distinction between virtuosos and mass religion was especially appropriate in the Hindu and Buddhist contexts, where it was reinforced by the differences in soteriological goals and paths. In Hinduism, only the virtuosos born as Brahmans could hope to achieve ultimate salvation; apart from the essential requisite of their birth, only they had the resources and time that would allow them to distance themselves from worldly activities and devote themselves to contemplation. In contrast to the contemplative, ascetic techniques and knowledge seeking of the virtuosos, the familiar elements of popular religion included "alcoholic, sexual and meat orgies, magical compulsion of the spirits, personal deities, living and apotheosized saviors, ardent cultist love of personalized helpers-in-need, conceived as incarnations of great merciful gods."[42] For the vast majority of peasants and laborers, and for many of the middle classes, the magical spell remained the core element of religion. Even Hindu soteriological sects, centered on various gods, did not address themselves to the real masses; they probably appealed to no more than 5 percent of the population, mostly from the middle strata.[43]

Popular religion in India did not go entirely unaffected by the rationalizing tendencies of the elite. By making extensive concessions to the needs of the masses, the Brahmans were also able to moderate the popular orgiasticism they detested. These changes occurred in conjunction with the so-called Hindu restoration in India, when the Brahmans sought to provide an alternative to Buddhism and Jainism by organizing cults for the laity through an organized, professional monkdom. Various gods, especially Shiva and Vishnu, although not new, were now officially accepted. Folk deities, especially goddesses, were recognized by the Brahmans, and some goddesses were elevated to the status of wives of Brahmanic gods. Weber was describing here a process of mutual influences between elite and popular religion.

Folk ecstasy, with its aim of self-deification for magical purposes, made its entrance into Brahmanic literature in the form of Tantra magic. Some degree of rationalization of popular religion was evident in the Brahmanic transformation of the alcoholic and sexual-orgiastic character of the adoration of the phallus into a purely ritualistic temple cult that spread throughout India. The Brahmans conceded the adoration of the phallus (*lingam* or *linga*), but in contrast to traditional sexual orgiasticism, the god was happy when the lingam remained chaste. This modification was limited, however, to orthodox Brahmanic Shivaism. In mass religious expression, sexual orgiasticism continued to dominate.

Another important element in the Hindu restoration was the spread of redeemer or savior religion, as in the Krishna and Rama cults. The savior was often a guru, a corporeal, living person and object of worship who performed magical therapy, heard confessions, and helped his followers in need. Brahmans who became gurus were living gods whose followers would eat from their leftovers and drink the water in which they had put their toes. The gurus would designate their successors, or their charisma would be inherited, and these, in turn, would become the objects of worship.[44]

Hagiolatry and idolatry were also dominant features of later Mahayana Buddhism. As in Hinduism, but without the overlay of the caste system, there was a vast gulf in Theravada Buddhism between the soteriologies of the virtuosos and the masses. The Buddhist masses had no wish for nirvana; they did not have the time that was required for the seeker of salvation to devote to meditation; and they could find little satisfaction in the figure of the Buddha when he was presented exclusively as an exemplary prophet of self-salvation. The masses demanded supernatural assistance in this world, and their interest in salvation was restricted to seeking paradise in the hereafter.

Buddhism was transformed into a world religion through the Buddhist monks' accommodation to the religious interests of the masses. The monks' preoccupation with their own salvation disinclined them to cater to the majority, but they had a material interest in increasing the number of givers of subsistence, and the compassionate divine filled life, which is almost always found together with mystical holy states, justified reaching out to others. The secular authorities reinforced the outreaching of Buddhism because they were interested in using the monks to domesticate the masses. The organization of Buddhist monks into professional orders enabled Buddhism to become one of the greatest missionary religions, and even though early Buddhism was inimical to magic, its diffusion included the incorporation of magic and saviors: "Magical therapy, apotropaic and magical homeopathic ecstasy, idolatry and hagiolatry, the whole host of deities, angels, and demons made their entrance into Mahayana Buddhism." The Buddha as a prophet of self-salvation was replaced by the supernatural redeemer who appeared ever anew on earth in a series of rebirths.[45]

The incorporation of the masses into Hinduism and Buddhism involved some rationalization of popular religion, especially in the middle strata, but the intellectualist form of rationalization and the nature of the soteriologies of the Eastern religions greatly limited the contact between virtuosos and mass religious practitioners. Developments were entirely different in the monotheistic religions of the Near East and West. Even though the conception of God that the prophets and teachers of Ancient Israel sought to impose on the masses often met resistance, Ancient Judaism had a popular character insofar as the Covenant was made not with an elite but with the entire people, and the punishments for its contravention were imposed not on the rulers alone but on the whole people. The ethical prophets appealed to strata who lacked political power, and their rationalist, ethical, soteriological message could be understood by all. They taught that historical events and the plight of the people were not a matter of blind chance or magical forces but were to be understood in terms of the relationship between a superworldly god, conceived in part as father and in part as king, and his people. When the people disobeyed their god, he would punish them sternly, but he could be won over by prayer, humility, and moral conduct. The holy texts could be understood by all, and the path to salvation, the observance of the law, was open to every person.

Such foundations did not favor an esoteric gnosis of aristocratic religious virtuosos. The religious elite that did emerge, the rabbinate, were interpreters of the law for the people and did not favor a severe asceticism or the intellectual mysticism of a salvation aristocracy. The guru worship that became common in the Eastern religions and in Christendom was precluded in Judaism by the Jewish conception of God and the authority of the rabbis, which rested on the interpretation of the law. Weber noted, however, that although the rabbi could not be a saint or mystagogue, such a figure did develop among eastern European Jews in the form of the *zaddik* (plural, *zaddikim*) of the Hasidic movement.[46]

Social Structures and Social Carriers

At the most general level of his explanation of the differences between the ancient Near East and China, Weber took a somewhat Durkheimian stance when he argued that the contrasting conceptions of the divine were projections of divergent political-social structures. The supreme deities in the Near East were, in some degree, modeled on all-powerful kings who "created" the harvest and ruled through centralized bureaucratic administrations. In Mesopotamia, the monarch's power was dependent on his control of the irrigation system, while in Egypt the regulation of the Nile was the source of the king's strength. The impression made by these controls was conducive to a conception of a god who had created the earth and human beings out of nothing. In China, the uncertainty of the weather meant that irrigation procedures could not be relied on; the Chinese emperor could only seek to avert meteorological disturbances through sacrifice, public atonement, and virtuous practices.[47]

It was not, however, in the ancient Near Eastern empires that the full development of monotheism occurred, but in a small society located on the margins of the empires. Ancient Israel was influenced by the neighboring civilizations, but its distance from the cultural centers increased its capacity to search for the meanings of events that affected the whole society. Weber made few and only very general comparisons of the social contexts of Ancient Judaism and Eastern religions: the situation of the small Jewish state on the periphery of hostile empires was conducive to a personal god in tension with the world, whereas the peaceful political and economic center of the postfeudal, pacified Chinese empire was conducive to an impersonal power in harmony with the world.[48] But insofar as Weber set his work on Ancient Judaism in a comparative context, the major comparisons were between Israel and its neighboring contemporary societies.

The importance of the Covenant was related to the sociopolitical structure of ancient Israel: it was a contractually regulated confederacy of seminomadic stock breeders and warrior tribes. The tribes and kin groups that made up the confederacy had, at first, their own separate gods, but as the confederacy became more powerful, it became increasingly bound to one God. The confederacy was an unstable war association that, until the period of the kings, did not have permanent political organs, and only a religious organization, binding the confederation together by a sacred oath, could provide a solid basis for political and military actions. Common worship and priests unified an otherwise fragmented tribal association, and this unity was expressed insofar as a war hero or prophet, certified by Yahweh, could claim authority beyond the boundaries of his tribe. Weber did not want to suggest that the Covenant was the inevitable consequence of the absence of strong sociopolitical bonds. The religious formation that emerged was the consequence of highly particular historical and religious circumstances and vicissitudes, but once that order emerged, its sociopolitical advantages meant that it was likely to survive.[49]

The appeal of the prophets can be understood, in part, against the background of the development of the monarchy into despotic states, the demilitarization of the peasants, and the mounting external threats to the Israelite kingdoms. Weber stressed that political factors did not cause the prophets of doom to arise; their visions can be traced to their "psychic" or "preformed" dispositions. Nevertheless, the historical fate of Israel conditioned the importance of prophecy. The tradition preserved those prophecies that appeared to have come true, and it was during the Babylonian captivity, when the predictions of doom were seen to have come to pass, that the prestige of prophetic religion reached its height.[50] Although the Israelite prophets themselves came from privileged strata and their opposition to the orgiasticism of rural fertility cults and the shrines of Baal meant that they did not obtain the support of the peasants, their opposition to kingship and the priesthood helped them gain the support of powerful kinship groups of pious laity.[51] Rabbinical Judaism's emphasis on legal interpretation and practical-ethical rationalism corresponded to the lifestyle of the bourgeois stratum who strongly influenced how rabbis handled the law.[52]

The movement around Jesus appealed at first to small-town and rural inhabitants who were close to magic and sought salvation through saviors.[53] Beginning as an anti-intellectualist doctrine of itinerant artisan journeymen, Christianity became an urban civic religion, and the major carriers of the later stage of its rationalization, ascetic Protestantism, tended to be merchants and artisans from the middle classes.[54]

The differences with respect to social structures and the position of cities in Western and Eastern societies are of great significance in an interpretation of the world religions and their principal carriers. The Chinese literati were prominent in a relatively centralized, unified, patrimonial state; the Brahman were prominent as the highest caste in a decentralized society built on the caste structure; Islamic warriors were prominent in a tribal, military society; and merchants and artisans were prominent in the Occidental cities that became the major social contexts for both the pariah Jewish people and developments in Christianity.

The Occidental city attained an important degree of independence within the framework of European feudalism. Its burghers viewed themselves as separate from peasants, and they organized themselves into guilds, whose membership was defined in terms of abstract legal principles rather than on particularistic familial or clan ties. The emergence of relatively autonomous, self-governing civic organizations based on coalitions of guilds made possible the development of citizenship rights and relatively free economic activities. This milieu, which allowed the growth of relatively independent religious communities of laity with a rational, inner-worldly ethic, had no parallel in China and India.

From an early date, China had many cities and a flourishing long-distance trade, but the cities were principally administrative centers of government and were internally divided by strong, cohesive clans. In these circumstances, civic coalitions did not emerge, and the socially mobile were absorbed within the patrimonial state. The merchants and craftspeople of Indian cities were organized into guilds, but they remained weak under the pressures of the princes and the caste system. Urban groups were sometimes attracted to heterodox salvation religions, but these were suppressed or their activities limited by the alliance of princes and the Brahmans.[55]

The major carriers of the religions of China and India did not, therefore, come from the middle urban stratum. The adoption and dominance of Confucianism as the state religion was intimately tied to the emergence of a patrimonial state, whose victory over feudal rulers led to the decline of personal warrior gods and provided for their replacement by an impersonal Heaven. A status group of nonmilitary, genteel officials emerged with the unification and pacification of the empire, and its interests and lifestyle had been greatly influenced by the institution of an examination system on which depended qualifications for office and rank. The educational system of the literati provided them with knowledge of the Confucian texts as well as of the calendar and stars in order to discern the heavenly will and to conduct themselves according to the appropriate rituals, ceremonies, and ethical behavior.

Without competition from a powerful priesthood or prophecy, the intellectual rationalism of a stratum of officials was able to develop freely in China. They evolved and maintained an inner-worldly morality for politically involved laypeople, a code of political maxims, and rules of propriety for cultural persons. The order of society was seen as part of a harmonious cosmos; tension with the world was kept to an absolute minimum, and the ethics of this stratum consisted of an unconditional affirmation of and adjustment to the world.[56]

Some rulers sought to free themselves from dependence on the literati by making use of eunuchs and plebeian parvenus, and in these struggles they found support among Taoists. In addition to political divisions, the Confucianist-Taoist divergence followed class differences: the aliterate and antiliterate character of later Taoism attracted circles of traders. For the most part, however, Confucianism and Taoism existed side by side, and Confucian mandarins even used the Taoists for certain services.[57]

The major carrier of Hinduism, the Brahman caste, began as a loosely knit group of intellectuals who gradually gained a superior position over the Vedic priesthood to become, by the sixth century B.C.E., the possessors of religious authority. Unlike the Chinese literati, the Brahmans did not rule politically, and they entered into an alliance with the princes and kings of the Kshatriya caste. The Brahmans' relative lack of involvement in political rule and their economic independence, based on rent from land and on tribute, allowed them to ponder ultimate meanings and cultivate an other-worldly religion. Their ranks included world renouncers as well as the religious counselors, teachers, and priests who served the many autonomous princes of a highly decentralized society. Another difference from China was that the material interests of the Brahmans were advanced by diffusing Hinduism in the population, and they were supported in this by the kings and ruling stratum, who thereby acquired religious legitimation. Despite the fact that other groups and strata were not expected to aspire to the salvation goals of the Brahmans, they adopted Hinduism because its integral relationship with the caste structure gave them monopolies over work opportunities.[58]

Tension was felt between the Brahmanic emphasis on escape from the world as a prerequisite to ultimate salvation and the worldly dharma of the high-status warrior caste. An attempt to solve this problem was made in the epic poem the Bhagavad Gita; the message was that inner-worldly caste duties could increase the chances of ultimate salvation if they were performed in a completely detached way, with no seeking after success.[59] The emphasis remained, however, that only those who detached themselves, outwardly as well as inwardly, from involvement in the world could attain final salvation. Others, including the Brahmans who performed priestly offices, could expect only higher rebirth.

Detachment from the world as the path to salvation remained the message in the heterodox religions that emerged in India, Jainism and Buddhism, but their rejection of the doctrine that birth in the highest caste was a precondition for salvation gave them an appeal to non-Brahmanic high-status strata. Jainism stemmed from Kshatriya speculation and lay asceticism, and it was favored by princes who wished to be free of the Brahmans' power. It appealed also to traders, but Weber emphasized that it was not a product of the bourgeoisie.[60] The teachings of the Buddha were addressed to a group of apolitical, cultivated intellectuals, the product of a privileged stratum who, although anti-Brahmanic, had no desire to change the social order. Buddhism was a religion of world renunciation, carried principally by medicant monks who soon after the time of the Buddha became organized into orders. The early Buddhism of the canonical Pali text can be designated a status ethic of a contemplative monkhood.[61]

The fact that the initiators and major carriers of the Eastern religions came from highly privileged backgrounds helps explain the nature of their soteriologies and their distance from the masses, who remained in a "magical garden." The relative disenchantment in Judaism and Christianity was related to the far greater importance of disprivileged strata among the major carriers of those religions than among the carriers of Eastern religions. It was not the most disprivileged strata, the peasants and urban poor, who were the carriers of an ethical, salvational, rational religion; the unpredictability of their lives disposed them to depend on magic to improve their life chances. The major carriers came rather from the middle and lower-middle strata, the merchants and artisans, whose lifestyles were based on the manipulation of materials and rational calculation.[62]

Religious Institutions

In addition to variations in the lifestyles and sociopolitical characteristics of the principal carriers of the world religions, variations in religious institutions were an important context for the patterns of religious action. The religious elites' religious actions and orientation toward the masses were influenced by the extent of their differentiation from, and their relationships with, political rulers. Where political rulers were not considered deities, they depended on religious elites for legitimation and sought their help in the pacification of subjects. In return, the rulers provided hierocracies with the machinery for the persecution of religious opponents or heretics and the exaction and collection of taxes and contributions. There was a greater possibility of control of a hierocracy by political rulers where the religion was magical and ritualistic and where the ecclesiastical organization was minimal, but rulers had to compromise with hierocracies that proclaimed ethical-soteriological doctrines and had solid hierarchical organizations with educational systems. Ecclesiastical organizations with an extensive autonomy from political rulers were rare in the East, developed to a limited extent in Islam and Eastern Christianity, and reached the highest level in the Roman Catholic Church.[63]

Weber's comments on the implications of religious organizations for religious action are less extensive and more fragmented than his discussion of carriers, but a number of his points are of relevance in a discussion of the differences and relationships between elite and popular religion. One important variable is the extent to which a religion took a congregational form. The laity could have an influence even without a local congregational organization, but priests were more likely to consider the needs of laity who were organized in a manner that allowed them to participate actively in the religious organization. The parish, an administrative unit that delimited the jurisdiction of priests, was by no means universal among the world religions, but even parishes did not guarantee that laypeople would be organized as congregations. In medieval Christianity, Lutheranism, and Anglicanism, the parish was "essentially a passive ecclesiastical tax unit and jurisdictional district of a priest,"[64] and where the congregational type of religion developed, it was connected with the urban middle classes.[65]

Congregations were likely to develop in association with churches that emerged out of hierocracies that had succeeded in overcoming the obstacles of blood groupings of kinship and tribal divisions to their monopolization of the distribution of religious benefits. Churches did not develop, even in a restricted sense, in most Eastern religions, and in the full sense of "church," as bearer and trustee of office charisma, churches existed only in Christianity, Islam, and Lamaist Buddhism.[66]

The organization of priests and monks in the Eastern religions remained amorphous, with loose obligations of membership and little hierarchy. China had no independent powerful priesthood, but Taoist priests occupied positions in some state temples; they were responsible for some systematization of the pantheon of folk deities and spirits; and there was a Taoist hereditary hierarchy modeled on Buddhist examples.[67]

The development of professional monasticism in Hinduism made possible the Hindu restoration among the population in India, but discipline within monasteries remained lax and rules were loosely defined.[68] Weber argued that the highly amorphous character of Buddhist monastic communities was an important factor in the disappearance of Buddhism in India. There was little in the way of an official hierarchy in Buddhism, and like Hindu monks, it was possible for Buddhist monks to resign from a monastery at any time. Of particular relevance for the relationship of elite and popular religion was that families were not attached to monastic consociations; areas were demarcated as associated with particular monasteries, but these were mere measures of convenience for the monks, who performed few communal ceremonies and provided little instruction or preaching.[69] In the Catholic Church, by contrast, laypeople were administered to by monks as well as by priests, and although some monastic orders were encouraged by the hierocracy to become missionaries and fulfill priestly roles among laypeople, local churchmen resented the competition of monks, who were often popular and undemanding confessors.[70]

To summarize: Weber dealt with the relationship of elite and popular religion mainly in terms of the relative influence of the virtuosos over the masses, and the nature of the religion of the virtuosos can be considered as one of three interrelated factors that are important in an explanation of the differences and relationships between elite and popular religion. The first factor concerns the religious values of the virtuosos. The influence of the virtuosos was smaller in the East than elsewhere because their other-worldly, contemplative mysticism separated them from the masses, whose religion remained predominantly one of magical tradition. Laypeople materially supported the virtuosos, who were worshiped as saints or were sought for their magical powers as a means to achieve salvation and worldly goals. This-worldly asceticism, with its practical ethical elements, was more typical of virtuosos in the West and was more likely to relate to the daily life of the masses.[71]

The second factor is the difference among world religions in the carriers and supporters of virtuoso religion. Virtuosos in the East came from the intelligentsia of aristocratic strata, whereas in the Middle East and the West, a different form of intellectualism emerged from urban, petit-bourgeois and bourgeois strata, who supported the rational-ethical development of religious thought and the rational organization of hierocratic domination.[72]

The third factor relates to the structure of religious organization. In the East, religious organizations were mainly limited to monks, whereas in the West, the congregational form of organization and the church incorporated the elites, monks as well as priests, and the masses.[73] Thus, religious values, social carriers, and religious organization interrelated to produce a greater influence of virtuoso religion on the religion of the masses in the West, but it was Weber's contention that, with the exception of Protestantism, the religious activities of the masses in both East and West remained in a magical tradition and were rarely directed toward soteriological goals.

Religious Elites and Masses: Weberian Scholars

The relationships of religious specialists and lay strata have not been a prominent issue in most interpretations and reformulations of Weber's comparisons of the world religions. The issue has arisen, however, in discussions of the relative importance in Weber's accounts of rationalization of the inner logic of religious ideas in comparison with the influence of social carriers and other material factors. Whereas Fredrich Tenbruck makes the inner logic of rationalization a universal process, equally relevant to all the world religions,[74] Talcott Parsons suggests that the inherent dynamism of the intellectual function was a more important factor in the Eastern religions and was responsible for the immanent conception of the divine order, pantheism, and seeking salvation through mystical, contemplative channels. Parsons contrasts the Eastern intellectuals' focus on the question of meaning with Middle Eastern and Western developments that were more affected by external social factors and were carried by relatively nonprivileged groups who sought solutions to suffering and to their exposure to evil.[75]

The implication in Parsons's comparison of a greater distance in the East between religious elites, especially intellectual virtuosos, and the masses is echoed in the writings of other interpreters. Jürgen Habermas writes that the contrast between virtuosos and the masses was found everywhere, but it was the Asiatic religions that had the greatest affinity to the world outlook and life experience of the intellectual elite.[76] Habermas's criticism of Weber—that he judged Confucianism and Taoism only from the standpoint of ethical rationalization and did not consider the Chinese tradition from the standpoint of cognitive rationalization, which, as in ancient Greece, was extensive in China[77]—would appear to reinforce the impression of an especially great divide between religious elites and the masses in China.

Schluchter writes that the greater distance between the religions of virtuosos and masses in the East was a consequence of the virtuosos' emphasis on the cognitive rather than the ethical components of salvation and its achievement. The idea of salvation through literacy or gnostic knowledge imparted to Asian religions an intellectual and aristocratic character, and although intellectualism and religious aristocracy were by no means absent in the Near East and West, the religious tradition's ethical emphasis resulted in a tendency to universalism rather than particularism of grace.[78]

The interpreters of Weber tend to assume that the nature of the Eastern great traditions (contemplative, cognitive emphasis, etc.) and the typical aristocratic intellectualism of the major social carriers must have resulted in a greater divide between the elites and the masses than in the West. They have paid little attention, however, to the patterns of religious action among the masses. Schluchter, for example, writes that the typology of stances toward the world that he extracts from Weber's writings is one that applies to elites or religious virtuosos and not to the masses, who continued to naively affirm the world even within the context of salvation religions.[79]

Religious Elites and Masses: Marxist Analyses

The religion of the masses has been a concern of Marxists, who have frequently interpreted it as a compensation for suffering and alienation.

Other-worldly or transcendental goals among the subordinate classes have been viewed as part of the "false consciousness" that inhibits the development of their "true" class consciousness. Depending on the type of Marxist analysis, the "illusory" compensations of religion will either become self-evident to the subordinate classes as the laws of historical materialism work themselves out or there will be a need for an educational program that will demonstrate the falseness of these compensations and eradicate them. Marxists mention the compensatory element mainly with respect to the subordinate classes, but it is rarely viewed as negating all resistance, and some Marxists believe that religion can become a framework for class consciousness and organized rebellions against the dominant classes.

Both religious compensation and religious rebellion can be placed in the utilitarian action scheme that is adopted by most Marxist theoreticians.[80] Religious compensation among the subordinate classes represents a deviation, as a consequence of ignorance or error, from the pursuit of their rationally conceived class goals. If there is an emphasis on rebellion, religion is interpreted as a means, although not necessarily the most appropriate means, to attain the this-worldly ends of social transformation. Religious ideas and practice are also interpreted as means the dominant classes use to maintain or strengthen the social order. This is part of the dominant classes' instrumental orientation toward the production and dissemination of ideas that are intended to indoctrinate the subordinate classes and obscure their real interests.

The utilitarian action scheme of Marxists has inhibited an interest in variant forms of such non-utilitarian ends as religious salvation, but interesting analyses of religion have been made by Marxists who have rejected "vulgar" interpretations of religion as an epiphenomenon of material factors and have taken a special interest in the components of the "superstructure." Antonio Gramsci, perhaps the most prominent Marxist theoretician of the superstructure, made a number of observations relevant to subjects central to this work: the differences and relationships between official and popular religion. With respect to official religion, Gramsci's comments on the medieval Catholic Church qualified his portrayal of the dominant classes in precapitalist societies as closed castes who did not attempt to extend their ideology to the subordinate classes. Gramsci wrote that, although precapitalist societies were built on inertia and indifference rather than consensus, the Catholic Church felt the need for the doctrinal unity of all believers. The church sought to prevent the formation of two religions, one for "intellectuals" and another for "simple souls," by imposing a strict discipline on its functionaries and by founding new religious orders that absorbed popular movements.[81]

The ecclesiastical hierarchies of the church were a good example of what Gramsci called "traditional intellectuals" who justified their position by a historical continuity that was uninterrupted by even the most complicated and radical changes in the political and social structure.[82] Although traditional intellectuals were not necessarily passive agents of the classes they served or represented,[83] the ecclesiastics were bound to the landed aristocracy, sharing their feudal ownership of land. The concern of the church to bridge the religious differences between intellectuals and the lower strata can be seen as part of a strategy of hegemonic control by the dominant class or "historical bloc" of social groups. The notion of hegemony was given a number of meanings by Gramsci, but with respect to a dominant class's dual strategies of coercion and the production of consent, hegemonic social control was generally understood to be predominantly consensual. Two major superstructural levels were involved in the control of a society by a dominant class or historical bloc: the political society or state, which was the primary vehicle of coercive domination, and the civil society, including the church, which was the primary source of consensual hegemony. Civil society did not operate exclusively by consent, but coercion by religious authorities was more likely to operate on a spiritual than on a physically violent plane.[84]

The Catholic Church did not, however, lead the "simple folk" to a higher conception of life; it left them in their primitive philosophy of "common sense," and it maintained only an external unity, based primarily on the liturgy.[85] Where there is a gulf between the religions of the elite and of the masses, ritualization may be the primary means by which the rudiments of elite religion are infused into popular religion. The rituals embody the ideology of the elite, but the symbolism of the rituals is able to accommodate the magical interpretations and worldly ends of the masses.[86]

Popular religion, which Gramsci described as crassly materialistic,[87] appeared in his categorization of cultural forms to overlap with folklore, which he considered to be the lowest form of culture, associated with the subaltern masses living at the periphery of the dominant hegemonies. As a factor influencing daily lives, folklore should be analyzed seriously, but its conceptions of the world lacked systematization and coherence. It contained a fragmented and unelaborated mosaic of remnants from the high, official cultures, both of the present and of the past. As a debased spillover of cultural hegemonies, folklore was essentially conservative, and it contributed to the subordinate position of the subaltern classes. The negative characteristics of folklore far outweighed the positive elements that were to be found in it, and it was necessary, therefore, to replace it, together with other religious notions and common sense, with a new mass culture.[88]

Nicholas Abercrombie, Stephen Hill, and Bryan Turner dispute that there was an incorporation of the medieval and early modern peasantry into Christianity by the church. Their portrayal of a religious division in the European Middle Ages between the "Christian" dominant class and the "non-Christian" peasant majority is part of their critique of those neo-Marxist theories that have attempted to explain the acquiescence of subordinate classes through their acceptance of a dominant ideology formulated and imposed by a dominant class. Abercrombie, Hill, and Turner argue that it was not ideological indoctrination but military and judicial force that accounted for the compliance of the subordinate classes in feudal Europe. Christianity was the dominant belief system in the medieval period only in the sense of its influence among the ruling class. For this class, the church's teachings on sexuality, monogamy, and family duty, emphasizing the need for the virginity of brides, the chastity of wives, and the fecundity of mothers, were of central importance. These doctrines provided support for a system of stable inheritance, the preservation and concentration of the ownership of land among a few families, on which the feudal mode of production was based. Conflicts did arise within the dominant class between the ecclesiastical and secular sectors, over such issues as the appropriate rules of marriage, but in general, the teachings of the church succeeded in providing a coherent ideology for the dominant class. One example is the conception of chivalry, formulated by churchmen who depicted knighthood as a religious calling and who drew parallels between the asceticism of the monk and the warrior.

The church attempted to achieve social control over the peasantry by means of the confessional and the sacrament of penance, but these proved neither reliable or affective, and churchmen constantly complained about the difficulties of bringing the laity to confess on a regular basis. The majority of peasants did not attend church regularly to hear sermons or take the sacraments; they remained largely ignorant of the Christian faith; and they preserved many of their pre-Christian beliefs and festivals within the context of a localized sense of identity and solidarity. Certain practices, such as black masses, the recitation of Christian prayers backward, and the burlesque of church rituals in holiday celebrations, point to the rejection of the official religion. The invention of printing, the Reformation, and the Enlightenment only served to increase the cultural distance between the dominant and subordinate classes. There were important religious components in the ideology of the bourgeoisie in the period of early capitalism, and religion retained a firm basis among both the landed and industrial sectors of the dominant class, but the working class remained impervious to formal Christian religion.[89]

Abercrombie, Hill, and Turner tend to conflate their distinction between Christianity and folk religion with both the division between clerics and laypeople and the division between dominant and subordinate classes. Similar conflations are to be found in the writings of social scientists, influenced by Marxism, who have investigated the religion of peasants and poor urban strata in Central and South America and in Asia. An exception is Otto Maduro, a Venezuelan Marxist sociologist of religion, who distinguishes three types of divisions with respect to religious interests: dominant and subordinate classes, religious specialists and laity, and the higher and lower religious specialists. The interest of the dominant class to legitimate its position by religion diverges from the interest of the subordinate class to receive religious compensation for their position or to demand a reversal of the religious legitimation. The interests of the religious specialists or clergy to preserve and extend their power over the production, exchange, and distribution of religious goods or means of salvation diverge from those of the laity, who wish to restrain or possibly to reverse the process of expropriation or to obtain religious goods from the clergy at a minimal cost. Among the religious specialists, there is a division between the higher clergy, who wish to preserve and deepen their religious power, and the lower clergy, who wish to acquire more of that power.

The dominant class will seek to incorporate the clergy into its hegemonic strategy by promoting economic, political, and familial links with the higher ranks of the clergy, bestowing privileges and property on them, and creating feelings among the clergy of indebtedness and dependence. If the dominant class succeed in this strategy, the clergy will produce religious discourses that reinforce the social order and turn attention away from class conflicts.[90] The subordinate class may find allies among the lower clergy, but the dependence of the lower clergy on the higher is likely to make for a weaker clergy-laity alliance than that between the dominant class and the higher clergy. The dominant classes, however, may not succeed in placing the religious system under their direct or indirect control, and it is unlikely that the clergy's religious production will be devoted solely to satisfying the demands of the dominant classes.

Maduro's sophisticated analysis allows for the relative autonomy of religion within a Marxian framework. In contrast to Gramsci, however, who believed that popular religion and folklore narrowed the mental perspective of the masses and served the interests of the dominant classes, recent Marxian writers have emphasized themes of rebellion within popular religion and the little tradition. Roger Lancaster, for example, writes that although fiestas centering on patron saints appear to be about magical cures and favors, their symbols of inversion and reversal reveal that their real subjects are popular revolt against social inequality and the possibility of transforming the social order.[91]

Elites and Masses: A Framework of Relationships and Environments

The themes of inversion and revolt in popular religion have been subject to contradictory interpretations. A functionalist interpretation that has been made by radicals as well as nonradicals points to the cathartic effects of symbolic inversions and the defusing of pressure that results from the periodic acting out of revolt. Once they have given expression to their resentments and exorcised their frustration in a symbolic fashion, the subordinate peasants and workers will return and accommodate themselves to their positions of subordination. The implication of this interpretation from a radical viewpoint is that the development of an advanced class consciousness requires the eradication of popular traditional religion. An alternative interpretation proposes that the periodic rituals of transgression keep alive the possibility of revolt in the consciousness of the poor, and that revolutionary thought and action should build on those themes in popular religion that express opposition to the established order.

It would appear to be premature to characterize popular religion as either essentially conservative or essentially radical. As Maduro writes, the effect of class struggles can have a variable effect on religion, not only because of the circumstances of those struggles but also because of the internal conditions of the "religious field," a complex of social agents and institutions that may impede, filter, or facilitate the forces and influences of the wider society.[92] Thus, the orientation of lay masses toward elite religion may range from indifference to appropriation to resistance. Popular movements of resistance are outside the purview of this work, but protests against official religion may be included in the symbolic reversals of hierarchical relationships and satires of official rituals in popular carnivals.

The policies and strategies of religious elites toward popular religion also range widely: they include indifference, toleration, persecution, appropriation, and superimposition. An example of elite appropriation is when a local god is identified as a member of the official pantheon. An example of superimposition is when the elite succeed in superimposing their own supramundanes on those of the masses, as occurred in Christianity when official saints were superimposed on local nature or fertility spirits. Laypeople may, however, transform the elite supramundanes into local community deities who are believed to be instrumental in achieving goals quite different from those proposed by the elite.

The strategies of elites toward popular religion are influenced by two types of interests that can exist in tension: first, the exclusion of non-elite persons from the religious benefits enjoyed by members of the elite, such as access to the means to achieve valued religious goals; and second, the control over the distribution of religious benefits among the population. Insofar as a religious elite constitutes a status group, its members are likely to exclude from their religious ceremonies the participation of persons from subordinate groups and to regard the popular religion of subordinate groups with indifference and disdain. In contrast, the concern of hierocratic elites to control the distribution of religious benefits necessarily involves active strategies toward popular religion, which, depending on values and circumstances, may take the form of superimposition, appropriation, or repression.

The orientations and strategies of elites and masses that affect the extent to which elite and popular religions differ and overlap depend in turn on the "environments" of religious action, the values and institutional contexts that both limit and enable religious action. Three environments of religious action are distinguished here: first, the religious value complexes that underlie the patterns of religious action (of special importance is the extent to which values emphasize common or different goals and paths for elites and masses); second, the characteristics and structure of religious organizations (these include the extent to which religious elites and lay masses participate in encompassing or separate religious organizational contexts, as well as the levels of hierarchization and centralization of the organizations); and third, the wider socioeconomic and political environments (of special importance is the extent to which religious elites are differentiated from or associated with the dominant classes and political rulers).

PART II

Religious Action in the World Religions

There is no agreement among scholars over what constitutes a world religion, and there is necessarily some degree of arbitrariness in the choice of cases to compare. This work follows Max Weber in his focus on six of the world religions, but my choice of cases has been determined in part by the availability of sufficient information to permit the delineation of patterns of religious action of both elites and masses. The summary of Weber's work on the world religions in the previous chapter made no attempt to "correct" his descriptions and interpretations in the light of new material and scholarship. Weber's scholarly achievements were phenomenal given the material available to him, but there have been extensive revisions of many of his characterizations, especially of the Asian religions, as well as criticisms of his interpretations.

In the following chapters, the differences between contemporary interpretations and those of Weber are only occasionally made explicit, and an attempt is made to build on Weber's considerable achievements, especially with respect to the description and analyses of popular religion. What we have now is a substantial accumulation of studies on popular religion—anthropological, historical, or both—among rural populations in China, India, Southeast Asia, and Catholic Europe, with a somewhat more limited number of studies on other Christian streams, Islam, and Judaism.

The availability of source data on popular religion has been a major determinant of the relative foci on the past or the present in individual chapters. Since the Communist Revolution in China, Western anthropologists have had few opportunities to conduct research on popular religion in mainland China, but we do have many historical studies of popular religion in late imperial China. A comparison of the data from the historical studies with the data gathered by anthropologists in contemporary Taiwan show remarkable continuities in Chinese popular religion. There are relatively few historical studies of the popular forms of religion in Hindu India and Buddhist Southeast Asia, but we do have a considerable accumulation of anthropological studies that provide much of the data in the chapters on Hinduism and Theravada Buddhism. With respect to popular religion in European Catholic countries, we have the advantage of a considerable number of both historical and anthropological studies. This enables us to point to both change and continuities in popular religion over a considerable time frame.

The chapters on China, Hinduism in India, Buddhism in Southeast Asia, and "traditional" Catholic Europe have a common framework: the characteristic patterns of elite and popular religion are described; their interrelationships are analyzed; and the data are then contextualized by reference to religious values, religious institutions, and the wider sociopolitical environment. The cases here include one, China, where an emphasis is placed on the total complex of religions (Confucianism, Taoism, Buddhism) that constitute "Chinese religion." In the other cases, the focus is on a single religion within a geocultural unit (Hinduism in India, Theravada Buddhism in Southeast Asia, Catholicism in Europe). Japanese religion is similar to Chinese in its syncretism of a number of religious traditions, but in a brief section appended to the chapter on Buddhism, I have, for comparative purposes, chosen to focus on the place of Buddhism in Japanese popular religion.

The focus on a particular religious tradition in most of the chapters is not intended to suggest that what we call the world religions are single, monolithic traditions or that we can understand the development of religion in a particular area or country by focusing exclusively on the dominant tradition. It is evident, for example, that what we call Hinduism today developed in interaction with other religious traditions, especially Jainism and Buddhism in ancient times and Sikhism and Islam in later times. The understanding of the total religious scene of a particular society, such as India, or the historical development of a particular tradition are not, however, the major concerns here. This work is an attempt to compare and analyze the interactions of elite and popular forms of religion, and for this purpose an analytical differentiation of the religious traditions appears justified.

The short chapter on Islam and Judaism does not attempt to provide a comprehensive review of elite and popular religion or follow strictly the framework of the preceding chapters. Instead, the dynamics of popular religion are demonstrated by focusing on popular communal religion and popular religious movements organized around saints who present an alternative leadership to the scholarly elites of ulema and rabbis. Chapter 9 also deviates somewhat from the framework of the preceding chapters on China, Hinduism, Buddhism, and traditional Catholicism by analyzing the effects, both short and long term, of the Protestant Reformation and the Catholic Counter-Reformation on popular religion. A section on the United States looks at the relationships between churches and popular religion in a society without a peasant class and where church and state were separated. The concluding chapter highlights comparisons of elite and popular religions and their interrelationships and considers the new forms of popular religion in advanced modern or post-modern societies.

4

China

State Religion, Elites, and Popular Religion in a Syncretistic Milieu

The analysis here focuses on typical patterns of religious action of three social categories: the dominant class of scholar-officials (the literati), the religious elites of Buddhist and Taoist religious institutions, and the subordinate class of peasants and urban workers. Data on the patterns of religious action of Confucian literati are necessarily drawn from historical studies, whereas the accounts of Taoist and Buddhist elites and popular religion draw on both historical research and recent anthropological studies. The section on the relationships of official and popular religion relates especially to the late empire period (eighteenth and nineteenth centuries). In general, the material is presented in the past tense, but many of the patterns (and especially the popular patterns) of religious action are to be found today—especially in Taiwan, which, because of the repression of religion and problems of undertaking fieldwork in Communist mainland China, has been the major site of anthropological studies of Chinese popular religion.

Syncretism and Great Traditions

The vast majority of the Chinese population, past and present and from all strata, cannot be identified with, or internally distinguished by, specific religious traditions. The majority of Chinese participated in religions that have been portrayed as syncretistic amalgams of Confucianism, Taoism, Buddhism, as well as additional elements that cannot be linked to the three major traditions.[1] The syncretistic combinations have differed considerably over the vast expanses of time and space of the Chinese empires, and some scholars have argued that the range of beliefs and practices is so great among locales and communities that it makes little sense to refer to "Chinese religion" as a single entity.[2] Other scholars have argued, just as forcibly, that Chinese religion has a unity that transcends the variety among regions and strata.[3] They do not deny the numerous local deities and ritual forms, but they point to common features such as cosmological notions (the Tao, yin-yang, the five elements), geomancy, ancestral worship, the belief in the supremacy of Heaven (T'ien) over all other deities, annual festivals, similar forms of ritual offerings to deities, and common patterns of exorcism of harmful spirits.[4]

Traditional China had great traditions in the sense that three identifiable elites promoted and interpreted three particular systems of religious beliefs and practices that were based on three distinctive canons: Confucianism, whose major social carrier was the group of scholar-officials (gentry or literati), especially its more intellectual sectors; Buddhism, whose major carrier was the Buddhist monks, and Taoism, whose carrier was the Taoist monks and priests. The distinctions among the three traditions can be made at self-conscious literate levels, but at the level of practice, the distinctions are difficult to maintain.

The difference between great tradition—the canon formulated, promoted, and interpreted by a religious elite—and elite religion—the overall system of religious action of an elite—is of relevance here. Whereas it is possible to distinguish many religious items that can be identified with distinctive great traditions, such as T'ien with Confucianism and bodhisattvas with Buddhism, the traditions themselves were not exclusive to any particular group or stratum, nor did any particular group or stratum practice only one of the traditions. The literati, for example, were the major carrier of Confucianism, but their patterns of religious action contained many elements of non-Confucianist origin, and the influence of Confucianist notions is evident in the religious actions of other strata.

Official Religion and the Literati

The literati or "gentry" were a group whose status and political authority were based primarily on members' knowledge of the Confucian classics, which was demonstrated by success in the civil service examinations that enabled them to hold official titles and positions in the state bureaucracy. There were scholars who did not take the examinations or hold official positions, but they shared the educational experiences and social identities of the "scholar-officials." Most of the literati read the same books, wore clothing that identified them as members of the gentry, and participated in rituals appropriate to their status.[5]

A distinction can be made between the nomic goals of the literati, who as state officials participated in the formulation and administration of the official religion, and the transformative goals of the literati, who as followers of Confucius sought completion of the Tao, or Way of Heaven. Confucianism was the major canonical tradition in official religion, but among literati tension could arise between their position as servants of the emperor, located within the ruling elite, and their self-perception as noble sages and autonomous custodians of the Confucian Way.

Unlike Taoism and Buddhism, the Confucian canon was constructed and interpreted not by priests and monks but by an ongoing interaction between the imperial courts and members of the literati. More than any other religion, Confucianism was tied to official religion, an extensive system of religious items that were formulated in legal documents by members of the state bureaucracy. The boundaries of official religion were a matter of state, and special departments and officials of the state organized and administered official religious institutions. The Ministry of Rites was divided into a number of bureaus that approved and supervised such activities as the erection of new temples, the licensing of priests, the recognition and incorporation of gods into the official pantheon, the ritual calendar, and the correct formulas for sacrificial and other rituals. The actual administration of officially sponsored temples was devolved to local elites, who had a vested interest in maintaining good relations with state officials.

Official religion should not be confused, however, with Confucianism. The official temples and shrines contained many Confucianist features, but as the outcome of the influences and sometimes conflicting interests of emperors, literati, Taoist priests, and local elites, they also included Taoist and popular religious elements. Religious institutions identified with Buddhism and Taoism were not promoted by the later dynasties of the Chinese empire, but they were subject to political regulation and supervision. Neither Buddhism nor Taoism had an empirewide or centralized system of religious authority that could stand up against the state.[6]

Official religion in China was initiated, organized, and administered by agencies of the state whose major goal, at the most general level of formulation, was the accomplishment and continual reassertion of a hierarchical order, encompassing both the supramundane and society. Order and harmony of the interwoven human and supramundane worlds were always conceived as hierarchical, and official religion provided that clear lines and distinctions should be made between the ranks of both deities and humans. The emperor was not only the highest human participant in the official religion; he was also held to be superior over most deities, and he used his authority to grant honorific titles to deities, promoting some and demoting others.[7] He had the exclusive right to sacrifice to Heaven, a ritual that was allowed to take place only in the imperial capital. Others were forbidden to make sacrifices to Heaven because such ritual accessibility could uphold a claim that Heaven was supporting a struggle against the emperor. For similar reasons, the government claimed a monopoly on the interpretation of heavenly portents; any unusual phenomenon of nature could be interpreted as Heaven's anger over the misconduct of an important individual or group.[8]

The emperor was the leading participant in the worship of his ancestors and of great statespersons and warriors, to whom sacrifices were exclusively conducted in the imperial capital. The worship of Confucius, the "patron saint" of the literati, was an important component of official religion (sacrifices to Confucius were included among the limited number of sacrifices performed personally by the emperor), and many state-sponsored shrines were dedicated to celebrated former officials. In accord with their ranks, officials conducted the middle and lower levels of sacrifice to a multitude of ranked deities in the provincial capitals and other towns. Rituals were held for some supramundanes, such as the soil and grain gods and the hungry ghosts, at all administrative levels.

By establishing altars for gods, based on their prototypes in the capital, and by matching a hierarchy of city gods with the civil administration, it was intended that all communities would be integrated into the hierarchical structure of the state. The Record of Rites stipulated how the gods were to be worshiped at the various administrative levels, and there were also specifications for the number of ancestral generations to be worshiped, according to social rank. All such restrictions and obligations were intended to reinforce status distinctions, encourage submissiveness to authority, and express the pervasive notion of harmony based on hierarchy.[9]

The temples of official gods were modeled on the residences of government officials, and the gods were dressed in robes typical of civil and military officials. The fashioning by state officials of supramundanes after their own bureaucratic structure was especially apparent in the case of territorial deities, who were known not as individuals but by their posts;

they served given terms of office and were promoted and demoted according to their performance.[10] One of these gods, the City God, held a bureaucratic rank in the supramundane world equivalent to his earthly counterpart, the district magistrate. When a magistrate took up his post, he would visit the City God to enlist his help in governing the people, and during his term of office the magistrate called on the City God to help him resolve judicial cases.

Apart from the City God, magistrates made sacrifices and offerings to many gods and spirits in their full schedule of rituals prescribed in the official statutes: they included the deities of war, literature, soil, and grain; the spirits of the winds, clouds, thunder, rain, mountains, and streams; the spirits of local worthies; and the potentially troublesome ghosts. Ritual performances by the appropriate officials to the many supramundanes were believed to harmonize the forces of yin and yang and thereby maintain the natural and social order.[11] The maintenance of a harmonious cosmos, and at the individual level, the achievement of oneness with this cosmos, required also the discernment of the will of Heaven and conformity to the codes of ceremony, social propriety, and ethical behavior appropriate to the Confucian gentleman.

Weber's portrayal of the religious actions of the literati as accommodations to, and affirmations of, the existent society has been modified by historians of imperial China who have argued that, beginning in the Sung dynasty (960–1126), a transcendentalism, albeit a worldly one, can be discerned in the writings of the "neo-Confucianists." Wm. Theodore de Bary writes that, although neo-Confucianists did not conceive of T'ien as an active deity who communicated with them, they understood Heaven's imperatives to provide ideal moral standards and a basis for a radical critique of the established order. De Bary believes that a prophetic stance is to be found in the writings of some neo-Confucianists who protested against the despotism of imperial dynasties. The protests remained, however, at a literary and theoretical level, for scholars had no power base of their own to challenge the state.[12] Thomas Metzger has argued that, after the eleventh century, neo-Confucianists saw little hope for sociopolitical transformation, and that although a concern with the "outer realm" never entirely disappeared, the transformative goal came to be focused on the individual. It was individual perfection, a personal harmony with the Tao, that became the central quest. This was a goal that was sought even though it was felt to be extremely difficult, if not impossible, to achieve.[13]

Neo-Confucianists believed that the cultivation of self required the development of the seeds of goodness that were inherent in human nature. The principle of heavenly order, already actively present in the self, had to be located, developed, and protected against the disturbances of the passions and egoistic thoughts. This could be done only by a mastery of the Confucian canon and by conforming both to the basic principles of conduct, such as filial obedience, and to the minutiae of ritual, propriety, and deportment. An important additional means for the achievement of this personal state, which was observed among some neo-Confucianists, was the cultivation of quiescence through meditation or "quiet sitting." Meditation among Confucianists was practiced in the home or study and appears to have been interspersed with normal activities.[14]

The supramundane entities relevant to these goals—Tao, T'ien, the five elemental operative qualities or phases (metal, wood, water, fire, and earth), and the yin-yang forces—tended to be conceived by the literati in an impersonal idiom. In its most general sense, the Tao was the essence of all that exists, the cosmic force behind all phenomena, the absolute reality behind or within all appearances. As an ultimate essence, the Tao was ineffable and inaccessible to human description, but it was also conceived as the ideal, true, normative way or order of society and behavior. More concretely, the Tao was believed to have been accomplished at the beginning of certain dynasties under exemplary emperors. According to this understanding, the collectivist, transformative goal represented a return to a golden age or ages of the past when the Tao had been realized.[15]

T'ien was also attributed with various meanings that differed with respect to impersonal or personal and passive or active idioms. In its pre-Confucian form, T'ien had been an anthropomorphic being at the peak of a pantheon, and although in many Confucian texts it was personified as the supreme Emperor, the father of all earthly Chinese emperors, the dominant Confucian conception was of an impersonal, amorphic, supreme principle or force that expressed and sustained an order that was both divine and natural, cosmic and social. The most sophisticated among the literati believed that T'ien acted only in an indirect fashion, in a spontaneous and impersonal fashion, without intention and with total impartiality. There was, however, a tendency to conceive of T'ien in a more active idiom than that of the Tao. T'ien was seen as the greatest controlling power, with a moral will that judged the behavior and determined the destiny of individuals and dynasties. It was the support of T'ien that Confucians sought in order to reestablish the Tao.[16]

Somewhat more differentiated impersonal conceptions in Chinese cosmology were the five elements or phases, which were seen to compose the fundamental qualities of all phenomena, and the yin-yang forces, which were seen to produce and animate all things and beings. These were central notions in a system of correspondences and complementarities between the cosmic and human orders that were pertinent to the means for achieving the neo-Confucianist goals.[17] They were relevant to the practice of geomancy—the harmonization of landscape, time, and persons—which was common among all strata, and to the more elitist concern with the cultivation of self.

The emphasis on self-cultivation and the perfection of heart and mind among neo-Confucianists left intact a society that some saw as only an imperfect approximation to the Tao. The goal of changing society was transformative only in a limited sense. The ideal society, which was believed to have existed in the past, and the existent society shared basic values, such as filial piety, that contributed to the acceptance of the status quo and the perception of the existing state as the expression of Heaven's will. And even at the level of the individual, many of the means to achieve the transformative goal involved conformity and adjustment to the existent society. Thus, Weber's analysis has been modified rather than shown wrong. The literati were carriers of a great tradition, articulating the goals and means of Confucianism, but as state bureaucrats, their transcendentalism or transformationism was bound to be limited.[18]

At a more mundane level, the goals of the religious action of the literati included the passing of examinations, official appointments, upward mobility, longevity, health, and prosperity. The gentry could refer to "ledges of merit and demerit" for assistance in planning their behavior and accumulating the merits required to attain their goals. The specific deeds to be followed and avoided were assigned points that provided precise measures for calculating, in numerical terms, the values of good and bad deeds and their rewards and punishments.

The earliest known ledges of the twelfth century were influenced by Buddhism and Taoism, and the rewards and punishments they promised were predominantly other-worldly: immortality or a good rebirth on the one hand and sufferings in hell or reincarnation in a lower form on the other. Soteriological rewards, such as deification, were still included in the ledges in later centuries, but this-worldly rewards and punishments, such as examination success or failure, longevity or premature death, appeared more often. The lists of good deeds varied little throughout the history of the ledges: conformity to the rules of the basic social relationships, the exercise of self-restraint, frugality and humility, acts of charity, and the worship of appropriate spirits.

The connection between good deeds and personal rewards that was made in the ledges contradicted a classical Confucian view that good should be done for its own sake or to bring order to the world, and not for personal rewards. The more common view among literati was that moral and immoral acts called forth rewards and retribution from supra-mundanes, although there were different views with regard to how this relationship operated. Some argued that retribution occurred "naturalis-tically," as an automatic process of action and response in accord with the transcendent moral order of T'ien. The alternative view was that retribu-tion was the work of the supramundane bureaucracy of gods and spirits, who kept a close surveillance over human behavior and dealt appropri-ately with the individual's smallest acts and innermost thoughts.[19]

Beyond their nomic and thaumaturgical patterns, some literati dem-onstrated transformationism in the sense of their concern to sacralize (or ethicalize) the world, but the Confucian canon offered little in the way of other-worldly salvation. The literati could take comfort in the belief that their actions would bring them a good name after death, and they could expect to be remembered and worshiped as ancestors, but conceptions of death and the afterlife remained undeveloped in Confucianism. Although Confucianism was an important basis of ancestor worship, its emphasis was on caring for the dead as a filial duty, with little or no attention to the ancestors' supramundane status or powers. Those who were concerned with existence after death were likely to turn to Buddhism, and although many literati distanced themselves from Buddhism and condemned its rituals, Buddhist ideas, especially karma and transmigration, were widely accepted. Some literati employed Buddhist priests to conduct funeral ser-vices, with the object of helping the deceased expiate their sins and avoid suffering in the netherworld prior to reincarnation.[20] Like other Chinese, the religious actions of literati were not confined to a single religious tradition.

Taoist and Buddhist Elites

Among the Taoist and Buddhist elites, a distinction can be made between the virtuosos and the priests and monks who provided religious services for laypeople. Virtuosos of historical Taoist movements have been categorized into two groups: (1) those who sought union with the Tao and (2) those who sought physical immortality. The former adopted Buddhist meditation techniques and cultivated a state of serenity and emptiness that was intended to lead to the dissolving of subject/object distinctions and a return to an undifferentiated, primordial, pure cosmos.[21]

Rarefied mystics were probably always few in Taoism, and the greater number of Taoist virtuosos sought physical immortality, or at least longevity, a goal that was seen to represent a reversal of the normal progression from yang to yin. Once the virtuoso had liberated himself from all physical limitations, he could choose either to remain in his physical body and enjoy mundane pleasures or to wander freely in space and visit or dwell in one of the abodes of immortals.[22] The appropriate religious actions were the concoction through alchemy of an elixir of life, seeking out a mushroom that would prevent death, and the preservation of what were regarded as the vital components of the life force—breath, blood, semen. Breathing exercises and gymnastics were practiced; dietary regimes were followed in order to reduce the excreta that clogged passages in which the life force circulated; and techniques were used to prevent the ejaculation of semen during the sexual act.[23]

Union with the Tao and physical immortality were goals that were rarely sought outside virtuoso circles, and Taoists were no doubt influenced by Buddhism when their soteriological goals shifted toward a concern with an afterlife in heaven and avoiding or reducing the tortures of hell.[24] These were goals that were more likely to be shared among priests and laypeople, and in recent times, the emphasis upon the personal salvation of Taoist priests has appeared less prominent than the services they have performed for communities and for individual laypeople. Many Chinese regard Taoist priests as indispensable for the consecration of temples and newly made statues of gods, the blessing of gods on their birthday festivals, purification ceremonies, leading religious processions, and placating dangerous spirits. Buddhist monks also act as liturgical specialists, sometimes together with Taoist priests in community rituals, but their ritual participation is generally less than the Taoists'. A common type of Taoist priest has been the "hearth-dwelling" priest who works out of his home and performs rituals within a large area when invited by individuals, families, and temples.[25]

At the collective level, an important and complex set of rituals performed by Taoist priests is the *jiao*, the rite of cosmic renewal, which is held when new temples are opened and at regular intervals of twelve years or so. Its major nomic goal is both cosmic and social: a reversal of the cosmic process of disorder and entropy and a purification and renewal of the particular territorial community. A union of humans and nature with the transcendent Tao is effected as the Tao's primordial breath circulates through the entire cosmos, bringing a renewal of the five elements, crops, and children.[26]

The formal rituals the Taoist priests conduct on these occasions are regarded as essential by members of the community, but the complex meanings involving the purging of yin influences and the restoration of yang forces are only vaguely understood, if at all, among most participants.[27] The restrictions the Taoist priests impose on access to their religious knowledge have contributed to divergent priestly and popular interpretations of the rituals. In a jiao ritual, for example, laypeople singled out the worship of the Emperor of Heaven and the ghosts as the most significant because these elements resemble those of popular rituals outside the context of institutionalized religion.[28]

The most commonly sought services of Taoist priests are directed to thaumaturgical goals of families and individuals, especially the diagnosis and curing of illnesses. A combination of divination techniques and some traditional Chinese medicinal knowledge is used to diagnose minor ailments, and the simplest and most common cures involve writing charms, which the patient places in his home or burns so that he can drink the ashes or wash with them. Complex diseases require more complex ritual solutions, such as exorcism, for which the Taoist priests draw on their esoteric knowledge.[29] The names of spirits, the mantras for summoning them, and the techniques for bringing them under control are among the most carefully guarded secrets of a Taoist priest's liturgical repertoire.[30]

The Taoist priest's rank is connected to the extensiveness of his talismanic list of deities who will obey his commands and enable him to communicate with higher spheres. One method of communication is for the priest to summon the gods from the microcosm of his body and to merge with the gods' counterparts in the macrocosm. The self-transformation of Taoist priests into gods is a voluntary process that enables them to command exceptional powers. It differs from the process of mediums, who are often forced into a trance by the insistence of a deity.[31] Mediums and other popular practitioners also perform healing and exorcism, but the Taoist priests are more likely to use "literalized" techniques and to chant written prayers.[32]

Like the Taoist priests, Buddhist monks are called on by communities and individuals to act as liturgical specialists in the achievement of thau-maturgical goals such as praying for rain, healing, and exorcism.[33] With regard to soteriological goals and their appropriate means, Buddhism has undergone considerable transformation in China. The ultimate goal of nirvana, its doctrinal grounding in the utter unreality of all phenomena, and the appropriate means of other-worldly contemplation were not in affinity with the this-worldly orientations and social foci of the Chinese. The Buddhistic monastic ideal of rejecting worldly ties was in conflict with the social ethics of filial piety and the ritual obligations of ancestral worship. Dependent as they are on donations, Buddhist monks tried to meet, in part at least, the demands of laypeople and to find an acceptable accommodation with the family. Texts were written that praised parents and enumerated the obligations of children, and it was ruled that no son could enter a monastery without his parents' permission. Many monasteries took family organization as their model, with an older monk playing the role of father by setting up ancestral tablets and by performing rituals that signified the adoption of monks into the "lineage."[34]

During the entire history of Buddhism in China, it is probable that the rank and file of the Sangha (monks) were only semiliterate, and that they were only able to recite by rote a smattering of the Chinese versions of the sacred texts and what were, for them, unintelligible Sanskrit formulas. Special competence in the enormous Buddhist canon was limited to an elite of scholar-monks.[35] Of the major monastic movements, only the Ch'an movement included patterns of religious action that focused on the goal of nirvana. This movement taught that salvation meant enlightenment of the true nature of the Void, the non-existence of the ego, and escape from the illusory conditions of the phenomenal world. There were no bodhisattvas or other deities to assist in the elimination of suffering anchored in this-worldly desires, and only meditational techniques could lead to transcendental awareness and ultimate salvation.

A larger Buddhist movement in China was the Pure Land movement, whose typical soteriological goal was entrance into the Western Paradise of the Buddha Amitabha. This was to be achieved not by arduous self-discipline or meditation but by meritorious deeds, devotional practices, and genuine faith. A central practice of this movement, the repetition of the sacred formula "Hail to Amitabha Buddha," served to reaffirm faith in the savior Buddha.[36] Rebirth in the Western Paradise or Pure Land was also the soteriological goal of predominantly lay Buddhist-influenced movements such as the White Lotus movements. This was a meaning of salvation that was inconsistent with the beliefs of the soul associated with ancestor worship, and only a small minority of Chinese became members of these movements. Moreover, Buddhist monks sometimes expressed a concern that lay followers turned to the Buddha savior to solve problems of a this-worldly nature.

The contrast made by the Buddhist elite between the worldly life and salvation has encouraged the masses to perceive Buddhism as focused on the afterlife rather than on their daily needs, and in China there has been some division of labor between the Taoist priests, who specialize more in protection against harmful spirits and demons in this world, and Buddhist monks, who specialize in the care of souls in the afterlife. This division is by no means clear-cut, if only because many of the spirits who visit the living come from the underworld, but it is generally the Buddhist monks who are requested to offer chants for the deceased in order to free their souls from the hells and effect their ascent to heaven. When the limitations on religious practice were lifted in 1979, many Chinese requested that Buddhist monks and nuns chant sutras for those who had died during the long period when such activities had been forbidden.[37]

Popular Religion

There is a considerable interrelationship of soteriological and thaumaturgical goals in Chinese religious action. Two major goals of the Chinese masses are integrally linked: first, to assure the dead a peaceful and comfortable afterlife, and second, to avoid or minimize misfortunes and to maximize the fortunes of the living. Impersonally conceived supramundane forces, particularly yang and yin, are relevant to these goals, but at the popular level, these forces tend to take on personalized characteristics or to become associated with personalized entities and beings. The achievement of most goals of religious action is seen to be dependent on the relationships between the person or group and the various categories of supramundane beings, many of whom are believed to have been past humans who continue, in their transformed states as ancestors, gods, and ghosts, to affect the lives of the living. Even gods and spirits of natural phenomena such as mountains and rivers came to be identified with the souls of historical or pseudohistorical persons and were attributed with specific roles within the supramundane hierarchy. For example, the mountain god of T'ai-shan, which is popularly known as the Eastern

Peak, was a judge in the Ten Courts of Hell and was believed to bring peace and order to communities.[38]

Deities that are found in the highest positions of the pantheon are the least relevant to the achievement of goals. T'ien is not absent from the religion of the Chinese masses, but as a remote being or force, it is of little relevance to people's goals. In many contemporary Taiwanese temples, T'ien is represented by a plaque with written characters, whereas other deities are represented by carved images. Somewhat more personal but still remote for most purposes is the Jade Emperor, or Emperor of Heaven, who reigns over a heavenly hierarchy. The population of the underworld and its various courts and hells are also hierarchically conceived, but it is those supramundane beings who reside on earth or in the liminal areas between earth and heaven and earth and underworld that tend to be of most relevance to people's goals.

Supramundanes of the official, state-sponsored pantheon were also to be found in the pantheon of popular religion. The lowest ranked of the territorial gods was the stove or kitchen god, whose location in the family stove put it in a good position to report to the Emperor of Heaven on the state of the household. The stove gods were subordinate to the earth or place gods, who were in turn subordinate to the city gods, continuing up to the Jade Emperor. In addition to their responsibility for the public welfare of their respective territories, these deities were also approached by individual residents for help in achieving their personal goals.[39]

The analogies between many male gods and bureaucrats were often made explicit by Chinese, as were the analogies with other categories of supramundanes: goddesses to mothers, ancestors to living family members, and ghosts to strangers or bandits. The relative importance attributed to the various categories and ranks of supramundane beings varied according to the goals people sought at any particular time and place, and the appropriate rituals varied according to the type of relationship between categories of persons and the particular kind of supramundanes. The analogies between humans and supramundanes gave some indication of the appropriate type of ritual behavior to be followed.

Just as they would hire experts to write their requests to human bureaucrats, people hired experts (possibly the same ones) to write in the appropriate administrative jargon to the bureaucratic-type deities. The applications might then be burned in order for them to materialize in the divine courts to which they were addressed. Like human bureaucrats, the deities were informed of the applicant's full name, address, and birth date, to allow them to locate the appropriate file. On occasion, people asked lower-ranking deities to make requests to higher deities on their behalf, and they bribed lower deities so that they would make good reports about the people under their jurisdiction. Communication with the Jade Emperor could be made only by way of another god, who would normally be of high standing.

The supramundane bureaucracy was thought of as parallel to, rather than superior to, the human bureaucracy. There were, however, differences between them. People believed they had greater access to the higher ranks of the supramundane than to the higher ranks of the state bureaucracy, and that it was not usually necessary to seek the mediation of lower deities. If lower deities were asked to transmit a message to higher deities, it was believed that, unlike human officials, they would not hold them up.[40]

The rank of a deity was taken into account by people in their approaches to the gods, in the form of etiquette that was expected and in the type of offerings that were given. Offerings were made in temporal sequence: first to the highest gods and then to those beneath them. Because the high gods were assumed to be impartial and benevolent, offerings to them were seen as tokens of respect, given to perpetuate a valued relationship, rather than as payments for particular services. Lower gods were believed to be more susceptible to the influence of special gifts.

Appeals on behalf of communities were likely to be made to the territorial gods, who were believed to intervene in their defense against floods, epidemics, and bandit gangs. The stated purposes of communal rituals held on the birthdays of territorial gods were to honor the god and request that the god bring peace, protection, and prosperity to the community. On these occasions, households brought offerings to the shrine or temple of the god, offerings they would later take home to share with other members of the community. The higher the ranking of the god, the more likely the god would leave the human offerings untouched, because the deities were believed to have sufficient resources to sustain themselves. The offerings of untransformed food, live animals, and raw food that were presented to high-ranking gods marked a recognition of the distance between them and humans. Lower-ranking gods were offered food similar to that of humans, although it was often uncut and unseasoned.[41]

Among the most important deities who fell outside the bureaucratic system were the numerous goddesses, ranging from the Eternal, or Venerable, Mother to the goddess of the toilet. The Eternal Mother was the major deity of some of the major heterodox movements, including the White Lotus and its offshoots; as the creator and controller of heaven and earth, she was regarded as superior to all male deities. The Eternal Mother has remained a major deity in modern Taiwan, as has the goddess Guanyin, who, among the Taiwanese deities, has the second largest number of temples dedicated to her. (The largest number are dedicated to semidemonic plague gods.) Guanyin originated as a bodhisattva, underwent a gender transformation, and came to be worshiped throughout China. Like Ma Tsu, another popular goddess who was worshiped in the eastern and southern areas and in contemporary Taiwan, Guanyin was represented in myths as having refused her father's order to marry, preferring death to marriage. The premarital deaths of the goddesses guaranteed their ritual purity, and although their myths do not present them as real mothers, they were considered fertility goddesses who had the power to grant sons, protect pregnant women, and assure safe childbirths.[42]

The protective role of Ma Tsu, or T'ien Hou ("Empress of Heaven," her official title), extended beyond pregnant women to include a number of groups who differed in their conceptions of the goddess: for those connected with the sea, she was a guardian of seafarers and a defender of the coast; for landowning lineages, she was a symbol of territorial control, with jurisdiction over land as well as sea; for many women she was a fertility goddess; and among the literate elite, she was seen as a bearer of civilization and guardian of the social order.[43] In contemporary Taiwan, Ma Tsu stands for a cultural identity based on the shared historical experiences of Taiwan's settlers, and pilgrimage to the major shrine of the goddess has come to signify a Taiwanese ethnic identity that transcends local identities. The majority of Ma Tsu pilgrims, however, undertake the journey to the shrine as members of villages, displaying the banners of their villages, dressing in a distinctive manner, and performing their local customs at the site. Thus, the ritual expression of solidarity at the pan-Taiwan level is accomplished partly through the expression of ritual differentiation of the separate village groups participating in the pilgrimage.[44]

Clown or eccentric gods and martial deities also fall outside the bureaucratic system. Some of the humorous gods were incorporated from Taoism; their eccentric traits were accentuated in popular religion, and in certain areas they exhibited a rebellious nature by making fun of officialdom. The jokes and pranks of the comic gods were not seen to diminish their efficacy in assisting supplicants, and although they were never incorporated into official pantheons, they became popular throughout China.

A rebellious nature was also one facet of some of the martial figures, whose military skills were utilized in the battles against demonic forces who caused calamities such as epidemics.[45] Whereas some epidemics were believed to have been sent down by the Jade Emperor to punish individual wrongdoers and sinful communities and were countered by rites performed by state priests and other religious specialists, other epidemics were believed to have been brought about by plague demons, who would strike at random intervals, regardless of the moral condition of their victims. People turned to the martial deities to capture and expel the demons threatening their communities.[46]

Some martial deities, like many other supramundanes, were believed to be historical figures whose unusual abilities and outstanding, meritorious behavior during their lifetimes qualified them to become spirits with extraordinary powers.[47] The exceptional characteristics of such deities put them in a class apart from most ancestors, who were understood to be the souls of peoples' paternal forebears who had attained parenthood, actual or potential, before they died. Most ancestral spirits were not believed to have extensive power, and their concerns were thought to be centered on their own welfare and that of their descendants.

The food offered to ancestors, and ancestral worship in general, reflects the assumption that the needs and purposes of ancestors are similar to those of living people. Certain meanings of ancestral worship do not appear to require the assumption that the deceased have a existence beyond death: they signify remembrance of the dead, perpetuation of their good names, and expression of a continuing indebtedness to those who gave life, love, support, and possibly a material inheritance. A "rationalistic" Confucian interpretation was that ancestral rites cultivated moral values, especially filial piety, and were of benefit to the living and not to the dead, who lacked consciousness. Among most Chinese, however, ancestral worship had meanings and an efficacy that went beyond remembrance, the celebration of past lives, and the reinforcement of moral values. It acted out a continuing reciprocity that had material benefits for both sides, even though, in parallel with the relationship of children and parents, the heaviest obligation fell on the descendants rather than on the ancestors.

The obligation of the living to guarantee the continued well-being of the deceased was carried out by appropriate ritual behavior at domestic altars, which usually included a tablet representing the collective ancestors as well as tablets of individual ancestors going back three or four generations. In addition to each household's domestic altars, some lineages had ancestral halls containing tablets of ancestors going back many generations. Family members regularly bowed before the ancestral tablets and burned incense, and a more elaborate ritual was performed on anniversaries of the ancestors' deaths, when the favorite food of the deceased was set before them, and on festival days, births, and weddings. The ritual media, such as incense, libations, and offerings, were much the same as those used in rituals directed toward gods, and in return, aid was solicited from ancestors just as it was solicited from gods. Ancestors were seen as having greater obligations toward their worshipers than gods, but they were generally believed to be less powerful than gods.[48]

When misfortune such as illness occurred to a family, members of the family or their spirit medium may have attributed it to the neglect of ancestral worship. Misfortune was more frequently attributed to ghosts, however, the spirits of the dead who for various reasons had not made it through the underworld to enter a heaven or be reincarnated. They may not have been properly buried, or they may have been neglected after their deaths by the living. There were those who died as infants or small children and had no descendants to worship them. Others had unfilial children who did not worship them. And there were those who died violent deaths—the suicides or murder victims who sought revenge among the living.[49]

Ghosts were socially marginal beings who, unlike gods, had an urgent need for the substances given to them by humans, and if these were not forthcoming, they became malicious and attacked the living. As strangers, offerings were made to them outside the home, or as bandits, they were to be bribed or paid protection money to forestall harmful actions. In cases where they sought sustenance by entering living persons, rituals of exorcism had to carried out. Their powers were sometimes used by the living to gain thaumaturgical goals, and because they fulfilled requests without regard to morality, it was said that criminals and prostitutes frequently appealed for their assistance.

Most people feared ghosts, and the great attention given to funeral ritual was intended to prevent their creation. The appropriate location of the grave, according to the rules of geomancy, and the proper performance of the funeral rites aided the passage of the deceased through the underworld. Priests were hired to undertake and supervise the rituals, and possibly to bribe the appropriate officials of the underworld. If the deceased was improperly buried or if the rites were carried out incorrectly, the souls would be trapped in a hell, and it was believed that they might return to earth as "hungry ghosts," causing harm to the living. One common means of assisting the dead through the underworld was to burn imitation money, miniature houses filled with symbols of wealth, paper carriages, and, in more recent times, paper Mercedes Benz. The burning of the offerings, often accompanied by the chanting of Buddhist texts and sutras, represented the transfer of merit to neutralize the demerits caused by the misconduct of the deceased in their lifetimes.

The Universal Salvation ceremonies, held during the seventh lunar month, were intended to protect the community from hungry ghosts. This is the time when the gates of the underworld are opened and spirits are free to roam in the world. The goal of the ritual was to effect the release of suffering souls from the hells and then to feed them. This gave them relief from suffering and appeased their anger and resentment, which could harm the community. The ritual constituted an act of mercy and kindness toward the miserable ghosts, as well as an act of propitiation, forestalling the exercise of their malevolence. Buddhist and Taoist priests were involved in the ritual, seeking to purify the ghosts from pollution and thereby gaining them admission into paradise or effecting their reincarnation at a higher level. The priestly functions were complemented by the activities of the shamans, who held at bay the malevolent spirits of the discontented dead and traveled to the underworld to discover how the spirits were faring.

The transformation of hungry ghosts into ancestors who can be worshiped remains a goal among contemporary Taiwanese, who perform rituals for that purpose within the context of the family. Girls who are ghosts because they died in childhood are believed to appear before members of their family and to ask to be married. A living groom, often the husband of a married sister of the ghost, is married to the ghost bride in a ceremony that resembles an ordinary wedding. The groom and his family are then obliged to incorporate an ancestral tablet of the bride on the family altar, to worship it, and to provide it with offerings.[50] Thus, many rituals of popular religion have simultaneous salvational and this-worldly aims. By providing for the salvation of the deceased, preventing the creation of ghosts, or transforming them into ancestors, the living can minimize this-worldly misfortunes.

Religious Overlaps and Interrelationships

Some scholars have followed Weber in emphasizing a religious gulf between a Confucian elite, for whom ritual was a matter of social convention, devoid of emotional elements and any concern with salvation, and popular religion, characterized as magical and animistic;[51] but the dominant tendency among both anthropologists and historians has been to emphasize links between elite and popular religion and their common foundations.[52]

Scholars who have emphasized a religious gap between the elite and the masses have tended to portray the Confucianism of the elite as a philosophy rather than a religion. They have pointed to passages in the Confucian classics where skepticism is expressed toward the existence of gods and spirits.[53] Some Confucianists interpreted ancestor worship in non-supernatural terms, as a means of expressing longing for the dead and of strengthening the kinship system, which they saw as tied to the maintenance of the sociopolitical order. Sacrificial ceremonies were interpreted in a rational fashion as affairs of humans, and the use of supramundane notions as instruments for the enforcement of social values and the control of the masses was explicitly recognized. It was, however, only a minority within the elite who offered such rationalistic interpretations. The majority of Confucians conceived of T'ien in an anthropomorphic fashion, believed that the fate of humankind and the world was ordained by it, and used their knowledge of yin-yang and the five elements to decipher its intentions.

Like other Chinese, most literati believed the cosmos was populated by many varieties of supramundane beings, gods, ancestral spirits, ghosts, and so on, who could be propitiated and appeased by the appropriate forms of offerings and sacrifice.[54] There was a greater tendency among literati than among other strata to view gods and ghosts as disembodied positive and negative forces, as yin and yang, rather than as personalized beings,[55] but links between impersonal and personal idioms existed among all strata. For example, it was a common belief that people had two souls, one made up of the spiritual or yang component, the other of the material or yin component. It was the yin soul that could turn into a malevolent ghost if not placated by suitable burial and worship. The yin-yang distinction not only encompassed the distinction between ancestors and ghosts; it also distinguished between the status of the ancestor in the tomb, where it was a corpse and therefore yin as well as a soul, and the ancestor's status in the shrine, where it was yang.[56]

All supramundane beings, including those of Taoism and Buddhism, were encompassed by the idiom of yang and yin, and because low-ranking deities were believed to mediate between yang and yin in the supramundane hierarchy, they were often of greater ritual importance than high-ranking deities. In contrast to the pure yang of abstract forces such as Heaven, lower-ranking deities retained some yin aspects, thereby increasing their practical efficacy.[57] Of course, literati and peasants differed in their conceptions of these forces. The literati tended to conceive yang and yin in abstract modes and as complementary, whereas peasants were more likely to personify them and see them as potentially or actively hostile toward each other. Even this difference was a relative one; literati were likely to emphasize the need for harmony of yang and yin, but they were also inclined to regard yin as inferior and evil in relationship to yang.[58]

Thus, although the "classical" idiom differed from the "vulgar" idiom, and although certain patterns of religious action were more typical of one stratum than of another, both were conducted within a single religious culture. The literati and the peasants adopted religious items from each other and "translated" them into more familiar idioms. Examples include the supramundane stories from folklore that were adopted and "literalized" by the elite[59] and the hanging of the imperial calendar on sickbeds by peasants who believed it carried the curative power of the stars and the emperor.

Mutual religious influences and accommodations among the strata are particularly evident in the relationships between official religion and popular religion. Whereas some deities were exclusive to official or to popular religion, many were common to both. Deities sanctioned by the imperial Ministry of Rites were promoted by local elites who sought to gentrify themselves by cooperating with the state authorities in the standardization of cults, and during the Ch'ing dynasty many purely local deities were superseded by a few officially sponsored deities. The process of standardization also involved the incorporation of popular deities into official religion, and there were well-established bureaucratic procedures for this purpose. A good example was Ma Tsu, which began as a minor folk goddess protecting fishermen in the tenth century and was promoted through official sponsorship to become the Empress of Heaven, a bearer of "civilization" and guardian of the social order.[60]

The Confucian gloss the elite put on popular gods did not necessarily penetrate the masses, and a god depicted in the state-sponsored literature as a filial son and scholar could retain its rebellious and irreverent character among the populace. The more popular representations of deities were transmitted by dramas and novels written in the vernacular, which reached a wider audience than the hagiographic collections written in the classical language by members of the elite. Deities who deviated from the

Confucian ethos were especially prominent in locations on the periphery of the empire, where local elites did not necessarily collaborate with state officials in promoting the official representations of deities.[61]

With regard to deities that were believed to be of human origin, such as local heroes and other eminent persons, the form of their worship did not differ significantly in the official and non-official temples. The same was true of deities of Taoist origin. There were other deities whose official forms were quite distinct from their popular manifestations. One example is T'ai-shan, the chief deity of the five sacred peaks: in popular religion, it was considered primarily to be ruler of the underworld; in official religion, it ruled over lesser territorial spirits, such as city, local, and domestic gods, and played an important role in the regulation of water and the prevention of natural disasters.[62] In the case of the City God, there developed a pseudoclassical altar form that was connected with the primordial spirits of mountains and rivers and a temple form that overlapped with popular religious activity under Taoist auspices.[63]

One method of "Confucianizing" local, popular deities was to manufacture an association with, or conflate them with, state-sanctioned deities. An example of this occurred in the nineteenth century when a group of popular plague-dispelling deities, known to local people in the Fuzhou area as the Five Emperors, were represented by officials as state deities, first as gods known as the Five Manifestations and later as Guandi, the God of War. The rituals centered on the Five Emperors were criticized by some members of the local elite and officialdom as heterodox and dangerous to public order, and the apparently deliberate misidentification by officials concealed the local tradition and gave the impression of standardization of deities by state authorities. In this instance local people did not accept the substitution of state deities, and the conflation by officials had little effect on the ritual practice and iconography of the cult, which continued to focus on the prevention and relief of disease.[64]

Deities in official religion were far more differentiated, categorized, and standardized than in popular religion. The agents of official religion made clearer distinctions between the celestial and territorial, the natural and human, and the civil and military character of deities, and they sought to establish appropriate histories and authentic classical forms of worship for the deities. Regulations specified the exact amount of offerings appropriate for the various deities, the kind of music and obeisance required, and the appropriate worshipers. In administrative capitals, where both official and popular, unofficial temples were to be found, the contrasts in patterns of worship were clearly visible. The noise and bustle in the popular temple contrasted with the atmosphere of decorum that prevailed in the official shrine. In popular temples there was little discrimination of worshipers by social rank, and all participants were likely to make offerings; in the official temples, only the leading participants made offerings.[65]

In accord with the concern for order and the bureaucratic ethos, the rank of deities and the practices associated with them tended to become relatively fixed in the official religion. The position of deities in popular religion was not confined by classical traditions or written rules, and their ranks and relative prominence varied from place to place according to their perceived efficacy. Even within a single village, apart from an agreement that the Jade Emperor was at the top of the pantheon, there was no consensus over the ranking of deities, and indeed, most people paid little attention to the ranking of deities in a formal and systematic fashion.[66] Whereas in official religion it was sufficient that an official to whom a shrine had been dedicated be regarded as an exemplar during his lifetime in order for him to be worshiped, in popular religion he had to manifest efficacy in order for people to continue to worship him.[67]

More systematized and clearly delineated pantheons than those of popular religion were also to be found in the institutionalized locations of Taoism and Buddhism. The Taoist pantheon grew and changed considerably over the centuries, and its considerable overlap with popular pantheons presented Taoist priests with the problem of drawing boundaries between themselves and forms of worship they regarded as excessive. Taoist priests refused to incorporate blood sacrifices into their rituals, but they absorbed many local, popular deities into their pantheon. The writing of scriptures for the god in classical Chinese was a major step in its incorporation into the Taoist framework, and this often involved the identification of the god with a Taoist astral deity.

Taoists incorporated local rituals without altering their own liturgical structure, which provided a framework even for those local deities that remained outside the Taoist pantheon. In place of blood sacrifices, which were allowed to continue under certain restrictions outside the temples, a sacrificial form of communication with deities was accomplished within the Taoist framework by the burning of sacred texts and symbols. When Taoist priests conducted the jiao rite, the statues of popular deities were either taken outside the temple or, if left inside, covered from view. The goal sought by the Taoist priests, who taught that the "emptying" of the deities induces an awareness of the transcendent Tao, may have been accompanied by the more material goals of laypeople who addressed the deities with their worldly concerns in the temple courtyard.

Some historians have argued that the accommodations, appropriations, and transformations of the Taoist elite brought a degree of unity to Chinese popular religion and made Taoism the indigenous higher religion of the Chinese masses.[68] Taoism is presented as the centripetal agent within the syncretistic context because it provided a conduct for almost all deities and ritual forms. Taoists built on widely shared Confucian beliefs, such as the five elements; they incorporated Confucian lineage and ancestral worship; and they also performed rituals that were associated with Buddhism, such as funerals and the transfer of merit to the dead. Taoists played a major role in the structuring of religious action at the popular level, and local gods who were incorporated into the Taoist liturgical structure had a better chance of being absorbed within the imperial pantheon. A Buddhist monk known as the Patriarch of the Clear Stream was transformed into a popular deity and worshiped through rituals structured by the Taoist framework.[69]

Reservations about the impact of Taoism on popular religion have been expressed by Paul Katz, who finds that the influence of Taoist priests over the representation of local deities was often limited. In his study of Marshal Wen, a deity specializing in preventing and overcoming epidemics, Katz writes that the spread of its worship in South China and Taiwan appears to have been largely due to popular novels and folktales and occurred without the support of Taoist priests. Even when Taoist priests contributed to the hagiography and rituals of particular deities, the growth and spread of their worship depended largely on the support of scholar-officials and local lay elites. Katz also disagrees, however, with those historians who have drawn a sharp line between the deities worshiped by Taoist priests and popular deities. While Taoist priests have on occasion distanced themselves from local gods and have cultivated the esoteric facets of their religion, they have nevertheless co-opted deities from popular religion and shared in their worship.[70]

In contemporary Taiwan, the names and ranks of Taoist deities are more clearly delineated than in popular religion, but it is the Buddhist priests who present the most systematized view of the supramundane world. They distinguish ten types of beings that fall into two main categories: the buddhas, who have transcended the wheel of reincarnation and no longer take an active part in the world, and all those who are still subject to rebirth (gods, ghosts, demons, etc.). The supramundane beings of the popular pantheon are interpreted by the Buddhist elite in terms of the dichotomy between buddhas and all other beings. For example, the hungry ghosts are seen as a metaphor of the human desire for material things and as a particularly vivid illustration of the sufferings of beings caught in the world of illusion. The ghosts did not simply undergo an improper death; they are metaphors of the greed typical of all unenlightened beings.[71]

The Buddhist interpretation of ghosts illustrates the concern of a religious elite to transcend particular contexts and to explain the world according to universal and eternal principles. The elite's consistent treatment of ghosts within a broad system of meanings contrasts with the popular tendency to treat ghosts differently according to particular goals and situations; the conception and ritual treatment of the pitiful ghosts on the occasion of the Universal Salvation rites may be quite different from those that take place when people attempt to appease the vicious ghosts who are held responsible for illnesses.[72]

The differences between the elite and popular levels should not obscure the considerable interpenetration that occurs between them. In China, where people frequently called on Buddhist and Taoist priests to perform rituals in a wide variety of contexts, the transformation of great into little traditions has been particularly extensive. Guanyin, who was transformed into a compassionate mother figure of popular religion, is the most prominent of a number of bodhisattvas who have lost much of their particular Buddhist character in the process of absorption through adaptation. Elitist forms of Buddhism and Taoism have continued in some of the temples and monasteries, but even where their rituals appear exclusively Buddhist or Taoist, the monks' interpretations have clearly been influenced by widespread notions among the populace.[73]

Values and Social Structure

An examination of values and social structure points to the bases of both divergence and overlap of elite and popular religion in China. The promoters and agents of official religion were influenced by two somewhat contradictory orientations toward popular religion. On the one hand, as holders of a status ethic, the literati were disdainful of popular religion, tried to keep aloof from it, and sought to construct an official religion that would represent a classical tradition uncorrupted by popular elements. On the other hand, as state bureaucrats concerned to uphold the hierarchical order, they advocated the influence of official religion over the subject population, thereby reducing the possibility of social disorder and political revolt.

Officials' absorption of certain local gods into the elite pantheon reaffirmed the role of the polity in the cosmic continuum of power,[74] but the accommodation of popular customs into the ritual domain of Confucianism posed a danger to the status claims of literati. Ritual behavior was an important way of asserting and maintaining social status in China, and adherence to a distinctly Confucian schedule of rituals validated the standing of the gentry. When ritual actions spread from the elite to popular religion, as in the case of spirit tablets, the rites lost their status connotations, and the gentry would highlight other practices from the Confucian liturgies to reassert their superiority.

Family rituals such as weddings and funerals provided particularly good opportunities to display not just wealth but also, through the appropriate ritual behavior, status. To conform to the canonically derived forms of ritual, gentry families could refer to ritual codes and guidelines, but the aim of harmony and order of society through "civilizing" the population encouraged officials to make the ritual guides available to wider circles.[75] The Chinese state did not attempt to compel the "correct" practice of rituals, and sources from the eighteenth century indicate that many literati believed their class was too tolerant toward the religion of the masses. Statements were made of the need to reassert official religion, but in practice, popular religion in its nonsectarian forms was normally tolerated.[76]

Subordinate strata were encouraged to participate in certain rites at particular temples, and the state sought to encourage cultural conformity and minimize regional diversity and social deviance through prescribed rituals and lectures on Confucian ethics, but there were no sustained efforts to incorporate the masses into official religion. People without degrees or without aspirations to join the scholar-official class did not generally attend the school-temples that were the centers for the worship of deceased sages and bureaucratic exemplars of official virtues. Commoners and officials did participate together in other temples, and it was generally the officials who made the offerings to the gods, which, in many cases, were former occupants of their positions.[77]

It was, in fact, the literati—the state bureaucrats and local elites—who were the major intended objects of control by official religion, and insofar as it is appropriate to use the term *orthodoxy* (or *orthopraxy*), its applicability is toward the literati. Confucian classics were effectively given canonical status when questions were asked about them in the examinations and when the appropriate way to read them was taught in the state schools. The examination curriculum, based on the Confucian classics and the commentaries, was distributed in the late imperial empire by the directorate of education to the schools that prepared students for the degrees or credentials necessary for bureaucratic appointments. The examination system regulated and reproduced Confucian orthodoxy in the sense of acceptable knowledge and correct readings of the classics, and this orthodoxy was reinforced by its ritualization in official domains, such as the state temples. The meticulously scripted official rituals were based on principles formulated in court, and even those literati who did not fully endorse the court's position on orthodoxy contributed to its reproduction by their participation in the rituals.[78]

The examination system ensured that literati aspiring for office would have some grounding in official doctrine, but even among the literati, the notion of orthodoxy in the sense of an obligatory adherence to a precisely defined body of doctrines is difficult to apply. Although the majority of literati were no doubt conformist in accepting the appropriate readings of the official canon, many of the more intellectual literati regarded the exams as a mere formality, and some scholars purposely avoided recruitment to the bureaucracy.[79] For those literati in employment, there was little supervision or use of sanctions by the state to ensure conformity in the performance of important ritual areas, such as family rituals.[80]

Despite standardization, the Confucian canon remained relatively open and a variety of interpretations were permitted, including different emphases or de-emphases on the religious as opposed to the more purely philosophical dimensions of the classics.[81] There was certainly no persecution of non-official Confucian doctrines, and if the term *heresy* is to be used at all, it was less a matter of doctrine than of politically relevant practice. Many laws were passed forbidding particular practices, such as unauthorized worship of Heaven and the North Star, which were the exclusive prerogatives of the emperors, and the publication of unauthorized calendars or almanacs. Such practices were regarded as challenges to political authority and to the accompanying codes of social relationships.[82]

The policies of political rulers toward the institutionalized forms of

Buddhism and Taoism were also dictated by political rather than doctrinal considerations. Although some official sources defined heretical teachings as anything outside the Five Classics and Four Books of Confucianism, most political rulers displayed wide latitude toward non-Confucian religions. Buddhist and Taoist temples were sometimes located on the same streets as Confucian temples, and their priests frequently took a major part in local community festivals that were independent of official religion. Taoist priests in particular were important in both the central and branch temples of deities, such as the Eastern Peak, that were worshiped throughout the empire. The ritual participation of the Buddhist and Taoist elites and the religious actions of virtuosos were tolerated as long as they were not accompanied by challenges to state authority, social ethics, or the norms of ritual propriety. This meant that, in addition to the display of loyalty to the emperor, Buddhists and Taoists were expected to conform to the norms of filial piety within the strongly hierarchical family structure.[83]

Buddhist and Taoist orders were subject to political supervision, and any organized religious movement outside political sponsorship or regulation was regarded with suspicion by political rulers. Popular religious movements were persecuted, not for their beliefs, which were often a blend of Buddhist, Taoist, and Confucian elements, but because they were regarded as politically dangerous. Government fears of political intrigue and subversion were, on occasion, justified, and some movements did initiate uprisings. But even quietest movements were persecuted, because the recruitment and organization of members across communities was sufficient to arouse the suspicion of state agents.[84] In comparison, unofficial, popular religion anchored in existing communities was little affected by state supervision or intervention. Local communities, groups, and organizations, such as villages, town neighborhoods, guilds, and those based on ties of kinship, built temples, installed their deities, and ran their festivals quite independent of any authorities. Official edicts were intended to limit the number of temples, but C. K. Yang notes that 84 percent of the temples in the seventeenth century were built without official permission, and this figure does not include numerous small shrines that were built privately.[85]

The values represented by officially sponsored temples and rites were promoted by primers and other literature directed at the semi-educated and by state and gentry-sponsored lectures, but the effect of such media on a predominantly oral culture is difficult to assess. Some deities promoted by the bureaucracy were worshiped by peasants, but so were deities who violated Confucian morality. Data from both nineteenth-century mainland China and contemporary Taiwan show the popularity of gods known more for their sex, drunkenness, and gambling than for their dedication to bureaucratic organization. Among popular gods were those who challenged the bureaucracy and presented a reversed image of the ideologies of official religion.[86]

Among the mediators of elite and popular religion were the lower ranks of the literati, who, having passed only the basic-level examinations, were not normally appointed to imperial offices but who typically possessed prestige and power in their local communities.[87] To gain support in their areas of jurisdiction, local officials assisted, often without official sanction, in the building and repair of popular temples. On their part, peasants attempted to draw local officials into the worshiping of a local god whom they believed would be influenced more by the prayers of an official, who occupied a rank in the human realm similar to that of the god in the spiritual realm. Officials were forbidden to worship deities who were not on the official lists, but they risked resentment and disturbances in their areas if they refused to participate. In some instances, local officials represented popular deities to their superiors in a way that brought them in line with state-approved cults but changed little, if at all, the popular religion. Attempts were made by local elites to bring the communities in conformity with imperially sanctioned forms of religious action, but local officials would normally limit their efforts to what they considered acceptable to their communities.[88]

In addition to the lower ranks of the literati, nonliterati literates were important in the translation of elements from elite culture into terms that the illiterate could understand. About a fifth of all males who were not degree holders possessed some degree of literacy; they were common in most market towns, and most villages probably had at least one literate. Located on the boundary between the written and oral cultures, nonliterati literates mediated cultural influences between the classes, and this function was also performed by the popular theater, which brought material from written histories and stories before the illiterate public.[89]

Like the agents of official religion, Buddhist monks and Taoist priests oscillated between condemnation and toleration of popular deities and the practices associated with them. Buddhist monks forbade various popular deities and certain practices, such as meat offerings, within their temples, but they accommodated to the demand of the Chinese masses for elaborate rituals on behalf of the deceased.[90] The situation of the Taoist priests was perhaps a more delicate one, because their greater involvement as liturgical specialists in popular ritual opened them up to the accusation that their own practices were identical or similar to those of popular magicians. Taoists have emphasized the distinction between gods and malevolent beings, and their policy toward popular practices has been to condemn offerings made to demons or to spirits who cause illnesses and to accept those offered to other popular deities, such as the stove god.[91]

For most of Chinese history there have been no strong differentiated religious institutions that might have allowed elites, if they had been inclined, to establish clear boundaries between great traditions and popular religion. The institutions of Buddhist and Taoist monks and priests were strongest in the early centuries of the common era, but with the establishment of political unity under the imperial state and the rise among the literati of what has come to be termed *neo-Confucianism*, Buddhism and Taoism were weakened and their influence fell among the intellectual elite. The weakness of institutionalized religion in late imperial times was evident in the small number of monks and priests, their low status, their lack of participation in education and community charity, and the autonomous functioning of each temple and monastery. The orders were organized on a local basis, linked to particular monasteries, temples, and religious schools, and it was rare for the head of a monastery or school to possess authority outside his local sphere of activities.[92]

With the exception of a tiny minority of devotees who became associated with Buddhist and Taoist monasteries, the institutionalized religions have not had the benefit of a strong commitment among laypeople, most of whom worship at a number of temples according to the occasion and the services that they require. Many temples were organized and governed by laypeople who have laid little emphasis on the relationship between their principal god and a particular religious tradition. Taoist and Buddhist priests were hired to perform certain rituals, such as the jiao and funeral services, but laypeople took daily care of the temples and often officiated at annual festivals and rites of passage. Some laypeople even chanted to free souls from afterlife punishments without the assistance of Buddhist or Taoist priests.[93]

The importance of laypeople in temple organization left the Taoist and Buddhist religious elites little autonomous power to produce or preserve a closed form of elite religion and contributed to the blurring of Taoist and Buddhist religious boundaries within the amalgam of popular religion. One reason for the weakness of hierocracies in China was the strength of the patrimonial state, which might appear to provide a structural basis for a clear religious division between the Confucian literati or nobility and the masses. Blocked from participation in the state cult, which was limited to the literati, popular religion in China has been characterized as going its separate magical and animistic way.[94] That the patrimonial state in China was conducive to the maintenance of religious differences between nobility and peasants is suggested by comparing its officialdom, whose power was based on positions within the state hierarchy, with feudal aristocracies, whose locally based power requires extensive association with peasant serfs.

A powerful, independent aristocracy based on nobility of birth and local power was undermined in China by making access to state offices dependent on passing examinations and by posting officials to positions some distance from their family estates. There was, however, a considerable interdependence between bureaucratic position and landownership. Although some moderately rich landowners did not hold any form of academic degree and some degree holders owned no landed property, these were the exceptions, and most officeholders used the financial rewards of their positions to increase their family's land.

The acquisition of more land was important in a system where the absence of primogeniture and the equal division of inheritance could progressively undermine the material basis of a family's status. Officials were not paid high salaries, but it was recognized by the political center that bureaucrats would use their positions to generate additional income, and it was this "extralegal" income, far in excess of the official salaries, that enabled officials to advance their familys' fortunes.[95] Although the "feudal" inclination of the literati to extend their landownership and local power was perceived, on occasion, as excessive by the emperor and his chief ministers, who used their power to check it, the late imperial state generally supported the local privileges and the official titles and symbols of status that differentiated the gentry from the rest of the population.[96]

The structure of landownership and agricultural production only marginally increased social contacts between gentry and peasants; the scholar-landlords put pressure on the government to construct irrigation systems, but they took no part in the cultivation of crops, which, after harvesting, were divided between themselves and the tenant peasants. Nor were social boundaries weakened by class mobility. Although there were no legal or formal restrictions preventing a male from any class taking the official examinations, and a number of degree holders were recruited from nongentry families, the absence of a system of popular education meant that prospective scholar-officials depended on wealthy families to support them in their studies.

There were components of the Chinese social structure that contributed to cultural interaction of literati and peasants. Officials used their positions to obtain land for their patrilineal lineages, which in some areas, especially the south, took the extended form of the clan. The lineage or clan was led by the gentry but it included many peasants, and it is through extended kin networks that certain Confucian values, such as respect for ancestors, filtered down to the peasants.[97] Most features of the Chinese society and state, however, were likely to induce feelings of cultural difference and antipathy between the literati and the peasants. As we have shown, the status ethic of the literati caused them to distance themselves from popular religion, and as officials of an oppressive state, as well as landowners who had little contact with the peasants whose surpluses they appropriated, they were likely to arouse considerable resentment among the masses.

Peasant proverbs from the late empire period suggest that peasants were not inclined to express loyalty to the emperor or deference to the literati. In fact, the proverbs indicate cynicism toward Confucian moralism and some distance from the kind of orthodoxy represented by official religion.[98] Popular religion was too diffuse in family and community structures to become a focal point of resistance, but it provided many of the ingredients for religious movements. State repression of the more sectarian forms of popular religion was a major factor in the massive revolts of the nineteenth century that weakened the late imperial system and contributed to its fall.[99]

Chinese governments' repression of popular religion began early in the twentieth century and continued through the Republican period (1911–49), when modernizing state reformers saw popular religion as an obstacle to their programs. The suppression of all forms of traditional religion by the Communists was intensified during the Cultural Revolution of the 1960s and 1970s, but since 1979, when the Chinese government relaxed its controls, there has been a considerable resurgence of openly displayed religion, including ancestral worship and the rebuilding of temples to local gods. Although religious activity remains extremely limited in the cities, large traditional festivals and funerals are being held in the countryside, and in his recent research on religion in Southeast China, Kenneth Dean found many similarities to the religion described by J. J. M. de Groot in the 1870s and 1880s.[100]

A renewal of religious repression by the Chinese government has been directed against Falun Gong, a popular religious movement that was established in the early 1990s and gathered millions of adherents throughout China in the late 1990s. The Falun Gong mixture of Buddhism, Taoism, and various techniques, such as breath control, to channel the body's vital life force is directed to thaumaturgical goals, such as overcoming illnesses; but the movement also appears to have a millenarian component, which has become more apocalyptic in the face of persecution by the regime.[101] As in imperial China, the present regime appears willing to tolerate popular religion as long as its organization does not extend beyond the local level.

5

India

Brahmans, Renouncers, and Popular Hinduism

In contrast to China, where religious identities are too diffuse and flexible to allow their categorization according to religious traditions, the populations of India have come to identify with what are seen as distinctive religious traditions. Today, the vast majority of Indians identify themselves as Hindu; about 11 percent identify as Muslims, the largest religious minority; and about 6 percent identify with the other minority religions, including Jainism, Sikhism (which is the major religion in some areas of the Punjab), and Christianity (which is the major religion of a few areas of South India).[1]

The relatively diffuse religious boundaries of Hinduism were constructed by an indigenous religious elite or elites, predominantly from the Brahman castes, who were responding to the challenge of indigenous counter-elites (Buddhists, Jainists) or to the threat of religions that originated outside India (Islam, Christianity). Although "Hinduism" has become part of the discourse of many Indians, scholars have questioned its appropriateness as a designation for the extraordinary diverse range of beliefs, practices, and movements it is purported to cover.[2] Among the vast sacred writings of Hinduism, certain texts such as the epics (Mahabharata, Ramayana) and the Puranas (Ancient Stories) are popular throughout Hindu India, but each region has its own body of folklore concerning the gods and heroes of the epics, and although certain festivals are very common, their actual content differs markedly from place to place.[3]

If the boundaries of Hinduism cannot be delineated by a core of texts or common beliefs and practices, a possible alternative is by reference to the caste system, a system of social stratification that is integrally related with religion in India. The four social categories known as *varnas* were described in the ancient Vedic literature. A hymn of the Rigveda, the oldest of the four Vedic texts, relates how the varnas were constituted at the creation of the world: a primeval being called Purusha was sacrificed, and from his mouth the Brahman varna was created, from his arms the Kshatriya (kings and warriors), from his thighs the Vaishya (merchants and farmers), and from his feet the Shudra (servants). Below the four varnas and positioned in a sense outside the system are the *harijans*, or "untouchables," whose very contact can defile the higher varnas. The laws of the system appear in their most detailed and concise forms in the Manu Smriti ("traditions according to Manu," circa 200 B.C.E.), which held that birth in a particular varna was a consequence of *karma*, or actions of previous lives, and that it was the essential duty of every person to fulfill the *dharma*, or moral obligations, of whatever position they were born into.

A differentiation should be made between the varnas, which are an idealized scheme used to justify a simplified hierarchical image of the society, and the *jatis*, or castes, which number two to three thousand in India. Although it is not possible to account for all castes and subcastes as divisions and mixed unions of the varnas, it is generally presumed that jatis can be categorized into varnas. Most villages include between five and twenty-five castes, and most local areas include at least one Brahman caste and a number of Shudra castes. In most regions the bulk of the population, 70 percent or more, are Shudras or some mix of Shudras and untouchables, and there are many areas where there are no Kshatriya or Vaishya castes. As agrarian laborers, Shudras have necessarily constituted the majority in an agrarian society, and they have also acquired occupational functions that traditionally were associated with the Kshatriya and Vaishya. Today, there are few jatis in which the majority work in the occupations traditionally associated with their castes.[4]

Hinduism has assimilated formerly isolated tribes, religious groups originating outside India, and innovative religious movements arising among the indigenous population by incorporating them as castes or subcastes, each defined and regulated by religious rules, especially those of purity and pollution. Thus, a considerable variety of beliefs, practices, and identities are to be found under a broad religious canopy characterized by socioreligious differentiation as well as socioreligious interdependence and linkages. Among the diverse parts there has generally been mutual recognition, with few claims of an exclusive truth. Hindu inclusivism with respect to beliefs and practices has been accompanied, however, by exclusivism toward other religions; there was extensive persecution of Buddhism in the past, and in recent years Hindu nationalist groups have refused to recognize Muslims as part of the Indian nation. Hindu inclusivism also has its spurious and intolerant features. The official classification of various tribal groups with animist religions as Hindu is questionable when they do not worship any of the major Hindu deities, and there has been tension between the tendency of Hindus to consider Sikhism as a branch or caste of Hinduism and the demand of Sikhs to be recognized as a separate religious group.[5]

Elites and the Great Tradition

In addition to its importance in drawing the boundaries of Hinduism, the caste system is central to the distinctions between religious elites and masses in India. There is no single rank order of castes across India, but there is a wide consensus that Brahmans are ranked at the top and harijans at the bottom, although both are divided into subcastes whose ranking varies from region to region. In the sense of an elite as superior in a certain quality, the whole of the Brahman caste might be considered a religious elite because of their relative ritual purity in comparison with other castes. This would establish the elite by an ascriptive criterion, but the sacred status of religious virtuosos, who have come from all castes, is understood to be an achieved one, accomplished by renunciation, asceticism, and meditation. Brahmans have had a highly ambivalent attitude toward renunciation, and in the past they made unsuccessful attempts to restrict the path of renunciation to their own caste or, alternatively, to the three upper varnas.

In the sense of the elite as constituting those who occupy the upper positions of the major religious organizations, the Brahmans are dominant. Only a minority of Brahmans act as priests, and not all priests are Brahmans, but Brahmans generally occupy the position of priest in the important temples of the major gods, whereas in other, less important temples, non-Brahmans as well as Brahmans may function as priests. The involvement of priests in activities involving pollution, such as negating the sins of others, means that Brahman priests are generally considered to have a lower status than Brahmans in other occupations, and they are certainly considered to have lower status than genuine renouncers from a Brahmanic caste. The question of religious status does not detract, however, from the Brahmanic predominance within the religious elite in its institutional sense. Thus, although only a small proportion of Brahmans can be counted as members of the religious elite in the two senses that have been distinguished, they have a close association with the priestly elite and, to a somewhat lesser extent, with the elite of virtuosos, many of whom are monks in religious orders.

It is the religious elite of Brahmans who have expounded a great tradition, or in their terms, a Sanskritic Hinduism, as the prestigious standard by which all forms of Hinduism are to be evaluated. Brahmans in the sacred city of Varanasi (Banaras or Benares) make a sharp distinction between *shastrik* (scriptural) beliefs and practices, which are eternally valid and binding on all Hindus, and *laukik* (popular) beliefs and practices, which are not authoritative. There is no general consensus on what belongs to the two categories, but the Brahmans hold that only their interpretations are valid, and their claim of conformity to Sanskritic Hinduism is an assertion of religious superiority over the beliefs and practices of lower castes.[6] Thus, although the great tradition is presented as universally valid and relevant for all Hindus, it is also used by Brahmans as an assertion of closure and higher status. Its content has been selected and adopted from the supposed contents of Sanskrit texts by Brahman priests and monks, who have taught it to other Brahmans and to members of some other castes whose status is considered appropriate to receive the knowledge.

The particularism of the Brahmans and their emphasis on restricting religious knowledge and certain practices to the higher castes have not inclined them to draw on the patronage and material support they have received from political rulers in order to promote an official form of religion among the general populace. India had neither the political centralization, which was the basis of official religion in China, nor the appropriate religious ideology (ecclesiology) and other conditions for a hierocracy, which was the basis of official religion in Christian Europe. Thus, the distinction between official and unofficial religion is of little relevance in India, whereas the distinction between great and little tradition takes on meanings associated with caste status. There is, of course, a considerable difference between the great tradition expounded by the mainly Brahmanic elites and the actual religion practiced by the elites. As in other religious cultures, the religious elites in Indian Hinduism participate in the little traditions and popular religion of the Hindu masses.

Elite Patterns of Religious Action

The nomic pattern of action, the preservation and renewal of the cosmic and social order, can be recognized in the ancient Vedic religion. Sacrificial and other rituals were performed to nourish those gods and powers that sustained the fertility and well-being of the world and protected it from demons and forces of destruction. For individuals and families, rites were performed to secure health, wealth, sons, and a long life, with the afterlife conceived in earthly terms. It has remained a cardinal principle that only Brahmans have the authority to perform the most important rituals that preserve and renew the sociocosmic order. Such rituals are for the benefit of all castes, but Brahman priests have often undertaken them on behalf of patrons, especially from the higher castes, who have sought the ritual services of priests not just for nomic and especially life-cycle rituals but also for their particular soteriological and thaumaturgical goals.[7]

Dharma is a central concept in the model of religious action espoused by religious elites in Hinduism. The various meanings of dharma encompass the appropriate supramundane principle to which action is oriented, the goal of religious action, and the appropriate means or behavior. At the most comprehensive level, dharma is "that which maintains" all other entities; it is the power underlying the cosmos, self-sustaining and independent of any antecedent being. Dharma is manifest in the ethical and social laws of humankind, and in conformity to this order, dharma is presented in the great tradition as the highest of the three "human ends," followed by *artha*, the pursuit of power and wealth, and *kama*, the pursuit of love and physical desires. In the most common formulation, each of the two lower goals is to be pursued as long as it is not in conflict or does not interfere with the goal or goals above it.[8]

Conformity to dharma in its meaning as appropriate behavior can be understood both as an end in itself and as the means to the achievement of dharma in its wider meanings: the maintenance of the cosmic and social order and the rebirth of the individual in a higher state. All persons can increase the store of merit and cancel out former sins by performing such actions as going on pilgrimage, bathing in a sacred river, giving charity, and honoring Brahmans. In addition, all persons are expected to conform to the particular dharma of their caste, to practice their *svadharma*, the specific lifestyle and duties whereby people express their own particular, ideal nature. Thus, not just specific rituals but human actions in general, including those of the lowliest born, are believed to uphold the sociocosmic order and to effect the rebirth of the individual within that order.

Although ritual and moral acts are understood to take effect through the impersonal, lawlike workings of karma, most Hindus believe that the future of the world and the future of every person are in the hands of the gods. For this reason the gods are worshiped and propitiated, and as focal worshipers, servants, and intermediaries of the gods, the priests play cru- cial roles in Hinduism. The performance of public worship "for the well- being of the world" is the most important religious action of the priests of the major temples of high gods, such as Shiva and Vishnu. The acts of worship performed by the priests include bathing and decorating the gods, burning incense sticks whose smoke wafts over the gods, and mak- ing offerings that are later distributed to worshipers as transvalued food.

In the important Shiva temple of Madurai, the justification of the ex- clusive rights of priests from a Brahmanic subcaste to perform public worship is their descent from the god himself. As in all major temples in South India, the priests' rights are hereditary and do not depend on for- mal educational qualifications, although a few priests have an elementary knowledge of Sanskrit. In addition to their ascriptive requirement, how- ever, candidates for priesthood are required to undergo initiations and consecration that are believed to transform their souls, so that they be- come forms of Shiva. Another requirement before they can perform pub- lic worship is marriage; the priests must have access to *shakti*, the divine power personified as feminine, which they gain through sexual relations with their wives. In this, they follow the example of the god Shiva, who is taken from his temple each evening to the nearby temple of his consort, which in Madurai takes the form of the goddess Minakshi. Shiva spends the night with Minakshi and is returned to his temple in the morning.[9]

Much of the priests' worship and serving of the deities is carried out without lay participation or observation, but laypeople often seek out the priests as intermediaries when they come to the temple on an individual basis with a special request for the attention of the deity. Ceremonies such as investiture of the sacred thread for Brahman boys, marriages, and oaths for civil and criminal cases also take place in temples.[10] Domestic priests, who generally have a higher rank than temple priests, belong to subcastes who have the hereditary rights to perform rites of passage and ancestral and festival rites for families in particular, usually high castes. Ceremonies in the home can be conducted without the assistance of a priests, but if there is a wish to perform the rites in a textually elaborated style or to gain status, a Brahman priest is required.[11]

Beneath the domestic and temple priests in status are the funeral priests, who perform and supervise rites with the aim of separating the soul from the dead person's body. The essentially pure soul has to be re- leased from the physical body, the location of impurity, which acquires added pollution when it dies. Prior to cremation the body must itself be purified by such acts as bathing the body and clothing it in clean, white cloth, but the release of the soul in the cremation fire is the essential purifier. If the transition from a relatively impure being into a pure being is not completely accomplished, the deceased will not reach heaven or be ready for rebirth. Instead, the dead person may become a malevolent spirit.[12]

In addition to their soteriological goal, the funeral rites are also interpreted within a nomic frame of reference. Death and cremation, when conceived as sacrificial offerings of the self to the gods, are creative acts that not only result in the rebirth of the self but also renew the cosmos. A recurrent theme in Hinduism is the homology between the body and the cosmos, and the death of an individual is assimilated to the process of cosmic regeneration.[13]

The engagement of priests in cosmic renewal and rebirth diverts them from the goal of *moksha*, the ultimate salvation understood as escape, release, liberation from samsara (literally "wandering" or "keeping going"). *Samsara* refers to the phenomenal world, the realm of conditional reality characterized by instability, fluctuation, and contingency. A manifestation of this ultimately unreal or illusory realm is the transmigration of the soul that is effected by karma. Even rebirth as a god in heaven must eventually be followed by redeath and the suffering this involves, and it is taken as axiomatic in the great tradition that never-ending rebirths are undesirable. Moksha goes beyond and in a sense cancels the "worldly" goals of dharma, artha, and kama; it is the transcendence of moral existence, and is often characterized as an anonymous, impersonal, and blissful state.

Moksha and the appropriate means to attain it have been subjects of considerable speculation among the philosophical schools and orders of the religious elite. The monists conceive moksha as the absorption of the person's inner soul (*atman*) into the Brahman, the single, unchanging, and eternal Absolute or ground of being. The atman that realizes its identity with the Brahman looses its individuation. The conception of moksha among the theists or dualists is of the soul retaining its identity in an eternal proximity to Brahman or to a more personalized manifestation of the divine (Vishnu, Shiva, or Krishna) in heaven.[14]

Ritual and virtuous actions can improve a person's chances of a better rebirth, but they cannot lead to moksha. The necessary effects of such actions can only prolong the cycle of rebirth and redeath. The only path of escape from samsara and the mechanism of karma is through renunciation of involvement in society. Separation from social groups in a socially unorganized space (the forest) is believed to provide the ideal condition for the abolition of individuality and fusion with the Brahman. Just as society with its social obligations may be viewed as an analogue for samsara, a life with no social ties may be viewed as an analogue for release from rebirth.

The acceptance by Brahmans of the path of renunciation gave rise to the problem of reconciling contradictory goals and modes of action. On the one hand, the Brahmans had the major responsibility to uphold the sociocosmic order; they were required to officiate at auspicious rites that affirmed and renewed that order. On the other hand, the pure state of the Brahmans, relative to other castes, made them the most suitable candidates for the attainment of moksha by renouncing the world and its caste divisions. One solution in the texts of the great tradition was to divide the life of the Brahman into stages (*asramas*) and to relegate renunciation to the last stage. The fundamental distinction here was between the stage of the householder and that of the renouncer; the priority of social obligations was underlined, and the threat of the renouncer to the dharmic order of the world was contained. This was, however, an ideal portrayal that was rarely practiced, and the patterns of world affirmation and world renunciation have been associated with two distinctive elites—Brahman priests and renouncers.[15]

Unlike priests, who are sexually active "householders," monks and other ascetics (known as *sadhus, sanyasin,* or *yogis*) are set apart from laypeople by their path of celibacy and renunciation. The image of the renouncer is of one who has abandoned all the social relations and activities of the householder; he or (less often) she severs links with family and leads a life that negates the world of work, authority, and ritual. There is, however, no general agreement among orders of renouncers concerning the distinction between "householder" and "renouncer." One order believes it is not necessary to leave the family; sexual abstinence or "celibacy in marriage" is regarded as sufficient to attain a desireless state. Other orders emphasize the need to renounce the family; the belief that the houses and hearths of householders are permeated with desire obliges the members of one group to avoid sleeping in houses and to refuse to accept cooked food from householders.[16]

Outside the web of social obligations, renouncers seek to erase their past karma and attain moksha by means of asceticism, yoga techniques, and meditation. Whereas in the society of householders it is assumed that actions are usually aimed at satisfying material or bodily needs, renouncers believe that outside such a society they can master their bodies by self-mortification and yoga. Austerities include courting discomfort, such as remaining unwashed and subjecting the body to extremes of heat and cold, hunger and thirst. Some impose on themselves extreme penances, such as burying their heads in the ground or standing on one leg or holding one arm up for long periods.

Lifestyles of moderate forms of asceticism, involving a denial or indifference toward worldly desires, have frequently accompanied an emphasis on meditation among renouncers. Meditators sit quietly in secluded places and attempt to withdraw their senses from desirable objects of the phenomenal world. By an essentially inward orientation, meditators attempt to transcend their individualities and realize their knowledge of, and identity with, the Brahman.[17]

Renouncers attach themselves to the higher gods, whom they regard as the most distant from human affairs, and although there are orders for whom Vishnu is the central god, Shiva is the god most associated with renunciation. In one of his forms, Shiva is depicted as a lone ascetic with a head of matted locks and other marks of the renouncer, living on the margins of settlement, in the forests, mountains, and cremation grounds.[18] Many sadhus carry a trident and mark three stripes of ash on their foreheads to symbolize their identity with Shiva's destruction of the three impurities: selfishness, action with desire, and *maya* (illusion). Some use a two-sided drum that represents the union of Shiva and Shakti and wear saffron-colored robes or loincloths, which signify that the renouncers have been symbolically washed in the blood of Shiva's goddess consort.[19]

Priests and monks worship common deities; but whereas the priests worship the deities and unite with them for cosmic regeneration and the attainment of their own and their lay clients proximate salvation and worldly goals, the renouncers worship and imitate the deities on their path to the ultimate salvation of moksha. As in many other religious traditions, however, lay recognition of the accomplishments of virtuosos who renounce the world draws those virtuosos into thaumaturgical religious action.

The belief that asceticism, yoga techniques, and meditation enable sadhus to subjugate nature leads laypeople to request their help in the attainment of worldly ends. It is the ascetics' recognition of the world as illusion that is seen to give them the power to manipulate the world for the benefit of others who remain in it. Religious texts advise sadhus not to seek supramundane powers but to recognize them as an inevitable product of the actions or non-actions that they perform on the path to moksha. The sadhus are also advised to keep their powers hidden from people, whose demands on them will bring karmic entanglements and lead the renouncers away from their chosen path. Such strictures have frequently been ignored when sadhus gain lay followings who, in return for the sadhus' thaumaturgy, reward the sadhus with their worship and devotion. It is the more sedentary renouncers, whose residences are located near their communities of origin, who are the more likely to direct their religious action to the goals of their lay devotees.[20]

Patterns of Religious Action in Popular Hinduism

Weber made a sharp distinction between the soteriological goal of the Brahmanic elite (moksha) and the soteriological goal of the masses (a good rebirth). It could be argued that rebirth in a higher caste or as a god in heaven was perceived as one stage in the journey toward the final, ultimate goal, but for the masses, moksha was too distant a goal to be considered. The supramundane principles and beings and the appropriate forms of behavior were entirely different for the two goals. Moksha was a fusion of the atman with Brahman and was to be achieved through renunciation, self-mortification, and meditation. A good rebirth was dependent on good karma or a salvation god, and it was to be attained through ritual action, conformity to dharma, and devotion to high gods.

Moksha, in the sense of fusion with Brahman, is not regarded as a realistic goal for the majority, but large numbers have been drawn to *bhakti* (devotionist) movements that promise a salvation of being perpetually in the presence of the devotee's deity. The preoccupation here is with heaven rather than a good rebirth. Heaven, a pleasant celestial realm of the gods, is the karmic reward for one's good actions. Some Hindus think of heaven as a temporary sojourn; it will last until the person's accumulated merit has been appropriately awarded, and it will be followed by rebirth.[21] Others conceive of residence in heaven as eternal salvation, or they regard what follows heaven as too remote and unknowable to warrant reflection. Many are quite vague in expressing beliefs about the afterlife or the fate of the spirit after death.[22]

There is no obvious parallel in popular religion to the tension in the great tradition between the patterns of world affirmation and world renunciation. Villagers may acknowledge that ultimate salvation can be achieved only by renouncing the world and abandoning caste and family, but their taken-for-granted path is that of the householder. They believe that in order to achieve proximate salvation or conditional immortality, they must follow the rules, rituals, and morality of their dharma, and they must produce male offspring who will perform the appropriate rites after their death. They acknowledge the appropriateness of the ascetic path to transcendent immortality, but villages will often voice skepticism about the motives of actual renouncers who come begging. "Ascetics" are often portrayed as lazy, untrustworthy persons who took up a life of mendicancy for material rather than religious reasons.[23]

The preservation or continual rebirth of the cosmos and the social world is a principal concern of both the great and little traditions, but the little tradition and popular religion in general focus on more immediate and parochial concerns, such as the family's or village's crops, the health of the animals, and the birth of healthy children. No contradiction is felt between the worldly, "pragmatic" goals and the soteriological, "transcendental" goal. There is little consciousness of such distinctions, and in many cases the observer finds it difficult to tell whether a particular religious action is directed toward an ultimate goal or to individual welfare.[24] For example, pilgrims believe the merit they accumulate through pilgrimage determines both earthly and heavenly awards. Different pilgrims choose to direct the merit to different ends, but the approach to the deity and the ritual actions are the same regardless of whether the merit is intended to produce immediate material changes or whether it is to be stored.[25]

The supramundane beings and processes that are believed to participate in the field of religious action can be divided approximately between impersonal processes or laws, of which karma is the most prominent, and personal beings. Deities and impersonal forces should not, however, be regarded as clearly differentiated categories in popular religion. When Hindus say they will die at a particular time because of karma, fate, or God, there appears to be little difference in the meanings attributed to these terms,[26] and the relatively impersonal gods or idea of God (conveyed by multiple names, such as Bhagwan and Ishwar, that vary over India) are referred to interchangeably with karma. These gods rarely assist in the achievement of worldly goals.

Karma and the Little Tradition

In the pursuit of their goals, individuals take into consideration both the conditions they cannot alter and the means that can facilitate their attainment. In the framework of religious action among Hindus, there is considerable variation in the extent to which karma is considered a condition or a means. Building up "good karma," or accumulating merit, is a means for achieving both proximate salvation and this-worldly goals. Merit is gained by moral behavior, such as honesty, marital fidelity, and charity, and by ritual behavior that may keep the "karmic score" even, restore a positive balance by canceling out previous sins, or increase the scale of merits over demerits. Passionate devotion to a particular deity, such as Krishna, is regarded by many as a major means of increasing merit, and conformity to the rules of purity and pollution, in which the deities are deeply involved, is also of great importance in the determination of karma. The highest divinity keeps track of good and bad deeds over countless incarnations and is especially pleased by ethical acts and the giving of alms.[27]

In Weber's formulation, karma was a condition par excellence. He was impressed with karma as a supremely rational and ethical theodicy that explained why people had been born in particular castes and why they experienced happiness or suffering, fortune or misfortune, in this life. Anthropologists have found, however, that most Hindus do not attribute their birth in a particular caste to their actions in previous lives, and that explanations of physical defects or specific misfortunes in terms of karma are not common. Even when there is an appeal to karma as an explanation, there are no feelings of responsibility, guilt, or remorse for the unknown offenses that may have been committed in previous lives. Hindus sometimes refer to karma when they wish to account for luck or misfortune in general terms, and when events are understood to be beyond their control and understanding.[28] A general term for "fate" that is not understood to be related to past actions is used interchangeably with karma, and either may be referred to when things go wrong. When things go right, credit is more likely to be ascribed to a god, although general terms for God are also used interchangeably with karma.[29]

Karma overlaps and fuses with other notions of causality and explanation. Religious texts relate that the gods or their representatives total up the good and bad actions of individuals and "write" on their foreheads their fate as determined by karma.[30] In popular religion, "headwriting" is not just a consequence of karma and is presumed by some to be more deterministic than karma. Villagers believe they can alter the consequences of their karma through ritual, and that karma works itself out inexorably only when they have not made enough effort to prevent its consequences. In contrast, only "God" can change headwriting, and most believe that it cannot be changed, despite efforts at persuasion through vows and offerings.[31]

Hindus are able to justify inconsistent notions that it is both impossible and possible to change their fate by reference to the remarkably inconsistent gods of their religion. Weber has been criticized for assuming that popular ideas of karma were the same as those found in religious texts,[32] but it should also be emphasized that inconsistent, contradictory, and paradoxical statements concerning human fate and effort, and both deterministic and voluntaristic models of humans, can be found in the Hindu canon. The Puranas, for example, constantly invoke karma as a "condition," but they also insist that karma can be reversed by antidotes, including meditation, renunciation, yoga, devotion to a god, and pilgrimage to sacred shrines.[33] In the epic Mahabharata, the notion that a person reaps the consequences of his actions in previous lifetimes is counterposed with claims that it is the actions of gods or the machinations of blind fate that are the primary causes of a person's situation. The characters of the epic present alternate views: for one, God alone is determinative; for another, it is man alone, or man in interaction with the god. And it is not just that different events are accounted for by different factors; single events are explained by alternative factors.[34]

Both the elites and the masses are selective in their readings of the references to karma in the sacred texts. Whereas the more philosophical texts have been selected by members of the elites, the folk prefer the mythical texts that demonstrate the meaning of karma in the lives of gods, demons, saints, and sinners and are given form in the songs and rituals of temples and village festivals. The stories taken from the Puranas and local mythologies do not focus on how past actions resulted in present karma but on how present karma influences people's lives.

A common theme in popular myths is how the karma of one person affects the lives of others. The transference of karma is not a popular transformation and distortion of a textual doctrine; it is found in the Manu, the epics, and the Puranas. The assumption that karma cannot be transferred is found in certain philosophical traditions, such as Yoga and Vedanda, but this was an elitist notion of a few virtuosos. The vast majority have believed in the possibility of its transfer, including its transfer from one generation to another. For example, an illness is explained as a consequence of a parent's bad karma, or an early death is believed to be the consequence of the sins of an ancestor who lived two or three generations earlier. Karma can be transferred through sex and food, and dangers may therefore accrue not only from sex with a prostitute but also by accepting food from her. In contrast, the acceptance of the "leavings" of gods, Brahmans, and holypersons can increase a person's good karma.[35] Thus, karma is not only a condition of action; it is also a means that is relevant to the improvement of people's situation in this lifetime as well as the next.

Within an exclusively karmic frame of reference, people's life situations are a product of the entire moral history of their transmigrating selves. Specific misfortunes in this lifetime cannot be predicted or avoided because they are understood as symptoms of general moral conditions that derive from the unknown actions of past lives. Present actions will have karmic consequences, but without the knowledge of the past, the future is also hidden.[36] Many Hindus cope with the problem of the hidden character of karma by turning to astrology. Hindu astrologers state, and many of their clients believe, that a correct reading of the planetary configurations present at the time people were born will reveal their karma and its effects on their present and future circumstances and actions. After "readings" suggesting that clients may have to suffer because of bad karma, astrologers are able to recommend preventive measures, such as worship, wearing charms, special diets, and giving alms.[37]

Astrology is largely popular among the middle and upper social strata, and it is possible that the absence of exact records of the date of birth in the poor stratum makes the practice less attractive to them.[38] Even if astrology is used to discover the consequences of karma, however, the determination of specific remedies remains problematic. This is because karma is still an indeterminate cause: no meaningful links are made between specific consequences (illness, injury, etc.) and specific causes (specific actions in previous lives). When particular misfortunes are attributed to specific causes in this lifetime, such as the annoyance of a spirit, witchcraft, or the evil eye, a diagnosis can be directly linked to the prognosis: offerings are given to the spirit to assuage its anger, or help is sought from a magician to use countermagic against witchcraft or the evil eye. Success may not be guaranteed, but it is important to feel that the remedy is an appropriate response to the specific causes of the condition. Explanations in terms of the actions of gods, spirits, and witches are more common than explanations in terms of karma because the former have practical applicability.

Supramundane Beings: The Hindu Pantheon

The Hindu pantheon is populous, complex, and fluid: the number of deities worshiped by the residents of a single village can total up to one hundred; deities are known under a multitude of names and take numerous forms; and one deity can become many and many deities become one. The doctrine that all supramundane beings are ultimately one is not confined to philosophers and is reiterated among illiterate villagers.[39] Some Hindus say that the plurality of gods are "parts," "divisions," "forms," or "manifestations" of one Shakti in the sense of one power, energy, or force. Others emphasize that the gods have separate and distinct natures; there are different shaktis that answer different needs and require different offerings.[40]

The most abstract and impersonalized formulation of divinity is Brahman, the unknowable and ultimate source, which encompasses all that is manifested in the universe. Brahman is a focus of contemplation for the sophisticated, but as an undifferentiated and non-active principle, it rarely intrudes into popular religion.[41] In speaking of an encompassing divine power Hindus more often refer to Bhagwan (or Bhagavan), a name that encompasses all male deities but that may also be attached to a specific god, and Devi, which refers to an undifferentiated form of female divinity. Somewhat less abstract and more personalized are the high gods Shiva, Vishnu, and Brahma, who make up the Trimurti, or Hindu trinity; Krishna and Rama, who are two of Vishnu's avatars; and Shakti, the female deity in its "high" form.[42]

A large proportion of Hindus can be distinguished by their devotion to Vishnu (Vaishnavas) or Shiva (Shaivas), each of whom is worshiped as the Greatest or Supreme God in the sense of Supreme Person rather than Supreme Abstraction. As ultimate sources of being or supreme principles of the universe, Shiva and Vishnu are regarded as formless, unknowable, transcendent, and immanent, but in contrast with Brahman and Bhagwan, they are subjects of a large mythology; they have particular names, locations, and attributes; they are manifested in objects; and each has his temples, priesthoods, ritual styles, and festival cycles.[43]

Shiva and Vishnu in their high manifestations are associated with values and goals that extend far beyond the immediate goals of individuals and groups.[44] They are associated with the general welfare rather than specific advantages, with general principles rather than immediate exigencies, and with the encompassing order rather than the encompassed realities of everyday life. They are worshiped on occasion for individual benefit, but as remote deities, they may not deem to involve themselves in the petty affairs of individual people. The high gods are also not directly accessible to ordinary worshipers, because the conventions of their worship and the need to guard them from pollution require the specialized knowledge and mediumship of the Brahman priests. Local deities have less power than the high gods, but people often feel it is more efficacious to appeal to and worship lower deities who are willing to enter directly into the affairs of humans, do not require elaborate ritual styles, and are not insulated by the priests, who are concerned to protect the high gods' purity.[45]

Many of the lower gods and goddesses are local manifestations, offspring, and relatives of the high gods. The ambiguities of Shiva, who is a god of both chastity and eroticism, renunciation and sexual energy, would appear to make him ritually accessible, and he is one of the most commonly localized of the high, textual gods.[46] He is the focal deity of many large temples and pilgrimage sites as well as of numerous small temples and local shrines, where he is known by different names and is given different consorts.[47] The universal Shiva, the higher form of the god, is understood to have given his subordinate forms the powers to protect particular villages and urban quarters. These subordinates include his sons, the elephant-headed Ganesha and, in southern India, Ayyappan and Murugan, who unlike the distant Shiva are believed to be active in their devotees' lives, protecting their villages against the forces of darkness. Vishnu takes on localized, more particularistic forms in his fourth incarnation as the man-lion Narsimba. Hanuman, the monkey ally of Rama, is among the most commonly localized of the textual gods.[48]

Whereas the high forms of Shiva and Vishnu are associated with nomic themes of creation, destruction, preservation, and moral order, their consort goddesses concern themselves with the mundane problems of ordinary people. Vishnu upholds the moral system and hierarchical institutions, which are intrinsic to the cosmic order, while his consort Lakshmi represents worldly pleasures and is worshiped as a goddess of good luck and fortune. Parvati, the consort of Shiva, is one of the myriad forms in which goddesses associated with fertility are worshiped in the villages.[49] Many villages with Shiva temples and shrines have myths that relate how Shiva came to be worshiped there when he married a local woman-goddess. The goddess's identification with the indigenous and unique site of the shrine is seen to effect the link between Shiva and his local home.[50]

Parvati and other consorts of the major male deities are frequently presented as devoted and subordinate to their husbands and as benign sources of wealth and progeny. Whatever dangerous forces they may have are restrained within the social relationship of marriage, and the iconography of these gentle, submissive goddesses presents them, like Hindu brides, as literally bound. This is not the case of most local goddesses, who are often considered to be unmarried, in an ascendent position, and capable of disruption and harm. These blood-drinking goddesses are not controlled sexually by any male, and they are portrayed as unbound, with hair loose and flowing.[51] The unreleased sexual energy of the unmarried goddesses produces a hot anger that is manifested in the feverish diseases of their victims and is countered by cooling rituals.[52]

Many goddesses incorporate contradictions within their perceived natures: both nurturing and destructive, gentle and cruel, protective and harmful, bringers of children as well as disease and death. Some goddesses are believed to have once been women. These include the wives of god-incarnate kings, women who chose to die on their husbands' or sons' funeral pyres, and women who met a "bad" or premature death, which resulted in them becoming ghosts whose malevolence was controlled by deification.[53]

The fluid boundaries between deities and humans in the Hindu cosmology is also congenial to the claims of goddess-women and god-men, who are often conceived as incarnations of the major gods of the devotionalist communities and movements: Shiva, Vishnu, and Vishnu's avatars, especially Rama and Krishna. The focus of devotionalist movements on a single god entails conceiving other gods as subordinate forms of the god elevated by devotees, and some devotionalist followings of saints believe that the saint is superior to other manifestations of the divine, such as nonhuman deities, who are displaced or relegated by the saint. Divine saints include the dead, such as the founders of monastic orders, and the living, such as heads of monasteries who, as "perfect devotees," may be seen as continual manifestations of the original founder's divinity.

The transformation of ascetic renouncers into god-men or goddess-women does not originate solely in popular religion. The recognition of founders of religious orders as gods has come from the core groups of ascetic disciples around the founders, but a large following can come only from the laity who, without following the lifestyle of renunciation, aspire through their devotion to the saint to attain the renouncer's goal of salvation as well as this-worldly goals.[54] The most famous saint of recent times, around whom a religious movement has grown, is Sathya Sai Baba, whose claim to be an incarnation of Shiva and Shakti encompasses all the gods and goddesses of the Hindu pantheon. Sathya Sai Baba offers a good rebirth to his followers, a large proportion of whom come from the urban middle classes, but salvation is given relatively little attention compared with alleviating the misfortunes of this world.[55]

Below the local gods, goddesses, and human saints are the serpents, imps, ghosts, and spirits, many of whom are associated with or located in objects and places of nature. Women who died in childbirth are said to be among the most vicious and malevolent of the various minor spirits who haunt the countryside and seek the blood of attractive and unprotected women. Other people, who died young without fulfilling their desires, who committed suicide, or who were murdered, are believed to wander about the place of their death or burial. Such spirits are seen to exist on a plane very close to human life, and they exhibit disruptive human emotions, especially jealousy, which are a menace to the living and need to be warded off with the help of benevolent gods or folk remedies.[56]

Among the objects with supramundane power that are used to achieve beneficial goals and provide protection from evil forces are the products of the cow, the Tulsi plant, sacred trees, and rivers, especially the Ganges, which is worshiped as the goddess Ganga.[57]

Means: Symbols, Communication, and Appropriate Behaviors

The attainment of ends through transactions with supramundane beings requires the establishment of appropriate forms of relationships and the overcoming of problems of communication. Worship is performed in front of, and gifts and services are offered to, images that are believed to contain the power of the gods they represent. The images are "lifeless" until the installation ceremonies effect the embodiment of the otherwise immaterial and formless deities. The regular forms of worship in temples, performed four times a day by priests, include hymns that are recited to persuade the deity to take visible form by inhabiting the image. The image becomes the deity, but many still regard the image as a temporary, incomplete, and inadequate expression.

The belief that the shape and form of the deity are passing phenomena is manifested by deliberately making many sacred images in perishable materials or by destroying the image after the completion of the ritual. More permanent images are shown to be ephemeral by adorning them in different clothes for different festivals or even during a single festival. A goddess who is dressed differently each day during a festival is shown to loose its identity by becoming all the major goddesses. Almost all the objects that are used in ritual are impermanent: food is consumed; flowers fade; incense, oil, and camphor disappear in smoke; and ash and red powder quickly rub off the body. These perishable objects demonstrate the problems facing people in maintaining communication with the gods.[58]

The appropriate relationship of communicant and deity requires rituals that purify both the place of communication and the participants. The space in which the deity is approached is kept permanently in a pure state or is purified for the occasion. Prior to approaching the deity or making offerings, participants purify themselves, often by bathing and putting on special garments. The extensiveness and intensity of the preparations depend on the place of the deity in the pantheon, the status of the worshipers, and the importance of the ritual. Substances commonly used in the purification process are the products of the living cow, such as its milk and dung, and water from sacred sources, such as the Ganges.[59]

The application of substances in a particular order are believed to transform a deity from a lesser to a higher state of purity. In festivals that honor goddesses, participants first deal with the goddess in its low, impure form by offering it relatively impure foods. The goddess is then transformed into a higher, beneficent being as it receives offerings of purer food and expressions of devotion. This process is believed to neutralize the anger of the goddess in its low forms, thereby preventing diseases, and to attract the beneficence of its high forms, thereby bringing rain and providing protection for the village.[60] In these cases, purification is not just a preparation for communication with the deity but is part of the transaction.

The purity/pollution contrast is used in transactions with the higher gods in order to honor them and to show the deference of worshipers. A prominent example is when food is given to a deity, taken back, and distributed to the worshipers as leftovers. The exchange of food for leavings is to exchange a pure item for a polluted one, because it is believed that leavings are contaminated by the saliva of the eater. This transaction symbolizes the devotees' humility, but it is also a recognition of the deity's power of transformation: the deity is so superior that anything received from it is considered to be of great purity.[61]

The "sharing" of food with a god or goddess is an occasion of communion and intimacy with a deity. Another occasion of such intimacy is when a deity "gives *darsan*" (seeing), presenting itself to be seen in its image, and the sight is "received" by the people. The eyes of Hindu divine images are given prominence, and the exchange of vision, in which worshiper and deity "see" each other, is considered a central part of worship. Processions of the image enable everyone to receive darsan, including those who, by virtue of their low caste, are prohibited from entering the deity's temple.[62]

Understood as a transaction, the object of offerings and services is to please the deity, who, in return, will protect the worshipers. A variety of views is found among Hindus regarding the extent to which deities have needs that can be satisfied by worshipers. Some say the deities do not actually need offerings and services, such as food, washing, and beautification, because deities are never hungry, unclean, or ugly. According to this view, offerings and services are only symbolic demonstrations by humans of their respectful attitudes toward the deities. An alternative view, which is found especially among Vaishyas, is that a god such as Krishna does have bodily needs, that the god permits humans to satisfy these needs, and that the god will suffer if he does not receive the offerings and services.

Relatively sophisticated devotees say that the fulfillment of a deity's needs or the honor accorded to it by humans does not guarantee the deity will protect humans or fulfill their requests. Deities may be displeased by worship performed to persuade or induce them to bestow reciprocal favors on worshipers. A linguistic distinction is made in some regions between *puja*, which is worship understood as an exchange of benefits, and *seva*, which is worship without thought of any benefits in return. Many ordinary Hindus, however, are quite ready to admit that they worship with specific goals in mind or that they worship a deity only after it has met their request.[63]

Higher deities are believed by some to be unresponsive or even angered by efforts to persuade them to enter into bargains and provide favors. Transactions with lower deities, by contrast, are understood to involve hard-fought negotiations, and their potential malevolence requires that the worshiper take care not to neglect them or make mistakes that can invoke their angry retaliation. The objects that are offered to the lower beings, such as blood sacrifices, produce pollution, but they are believed to meet these deities' lowly needs.[64]

Religious Overlaps and Interrelationships

Blood sacrifice is still widely practiced in popular Hinduism and is one of
a number of religious practices that are widely criticized and condemned
by those who claim to represent a higher form of Hinduism. The question of whether Hinduism can be divided into two or more forms or levels associated with higher and lower castes or with elites and masses has
long been a perplexing issue for anthropologists writing on India. When
Robert Redfield presented his conceptual distinction of great and little
traditions and applied it to India, he emphasized that he was not suggesting there were two Hinduisms, one of an intellectual elite and another of
the masses,[65] but this is how the distinction has often been understood,
especially when it has been joined with a distinction between Sanskritic
and non-Sanskritic Hinduism. McKim Marriott used Sanskrit texts as a
measuring stick in assessing the importance of the great tradition in a village community and among the castes in the village. He found that fewer
than one-fifth of the deities worshiped by the lowest castes were Sanskrit,
but even among the Brahmans of the village, a little fewer than one-half
of the deities were Sanskrit.

Marriott described the processes of universalization, whereby elements of the little tradition are transformed into the great tradition by
elaboration, refinement, and systematization, and the processes of pa-
rochialization, whereby elements of the great tradition are transmuted
into more localized, less reflective, and less systematic elements. These
processes have gone on for so long that it is often impossible to judge
whether any particular item was a consequence of one process or the
other: a particular god may be either a parochialized Sanskrit god or a
universalized parochial god. Despite these processes of exchange, however, there remain "residual categories" that are found only within one of
the traditions: there is a huge Sanskrit philosophic literature that remains
outside the little tradition, and there are many gods and practices in festivals that have no relation to the great tradition. Thus, even after a millennium of interaction, the great and little traditions could still be distinguished in village religion.[66]

M. N. Srinivas also adopted the term *Sanskritic Hinduism* to denote an
"all-India Hinduism" that transcends the many regional and local Hinduisms, but the problems of distinguishing between Sanskritic and non-
Sanskritic Hinduism would appear formidable, especially since Sanskritic
epics and their associated rituals have been adopted in vernacular forms to

eulogize and worship local deities. It is difficult to separate two categories of deities when localized village deities are often understood to derive some or all of their powers from the great deities.[67] As C. J. Fuller has argued, Srinivas converted an ideological distinction, used by Brahmans to emphasize their religious superiority, into an analytical concept, which he used to distinguish levels of Hinduism. Some Brahmans do evaluate religious beliefs and practices by reference to this distinction, but anthropologists should not adopt these Brahmans' assumption that there is a clear division between scriptural and popular Hinduism when even among the Brahmans there is no consensus about their constituent elements.

Fuller warns against the reification of an indigenous distinction into a misconstrued empirical division within Hinduism, but he writes that it would be equally mistaken to overstate the unity of Hinduism. Temples of the great deities tend to attract a greater number of high-caste worshipers who are mainly served by Brahman priests, who make only vegetarian offerings and use Sanskritic ritual language. The worship styles in these temples are characterized by very formal modes of praise and deference to the deities. Temples of lesser deities tend to be patronized more by low castes, and their priests from non-Brahman castes make both vegetarian and non-vegetarian offerings and use vernacular languages in ritual. The worship styles in these temples tend to be informal and personal, emphasizing the accessibility of the deity and its intimacy with its devotees.[68]

Differentiation within Hinduism is especially evident when a comparison is made between temple deities served by Brahman priests and non-temple deities that are often mediated by religious specialists, such as healers and exorcists, who are drawn from a range of castes. In his study of popular Hinduism in the region of Chhattisgarh, Central India, Lawrence Babb counterposes the *baiga*—the non-Brahman curer-exorcist—and the Brahman priest as "two analytically separable complexes of religious idioms and practices." The Brahman priest is the focus of the "textual complex," centering on the deities and ritual styles of sacred texts, and he specializes in the performance of rituals that are derived from or refer to the sacred literature.

The major temples in which the Brahman priests serve have regional constituencies lacking clear-cut social boundaries, and they house gods and goddesses whose histories, attributes, and relationships are drawn from the sacred literature. The zone of purity that these deities require is relatively stringent, and only the purest of men, the Brahman priest, can approach them and act as a mediator for ordinary worshipers. The very presence of a Brahman priest in a temple is an expression of the need of the deity for an environment free of pollution.

The baiga is linked with nontextual deities, lower in the pantheon and less demanding of purity, and he also deals with the even lower category of malevolent ghosts, minor spirits, and witches. He comes from a lower caste, but he has special knowledge and characteristics that give him access to and a degree of control over various deities, both benevolent and harmful. These deities are likely to be associated with local constituencies (village, neighborhood, caste) whose social boundaries are relatively well defined, and they are believed to be intimately involved in specific human problems, particularly illness. The most conspicuous activity of the baiga is to diagnose and cure ailments by using his knowledge and power to attain good relationships between his clientele and the gods and spirits.

Babb emphasizes that the two complexes he distinguishes are not discrete entities. The village community incorporates textual passages and nontextual religious customs of local origin into what is, from the perspective of the villagers, a single religious system. Textual ritual "styles" will be employed in some ceremonies more than in others and by the higher castes more than by the lower. Two distinguishable complexes, centered on the Brahman priest and the baiga respectively, are evident, but this does not mean there is a strict division of clientele or of roles. The local complex and its representative have lower prestige, but they are patronized by high castes as well as low because, whatever their caste, people seek cures from supramundane sources. The textual-Brahmanic-regional temple complex deals with wider issues and larger social constituencies, but its prestige allows it to deal also with mundane issues. Brahman priests involve themselves in pragmatic concerns and will, on occasion, invoke even the highest gods of the pantheon to meet the demands of their clientele for good health, children, and business success. In contrast, the lower prestige of the nontextual-baiga-local temple complex does not allow it to encroach on the wider and supramundane concerns of the Brahman priests.[69]

Values and Social Structure

The caste structure is central to a discussion of both the values and the social structures that have shaped the divisions and interrelationships of elite and popular religion in India. The caste system is both a religious and a social system, and the hierarchical divisions of religious elements, such as pure and impure deities and vegetarian and nonvegetarian offerings, are closely related to the hierarchical divisions of castes. This association is especially emphasized by Louis Dumont, who argued that a single principle, the complementary opposition between purity and impurity, governs relationship of deities, including the higher and lower forms of a single deity, and the caste system.[70]

However much some Brahmans emphasize their separation from the lower castes, it is evident that the religious differences between the higher and lower castes are dependent on their relationship within a single system; the structural opposition is a complementary relationship of relative purity and impurity that can only be defined with one relative to the other. And within this system, the interests of both higher and lower castes have led to mutual influences and substantial interrelationships of patterns of religious action.

As a status group, the interests of Brahmans have inclined them to an orientation of closure; they have sought to monopolize access to religious knowledge, the performance of particular rituals, and the path of renunciation. As an institutional religious elite, however, it has been in the interests of many Brahman priests to extend their services to, and involve themselves in the religious enculturation of, non-Brahmanic, albeit "clean," castes. On their part, the status motives of lower castes have inclined them to adopt beliefs and behaviors from higher castes; this was seen as a means to raise the status of the caste, and those who were economically mobile or held political positions sought to make their caste status more compatible with their economic and political statuses. Brahmans sometimes opposed imitation of their ways, but Brahman priests facilitated the process by reciting and explaining sacred stories within the contexts of regular ritual occasions.[71]

The centrality of caste with respect to the differences between and interrelationships of elite and popular religion provokes questions about the nature and foundations of the caste system. Dumont has argued that religious ideas and values, and in particular the opposition between purity and impurity, determine the principles of the caste system, and although he admits that power can counterbalance purity at "secondary levels," he characterizes Indian society as one in which power is subordinated to status.[72] This view is uncomfortably close to that found in the Brahmanic Sanskrit texts, and it should not be assumed that the particular hierarchical values expressed in those texts have been accepted by all castes and classes of Indian society.[73] Alternative hierarchical models to that of the Brahmans, such as those of kings and of renouncers, were also justified in terms of religious notions that have come to be termed *Hindu*. Many kings or rajas did not accept the principle of an absolute distinction between royalty and religious status or their dispossession of religious prerogatives.[74] They made claims to an independent religious status by deriving their rulership from the cosmic kingship of a great god such as Rama/Vishnu or Shiva[75] or by presenting themselves as the sacred representation of the tutelary divinity of the country.

The attribution of divinity to kings did not in itself mark them off from many other humans who are also identified with divine beings, but as the ruler of a kingdom, a microcosm of the cosmos, the king was seen to preserve the dharma, or sociocosmic order, either as a god himself or in partnership with the gods. The warrior rulers of South India included Brahmans in their courts to reinforce their legitimation as divinely mandated kings; they incorporated Brahmans into their civil administration; and they endowed and protected temples served by Brahman priests. The rulers succeeded in absorbing Brahmanism into their kingly status, but they combined "Sanskritic" rites with the worship of fierce, blood-taking warrior deities and did not allow Brahmanism to dominate them.[76] In Rajasthan, the Kshatriya Rajputs claimed that they were the highest caste, and in some princely states they dispensed with Brahman priests and performed the worship of their clan goddesses themselves.[77] A sociohistorical study of a small South Indian kingdom found that the positions of castes were defined as much in terms of proximity to the king as in terms of purity and pollution, and that the highest-ranking Brahmans were those who generated the most merit and honor to the king.[78]

Dumont viewed the Brahmans as both preeminent in the hierarchical system and as priests; but as priests in the service of the king, they were highly dependent on the ruler for his patronage and gifts. Sanskrit texts that propagated the absolute superiority of the Brahmans advised them that they should not be priests, and especially not the priests of kings.[79] The assumption in the texts was that the king's protection and material support lowered the status of the Brahmans. In fact, Brahman priests were proud of the large gifts they received from the rulers, and they would attempt to improve their positions in relation to the king by accepting the gifts with as much detachment as was thought wise, by giving or withholding their blessings, and by threatening to use or actually using their powerfully perceived curse. The king, on his part, would attempt to improve his position in relation to the Brahmans by giving or denying gifts in such a way that the Brahmans would recognize that their purported detachment was thanks to the king.[80]

If kings represent an alternative hierarchical model to that of the Brahmans, the question arises of the effects of this model on popular religion. The analogy of god and king in India has been frequently commented on. In his study of a temple in South India, Arjun Appadurai notes that the word for "temple" means also "royal palace" and that the word for "temple servants" means also "servants of the king." The language addressed to the deity is in the idiom of bonded servitude, and the terms refer to the deity's universal lordship and sovereignty. This terminology is used only with reference to the high gods, with whom transactions are generally mediated by priests.

It is the pattern of worship performed by priests, laid down in detail in a series of texts, that evokes the reception and endowment of the deity as a royal guest: the awakening of the deity, the bathing and dressing of the sacred image, the offerings, and so on. Laypeople occasionally take part in these activities, particularly during the processions of the gods' festivals, when the paraphernalia that adorn and accompany the deity—umbrellas, elephants, and so on—are indistinguishable from the paraphernalia of royal processions.[81] Laypeople, however, relate more frequently to lower deities, whose status and characteristics bear no resemblance to those of kings.

Some writers with a materialist perspective have argued that it was the economic position of the Brahmans rather than their priestly roles that secured them the highest rank. Barrington Moore wrote that it is the caste that holds land in a particular locality, whether Brahman or not, that is the highest caste.[82] Such arguments might be extended to the claim that religious differences are in fact consequences and reflections of economic differences, rather than being rooted in the values of purity and impurity. Hostility of peasants toward Brahmans because of economic interests[83] might account for the disparagement of the high deities by low-caste Hindus who believe in the greater strength and effectiveness of their "lower" deities.[84]

Although Brahmans have been actively involved in the control of land and labor, they avoided making this control the primary basis of their power, which first and foremost has been based on their religious status. Murry Milner attributes the success of the Brahmans in retaining their high position in Indian society to their willingness to assign economic and political power to other castes. The means of violence and land and labor were alienable resources that could be appropriated by conquerors and rebellious groups. The Brahmans' religious status, in contrast, was a relatively inalienable resource; it depended on a highly elaborate ritual lifestyle, which was almost impossible for outsiders to copy or appropriate, and a strict regulation of their social contacts, especially with respect to marriage and eating companions. Thus, in most areas the local political and economic structures are not controlled by Brahmans; frequently the dominant castes are Shudras.[85] Some members of economically and politically dominant castes have questioned the preeminent status of the Brahman castes,[86] but when this occurs the economic hostility of low-caste peasants is unlikely to be directed toward the Brahmans.

Rather than provide the basis for religious differences or opposition, socioeconomic relations may provide models for transactions between people and deities. Susan Wadley notes the similarities between the transactions of worshipers and gods and those of patrons and clients in a North Indian village. The client provides a share of his harvest and his services and receives from the patron a plot for his house, foodstuffs, firewood, cow dung, fodder for cattle, and so on. The patron is committed to aiding his clients in times of crisis, such as providing grain when crops have failed, and he is expected to give special gifts on festivals and on occasions such as births, deaths, and marriages. When devotees say to their gods, "I am in your shelter," they are expressing a relationship similar to that of their relationship to their patrons.[87]

The hierarchy of economic classes in India may be relevant to a consideration of religious differences and interrelationships between religious elites and masses not because it is the foundation of the caste hierarchy but rather because it cuts across it. Modern trends have included a gradual dissociation of class from the caste structure, but there was probably always some degree of autonomy from the caste system of the relations of production.[88] Anomalies between caste ranking and class position were especially apparent at the highest and lowest levels: an economically impoverished Brahman retained a high caste ranking to which a wealthy member of a low caste could not aspire.[89] Where people from different castes have been united by economic class, they may be inclined to ignore the religious differences and rules of purity and impurity. There can be little doubt, however, that class consciousness, whether expressed directly or in religious terms, has been weakened by the strength of the caste system, especially in rural areas, where caste continues to determine many aspects of social and religious behavior.

The strength of the caste system has also been held responsible for the absence of strong central governments in traditional India,[90] which in turn has had implications for religious organization and the relationships of religious elites and masses. The caste system proved highly resilient when large parts of India were conquered by the Mogul and British empires. The Mogul Empire included a large part of India by the end of the sixteenth century, but its bureaucratic system was relatively weak, and its emperors ruled and taxed through many local chieftains whose territories varied greatly in size, resources, and autonomy. The chiefs and rajas did not unite into an aristocracy, and by the middle of the eighteenth century, after the disintegration of the Mogul Empire, the country was divided into a number of petty kingdoms.[91] The Hindu kingdoms of South India remained independent from the Mogul Empire, and the area lacked a stable ruling class. Each king or lord incorporated lesser chiefs and village elders, and a claim to kingship depended on the ruler's ability to maintain or widen a network of dependents and tributaries on whom he could bestow gifts of land, marks of rank and ennoblement. Military capacity was the basis of kingship, but there was no centralized military rule, revenue collection, or bureaucracy, and military mobilization depended on kinship connections and on alliances with chieftains and privileged landowners. This was a highly unstable political system; chiefs tried to expand their domains and claim new rights of kingship at the expense of other lords, including those whom they had previously acknowledged.[92] Decentralized political rule did not end with the British Empire. On the eve of independence in 1947, there were 565 kingdoms of "princely states" in the Indian subcontinent that were not under direct British rule.[93]

As noted, Brahmans provided rulers with religious legitimation, but they retained a detachment from political power; they rarely sought to influence state goals, and they did not attempt to use their position to create a hierocracy.[94] Rulers were not presumed to be heads of anything resembling a state church; individual temples became large landowners and amassed considerable riches, but they were amorphous in structure; they did not unite into more encompassing organizations, and they did not incorporate the vast majority of the population. The common relationship between priests with laypeople, whether they were family, temple, funeral, or pilgrimage-site priests, was that of functionaries and clients, and the only times priests have been likely to have contact with even loosely organized lay collectivities are the festival days of the temple deities.

The fact that priests have clients rather than congregations mitigates against them uniting in strong religious institutions. Castes or subcastes of priests are distinguished by the particular gods with which they are associated (an example is the Brahman *adisaivas* caste of temple priests in Shiva temples), but because they are divided according to their exclusive rights in particular temples and are often in conflict with one another, they have not united or developed an ecclesiastical organization. Monastic orders also vary with respect to their important god or gods and in their caste recruitment. Even within an order, there is little cohesion or uniformity. A leading ascetic of a particular order may exercise some financial control over branch monasteries and appoint their head monks, but he rarely interferes in their daily worship, annual festivals, and other activities. The orders have rules that relate to such matters as prohibited foods and celibacy, but there are no effective systems of discipline, and monks may choose to serve deities that are not the foci of their order's teaching tradition. Although the schedule of the monk's day is structured to some extent by the performance of morning, noon, and evening rituals, there are no formal assemblies; the monastic lifestyle is relatively casual and affords much time for reading, meditation, chatting, and other activities according to the preferences of the monks.[95]

Although priests perform services for laypeople, this does not necessarily lead to an exchange of more than a few words with them. There are more monks than priests with lay followings, but few of the monks' activities put them in contact with laypeople. Their daily rituals are performed in most cases without the presence of laypeople, and although the festivals in which monks play an active or leading role provide some of their most important contacts with laypeople, the most popular lay festivals are those in which the monasteries are least involved. Contacts with laypeople occur in some monasteries through the operation of schools, the provision of guest houses for lay pilgrims, and the operation of dispensaries.

When laypeople visit monasteries, they often come as clients or as devotees of particular monks or gurus. Laypeople who become disciples of gurus can retain their lay status and receive from the guru the appropriate initiation for laypeople. Lay communities of guru followers tend to be amorphous and unorganized because it is the particular guru who is of importance for the followers, not the doctrinal teachings or goals of the guru's particular order.[96] Thus, neither priests nor monks have been elites of strong hierocratic organizations, and this has limited their shaping of the religion of the masses.

6

Nirvana and Spirits
Buddhism and Animism in Sri Lanka and Southeast Asia

Unlike Hinduism, whose great majority of adherents are to be found in a single nation, Buddhism is associated with many Asian societies, either as the dominant religion or as a prominent tradition alongside other religions. Beginning in the northern fringes of Indian civilization, the diffusion of Buddhism throughout the Indian subcontinent and beyond occurred under the emperor Asoka (268–239 B.C.E.), who ruled over northern and central India. Buddhism lasted longer in southern India than in the north, but without continuing royal patronage and in competition with devotionist forms of Hinduism, it began to decline from the late seventh and early eighth centuries C.E. The Muslim destruction of Buddhist monasteries left little of Buddhist culture, and by the late fourteenth century, only vestiges of Buddhism were left in India. With the exception of Nepal, where Indian Buddhism survived in an unbroken continuity, albeit with considerable Hindu influence, Buddhism became associated with societies outside the cultural area of its origins.

What came to be known as Theravada (the Way of the Elders) Buddhism spread into Sri Lanka around the middle of the third century B.C.E., and for more than one thousand years it existed mainly in Sri Lanka and Southeast India. In the eleventh century C.E. it spread from Sri Lanka to Burma (now Myanmar), and over the next two centuries it entered those countries now known as Thailand, Laos, and Cambodia. The adoption of Buddhism in these countries was in large part a consequence of the conversion of kings, who cooperated with the Buddhist monks and used royal power to propagate the religion. The acceptance of Buddhism by the kings, their courts, and the upper stratum of the urban centers was facilitated by the fact that no other soteriological religion or established literate religious culture existed in these countries to challenge Buddhism.[1] The time frame over which

Theravada Buddhism spread from the religious elites and upper lay stratum to the masses is uncertain; one estimation is that the "downward spread" began in the thirteenth century, but some historians maintain that Theravada Buddhism has become a popular or peasant religion only over the last two centuries.[2]

Canon and Sangha

Although Buddhism has taken diverse forms, a historical founding figure and a codified canon have provided foci of a common Buddhist identity. This is especially the case for Theravada Buddhism, the focus of this chapter, which presents a far more unified picture than Mahayana, the other major stream in Buddhism.

Buddhists trace the historical origin of their religion to Siddhartha Gautama, who was born in what is now Nepal in the sixth or fifth century B.C.E. Buddhists believe Gautama's birth was the last of a great number of incarnations, and that he became the Buddha, the "awakened" or "enlightened," when he achieved knowledge of the ultimate truth and thereby freed himself from all suffering. The Buddha is believed to have taught his truths and the path to salvation to disciples, who transmitted his teachings orally for some centuries before they were committed to writing in the Pali language in Sri Lanka in the second half of the first century B.C.E.[3]

The Buddhist canon and its commentaries were the work of a religious elite, the learned monks of the Sangha, the "gathering," "community," or "order." In contrast with Hinduism, Buddhist religious elites have not been associated with a caste hierarchy. (Sri Lanka is a partial exception.) The Buddha accepted the structure of the social world, including the caste system, but he did not sanction the religious authority of the Brahmans or the notion that birth in the Brahman caste was advantageous to salvation.[4] Another basis of religious elite status in India was renunciation of the world, and whereas Brahmans sought to link renunciation to their caste, Buddhism denied any such connection and made renunciation the single basis for religious status.

Buddhist soteriology differed considerably from that of Hinduism, but like Hinduism, the division between the Buddhist religious elite and others was established by a hierarchical separation of soteriological goals: only renouncers had any hope of achieving nirvana, and the realistic soteriological goal of householders was a good re-rebirth. By establishing the Sangha as the common organizational context of renouncers, however, the Buddhist religious elite developed a sense of corporate identity to a far greater extent than did the religious elites in Hinduism.

A mendicant-eremitic lifestyle remained an ideal among renouncers in all Indian religious traditions, but the Buddha did not advocate extreme isolation, and acceptance of the cenobitic community of ascetics as the appropriate social context for renouncers may have been present at the very beginnings of Buddhism.[5] One of the three "baskets" of the Buddhist canon, the Vinaya, provides an elaborate code of monastic discipline, and at bimonthly assemblies the monks recite the 227 rules by which they are expected to conduct themselves. Thus, the monks are distinguished from laypeople by the number of rules they follow (laypeople are normally expected to follow only five precepts); their appearance (shaven heads, colored robes); their lifestyle, including celibacy; and the formal entrance procedures to and communal residence in the monasteries. In most Theravada Buddhist societies, a large proportion of males spend at least one limited period as "temporary" monks in the monasteries. This may last as long as two years, but in many cases temporary ordination amounts to little more than a formal rite of passage, which has little effect on the distinction between "permanent" monks and the lay masses.

Only a small proportion of even the permanent monks pursue nirvana as a realistic goal, but this does not affect their status as monks, because laypeople are disposed to view the monks' appearance and monastic lifestyle as symbolic of renunciation.[6] In addition to renunciation, the status of monks is seen to derive from their role as preservers and propagators of the Buddha's *dharma* (truth), or what might be called the great tradition of Buddhism. A traditional account relates that the Buddha sent out the first sixty monks, whom he had ordained, to spread his dharma "for the benefit, welfare, and happiness of gods and men."[7] Access to the sacred texts was generally restricted to the Sangha, but unlike the Brahman elite, who normally taught only other Brahmans and a few other high-caste males, Buddhist monks were urged to teach the Buddha's dharma to all peoples in their local languages.[8] This does not mean that an identical great tradition was taught everywhere by the monks. The collection of texts available to communities of monks varied from one location to another, and the size and complexity of the canon provided wide opportunities for placing different emphases on its component texts.[9]

The diffusion and preservation of Buddhism did not involve the development of a hierocracy or organization encompassing all believers. An early meaning of *the Sangha* included monks, nuns, and laymen and laywomen, but the term came to be understood to refer to all those ordained, and after the ordination of women was discontinued in the fifth century c.e., it referred exclusively to monks and male novices.[10] Any male could become a monk, but the lay masses were excluded from the Sangha because their worldly involvements were seen to distract monks from their path of renunciation. Canonical Buddhism did, however, provide clear instructions for the relations between monks and laypeople.[11]

A basic ambiguity is evident in the monastic vocation: the requirement of detachment from the world is in tension with the demand to teach laypeople, whose acceptance of the teachings is a prerequisite for the support and survival of the monastic communities. The necessary removal of monks from worldly involvements, including food production, made them dependent on the laity for their material needs, and receiving food from laypeople, as well as teaching them, requires at least minimal interaction between monks and laity. The Sangha is believed to provide a "field of merit" for laypeople in that material support for monks, given in the correct spirit of selflessness, is understood as the most important way for laypeople to accumulate merit.[12] The involvement of the monks with the laity was reinforced by the Buddhist virtue of compassion, but in contrast with the bodhisattva in Mahayana Buddhism, the *arhat*, the enlightened virtuoso in Theravada Buddhism, is not expected to intercede to attain the salvation of others.[13]

The emphasis in Theravada Buddhism on the role of the Sangha in preserving the Buddha's dharma would appear to delegitimize any lay or little tradition adaptations and modifications of the monks' teachings. Theravada Buddhism leaves considerable room, however, for popular religions that concern themselves with worldly goals outside the soteriological focus of great-tradition Buddhism. Monks not only have tolerated but, in the majority of cases, have shared with laypeople beliefs in spirits and other supramundane beings and processes that help or hinder people in their worldly pursuits. The distinction made by some monks and sophisticated laypeople between "high" Buddhism and "low" popular religion provides an emic differentiation of elite and popular religion, although such a distinction is unlikely to be made with any clarity among the majority of village monks and laypeople.

The religious elite's tolerance of "non-Buddhist" popular religion provides little basis for a distinction between official and unofficial religion. In the absence of a hierocracy, another possible basis for the formulation of official religion, as occurred in China, is a patrimonial state that treats religious affairs as a branch of political administration. The rulers of southeastern Asian kingdoms supported the Sangha by grants of land and involved themselves in its organization by appointing its top ranks. Kings sought to unify the Sangha within their kingdoms and took measures that were intended to "purify" the Sangha by requiring the monks to adhere more strictly to the rules of discipline. Many kings titled themselves "Lord of the Dharma" and some believed themselves to be future buddhas. On their part, monks assisted in the formulation of the figures of the ideal or meritorious king and the universal emperor, the *cakravartin*, who brings the world under the aegis of the dharma. The image of a Buddhalike universal ruler was countered, however, by a tendency to confine the status of the king to that of a particularly meritorious layman and to characterize the social order over which he ruled as legitimate but irrelevant to the soteriological endeavor.[14]

Insofar as there was a state-supported official religion in Theravada countries, it was confined to the regulation of the Sangha. Some kings exhorted laypeople to practice Buddhism, and a few decrees proclaimed the subordination of local spirit cults to the way of the Buddha;[15] but even if they had been inclined to impose a state-supported, official religion on their territories, the kings of the southeastern Asian countries did not have the power to do so. The process by which Buddhism became the prominent element in the religion of most villages was, in fact, a slow one, and for a long period it may have been difficult to point to the effects of Buddhism upon what a number of investigators have called the "magico-animism" of the masses in southeastern Asia.

B. J. Terwiel writes that Buddhist monks were revered because their chants were believed to ward off evils; people placed images of the Buddha in their houses together with their ancestral shrines, and Buddhist monasteries were located at the shrines of the villages' spirit guardians. Under the influence of Buddhism certain changes in popular religion took place, such as the substitution of vegetable offerings for animal sacrifices, but it was only during the nineteenth and twentieth centuries, when the central governments achieved effective control, that Buddhism became a major part of rural religion.[16]

The focus in this chapter is on patterns of religious action in three Theravada countries: Sri Lanka, Burma (Myanmar), and Thailand. Two other countries, Laos and Cambodia, have been predominantly Theravada countries, but their Buddhist institutions have suffered in the modern period from governmental repression, and fewer anthropological investigations have been undertaken in them. The following sections highlight what is distinctive in the patterns of religious action of monks and laity, but the fact that each category participates, in varying degree, in the patterns that are prominent in the overall religious action of the other should not be forgotten.

Religious Elites

From the divergent emphases on practice or study in early Buddhism, a distinction developed within the religious elite between two types of monastic vocation: the vocation of meditation, which requires particularly strict limitations on interaction with laypeople, and the vocation of study and teaching, which includes the teaching of laypeople. This distinction overlaps, without fully coinciding with, the differences between forest dwellers and village or town dwellers, ascetics and preachers, renouncers and priests. The presentation here of two divergent patterns of religious action within the elite is somewhat ideal typical, as many monks combine the two patterns. A differentiation is recognized, however, by both monks and laypeople, and it is expressed by sectional and organizational divisions both among and within monastic orders.

A common historical pattern has been the emergence of new orders, sometimes splitting off from existing orders, that conform more closely to the forest-dwelling pattern, with a tendency over time for forest dwellers to drift back to the villages and towns. Some groups of monks identify themselves as forest dwellers even though their pattern of religious action does not differ from that of other monks. Michael Carrithers reports that out of approximately twenty thousand monks in Sri Lanka, about six hundred are listed in a government census as genuine forest dwellers.[17]

The pattern of the prospective arhat or virtuoso can be characterized by its soteriological goal (nirvana) and the path of meditation, which ideally involves little support from supramundane powers and restricts interaction with laypeople to a minimum. With the possible exception of the early beginnings of Buddhism, the virtuoso pattern has been that of a small minority of the Sangha. They are considered exceptional in their striving to attain the ultimate soteriological goal of Buddhism, nirvana, and their understanding of the meaning of that goal has often differed from that of other monks and the laity.

Nirvana is translated as a "blowing out," and it is described in the great tradition not as a state of being or existence but rather in terms of what is overcome or extinguished. It is a state of release from all suffering and impermanence. It is the destruction of desire and of the basic passions of craving, hatred, and delusion. It is the disappearance of the "five aggregates" of form, feelings, perception, volition, and consciousness. It is the ridding of the delusion of the ego or the self as something more than a bundle of physical and mental constituents.

If the virtuosos succeed in extinguishing all desire and overcoming the illusions of phenomenal existence, there is nothing left to be renewed, and they will have escaped from the wheel of rebirths and redeaths. Those virtuosos who have achieved the state of enlightenment and realized that all phenomenal things, including the self, are impermanent and without essence can live out the remainder of their natural lives in benign contentment. They are no longer conditioned by illusions, although a remainder of conditioning persists until it disappears with their death. The Buddha gave no answer to the question of what happens to the arhats after their death; they do not go to a place of eternal happiness, but neither would it be accurate to speak in terms of annihilation. There is the notion of an absolute, outside time and space, that cannot be conceptualized by human categories.[18]

This account of nirvana draws on the texts of the great tradition because, to my knowledge, there has been no empirical investigation of the actual meanings that virtuosos or forest dwellers attribute to nirvana. The virtuosos can be distinguished from other monks, however, by the prominence of meditation in their religious action. Meditation is the path that they believe will lead them to a wisdom unavailable to others. It is taken for granted that to be able to devote their time to meditation, the monks must have led many moral lives and observed fully the rules of the monastic code.

To practice meditation, the virtuosos renounce the social life of ordinary people, and to limit their social interaction with others, some go to live in a forest, either in relative isolation or with other renouncers in forest hermitages. The techniques of meditation, which are detailed in a classical Theravada treatise and traditionally learned on a one-to-one basis from a teacher, include restrictions on physical movement and practicing awareness of one's body, feelings, and states of mind. In the later stages of meditation, the virtuosos distance themselves from their sensory experiences and the confinements of space and time. They attempt to subdue their passions, uproot their desires, and arrive at a state of non-attachment and stillness of mind. Given that nirvana as the absolute cannot be described in a positive fashion, the psychological state of tranquillity and equanimity that results from the achievement of ultimate wisdom may itself be regarded as the goal of meditation.[19]

Meditation, the principal means by which the virtuosos achieve their transformative goal, does not depend on, but may be assisted by, supramundane beings or powers. The virtuosos follow the path of the supreme exemplar, the Buddha, and the accounts of that path in the great tradition give the gods a peripheral role. The future Buddha's birth was attended by supramundane events and blessings from heaven; gods were instrumental in showing Siddhartha the sufferings of life and death; and prior to his enlightenment, the demonic figure of Mara attempted to seduce Siddhartha from his concentration. The Buddha is believed to have visited the heavens, where he was praised and honored by the high gods, and to have exercised his power over harmful spirits on earth. When he achieved liberation from the wheel of rebirth, the Buddha transcended not only all other humans but also the gods.

As a human who died and was not reborn, the Buddha does not exist to assist others in their endeavors to follow his example, and the prayers of virtuosos to the images of the Buddha are commemorative rather than propitiatory or petitionary. The Buddha is believed to have urged his followers to make offerings to the gods, presumably for worldly goals, and to have encouraged the transfer of merit to the "hungry ghosts," who are badly in need of merit to escape from their pitiable condition in which they prey on the living. In some formulations, the powers of the gods are believed to be derived from the Buddha, who delegated them during his lifetime; but virtuosos are unlikely to seek the support of the gods in their soteriological goal, because it is clear from Buddhist doctrine that only humans can achieve nirvana. The gods have to be reborn in human form in order for them to achieve ultimate salvation.[20]

The virtuosos distance themselves from those humans who are involved in worldly matters, and they attempt to restrict their interaction with laity to the minimum necessary to provide the basic material needs of an ascetic lifestyle. The asceticism of virtuosos is believed, however, to produce extraordinary powers, which draws laypeople who seek a thaumaturge. The process of moving through the various stages of meditation is believed to have liberated the virtuosos from the limitations of corporeal and sensory existence. Having transcended the ordinary laws of nature, and having even reached a stage superior to the gods, who remain in the wheel of karma, the virtuosos are able to use their powers, if they so choose, to provide dispensations, such as the curing of illnesses. Whereas some virtuosos have resisted the intrusions of laypeople, others have submitted to or even encouraged lay supplications,[21] and they have adapted their virtues and powers to cater to the demand for thaumaturgy. On occasion, millennial expectations have emerged around certain virtuosos, some of whom have become foci of reform of the Sangha or of political resistance. But even though adepts may choose to use their powers to help laypeople, such activities are seen as at best an irrelevance and at worst an obstacle to the path of meditation and the goal of nirvana.[21]

The nonvirtuoso pattern of religious action among monks is characterized by a proximate soteriological goal, nomic and thaumaturgical goals, merit making as the principal means toward the soteriological goal, and an orientation toward supramundane beings. Most priest-monks do not consider nirvana a realistic goal or even appear to desire it.[22] As with laypeople, the soteriological goal of most monks is a good rebirth, either on earth or in heaven, and the principal means of attaining that goal is merit making, which adds to the karmic legacy from previous incarnations. Monks differ from laypeople in the far greater opportunities available to them to accumulate merit. They have more time than laypeople for meditation, but many priest-monks devote little or no time to meditation and regard it as less important than the study of the Buddhist texts and the ritualistic and pastoral roles they perform.[23] By activities such as studying and teaching the Buddhist texts and chanting the sacred texts, the monks increase their own merit or positive karma, and they also transfer merit to laypeople by the performance of such activities in their presence. Offerings to the monks, including providing them with their daily food, are the most important merit-making religious acts of the laity. The gifts that monks receive bear no direct relationship to their material needs, and by "conspicuous nonconsumption" monks can promote their religious status among the laity.[24]

The opportunities provided for merit making in the role of monk, both for themselves and for others, explain the common practice in most Theravada countries (not in Sri Lanka) for a large proportion of young males to become monks for a limited period. About half of the male population of Thailand and almost all Buddhist males in Burma are reported to spend some time as "temporary" monks.[25] A differentiation is made between the novitiate ordination, which in most cases functions as a rite of passage from youth to adulthood, and a higher ordination, which only a minority of novices choose to take. Even those who take the second ordination are not faced with formal obstacles if they choose to leave the monastery and return to lay life. Males may enter and leave the Sangha several times in their life, preferring to stay at monasteries during certain times of the year, especially the rainy season, and it is a common practice to retire to a monastery in old age.

The ceremony of ordination is associated with fertility, and on ordination days in Burma, the escorting of a novice to the monastery is accompanied by calls for rain and fertility. Ordination is also made the occasion of the propitiation of the guardian spirits of the household, family, and village. At a more individual level, men requesting supramundane help to obtain specific thaumaturgical goals will promise the relevant deity that they will become monks for a specified period. The merits accumulated through temporary monkhood are relevant for both rebirth and this-worldly goals, and parents are willing to allow their sons to become monks and forgo their economic contributions and social responsibilities because the act of ordination transfers merit to them.[26]

The higher ordination denotes a commitment to a more rigorous discipline and level of conformity to the monastic rules than are involved in the novitiate. The monk receives a new name, transforms his appearance, and removes himself from his family, friends, and all former associations. The purity of the Sangha is judged by the rigor of its members' adherence to the code that provides detailed regulations for the daily life of the monks, including their relationships with each other and with laypeople.[27] By strict conformity to the discipline of the Vinaya in their daily rounds, monks are expected to overcome this-worldly desires and anxieties, thereby achieving the goal of their way of life in the here and now. The life pattern becomes more than a means to an end, and it may be seen to become an end in itself, especially among those monks who retain a distance from laypeople and whose social life is confined largely to other monks.[28]

The major religious figure around which the life pattern and merit making of the monks are oriented is the Buddha. Most monks are likely to admit that the "historical" Buddha, who passed out of the realm of samsara, is not directly accessible, but their religious action is shaped by the Buddha's presence as mediated through images, relics, and texts. Monks chant before and make offerings to images of the Buddha. Food offerings are customarily offered to the Buddha three times a day, and monks demonstrate their respect by bowing, kneeling, and fully prostrating themselves before the images. Rituals of attendance on the Buddha include washing the image, brushing its teeth, and clothing it.

Relics of the Buddha, which include his purported bones, teeth, and objects used by him, such as begging bowls, are usually confined within the boundaries of monasteries and are venerated by the monks. Chronicles establish the relics' authenticity by tracing the chain of transmission through which they came to reside in particular *stupas* (dome-shaped shrines) and by documenting the marvels that occurred at their location. The marvels are explained not by the presence of the Buddha in a physical sense but by the efficacy of the vows he made before his death and the compassion he felt for those trapped in the cycle of samsara. While monks will acknowledge intellectually that the Buddha is not present, they nonetheless feel his presence and address him directly in rituals of veneration and when they request forgiveness for transgressions of the Vinaya.[29] The veneration of the Buddha is also performed through the study of the Buddhist texts, which many monks regard as their primary merit-making activity.

Teaching, preaching, performing special rituals, and receiving food are the most frequent regular occasions on which monks dispense merit to laypeople. Among the rites of passage of laypeople, the funeral is the only one at which the monks regularly officiate. Funerals are suitable occasions for expressing the Buddhist emphasis on impermanence, but of more immediate interest to the participants is the ritual transference of merit to the deceased, contributing to their good rebirths and guaranteeing their future assistance to the living, or at least forestalling any harm they might otherwise cause.[30] In addition to burial rituals, monks are often invited by the laity to recite merit-making chants on such occasions as a wedding ceremony, entry into a new house, or opening a school or business, and at the end of these ceremonies, the lay hosts present the monks with traditional offerings, such as incense sticks, candles, and lotus buds, which are all used in the worship of the Buddha image.[31] The rites the monks perform for laypeople tend to be simple and sparse, but the ceremonial role clearly differentiates such priest-monks from the virtuoso renouncers.[32]

The laity also request that monks chant for dispensational goals, such as an appeal to a particular deity to bring rain or protection against evil spirits.[33] This-worldly protection and prosperity are believed to be gained from amulets and charms that embody the virtue and powers of the monks who have purified them by their sacred words, sacred water, and other acts of transference. Amulets considered to be of particular power are those that have been placed close to monks who were meditating or chanting in unison. The sale of amulets, some of which depict famous monks, is an important part of fund-raising for the upkeep of some monasteries. Certain orders of monks are known to specialize in the making of amulets and charms that are believed to protect their wearers against demons and witches, and some monks achieve reputations as specialists in cures or as seers and astrologers.[34]

The involvement of monks in thaumaturgy may be thought of as part of their pastoral services, which in theory are less important than their study of the Buddhist scriptures but in practice often become their primary activity. Laity require from their monks that they cater to laypeople's everyday needs, and they seek advice from monks on such matters as marital problems, business matters, and community concerns. Monks who ignore such demands and focus instead on their own meditation or study are often criticized by laypeople as selfish. Thus, monks take on the roles of counselor and community leader as well as doctor and astrologer, and the functions of the temple or monastery are extended to those of hostel, community chest, and loan bank. Village and neighborhood temples are often the centers of community life.[35]

Popular Religion

As a consequence of their worldly involvement, the goals of laypeople are considered to be more modest than those of monks and are defined by the canon as wealth, honor, long life, and rebirth in one of the heavens.[36] Nirvana is not a relevant goal of the majority of laypeople, and although they may acknowledge that it is the ultimate goal of all Buddhists, it is too remote to be part of their active desires and expectations.[37] Many conceive of nirvana as eternal bliss rather than release from desire, but most feel they cannot aspire to reach such a state of perfection. The soteriological goal of most laypeople, like that of most monks, is a good rebirth, either in heaven for at least a temporary period or into a higher state on earth. Terwiel found that most of his informants believed they would be reborn in circumstances similar to those of their present lives, and those who felt their beneficial karma outweighed their bad could envisage that, instead of their present status as poor peasants or workers, they would become rich landowners, wealthy merchants, or government officials.

Those with exceptional merit might go to one of the heavens, where they would either retain their human form or become a god.[38]

Clearly, people wish to avoid a lower rebirth, which might take the form of an animal or ghost or involve a period in one of the hells. People are unlikely to see themselves as radically evil, and Martin Southwold reported that the villagers he investigated did not take the various hells seriously. Even if people fear punishment, they can take comfort in the thought that there is no eternal damnation in Buddhism, and that the punishment of demerits in a hell might even be followed by a period of reward for merits in heaven, before rebirth on earth.[39] Such reflections, however, are unlikely to be of daily concern to most laypeople, who are concerned more frequently to avoid or overcome misfortunes, such as illnesses and drought, and to obtain protection against the maleficent beings and powers that are understood to be the immediate causes of such misfortunes. As elsewhere, the goals of religion include health, finding a spouse, fertility, succeeding in making a living, and establishing good relationships with patrons or bosses.

As the appropriate means to nirvana, meditation is not relevant to the soteriological or thaumaturgical goals of most laypeople, and very few practice it. An exception is a section of the educated urban strata who believe that nirvana can be achieved by the appropriate behavior over only a few lifetimes, and who attach great value to the practice of meditation for laypeople as well as monks. Most village Buddhists, in contrast, show no inclination to practice meditation, and they are likely to make fun of those laypeople who do.[40]

Like most Hindus, most Buddhists conceive of karma as constituting an important condition and means of both transformative and dispensational goals; but unlike Hinduism, and unlike Mahayana Buddhism with its emphasis on the bodhisattva, who delays his final birth in order to help others, Theravada Buddhism does not provide saviors who override or minimize the relevance of the process of karma.[41]

Karma is the sum of the good and bad deeds of a person's lives, and although most do not claim knowledge of their previous incarnations, astrological readings are believed to indicate what a person can expect as a consequence of the moral balance of their actions from past lives. Karma and astrology can be reconciled by stating that a person with good karma from previous lives will be born at a time when the stars are favorable, but horoscopes tend to be vague on specifics, and Buddhists believe they can change their futures in this life by their acts of merit and demerit. Thus, the notion of karma encourages action centered on merit making: merits are stored up to ensure a good rebirth; they can be translated into virtues or powers in this life; they can serve as a protection against malicious spirits; and they can be transferred for the benefit of others, living or dead, human or divine.[42]

Unlike Hindu India, and with the partial exception of Sri Lanka, karma in Buddhist countries is not related to a system of castes, and merits and demerits are not calculated in terms of highly specific taboos and regulations centered on group relationships. Ritual tends to take simpler forms than in Hinduism, and those laypeople who are more conversant with Buddhist doctrines are likely to stress the importance of the ethical intention behind an act and to believe that they gain extra merit by benefiting others. Merits are gained by adherence to the five precepts incumbent on all Buddhists, by support of the Sangha, by observance of the holy days, and by giving offerings and participating in rituals that honor the Buddha. The five precepts, which proscribe killing (including most animals), stealing, lying, unchaste behavior, and use of alcohol or drugs, are recited daily by many, often before a Buddhist altar. The precepts are commonly used as a devotional before retiring or on arising, and they are frequently included in communal rituals.[43] As ethical guidelines without precise formulations, the precepts are interpreted to cover diverse moral injunctions and cultural norms.[44]

Support of the monks, including provision of their daily food, sponsoring novices, and contributing to the building and upkeep of monasteries is a major merit-making group of activities, as are listening to the monks' sermons and recitations of religious texts.[45] Laypeople who attend the Uposatha ritual, held at the monasteries on the quarter-month days of the lunar calendar, increase their merits by committing themselves for the day to eight precepts, and the ceremony closes with the presiding monk indicating the merit gained by those who took part. The benefits of the observance of the Uposatha are widely believed to include protection from evil spirits.[46]

Like monks, many laypeople will state that the Buddha, removed from samsara, cannot directly assist in the achievement of any goals, but popular notions of nirvana as a state of immortality provide more scope for the Buddha's involvement in religious action. The canonical account of the Buddha's life includes reports of his supramundane powers, and in the popular "birth stories" of the Buddha's former lives, the Buddha associates with a multitude of supramundane powers. Many of the approximately 550 "birth stories," to which local additions are often made, focus on acts of altruism.[47]

A common belief among laypeople is that a force resides in the images and relics of the Buddha. Offerings of incense, flowers, and candlelight are made frequently to images of the Buddha in homes as well as in temples. Relics have traditionally been restricted to the precincts of temples, although in recent times laypeople have obtained relics of arahats through people with special powers who are believed to have manifested the relics.[48] The temple festivals and the ceremonies celebrating the Buddha's birth, enlightenment, and death can always be justified as commemorative events, but many worshipers expect that offerings to the Buddha will be rewarded, and in times of misfortune, they appeal to the Buddha for assistance.[49]

The Buddha can be said to have a double role: he is both the supreme renouncer, uninvolved in the goal seeking of either the mundane or the supramundane world, and a ruler of the world and the heavens, a god of gods, who is the ultimate source of all authority, human and divine. In one formulation, the Buddha is not conceived to have a direct intercessory role, but he is seen to be the ultimate source of all supramundane conditions and means because he is said to have delegated his powers to the gods when he was alive. The gods who received their powers directly from the Buddha transferred, in turn, part of their powers to other deities.[50] Shrines to gods are often located on the grounds of Buddhist temples, and in the pursuit of thaumaturgical goals, both within and outside the temples, numerous associations are made between the Buddha and deities.[51] Rituals with communal nomic goals, such as harvest festivals, are linked to local guardian deities.[52]

Even those who wish to dissociate Buddhism from mundane goals will not deny that although the gods cannot provide the means of salvation, they can assist people in the attainment of worldly goals and defense against evil beings. The type of help a supramundane can give and the type of relationship that is appropriate to establish with it depends on its purported characteristics and its place in the pantheon. The major gods and many of the minor ones are believed to be bodhisattvas, aspirants for future buddhahood, and the closer the god is to buddhahood—the more it becomes like Buddha himself—the less involved it is in the affairs of the world.[53]

In the case of the four national guardian gods of Sri Lanka, a study of their four shrines has shown that one of the gods, Kataragama, has of late been receiving more requests and offerings than those of the other three put together. The reason for Kataragama's recent popularity would appear to be that, as a traditionally less morally scrupulous god, he is believed to be better able to cope with the particular demands and stresses of modern life. Thus, worshipers request that he help them in passing examinations, finding employment, and business success. Kataragama has been free to take on new functions because his traditional role as war god has been lost, and his moral ambivalence, signaled by having both a wife and a mistress, makes him more sympathetic to the newly formed desires and aspirations of modern worshipers.[54]

In addition to its role as defender of Buddhism, its institutions, and Sri Lanka, each of the four major gods has its area of special jurisdiction, where its authority is especially manifest. Under the four gods are their servants, the village and other local gods, who have territorial boundaries that can expand if they become more popular and shrink if their popularity declines. In contrast with Hindu India, powerful goddesses at the high and middle ranges of the pantheon have been almost absent in Theravada Buddhism. An exception in Sri Lanka is Pattini, a stern but generally benevolent "wife-mother" goddess who brings fertility and cures diseases caused by demons.[55] In recent years Kali, the demoness of Hindu origin, has risen in the pantheon of Sri Lankan Buddhists.[56]

Kings were frequently conceived as mediators with the gods and were associated with fertility rites. As builders of temples and protectors of the religion that linked their kingdoms to the cosmos, they were portrayed as embodiments of the dharma and as foci of merit. On occasion, kings were called gods or bodhisattvas or even, in Burma, buddhas.[57] And if kings were assimilated to supramundanes, supramundanes were sometimes assimilated to kings, with some of the gods referred to explicitly as kings and the Buddha's images and relics treated in a similar way to the king's person. The most famous corporeal relic of Buddha in Sri Lanka, the tooth relic, was enshrined in the precincts of the royal palace and moved from place to place with the relocation of the capital.[58]

Beneath the gods are the numerous forms of ambivalent and malevolent beings and powers, such as spirits, demons, ghosts, black magicians, and witches. The spirits, called *yakkha* in Sri Lanka, *nats* in Burma, and *phii* in Thailand, constitute the more structured aspect of the multitude of lower supramundanes and occupy a prominent place in the religions of Theravada countries. The Burmese believe that nats include spirits of people who died violent deaths; they tend to be jealous of humans, are quick to take offense, and will cause illnesses and other troubles if their anger is aroused. Beliefs in spirits and karma can be reconciled by stating that bad spirits attack only people with bad karma, but the tendency is to attribute specific events to the spirits and to evoke karma only on those rare occasions when no other explanation seems appropriate.

There are various types of nats: protective territorial nats, housed in a small nat house at the edge of the village, who keep malevolent nats from entering their territory; inherited nats, one from each side of the family, who are closely tied to birth and the health of children; and nats associated with particular realms of action or protection, such as house nats and rice nats. Although some nats provide protection, they are chiefly evil beings, similar in their intentions and behavior to demons, which in Burma and other Theravada countries are believed to inflict harm in an irrational fashion and to bring disorder and pollution to nature and society. Demons fall under the jurisdiction of some of the lesser gods, but their tendency to act independently and malevolently requires actions, especially of priests, to compel them to obey the gods' commands.[59]

An isomorphism, although by no means exact, can be traced between the structure of kingdoms and the cosmic model of supramundanes. Just as each king in Sri Lanka claimed rulership over the whole realm and exercised his power over that region or province where his palace was situated, so each of the major gods was believed to have general rulership over the whole of the country and special jurisdiction in its particular area. The organization of the pantheon, in which the lesser and local gods were subordinate to but often acted in an autonomous fashion from the higher gods, paralleled somewhat the relationship of the governors of provinces to the kings. The minor gods, like the governors of provinces, had authority over particular territories within the larger realm, and like the governors who sought to extend their authority and perhaps challenge the king, gods could become more popular, extend their territories, and come to share the attributes of the higher gods. Unlike kings, however, the overlap of jurisdictions of the major gods did not pose a problem for the divine realm. Although it shared an idiom and demonstrated parallels with the kingly structure, the cosmic model was not its replica.[60]

Like the king, the major gods were too distant to be of much relevance for most peasants. Of more relevance to their everyday lives were the lower supramundanes, whose patronage through processes of exchange was similar to that sought from the landowners and other local power holders whom the peasants served in exchange for protection and care. Clients competed with one another to obtain security and material benefits, and patrons attempted to strengthen their power by increasing the number of their clients. Competition in the system of patronage is expressed in the morally neutral spirit world, in which personal advantages are pursued through manipulation, with often unpredictable results.[61] R. L. Stirrat has argued that, in modern Sri Lanka, the increasingly strong patronage systems in which dyadic rather than hierarchical ties are important explain the rising popularity of the god Kataragama, which has no interest in moral issues but exemplifies all the qualities of the ideal patron.[62]

The encompassing of all beings, mundane and supramundane, by karma means that the places of supramundanes in the pantheon are not fixed; they can move in either an upward or a downward direction. Demons who are persuaded to desist from doing evil can be reborn as good Buddhists or they can move up the supramundane hierarchy and become deities. Those moving up the hierarchy can possess an anomalous status, a composite of demon and god, but their identities are often split in two, with the divine part increasing in importance and the demonic part decreasing. Thus, although there is a clear difference between the higher beneficent gods and the lower malevolent demons, in the middle stratum of the pantheon are ambiguous beings who combine features of protection and purification with those of danger and pollution.[63]

The nature of supramundanes, their place in the pantheon, and their relationships with humans are expressed by the types of offerings made to them and by the ritual contexts of these. Vegetarian foods, flowers, and soft incense are offered to the images of the Buddha and to the gods in demarcated areas that have been insulated from all sources of pollution and impurity. Burned meat and blood are offered to the demons in unconsecrated spaces.[64] It is common for village informants to say that they make offerings to the Buddha in gratitude for the dharma and to strengthen their commitment to it, and they repudiate the idea that they hope to receive a reciprocal favor. The merit that is believed to be earned by making offerings to the Buddha may lead some laypeople to feel there is a reciprocal element involved with the Buddha, but many say it is not the Buddha who bestows merit on worshipers and giving without expecting reciprocity is believed to enhance one's moral state and merit. As a basic form of human communication, the act of offering would appear to provide gratification quite irrespective of its supposed consequences.[65]

Offerings to the gods, in contrast, are readily recognized as part of a reciprocal exchange; the gods are thanked for what they did in the past or their assistance is sought in present or future endeavors, including the alleviation of suffering and protection from demons. One kind of offering to the gods is the transfer of merit acquired by the good actions of humans—for instance, when laypeople feed the monks—in order to help the gods on their path to nirvana.[66] The more remote gods, however, who are well on their way to buddhahood, are not typically asked for material benefits, and worshipers more frequently direct their requests to the lower gods, who are involved in the world. Once a god has moved up into the heights of the pantheon, his place in exchange relationships is taken by another who may have started as a demon and gradually risen to the status of deity. Supramundanes at the lower levels of the pantheon, such as ghosts, are especially dependent on humans, and people can pay for being left in peace by transferring merit to the ghosts, which is believed to improve the ghosts' chances of a human rebirth.[67]

As representations of disorder and symbols of destruction, demonic powers are believed to become effective when human relationships are in a state of disorder and motivated by such destructive emotions as anger, greed, desire, and passion. One way of breaking the power of demons is to reestablish their subordination according to the hierarchical principles of the cosmic order as defined by Buddhism. Priests neutralize demons by compelling them to obey the orders of gods or by reminding the demons of their promises to gods to desist from harming humans. Exorcists perform religious action that repairs the cosmic order, thereby breaking the illusion of demonic power and reducing the demons to their true absurdity. Another means of countering the harm caused by demons is to transform them into powers of good, thereby also achieving the nomic goal of restoring order.[68]

One Religion or More?

The question of the extent to which the religious patterns of the Sangha and the laypeople diverge and overlap has been tied up with debates over whether religion in Buddhist countries is divided into distinct systems. Scholars who have argued two or more systems of religion have often associated these divisions with the distinction between religious elite and masses. In the past, Western scholars of Buddhism distinguished between the Theravada Buddhism of the Pali scriptural canon, which they portrayed as a nontheistic philosophy espoused by monks and intellectuals, and the animistic-magical religion of the masses. To the extent that Buddhism was recognized as an element in the religion of the masses, it was presented as a thin veneer superimposed on a basically animistic religion or as a religion that had been corrupted beyond recognition by animism and magic.

Most modern scholars of Buddhism recognize that "pure" or "true" Buddhism is an essentially literary, idealized phenomenon that never existed in practice, even among the early Buddhist elite. "True" Buddhism was largely a product of Western scholars of the late nineteenth and early twentieth centuries, who influenced the way in which Western-educated Buddhists conceived of their religion.[69] There are no indications that the early Buddhist intellectual elite disbelieved in supramundane beings; on the contrary, the early scriptures contain many references to deities, demons, and miraculous events.[70]

Buddhism entered the countries of Southeast Asia as a religion with a whole array of supramundane beings, including those of Brahmanic or "Hindu" origins. Many indigenous supramundanes appear to have become identified with the imported deities, and those that were not so identified were more likely to be placed low in the hierarchy of supramundanes that eventually crystallized. Heinz Bechert writes that god cults were part of Buddhism from its beginnings in Sri Lanka, and that a distinction can be made between the cults of the higher deities, of Hindu origin, and the more popular cults, from which the stricter monastic orders have attempted to distance themselves.[71]

At no stage in the development of Buddhism should the canonical texts be identified with the religion of Buddhists, whether monks or laypeople. The beliefs and practices of the Buddha and the first generations of Buddhists can only be conjectures based on the texts written more than a hundred years after the death of the Buddha. The Buddhist scriptures were composed by a monastic elite who did not write extensively about supramundanes because, although they no doubt believed in deities, they regarded them as irrelevant to their goal of salvation. The written texts were preserved principally by memorization; manuscripts were rare and were confined to a few monasteries, so scriptures were not widely available for the majority of monks who resided outside the centers. Even without the commentaries, the canon was lengthy and complex, and the collection of texts available varied among monasteries. Recent studies have found that the canon expounded by learned monks in urban teaching centers touches most village monks little more than it touches village laypeople, and village monks tend to draw on the scriptures in only the most general way, emphasizing those texts they see as most relevant to the rituals that they perform along with the communities in which they live.[72]

Just as it is inaccurate to portray the Buddhism of monks as the religion of the canon, it is inaccurate to portray the Buddhism of the masses as a thin veneer over magico-animism. As the patterns of religious action discussed above have made evident, laypeople share with the majority of monks the goal of a good rebirth and regard merit making as the principal means to achieve this goal. Monks are supposed to live a way of life that enables them to accumulate far more merits, and this is regarded as appropriate by laypeople. Almost all monks, like almost all laypeople, perform religious actions directed to supramundanes, but monks are perhaps more likely to say that supramundanes are not part of Buddhism. According to this view, religion is a matter of salvation, and only the truth and the way of Buddha are relevant to salvation. Supramundanes can help only in the achievement of worldly goals and must therefore be considered to be outside religion.[73]

Distinctions that Buddhists make between Buddhism and supramundanes have been noted by a range of observers, from Western visitors in the seventeenth century to modern anthropologists. These distinctions, which are not confined to monks,[74] are made in stronger and sharper terms when attention is focused on spirits; this, at least, has been the argument of a number of anthropologists who have investigated beliefs and practices concerned with the spirits as the major element in what some call the magico-animistic system of Buddhist countries.

Michael Ames writes that although Buddhists frequently fuse Buddhism and magico-animism in practice, they do not confuse them intellectually. Rather than constituting syncretism, the placing of spirit shrines within the precincts of Buddhist temples is intended to bring the spirits under the control of Buddhism and the monks. When Buddhists participate in spirit propitiation, they reaffirm the supremacy of Buddhism by performing homage to Buddha before the rite directed to the spirit.[75] A. Thomas Kirsch notes the symbolic opposition made between Buddhism, which represents asceticism, self-control, predictability, and sobriety, and the spirits, who represent abandonment, unpredictability, capriciousness, chaos, and disorder. Involvement with the spirits tends to be intermittent, and because the consequences of spirit propitiation have an element of indeterminacy, they are resorted to only after offerings to the Buddha and to the gods have failed to bring about the desired ends. Unlike Buddhism, spirit worship is seen to relate to a limited segment of experience, and the superiority of Buddhism is expressed by the belief that monks are immune to spirit attacks and by the use of Buddhist symbols, such as holy water and inscriptions, to overcome the threat of spirits or to exorcise them.[76]

The most detailed counterpositioning of Buddhism and the spirit cults has been made by Melford Spiro. He wrote that Buddhism teaches that desire is the cause of suffering, whereas the nats, as the spirits are called in Burma, exemplify desires and material pleasures. The premise of Buddhism is moral action, whereas the amoral nats will punish those who offend them and reward those who propitiate them, regardless of the moral state of the person. Truth in Buddhism is attained by meditation, whereas truth in the nat cults is attained by possession. Buddhism represents the ideal of serenity, whereas nat festivals include frenzied shouting and screaming. Spiro states that Buddhism takes primacy over the nat cults with respect to the time and wealth expended; its symbols are assumed to embody greater power than that of the nats, witches, or other supramundane beings, who, if they dare to oppose Buddhism, will always be overcome.[77]

Some monks say that, from the point of view of Buddhism, which expresses the ultimate reality, nats are illusions, although this is qualified by noting that our life in the world of appearances makes it expedient to act as if the nats exist. Like most laypeople, most monks believe in the existence of nats, and they find no incompatibility in upholding Buddhism and propitiating nats.[78] Jane Bunnag reports that although monks rarely have dealings with house spirits or with the rites of exorcism, they often appear to give tacit approval to such actions, even though they may consider them inefficacious.[79]

Some anthropologists have postulated a clear-cut functional division between Buddhism and the spirit cults: the focus of Buddhism on soteriology has necessitated the cults of spirits to cater to the demands for worldly help and protection, and it is because the spirit cults have fulfilled the worldly needs that Buddhism has retained its singular concern with salvation.[80] Most recognize, however, that Buddhism also deals with dispensational goals. Ames wrote that Buddhism ministers to immediate and pragmatic concerns among the lower strata,[81] and Spiro has distinguished the apotropaic or nonsoteriological dimension of Buddhism from its "karmatic" dimension, focusing on rebirth, and the "nibbanic" dimension, directed toward the achievement of nirvana.

It would be misleading, according to Spiro, to refer to apotropaic Buddhism as the little tradition and to nibbanic and karmatic Buddhism as the great tradition, because apotropaic Buddhism is at least as old as canonical Buddhism. Nevertheless, nonsoteriological Buddhism is magical action "by any definition of magic"; it employs the symbols of Buddhism, its words, images, and relics, to create immediate merit or to enlist the assistance of supernatural beings or powers in the attainment of worldly goals. Magic was devalued in "normative Buddhism" not because it was believed to be wrong or false but because it was viewed as worldly. Nevertheless, monks as well as laypeople turn to magical ritual in order to alleviate stress and attain their worldly goals.[82]

The claim of anthropologists such as Ames and Spiro that Buddhism and the nat cults represent two religious complexes with contrasting and conflicting features was disputed by Stanley Tambiah, who wrote that the villagers he investigated did not differentiate their religion into conceptually separate elements. Tambiah wrote that Buddhism and the spirit cults are linked foci of religious actions within a single field; villagers interpret misfortunes as consequences of lack of merit and of spirit affliction, and they try to overcome their problems by performing rituals of merit making and rituals that propitiate the spirits. Tambiah admits, however, that villagers differentiate, implicitly, at least, when he writes that whereas offerings to the Buddha, the divine angels, and the monks are given freely to honor and respect them, offerings to the spirits are made in terms of a bargain.[83]

B. J. Terwiel found that a clear compartmentalization between Buddhism and animism is made more commonly by upper-strata Buddhists with secondary or higher education, and that the syncretistic incorporation of Buddhist concepts and beliefs into an animistic worldview is found among the lower strata, with little education. The differences between urban sophisticates and rural unsophisticates cut across the division between monks and laypeople. Rural monks participate as much as laypeople in the magico-animistic complex, and rules of monastic discipline are broken regularly when they are in contradiction with animistic principles.[84] The differences among social strata are noted also by Bruce Kapferer, who reports that middle-class Sinhalese distinguish between "true" Buddhism, whose ideals are to be found in the texts and the teachings of learned monks, and "folk" practices, which are to be observed among the working class and peasants. Thus, a distinction reminiscent of that made by anthropologists between the great and the little traditions has become part of the symbolic language of class and stratum.[85]

Martin Southwold reports that the Sinhalese villagers he investigated also made distinctions between non-Buddhist cultic practices concerned with this life and Buddhist practices concerned with the next. He explains that references to the Buddha in non-Buddhist cultic practices are not made because they are seen as linked elements within a single field of religion but because, as for all other significant public activities, including school days and political meetings, legitimacy is sought by formal homage to the Buddha.[86]

Anthropologists appear to be in general agreement that the Buddha, gods, and spirits are all part of what Buddhists perceive as a single cosmological system, and the differences among the anthropologists appear to be in the emphases they give to the hierarchical divisions within that cosmology. For some, the hierarchical distinction is conceptualized as two religious systems; for others, the levels are part of one overall system. All are agreed that Buddhists conceptualize the Buddha and his teachings as far superior to the spirits, but it would appear that the distinction between the soteriological relevance of the higher level of the pantheon/cosmology and the thaumaturgical orientation of the lower levels frequently becomes blurred in practice. Immediate worldly benefits are often expected from religious action that is associated with transformative goals, and such expectations are not confined to laypeople. Monks are seen to be linked to the higher aspirations of Buddhism, but when fulfilling the Buddhist injunctions, they can be as motivated as laypeople by thaumaturgical goals. Nevertheless, many Buddhists' emphasis that their religion is solely a soteriology has restricted its encompassing of nomic and dispensational goals. Whereas Hindus have incorporated folk practices in a syncretistic fashion, Buddhists have incorporated them by stressing their separate and inferior status.

Values and Social Structure

The patterns of religious action of the Sangha differ from those of laypeople, not so much with respect to thaumaturgical patterns, for even virtuoso meditators propitiate spirits, but rather with respect to the soteriological goals of virtuosos, and the soteriological means of virtuosos and priest-monks. The religious elite's patterns of transformative action are partial actualizations of two religious values that the elites have expounded, probably from the beginnings of Buddhism and certainly since its canonical writings: the renunciation of the world and the preservation of the Buddha's teachings. The tension between these values has been kept in check by the distinction within the elite between radical renouncers and scholars, and it has been the "forest-dwelling" renouncers, a small minority within the Sangha, who have tended to distance themselves most from laypeople and their worldly affairs. Only on special holy days are laypeople allowed to participate in the prayer and join the meditational sessions of the renouncers in their forest hermitages.

Even the most ascetic of renouncers, who have reduced their material needs to a basic minimum, are dependent on the laity for their needs, and this dependence necessarily compromises their position as individuals outside the society of laypeople. Some renouncers confine their interaction with laypeople to receiving food and occasional gifts, but others enter into more frequent interaction with laypeople when they agree to use their special virtues and powers acquired through renunciation to accommodate lay requests. Renouncers who have gained reputations as miracle workers may try to escape the attentions of the laity, but the more they have attempted to demonstrate their indifference to the world, the more they have impressed the laity who regard them as a means of achieving dispensatory goals.[87]

The response of the laity to the distancing of renouncers has elements of ambivalence; the virtuosos are revered by many for their attempt to achieve the supreme goal of Buddhism, but they are also criticized for their "selfish" behavior in refusing to assist others.[88] Some laity are more favorably disposed to the priest-type monk, whose action is focused more on the preservation and transmission of the dharma, the Buddha's teachings. Many of the Buddha's teachings are believed to have been given only to the Sangha, and the texts of Theravada Buddhism were composed by, and largely for, monks and nuns. Up to modern times the sacred texts were not readily available even to most monks, and for the laity, who did not understand Pali, access to the texts was highly restricted. Most lay Buddhists lived in an essentially oral culture, and only the development of schools and printing presses in the nineteenth century opened up possibilities for lay participation in the study of the religion.[89]

Both renunciation and the preservation of the dharma depend on the Sangha, whose survival in turn is seen to depend on their strict conformity to the Vinaya, the monastic code. The 227 rules of conduct not only distinguish monks from laypeople, who normally have to follow only the five precepts, but also constitute a rejection of the lay way of life. Monks are clearly identified by their saffron robes and shaven heads, and although they are often more comfortable than laypeople in terms of housing and food, their conformity to the rules means, among other things, chastity and giving up the attachments that make up the social world of laypeople. Heresy in Buddhism has meant deviance from the rules, and schisms within the Sangha have taken place over such issues as the methods of ordination, the wearing of silk robes, and the handling of money, matters unlikely to be of controversy among laypeople.[90]

The values on which the differences between monks and laypeople in the patterns of religious action are based have rarely been challenged by laypeople. It has been accepted that renunciation does not govern laypeople in their worldly affairs and that the centers for the preservation of the Buddha's teachings and the most complete Buddhist lifestyle are the monasteries. The importance of the Sangha as the major field of merit for laypeople is one factor in lay acceptance.

The differentiation within the Sangha between meditating monks and priest-monks has meant that criticisms of monks have not taken the form of opposition to the Sangha as a whole but rather as a criticism of one type in comparison with the other. Southwold found that, in Sri Lanka, while some urban lay Buddhists criticize those monks who do not meditate, village Buddhists tend to be either indifferent or critical toward meditating monks and to value those monks who minister to the social needs of the laypeople in their communities.[91]

The Structure of the Religious Institutions

From its beginnings, the Buddhist assumption that ultimate salvation and full conformity to the Buddhist way of life can be achieved only by members of the Sangha limited the incorporation of the laity into Buddhist religious organizations. Although laypeople have provided material support for the Sangha and have frequently requested religious services from the priest-monks, there have been no formal organizational links between the laity and the monastic orders, and it is the familial and community institutions that have provided the social bases of lay religion. An institutional differentiation between clerisy and laity nevertheless can exist together with considerable social interaction and mutual religious influences between them. In Burma (Myanmar) and Thailand, where a large proportion of males become temporary monks as part of their life cycle, the possibilities of mutual influences are greater.

The status of the permanent Sangha, based on the recognition that they represent the highest values of Buddhism, has constituted a resource enabling them to live a distinctive way of life within the organizational boundaries of the monasteries, but the interdiction against their accumulation of wealth and worldly involvement discouraged them from becoming an independent political-economic power and has made them susceptible to the religious influence of the laity. A partial exception was Sri Lanka, where land grants led to monks becoming the lords and heirs of vast estates from the ninth to the twelfth centuries. Large monasteries held lordships over small kingdoms within the country, and the elders acted like lords, with the rights to the labor of village populations. But even in Sri Lanka the economic activities of monks were limited, and the Sangha did not become an independent nucleus of political power.[92]

The Sangha evolved, in the first centuries after the Buddha's death, from a fraternity of wandering mendicants to loose associations of monasteries. The mendicant-eremitic ideal did not disappear entirely, but the dominant form of organization, both for the monks who settled in established communities and for the forest monks, became the settled monasteries, which entered into routinized relationships with the lay communities in which they were situated or which were located nearby.[93] The process from mendicancy to settlement in monasteries has repeated itself many times, when peripatetic meditation masters or "forest teachers" have established hermitages with cells of disciples at various points on their journeys. The networks of hermitages, which in some cases became more dispersed as disciples established branch monasteries apart from the main centers, were not normally tied by formal organizational bonds but rather by their loyalty to, or memory of, the revered founding masters and their particular teachings and practices. The laypeople who recognized the peripatic masters as saints supported them and their disciples but were not incorporated into the monasteries, and the religious differences among the monastic associations had little influence on differentiating patterns of lay religion.[94]

The hierarchical relationships between a central or large monastery and its branch monasteries have been limited, with the individual monasteries retaining considerable autonomy. A tendency toward greater fragmentation has occurred as groups of monks who desire to conform more strictly to the monastic code have seceded from established orders and set up their own fraternities,[95] and even where a number of monasteries are tied together by their recognition of the authority of an especially venerable monk, this figure's authority is limited to the discipline of individual monks. From time to time councils of senior monks have gathered and arrived at agreements on questions in dispute or doubt, but such bodies have not had the power to secure the implementation of their decisions.[96]

Attempts to achieve a unified Sangha have been initiated more by political rulers than by the monks. Rulers have perceived the Sangha as a factor in building a Buddhist state, and the kings of Burma were particularly successful in bringing the Sangha under the control of a central ecclesiastical organization, which in turn was controlled by the government. The absence of a Buddhist organization crossing national boundaries has made possible the securing of Buddhism to national or state identities, particularly in times of invasion and modern colonialism.[97]

There is a low level of centralization and hierarchization within as well as among monasteries. Authority depends largely on age and seniority of ordination rather than on formal positions. Formal organization is particularly weak in forest hermitages, where there is likely to be a greater turnover of members as individual monks seek their own ways, sometimes by leaving a monastery and joining another or by leaving the institutionalized setting altogether. Some monasteries have grades, such as novices, assistant or junior monks, monks, and chief monks or abbots, but the hierarchical authority of abbots rarely extends beyond granting or refusing the admission of novices and monks to the monastery and ensuring that the communal acts of the monks are conducted at the appropriate times. More important are the relationships between teachers and pupils, with the former taking personal responsibility for each novice or junior monk.[98]

Without the pressures of a hierarchical organization, monks have been open to the influence of their immediate social environments. Town-dwelling monks have become aligned with the political rulers located in the capital or town; monks who became custodians or even owners of land have come to share the views of landowners; and village monks, who were often born in the villages in which they reside, tend to share the beliefs and customs of their fellow villagers.[99] With the absence or weakness of a formal ecclesiastical authority, and with monks often living some distance from the informal authority of the learned, it is hardly surprising that village monks should participate in the popular forms of religious action, such as dealing with house spirits and the rites of exorcism.

The Wider Sociopolitical Structure

Unlike Hinduism in India, differences in the patterns of religious action of elites and masses in Buddhist countries were not built on a system of castes. The only Theravada Buddhist country to have a caste system is Sri Lanka, but its system might appropriately be called quasi-caste: it has fewer castes than in India; there are no castes of Brahmans or untouchables; and there is little connection between ideas of pollution and purity and the castes. The stratification of the peasant masses into castes has some relevance to religious differentiation because there has been a tendency to recruit monks from the higher castes,[100] but the castes are not divided by loyalties to particular deities.

If religious differentiation in Theravada Buddhist countries has not been anchored in castes, neither has it been structured by the hierarchies of a stable imperial empire. The polities of the Theravada Buddhist countries had what Tambiah has called a "galactic" character: a loose formation composed of a central entity surrounded by vassal states and, at the outer rim, by tributary states that replicated, on a smaller scale, the dominant center. The political centers varied in strength, sometimes dominating the lesser units and at other times failing to prevent the growth of considerable local autonomy. Hill tribes, in particular, were difficult to incorporate into the valley kingdoms, and many small, stateless societies remained entirely outside the major polities. Strong centers, which rested on military force rather than routine administrative machinery, were rare and short-lived; palace rebellions and wars of succession cut short the reigns of individual kings and of dynasties.[101]

The loose and unstable political structures have a number of implications for Buddhist religious organization and the interrelationships between monks and laypeople. Although a number of kings tried to centralize and hierarchize the Sangha, the frequent rise and fall of royal centers was not conducive to a stable Sangha organization.[102] Newly emergent rulers sponsored fraternities of forest monks to counter the already-established organizations of monks and monasteries that were tied to political centers that had been overthrown or were being challenged. Alliances with ascetic forest monks who were located on the frontiers of settlements could earn the kings greater support among laypeople and contribute to the expansion of their kingdoms. Kings also turned to forest ascetics to fortify their regimes in times of social and political turmoil.[103]

The relative influence of Buddhist religious centers tended to parallel the relative influence of the political centers in which they were located. The upland or hill peoples, whose dispersion over rough terrain made any organization above the village level difficult, were influenced less by elite forms of Buddhism than were the lowland villages, whose headmen were linked to the governors and officials of provincial capitals, who in turn had connections with the court centers. Some parallels existed between the political hierarchy and the hierarchy of the Sangha, but in neither case did the higher reaches penetrate deeply into village life. A large part of the political rule operated through kinship connections and informal patron-client relationships.[104]

The decentralized, cellular character of the political structure was a congenial environment for a village-based Buddhism in which monks as well as laypeople participated. Little interference came from higher levels, either from the king's administration or from aristocratic elites, which were weak and, like the kings, had little dynastic continuity. The status of the higher lay stratum was based on their personal vassalship to the kings, a status that was often lost as one king replaced another, and on their relations with their local clients. These conditions were not favorable to the development of a strong landowning aristocracy with a distinctive status-group culture to compete with the Sangha or with an authority to shape the religion of the peasant masses.[105] With few pressures from translocal religious or political organizations and elites, it was the religious principles of the segregation and interdependence of monks and laypeople, together with local conditions, that shaped both the differences between and the overlap of elite and popular religion.

A Brief Comparison: Mahayana Buddhism and Japan

The two-tier soteriology of nirvana and rebirth in Theravada Buddhism was questioned, from the first two centuries C.E., by Buddhist factions who came to call their alternative Buddhism Mahayana, the "great vehicle" or "large ferryboat." Their pejorative term for Theravada Buddhism was Hinayana, the "small vehicle" or "little ferryboat," because it provided room for only a religious elite to make the crossing to nirvana. As an alternative to the arhats, who were criticized as being selfishly preoccupied with their own salvation, the Mahayana emphasized the bodhisattvas, those figures who voluntarily delay their entrance to nirvana and suffer countless rebirths in order to help others reach salvation. Other innovations within Mahayana included the transformation of the Buddha into a transcendental deity and the reformulation of salvation as escape from the cycle of rebirths into a "Buddha field," or paradise.[106]

The single soteriological goal for all believers, in the form of paradise rather than nirvana, and the figure of the bodhisattva as a model of worldly action for religious elites have blurred the divisions between monks and laypeople in Mahayana and even erased them in some of its movements. Without a highly differentiated Sangha, Mayahana has been more open than Theravada to syncretism with other religious traditions. The syncretism of Buddhism with Confucianism and Taoism was noted in chapter 4 on China, but an even greater contrast with the Theravada Buddhist societies is Japan, where Buddhism took part in processes of mutual appropriation with Shinto, Confucianism, and Taoism among both elites and masses.[107]

Although Japanese emperors and governments used Confucianism to add legitimacy to their rule, it was Buddhism that became the major component of state-sponsored religion in Japan. From its adoption by the Japanese courts in the seventh and eighth centuries c.e. and until the reign of the Emperor Meiji (1867–1912), Buddhism overshadowed even Shinto as a state religion. By their support of Buddhist and Shinto organizations, rulers contributed both to the institutional separation of the two religions and to their syncretism, as when they required Buddhist monks to recite sutras in Shinto shrines for the protection of the country.

The official status of Buddhism reached its peak during the Tokugawa period (1603–1868) when all households were commanded to affiliate formally to Buddhist temples, which were obliged to act as registrars of births, deaths, and marriages. This status ended with the Meiji regime, which made Shinto the sole benefactor of state patronage and attempted to "purify" Shinto from Buddhist influences. Shinto parishes replaced Buddhist temples as official registrars, and Buddhist statues, images, and priests were removed from Shinto shrines. Opposition to the anti-Buddhist measures, especially in rural areas, led to their abrogation, and Buddhist monks were allowed to continue in their positions as long as they proclaimed their loyalty to the emperor. Buddhism retained its strength, and after the disestablishment of state Shinto at the end of the World War II, Buddhism continued to constitute a major element in the syncretistic forms of Japanese religion.[108]

When the Meiji regime passed anti-Buddhist measures, many Buddhist priests simply became Shinto priests. This is a testimony to the cooperation and similar patterns of religious action performed by Buddhist and Shinto priests, which have continued to this day. Shinto priests direct *kami* (gods and spirits) to defend Buddhist images and temples, and Shinto shrines are commonly found in the grounds of Buddhist temples.

Buddhist priests say prayers to extinguish the capricious side of the kami, and even those Buddhist monks who adhere to a strict monastic tradition perform acts of veneration at Shinto shrines that guard the location of their monasteries. Ian Reader describes a popular Shinto shrine dedicated to Inari, the kami of the rice harvest, which is run by Zen Buddhist monks who draw on Buddhist texts to invoke the deity and call on its help for thaumaturgical purposes.[109]

The dimensions of world rejection and meditation have been far less prominent in Japan than in the Theravada monastic traditions, and like their Shinto counterparts, the major role of Buddhist priests in Japan has been to mediate between deities and laypeople. Japanese Buddhist priests are not differentiated from laypeople by a higher soteriological goal, and in contrast with the Theravada monks' distancing from the social ties of laypeople, the Japanese Buddhist priests marry and, like the Shinto priests, pass on their positions and temples to their sons. The major religious activity of most Buddhist priests is not meditation to achieve individual enlightenment but the performance of rites for the dead, at the request of laypeople, with the aim of transforming the deceased into ancestors who attain peace and enlightenment.

The Japanese expression "born Shinto, die Buddhist" points to a differentiation between Shinto priests, who conduct ceremonies for newborn children, and Buddhist priests, who perform memorial services for the dead. There is, however, less differentiation between the priests in their provision of means to attain thaumaturgical goals. Although the deities with whom the Buddhist and Shinto priests communicate often differ in names and characteristics, and although there are differences in Buddhist and Shinto ritual formulas, a basic similarity lies in the transmission of this-worldly requests on behalf of lay congregations and clients.[110]

Without the two-tier soteriology of Theravada Buddhism, not only is there less differentiation between Buddhist priests and laypeople in Japan, there is also less of a differentiation within the religious elite with respect to the religious action of virtuosos and non-virtuosos. As in the Theravada countries, many of the Japanese Buddhist virtuosos are believed to have acquired extraordinary powers by following a path to enlightenment involving isolation and ascetic practices. In Japan, however, it is assumed that virtuosos gain their powers in order to intercede for the benefit of others in this world. A major type of virtuoso in traditional rural Japan spent a period of isolation in the mountains, where he underwent austerities such as standing for lengthy periods under waterfalls and walking long distances, and when he came down from the mountains, he would go from village to village, curing ills, exorcising evil spirits, and distributing talismans and amulets.[111] Like their Shinto counterparts, the Buddhist virtuosos who engaged in healing cooperated with shamanesses, who acted as mediums in rituals of exorcism.[112]

If religious elites in Japan have not attempted to preserve clear boundaries among their respective religious traditions, syncretism at the level of popular religion is likely to be even more extensive. Buddhism has retained a separate identity, however, at the popular as well as the elite level. Ritual demarcation of Buddhism and Shinto in the home is indicated by the separation of the *butsudan*, the Buddhist altar of ancestor worship, from the *kamidana*, the Shinto god-shelf of the kami who protect the home. The yearly cycle of rites connected with the renewal of the seasons, the growing of rice, and the harmony of the gods with human communities has centered on Shinto shrines.[113] Buddhist temples have also played a part in the cycle of production and fertility ritual, but such action has been less important than in Shinto, and it is soteriology rather than nomic concerns that has been the special province of Japanese Buddhism.

The notions of karma and reincarnation are inconsistent with the Japanese ritual focus on ancestors, and as in China, entrance into the Western Paradise, or Pure Land, rather than rebirth has been the soteriological goal of Japanese Buddhists. The major means for the achievement of this goal has been devotion to the Buddha Amida, which is expressed by continually chanting his name, and to the sacred text, the Lotus Sutra. The emphasis on chanting sacred names made salvation accessible to illiterate peasants, and although most laypeople have fewer opportunities and less time than the priests to chant, Japanese Buddhists have claimed that even one sincerely meant chant before a person dies can be sufficient to achieve salvation.[114]

For most Japanese, however, the salvation of the dead is dependent more on the memorial rituals for the deceased than on the behavior of the deceased during their lifetimes. Following a death, a series of Buddhist rituals are performed by members of the family and the local Buddhist priest in order to guide the dead spirit to the next world and transform it into an ancestor. The rituals are believed to purify the spirit from the pollution and dangers associated with death and to bestow a new identity, denoted by a new name, that is fitting to the world of ancestors. At the end of forty-nine days of mourning, the spirit is believed to enter the world of ancestors, and a mortuary tablet representing the ancestor is placed in the butsudan, the ancestral shrine of the household.

Once they are settled in the Pure Land or some other, often vaguely conceptualized afterlife, ancestors are believed to act as guardians and protectors of the household lineage to which they belonged. As in China, the soteriological goal of transforming a deceased member of the family into an ancestor is integrally related to the thaumaturgical goals of the living, who assume that their prosperity and success derive, in part, from the beneficent protection of their ancestors. Thus, people act on behalf of both their ancestors and themselves when they address their ancestors with reports and prayers and offer food and other items that enable the deceased to continue to have what they enjoyed in life.

Ancestors are rarely reported to be punitive, and when misfortune is attributed to them, the cause is seen to lie not in the malign disposition of a particular ancestor but in the neglect of the living in caring for the ancestors as a collectivity. When the dead are not worshiped by their living relations, they become hungry ghosts who, in their continual search for food and comfort, pose a potential danger to the living. Another source of danger are the unhappy spirits who died sudden, premature, or violent deaths. When people die in a state of jealousy, rage, or unpreparedness, their spirits are believed to remain possessed by worldly passions, and they wander the earth as horrifying or pathetic creatures, causing distress and possessing the living. In recent years many temples have been established containing deities whose purported aim is to bring salvation to the ghosts of embryos killed in abortions and miscarriages. The ghosts, existing in an unpleasant limbo, call attention to their plights by causing madness, sickness, and broken marriages in their families.[115]

Buddhist priests are called on to transform malevolent spirits and deliver them to Amida's Pure Land. They also perform exorcisms, as do Shinto priests and religious practitioners who are not identified with a formal religious organization or tradition. The overlapping of the religious traditions extends to supramundanes, and a number of deities from the different traditions are considered counterparts or manifestations of each other; Amaterasu, the ancestral goddess of the emperor, is identified with Dainichi, the Cosmic or Sun Buddha. Some supramundanes gain status and power when they become associated with more than one tradition. Inari, the fox deity, is regarded as a particularly powerful kami because of its associations with esoteric Buddhism; it is worshiped as the god of harvest in rural areas, as the god of fishing in fishing villages, and

— how to draw distinct between practice of rel. tolerance and privileging and are rel. of resources -- can have former while also doing latter; does this matter?

as the god of earth and hearth in urban areas, where it is believed to be efficacious in providing success in business and careers.[116]

In response to the syncretism of Buddhism and Shinto, members of the religious elites have proposed theories of prime entities and secondary manifestations: Buddhists have suggested that Shinto kami are manifestations of the primary buddhas and bodhisattvas, whereas Shinto scholars have argued that the reverse is true. Such distinctions have had little meaning at the popular level, where supramundanes adopted from Taoism as well as from Buddhism and Shinto have been fused into single objects of worship and placed in pantheons that include local deities unrelated to the traditions.[117]

Syncretism and indifference to religious boundaries among the religious traditions is perhaps most evident in popular religion, but the lay masses have differed little in these respects from the religious elites, who have shown relatively little interest in building and strengthening boundaries, either among the religious traditions or between official and unofficial religion. Political elites have, on occasion, sought to label certain traditions as "un-Japanese." Christianity was persecuted as part of the attempt by Japanese governments to remove all foreign influences, but at the level of popular religion, elements of Christianity have been incorporated into the syncretistic amalgam. The Virgin Mary has been identified with the Buddhist female bodhisattva Kannon, the popular, compassionate goddess who rescues people in distress and takes care of pregnant women and the elderly.[118]

The lack of concern in Japan with religious boundaries, both among religious traditions and between official and unofficial religion, presents a clear contrast with the case of Catholicism in Europe.

rel. pluralism or not

rel. pl.

3 variables salience of boundaries

alignment of rel. boundaries w/

other social boundaries

to extent of conflict and polarization

we are a rel. pluralistic society, +

one in which rel. boundaries are

relatively salient - but not alive

those boundaries w/

— religion can either divide or unite – religion itself is

neither divisive or unifying

inherently

7

Hierocracy and Popular Religion

Catholicism in "Traditional" Europe

The description and analysis here of patterns of religious action of the religious elites and lay masses of European Catholicism refer principally to a past Europe, a "traditional" Europe that has largely ceased to exist. Recent investigations by anthropologists are incorporated into the portrayal of popular religion in Europe, but there are fewer of these than of popular religion in Hindu and Buddhist societies, and it is the work of social historians of religion that provides a large part of the data that are synthesized and analyzed in this chapter. The major reason for the greater historical emphasis in the analysis of Catholicism compared with other religions is that the type of popular religion on which I have been focusing, a popular religion anchored in relatively autonomous and cohesive rural communities, is largely a phenomenon of the past in Europe. Anthropologists who have conducted studies of rural Catholic areas in recent decades have noted the effects on popular religion of urban culture, mass media, and secular and scientific values and norms.[1] This is not to say that popular religion no longer exists in Europe, but with few exceptions it has lost the comprehensiveness and coherence that it had in the boundaried communities of what has been called "traditional Europe."[2]

Although changes in popular religion are an important topic in this chapter, the major concern, as in previous chapters, is to delineate patterns of elite and popular religion at a level of generality that is applicable across the religio-cultural area (Catholic Europe) and a considerable expanse of time. With respect to the popular religion of rural populations, variations among areas and countries of Catholic Europe and from the Middle Ages through early modern to modern times are treated as secondary or as modifications to the broad patterns existing from the twelfth and thirteenth centuries until about the middle of the nineteenth century.

The historical boundaries of a broad delineation of patterns of religious action can only be approximate, but for a study of the differences and interactions of official and popular religion in Catholic Europe, the twelfth and thirteenth centuries provide an appropriate beginning. Historians have come to regard the twelfth century as a period of extensive change in medieval society, and of special relevance for this study was the development, already underway in the eleventh century, of a unified, hierarchical, and autonomous structure of the Catholic Church. The variety of local church practices of the early Middle Ages was replaced by a more uniform practice for the clergy that was formulated by a centralized ecclesiastical hierarchy with the pope at its head. Standard practices came also to characterize the monasteries of Western Europe. Most monasteries adopted the Rule of Saint Benedict, originally written in the sixth century, which laid down in detail the appropriate activities of monks. The important ecclesiastical unit for the lay masses was the local parish, and an extensive network of parishes had taken shape by the thirteenth century. Although the establishment of most parish communities had come from lay rather than ecclesiastical initiative, the parish was the unit by which the majority of laypeople were incorporated, at least nominally, within the church.[3]

The medieval Catholic Church should not be regarded as a unified monolith that spoke with one voice. The question of authoritative teachings was not settled in the Middle Ages, and to present the teachings of particular theologians or the decisions of particular church councils as church doctrine can give the false impression that disputes had been solved. There was no uniform elite in the sense of a consensus of beliefs or an agreement over which particular groups represented the "true" church. There was, however, a church in the sense of an institution of clerics, distinct from the laity, with a separate code of law.[4]

The establishment of the institutions of the church in Europe was accompanied by the emergence of a popular Christianity among large sections of the European population. Writing on Britain of the early Middle Ages, Karen Louise Jolly states that the intermingling and mutual assimilation of Anglo-Saxon and Christian religion had produced, by the tenth and eleventh centuries, a popular Christianity that included a "middle ground" of practices that cannot be fitted into tidy categories of native and imported religions. As evidence of the dynamic interaction that had taken place between native culture and imported religion, she gives examples such as a blessing for fields that appealed to the earth, sky, the Virgin Mary, and God. Vernacular invocations to Mother Earth were combined with the Latin liturgy addressed to Father God, who grants to Mother Earth the power to grow and prosper. The church integrated a number of folk practices, such as a blessing for sick cows, into liturgical texts, and it rejected or replaced various practices, as in replacing the worship of trees with worship directed to crosses. Jolly writes of a Christianization of folklore and a folklorization of Christianity; popular practices were textualized, and texts were accommodated into popular practice.[5]

The examples Jolly gives relate to the concerns of peasants, a class that had become firmly established with the conversion of large areas into arable land from about 1050 to 1250. Serf status was a unifying feature of the peasant class, and although serfdom began to decline in Western Europe as early as the twelfth century and was abolished by the fifteenth, the material life of peasants and the basic social patterns of village life changed little from the thirteenth century until the transformations of the modern period.[6] Concomitant with the establishment of the peasantry was the consolidation of the wealth, status, and power of the aristocracy, which was characterized by a high degree of cultural conformity by the eleventh century in Western Europe.

The emergence of powerful monarchs in the twelfth century modified the feudal structure and contributed to the diffusion of an aristocratic culture through the network of courts. The twelfth and thirteenth centuries were also a period of urban development, increasing contact of trading centers, and the crystallization of a burgher class, whose culture differed in many respects from those of the aristocrats and the peasants.[7] The lives of most urban residents continued, however, to be determined by agricultural activities and the seasons, and as in the countryside, most social relationships were of a face-to-face nature.[8] The precariousness of the physical environment and the local nature of social relationships for both rural and urban residents provide the contexts for a popular religion that the vast majority in "Catholic" Europe shared up to modern times.

Hierocracy and the Provision of Common Goals and Means

As in Hinduism and Buddhism, distinctions between virtuosos and ordinary religious actors and between priests and laypeople are important in Catholicism, but in contrast with the Eastern religions, virtuosos, priests, and laypeople are incorporated by a single religious hierocracy—the Catholic Church. The hierocratic framework has important implications both for the relationships of the religious elites to the lay masses and for the relationships of the virtuosos, of which a large number were monks, to the priests.

In seeking to monopolize the distribution of religious benefits, a hierocracy defines what religious beliefs and action are allowable and will often oppose religious action that is performed outside its auspices. From the perspective of the hierocratic elite in Catholicism (the bishops of the institutional church), the popular religion of the masses could be divided between those parts of little-tradition Catholicism that would fall within the limits defined as allowable by the elite and unofficial, popular religion, which would fall outside those limits.

The bishops' accommodation of and partial participation in popular religion extended the boundaries of official religion beyond great-tradition Catholicism, the ideal form that was promoted, but by no means always fully practiced, by the elite. The extent to which popular religion was included in or excluded from official religion was in part a consequence of negotiations between the elite and the masses, but that popular religion which appealed to supramundanes outside great-tradition Catholicism was almost inevitably categorized as unofficial. Rituals of little-tradition Catholicism that invoked and petitioned Catholic supramundanes in ways unauthorized by the elite could also fall outside the category of official religion.[9] The hierocratic framework made the distinction between official and unofficial religion more important in Catholicism than in the Eastern religions, but it was a distinction of the elite, unrecognized or ignored by most laypeople and by many in the lower ranks of the clergy. Religious actions that the higher ranks of the church regarded as illegitimate were often tolerated or even encouraged by local priests, and this was sufficient legitimation as far as most laypeople were concerned.

With respect to the relationship between the hierocratic elite and virtuosos, Max Weber wrote that hierocracies oppose any autonomous development by virtuoso religion because it is seen as a challenge to the general accessibility to sacred values provided by the organization. Rather than deny the legitimacy of all virtuoso religiosity, hierocratic organizations have admitted that full adherence to the religion's highest ideals is an extraordinary achievement that can be channeled for the benefit of the majority, who lack the qualifications or ability to achieve such heights. Thus, virtuoso religion, particularly as organized in monastic organizations, has been transformed into an instrument of hierocratic control, even though tensions often persist between hierocrats and virtuosos.[10]

By incorporating the monasteries into its ecclesiastical framework and by institutionalizing sainthood, the Catholic Church achieved a large measure of success in neutralizing the potential opposition of virtuosos and using them to strengthen its interests. The distinction between perfect and ordinary Christians was recognized within this framework, but in contrast with the Eastern religions, the church promoted a common soteriological goal and universal means for attaining that goal. There is no distinction in Catholicism between a proximate and an ultimate salvation, although hierarchical notions were introduced in the portrayal of ultimate salvation in heaven. There were also hierarchical conceptions of different paths to salvation, but the church taught that the sacraments were an essential means for the salvation of all Christians. The goal and means common to all Catholics are discussed here prior to the descriptions of the differences in patterns of religious action of religious elites and lay masses.

The common soteriological goal of the vast majority of Catholics, virtuosos and masses, is eternal "life" in heaven. By the time the church had become a pervasive organizational presence in Europe, the goal of eternity in paradise, with an emphasis on the salvation of the individual soul in another world, had long replaced millenarianism, with its stress on collective salvation in a transformed world. Millenarianism, the major soteriological goal of Christians during the early centuries of the religion, continued to surface in millennial movements that were treated as heresies by the church. Influenced by Jewish apocalyptic literature and drawing on the Revelation of Saint John, millennialists believed that upon Christ's second coming, which was imminent, Christ would defeat the devil and establish a one-thousand-year kingdom populated by the Christian faithful, including martyrs who would be raised from the dead. At the end of the thousand years, after the final destruction of Satan, who would be let loose for a short period, there would be the general resurrection of the dead and the final judgment, whereupon the virtuous would receive ultimate redemption and sinners would be sentenced to damnation.

After the adoption of the church by political regimes, the church supported the status quo and abandoned millenarianism, which was declared a heresy. The this-worldly, quasi-territorial, collective salvation of millenarianism was replaced by a metapolitical, other-worldly salvation of the individual soul, which would abide in heaven, freed from all matter. In the formulation of Saint Augustine, which became official doctrine, the millennium, the mystical City of God, had been realized in the church.[11]

NB: millenarism often an anti-clerical elite movement, best
— millenarianism is much sharper concept than "sectarian"

Hierocracy and Popular Religion | 171

As a condemned heresy, millenarianism had little appeal among the church elite. The major exception in the Middle Ages was Joachim of Fiore, a Calabrian abbot of the Cistercian order who, in the latter part of the twelfth century, prophesied an imminent age of bliss prior to the second coming and the Last Judgment. Joachim expected the church to endure until the end of time, and his doctrines were adopted principally by members of the religious orders, including the orthodox order of Franciscans. Radical interpretations of Joachim's prophecies, which castigated the church and the pope as forces of evil, were made in the middle of the thirteenth century by Franciscan spirituals who had broken from the main Franciscan order over the issue of absolute poverty.[12] Opposition to the ecclesiastical elite was a common feature of millennial movements, whose leaders included monks from minor orders and priests and monks who had left their parishes and monasteries to preach among the people. The movements rarely appealed to peasants who were socially embedded in village communities; instead, they drew their support from those on the margins of society, such as peasants without land, unemployed workers, beggars, and vagabonds.[13]

The dominant soteriological goal, common to most virtuosos, clerics, and laypeople, was to reside for eternity in heaven and to avoid damnation in hell. Although, in contrast with the Eastern religions, there was no two-tier soteriology, hierarchical elements were present in the categorization of the saved. Differences in personal holiness were believed to endure through eternity, and in heaven the highest group of the saved, closest to the angels and the Trinity, was the saints. Beliefs that personal holiness determined, in part, the ranks of the ecclesiastical hierarchy were linked to notions that this hierarchy was replicated in heaven, and those occupying the high offices of the church were sometimes called angels and gods.[14]

The number of laypeople who were to be saved was very few in some clerical formulations, and in ecclesiastical writings and on the decorations of churches, descriptions and representations of hell were more frequent and dominant than those of heaven.[15] Two judgments were posited: first, the judgment of each individual, to take place immediately after death, and second, the Last Judgment of all human beings, to follow the second coming of Christ and the rejoining of bodies and souls at the resurrection of the dead. At the Last Judgment, Christ, seated on the judgment throne and surrounded by the apostles and the Virgin and Saint John, who would act as intercessors, would judge each individual according to the balance of their good and bad deeds written in the "Book of Life."

The Last Judgment remained an official dogma, but the motif that each person was judged immediately after death and in isolation from the fate of others became dominant. Aron Gurevich surmises that it was difficult for most people to imagine rewards and retributions occurring in the distant and indefinite future, and he notes that reports of early medieval visions indicate that the notion of salvation and damnation immediately after death existed as early as the sixth century. The coexistence among medieval people of the beliefs in a general judgment at the end of time and judgments of individuals immediately after their deaths can be traced to the Gospels, but the early Christians, expecting an imminent second coming, were unlikely to perceive a contradiction. The distancing of resurrection from death accompanied the decline of millenarianism, and soteriological interests came to focus on the immediate aftermath of death, with little interest shown in the final stage of mankind's history.[16]

Popular beliefs may well have played a part in the changing emphasis in church doctrine from Last Judgment to judgment immediately after death, but the influence of popular notions was more evident in the development of church doctrines on purgatory. In contrast with Hinduism and Buddhism, in which residence in hells is conceived of as a temporary or finite state, Christianity postulated either eternal paradise or eternal damnation. In the early Middle Ages the church taught that few would be saved,[17] and possibly in response to such a grim outlook, the chance of salvation for the souls of sinners was expressed in popular representations of trials undergone in separate divisions of hell or on its threshold. Theologians began to organize conceptually the varied and sometimes contradictory visions of the next world among the populace, and purgatory gradually emerged as a place distinct from hell. The stark alternative of Christian soteriology was thereby softened; rather than suffering never-ending torture in hell, souls would enter heaven after their sins had been expiated in purgatory. Beginning in popular notions and then taken up and systematized by theologians, purgatory is an example of the complex interaction of popular and official religion in the Catholic context.[18]

The goal of members of the religious elite was to go straight to heaven after death, but they did not hold this as a realistic goal for most laypeople, who should seek to make their time in purgatory as short as possible. The extent to which the peasant masses absorbed these fears and directed their religious action to the goal of avoiding hell or reducing time in purgatory is difficult to assess. Alongside the soteriology expounded by the church, there continued among the populace the ancient idea that the body and soul remained together in the burial place in a condition resembling sleep. The belief in death as a neutral state and of the body and soul resting in a dormant peace[19] might be reconciled with Christian beliefs in the postponement of judgment until the resurrection of the dead at the end of time, but popular notions were more likely to conceive of the sleep of the dead as a permanent condition. Whether or not the dead did rest in peace or not depended on the nature of their death: those who had a "good death," a death of which they had foreknowledge and for which they had prepared, were in better stead than those who had died without warning or in abnormal or violent circumstances.[20] The latter were restless and were more likely to leave their graves to haunt the living.

Whatever meanings death and its aftermath had for the peasant masses, a large part of their religious action was directed to this-worldly goals of nomos and thaumaturgy. Peasants were concerned with the renewal and regulation of the seasons and with the avoidance of threats to daily life. Once the threats became real, they sought solutions or tried to limit the damage: animals and family members had to be healed; unsuitable weather had to be countered; thieves had to be discovered; and infertility had to be overcome.[21] Writing on religion in sixteenth-century Spain, William Christian states that one would be mistaken in concluding, from the little information we have on religious action among villagers that was directed toward salvation, that they were concerned only with this-worldly problems. It was to be expected, for example, that the vows villagers made to saints would refer to this-worldly goals, because the vows were made not by individuals but by the village, which, as a corporate entity, had no afterlife. In contrast, evidence of preoccupation with salvation among the wealthier classes, who had the money to pay priests to perform masses for the dead, should not lead to a conclusion that religious action directed to this-worldly goals was confined to the peasants: wealth was certainly no guarantee against illness and other problems of daily life to which religious means were applied.[22] The church presented its main function as the provision of the means of salvation, but as a hierocracy with monopolistic claims over the distribution of religious benefits among the population, it also provided the religious means to achieve temporal goals.

The sacraments of the church, and especially the Eucharist, were the common means necessary for the salvation of all, virtuosos, priests, and laity. The key position and authority of the clergy was based, first and foremost, on its sole rights to administer the sacraments and thereby mediate salvation. These rights were tied to the office of the priest: the church taught that the efficacy of the sacraments was dependent not on the personal qualities of the priests but on God's power, which alone was at work in the blessings of the priests. From the thirteenth century on, the number of sacraments came to be recognized as seven: baptism, confirmation, penance, marriage, ordination, unction or anointing of the sick, and communion or participation in the mass, partaking of the holy bread and wine of the Eucharist, which held the central place in the scheme of salvation. The Fourth Lateran Council in 1215 ruled that every member of the church should receive communion at least once a year at Easter, and it pronounced on the doctrine of transubstantiation, stating that at the moment of the priest's sacralization of the elements, the bread and wine were changed into the actual flesh and blood of Christ. As part of the ceremony, the priest placed the bread, in the form of wafers of unleavened bread, on the tongues of celebrants, although the priest alone drank the wine. By absorbing the bodily substances of Jesus, celebrants not only were commemorating and giving thanks for Christ's sacrifice but were providing for an eternal life in Christ.[23]

The Religious Elites: Monks and Priests

There was a tension in Catholicism between the doctrine that salvation was open to all through the sacraments of the church, on the one hand, and the teachings that restricted salvation to a select few who devoted their lives to the divine and the church, on the other. No single explanation of the effectiveness of the sacraments existed in church doctrine, and how the sacraments worked with respect to the achievement of salvation was open to a number of interpretations. Although theologians agreed that salvation was not possible without the sacraments, they did not necessarily consider them a sufficient condition, and many emphasized that benefits from the sacraments depended on the purity and moral state of the celebrant. Church leaders assumed that, if only a small minority were to be saved, they would come mostly from the ranks of the clergy; but even when salvation was extended to larger numbers (which the notion of purgatory made more feasible), many monks and priests believed they would be placed in a higher rank in heaven than most laypeople. There was no agreement, however, with respect to whether monks or priests such as bishops held the higher rank, both in this world and the next.[24]

The different conceptions of the hierarchy of clergy were related to evaluations of the differences between monks and priests with respect to their typical religious ends and typical religious means. It may be assumed that priests were concerned with their personal salvation no less than other Christians, but if only because of their administration of the sacraments, they were understood to have the goal of saving others. A relationship was purported to exist between saving others and saving oneself. By their celebration of the mass, priests not only provided the necessary means for the salvation of others; they also increased their own chances of salvation. The proviso existed that the celebration of the mass brought benefits only to the good priest; the same actions did not secure rewards for the bad or evil priest.[25]

How priests performed their official duties, including the administration of the sacraments, was one basis on which the heavenly tribunal was believed to make its decisions of the priests' destination after death, but the collective benefits from the priests' activities and their sacralization of the world on behalf of the entire church were emphasized both in theology and among laypeople. The religious actions of priests were understood to bring about not just collective salvation, which was emphasized in official religion, but also nomic and thaumaturgical goals, which were emphasized in popular religion. At least in certain periods of the history of eremitism and monasticism, individual as opposed to collective salvation was a more prominent goal, and the typical means of monks—withdrawal from the world—limited their involvement in the achievement of nomic and thaumaturgical goals. The desert monks of Egypt in the fourth century were early exemplars of the hermit or recluse who sought to achieve individual salvation through rigorous asceticism and self-abnegation.

As monks came to be clericalized and organized under the auspices of the church, at first in largely autonomous abbeys and later as orders, the eremitic (individual) type of monk tended to give way to the cenobitic (collective) type, and the religious action of monks tended to change from a focus on their individual salvation in relative isolation from others to a concern with the salvation of others. These "others" could be specific, such as the community of monks in a monastery or monastic order, but "others" could extend to all true Christians as defined by the church. All monks, cenobitic as well as eremitic, were expected to distance themselves from worldly concerns, renouncing personal property and refraining from sexual relations, and although most monks lived collectively within the boundaries of the monastery, the eremitic ideal was retained by such practices as isolation for long hours in cells, taking meals privately, and refraining from speaking.[26]

One indication of the change in the goal orientation of monks from individual to collective salvation was the increase in the time that monks devoted to collective prayer; private prayer and meditation continued, but meeting in chapel eight times over a twenty-four-hour day to recite set prayers took up a considerable part of the monks' time. According to the church's doctrine of vicarious oblation, the monks' prayers contributed to the salvation of all true Christians, living and dead; the church could draw on the disproportionate contribution of the monks to the store of merits in order to absolve the sins of less-worthy Christians. The doctrine of the "treasure of merit" strengthened the status of monks, but its extension by church leaders into a system of indulgences, by which people were encouraged to pay for absolution of their sins, undermined the distinctiveness of the monks' role.

Many of the monks' prayers and masses for the dead were performed either for the community of monks or for specific lay benefactors. In return for endowments and gifts, the religious actions of monks were seen as waging war against the devil and his demons and cleansing the lands of kings and lords from supramundane evil. The funerary role of monks expanded with the increased preoccupation with death in the later Middle Ages, and it became a major service of monks to say masses and intercessory prayers for the remission of sins of donors and the deceased members of the donors' families. In addition, monks could be relied on to perform religious actions that settled the penitential debts of their benefactors. These actions for the salvation of others, and the material rewards received by the monks for performing them, were not perceived to detract from the salvation of the monks themselves. On the contrary, actions performed for the benefit of others contributed to the accumulation of merits for the monks' own salvation.[27]

Laypeople's foundation of monasteries and contributions to their upkeep were signs of social status and political power, and although donations to monasteries were motivated by soteriological goals of an intangible and non-immediate kind, donors also expected that the use of their wealth for spiritual purposes would bring rewards of a more worldly nature. In addition, donors had access for thaumaturgical purposes to saints' relics located in the monasteries they supported. These benefits were no doubt relevant for kings, who established royal monasteries; for the high nobility, who often sponsored a number of monasteries; and for less-wealthy donors who gave to monasteries near their residences.[28] The system of exchange in which monks were involved—monastic spiritual goods for the material goods of laypeople—encompassed only a small minority of laypeople from the upper strata of society, and peasants in particular were unlikely to have much contact with monks.

Although there was a considerable overlap between the religious actions of some orders of monks and friars and those of the "secular" clergy, the distinction between the monastic clergy, who lived in monasteries, and the diocesan clergy, who administered the parishes, remained of central importance with respect to the relationships between clergy and laity. Many town dwellers had considerable contact with friars, but the main contact most laypeople had with the church was through the parish priest. The rural population had little or no contact with the elite of the church, the hierarchy of bishops, who normally resided in the towns.

Laypeople expected their parish priests to offer prayers and masses on their behalf, especially after their death, but much of the priests' religious action was undertaken without lay participation or presence. In the later Middle Ages, when many of the clergy performed the mass daily, often no laypeople would be in attendance. When laypeople were in attendance (and the mass was the only church service that many laypeople attended regularly), there was little opportunity for participation; the mass was conducted by the priest with his back to the congregation, and it was conducted in Latin, which few laypeople understood. The other main part of public worship, the Divine Office, was also supposed to be recited by the clergy every day, and those priests who did so would normally recite it in private, without lay participation.[29]

Preaching was added to the role of priest in the twelfth century, but not all priests preached, and although by the fifteenth century many urban priests preached regularly on Sundays and holy days, lay attendance was not obligatory, and it is difficult to evaluate the influence of this development on laypeople.[30] Another development of the later Middle Ages was the increase in the instruction and catechization of children by priests, and the church produced manuals that gave priests some guidance in the instruction of laypeople.[31]

Preaching and instruction were regarded as secondary to the provision and distribution of sacraments and blessings, which lent themselves to incorporation into popular religion. From the perspective of the church elite, the provision of sacraments through the priests established some ecclesiastical control in directing their use to the appropriate soteriological goal; but laypeople attributed their own meanings to the sacraments, and once distributed, the sacraments could be applied to purposes other than salvation. The sacraments and other objects blessed by the priests were applied to both nomic goals, particularly the insurance of a beneficent natural order, and thaumaturgical goals, ascribing the objects, especially the consecrated Host, with protective and curative properties.[32]

Lay Participation in and Adaptation of Official Religion

During the Middle Ages only a devout minority of laypeople made frequent communion, but a large proportion appear to have adopted the church's condition for inclusion within the church and for a Christian burial by making communion once a year at Easter. Another obligation required by the church was attendance at mass on Sunday and holy days, and although many people did attend, they tended to arrive at different times and to be present at only part of the service. It was common to be present when the priest elevated the Host, holding first the consecrated Host and then the consecrated chalice above his head. The gesture of elevation was understood to mark the point at which Christ became visibly present, to be gazed upon and to be available for supplication. One popular belief was that a person who saw the consecrated Host would be safe from harm for the rest of the day.

The church's teaching that transubstantiation was effected at the point of consecration was understood to mean that the pronunciation of words in a ritual transformed material objects, and this encouraged the thaumaturgical application of the Host. The Eucharist was brought out as a focus of supplication and as a protection against the powers of evil in times of crisis and misfortune; it was used to counter the plague and to protect crops from storms or drought. The healing power of the Eucharist was believed to extend to objects that were laid on the altar while Mass was being celebrated.[33]

Most clergy were ready to perform masses for a wide variety of purposes requested by laypeople: healing, protection against the plague and other epidemics, reducing the pains of women in labor, good weather, and safe journeys. There were, however, purposes for which many priests were unwilling to apply the Host, such as its use as a love charm, and for these objectives some communicants did not swallow the Host and carried it away from the church. Thefts of the communion bread for thaumaturgical purposes also occurred.[34]

A general distinction was made by theologians between the *sacraments*, which had automatic efficacy, and the *sacramentals*, whose effects were contingent on a number of factors.[35] Although understood by the elite to be primarily soteriological, the thaumaturgical value of the sacraments, which was recognized and advocated by the elite, was often uppermost in the minds of laypeople. This was even more the case for the sacramentals, which were ritually blessed elements and objects used in liturgical action, such as the holy water used in baptism and in other ceremonies. The sacramentals were understood to have automatic effects and, in comparison with the sacraments, could more easily be taken outside the control of the clergy.

Objects that had been blessed or from which harmful spirits had been expelled were numerous and varied greatly in their physical nature and components. They included the images, symbols, and remains of supramundanes, such as the crucifix and representations of Christ and the relics of saints; natural objects that were used in rituals, such as water and salt; and crafted objects used in rituals, such as the altar, candles, and church bells. Many such objects were blessed within the official liturgy but used for various purposes outside it. The rosary beads, which church leaders encouraged as a memory aid in the recitation of the rosary prayers, became an object with its own miraculous powers of thaumaturgy, and these powers were believed to be strengthened when the beads were brought into contact with other sacred objects.[36]

Objects of popular religion that were not part of church ritual included natural features such as fountains, objects such as the family hearth, parts of animals, excretions of the human body, herbs and other plants. Some objects were used for a wide variety of purposes: holy water, for example, was used to drive away evil spirits; to protect houses, people, animals, and food; and to overcome sickness and infertility. There was some specialization of purposes: herbs and animal parts were used to cure illnesses, whereas amulets would more commonly be used for protection against potential dangers. Objects that served as amulets, however, included parts of animals bodies as well as official items such as the breve, a slip of paper on which was written the names of the Trinity or words of the gospel, and the agnus dei, an image-bearing wax medallion made from paschal candles. Many objects were used in combination; for example, herbs were compounded with holy water.

Most priests and monks were willing to recite the appropriate prayers, pronounce the suitable blessings, and perform the exorcisms over the various objects as requested by laypeople. Belief in the thaumaturgical power of priests derived from the belief in the effects of their consecration, their decisive role in the transubstantiation of the Host, and their literacy, which, although limited among rural priests, was regarded as a basis for technique and knowledge of the correct formulas. The priest was unlikely, however, to be considered the sole provider or source of thaumaturgy. Apart from the fact that priests did not always succeed in achieving the purposes requested by laypeople, the church imposed restrictions, albeit not always effective, over the aims they could legitimately seek and the means they could legitimately use. In addition, the association of priests with an organization that imposed material obligations, such as tithes, on the people worked against them as exclusive religious practitioners.

Most villages had one or more residents in addition to the priest who had reputations for achieving worldly aims by religious means. They were known by a variety of names, such as wise or cunning men or women, charmers, blessers, conjurers, sorcerers, and witches. Although it was commonly believed that the power of wise people came from a supramundane source, such as God or a particular spirit, their reputations were based primarily on their purported knowledge and techniques that drew on both official and unofficial religion.[37] The religious actions of priests and wise people overlapped, but there were also differences in their goals, in the supramundanes they invoked, in the stances they took toward the supramundanes, in the types of objects they used, and in their religious formulas.

Healing and fertility were perhaps the most common temporal aims requested of priests and wise people, and both specialists would conduct exorcisms when they diagnosed an illness as possession by demons. Certain goals prohibited by the church were likely to be requested from wise people. These included charming or attracting loved or desired persons, inducing abortions, recovering or discovering valued objects, divination, and fortune-telling. Prior to the period of the official witch-hunts, an important service performed by wise people was detecting witches as causes of damage and illness. Certain supramundanes, such as the Holy Ghost and the Virgin Mary, were called on by both priests and wise people; other supramundanes, such as ghosts, fairies, and elves, were declared "superstitions" or were demonized by the church and therefore were less likely to be invoked or ameliorated by the clergy.

Wise people adopted prayers and objects of the church liturgy: paternosters, aves, and creeds as well as the cross, holy water, and many other objects associated with ecclesiastical ritual were assumed by priests and wise persons alike to be efficacious in the attainment of temporal goals. Common also was the belief that herbs with medicinal application would be efficacious only when gathered or applied with the accoutrements of prayers, holy water, and signs of the cross. However, the wise people's removal of phrases and sections of the Christian liturgy from their context and their use of these without regard for their official meaning or purpose were regarded as inappropriate and sacrilegious by church leaders.

In addition to non-official adaptations and reformulations of church liturgy, wise people used many prayers and objects, such as parts of animals and excretions of the human body, that were quite outside official religion. Scholars can trace to pre-Christian times some of the formulas wise people used, but the origins and former meanings of the formulas were of little matter to wise people and their clients, who were concerned, first and foremost, with their efficacy. Church disapproval meant that wise people rather than priests used such techniques as burning or burying an animal alive to effect a cure and employing girths and measures to relieve labor pains.

Even when wise people and priests applied the same prayers and objects to achieve temporal results, the perceived relationship of means and ends could differ. Whereas theologians argued that the means were supplications that might or might not be answered, depending on the moral state of the supplicant, wise people and their clients often assumed a mechanical efficacy or the coercion of the relevant supramundanes to answer their requests. It has been noted, however, that church leaders encouraged belief in the automatic effectiveness of practices by their teaching on the sacraments as operating quite apart from the character of the priests who administered them, and by their recommending the formal repetition of set prayers.[38]

Laypeople decided to approach priests or wise people according to their beliefs and perceptions of which specialist would be the most effective to achieve their particular goals in the particular circumstances, but they were inclined to regard religious action within the church and religious action outside it as parts of one composite religion. Few made distinctions between official and unofficial religion, which were, in fact, in a continual dialectic. Robert Scribner notes a dual process of appropriation: official practices were often reworked in unofficial and sometimes officially disapproved ways, but unofficial practices were also adopted, with appropriate modifications, by church leaders. He points to a number of examples from late medieval times of popular practices, developed on the fringes of the official liturgy, that came to be incorporated into the regular services of the church. The showering of wafers, water, and fire at Pentecost, which developed out of popular demands for more dramatic and participatory rituals with a fertility goal, was appropriated by church leaders who saw such practices as making the feast days more comprehensible to the populace.[39]

Pantheon: Official and Popular

An absolute division between the forces of good and the forces of evil pertained in the official pantheon of the Catholic Church. At the pinnacle of the forces of good was the one God in three persons: God the Father, God the Son, and God the Holy Spirit. Immediately below the Trinity were the Virgin Mary, the saints, and the angels, and at a lower level were the souls of the nonsaintly dead who had achieved salvation and dwelt in heaven together with the higher deities. The forces of evil were headed by Satan, or Lucifer, who was served by demons whose tasks included torturing the souls of the damned in hell. The only category that spanned the distinction of good and evil involved the souls in purgatory, who were destined, after receiving their just punishments, to be received by the forces of good in heaven. The popular pantheon differed from the official one in a number of ways: in the relative prominence of the various official supramundanes; in the additional, non-official supramundanes; in the features and behaviors of the supramundanes; and in the less categorical separation of good and evil.

As in other religions, the most abstract representations of the Supreme Deity, although formally recognized at the apex of the pantheon, were of little relevance in the goal-oriented religious action of most people. God the Father and God as Holy Spirit, represented as distant, pure, and intangible, were rarely approached in popular religion. God the Father was frequently praised in the prayer "Our Father" and was represented in human form, usually as an old man; but although his acts and judgments were invoked as explanations of worldly events, he had a less active role than other supramundanes in the attainment of either soteriological or worldly goals. God's images in the high Middle Ages included that of a feudal lord and judge, presiding over his court of angels and archangels. Peasants saw God as a farmer who understood about the weather and crops, but as a landowner, he did not soil his hands working, and he assigned such tasks to his underlings. There was an awareness of the Holy Spirit because of the formula that was frequently used in the liturgy, "In the name of the Father, of the Son, and of the Holy Spirit," and it was adopted as a popular advocate and seen as a symbol of charity in many parts of Europe from at least the early thirteenth century. The absence of a common iconographic image, however, appears to have limited the province of the Holy Spirit in popular religion.[40]

The backstage position of the Father and the Holy Spirit in popular religion reflected, in part, the Christocentrism of the church: the crucifix was its focal symbol, and the Eucharist, in which Christ was believed to be present, was its focal sacrament. The church taught that God the Son had appeared in the incarnation of the man Jesus to enable humans to return to the perfect state that had existed prior to original sin and the casting out of paradise. The crucifixion of Jesus was a sacrifice of redemption, and because salvation was possible only through him, it was appropriate that he would preside at the Last Judgment. The symbols of Christ were applied to worldly as well as soteriological goals, making him an important figure in popular religion; but the emphasis the church placed on the historicity of Christ's incarnation, death, and resurrection, together with the image of Christ as Judge, resulted in some distancing from the people compared with the Virgin Mary and the saints, who were believed to have "remained" to intercede on behalf of humanity. Although official religion positioned Mary and the saints as lower than Christ because they had no autonomous power and could only intercede with Christ or God the Father, their closeness to humans made them focal supramundanes in popular religion.[41]

The Virgin Mary is the great exception to the masculine gender of the important supramundanes. Mary was not a central figure in the Christian pantheon of the first four centuries, and her centrality in both official and popular Catholicism emerged over a number of centuries from the mutual appropriations and accommodations of the religious elite and the lay masses. Popular devotion of Mary increased from the fifth century onward; representations of the Virgin Mother had become almost as common as those of Jesus by the twelfth century; and most churches in the later Middle Ages had a chapel dedicated to her.[42] Although there was a decline in the number of saints' shrines in some countries during the early modern period, Marian shrines continued to proliferate, and the nineteenth and early twentieth centuries saw a number of signs of increased devotion to Mary: new religious orders of women and new lay organizations were dedicated to her; local Marian associations increased in number; and apparitions of Mary were reported more frequently. The church encouraged many of these manifestations, and only in the 1960s did it attempt to subordinate the worship of Mary to God.[43] A recent investigation of Catholic pilgrimage shrines in Western Europe found that about 66 percent of the shrines were devoted to Mary, 27 percent were devoted to other saints, and 8 percent centered on Christ.[44]

The Catholic Church has formulated four dogmas concerning Mary: her virginity, her divine motherhood, her immaculate conception, and her assumption, body and soul, into heaven. Virgin motherhood, which was declared by the councils of the early church, was the major sign of Mary's supramundane nature. In the early Middle Ages the theme of the Virgin's mother love was less prominent than the image of the Queen of Heaven, the mother of the God-Emperor. As a symbol of power, Mary's regal role supported the church's authority on earth, and the image also had an affinity with aristocratic notions of the pure lady, the object of courtly love.

The chastity of a wife was of special importance in a patrilineal society, in which inheritance passed in the male line; and among the aristocracy, where the rank and property of women were dependent on males, Mary, as a woman who owed her position to her son, was an appropriate object of devotion. Peasants encountered a contradiction between Mary in her image as a distant queen and Mary as a supramundane who was close enough to answer their worldly requests, and they found a greater affinity with the image, fostered by the mendicant orders, of a gentle, forgiving, indulgent, and merciful mother. The "feminine" virtues of humility, submissiveness, obedience, patience, and purity came to be associated with Mary.[45]

The doctrine of the immaculate conception, which declared that from the moment of her conception Mary was exempt from original sin, was only given the official imprint of the pope in 1854, but from the early centuries of Christianity, it was widely believed that the conception and birth of Mary had been a special miracle. The doctrine has been a popular one since the Middle Ages, and when it was explicitly formulated during the twelfth century, it quickly became a matter of controversy and continued to be discussed within the church for centuries.[46] The assumption of Mary was also given the status of official dogma centuries after it became commonly accepted among Catholics. Whereas the Feast of the Assumption is perhaps the principal and oldest of all Marian feasts, the pronouncement of the doctrine in a papal bull was made only in 1950.[47]

The church taught that salvation can come only from God, but its Marian teachings have given the Virgin Mother a central place in its soteriological scheme. Mary was understood to have influence both over humans on earth, inspiring them to repent their sins, and over the Judge in heaven. Present in body and soul by the side of her son-God, and untainted by original sin, she was the ideal woman and mother, submissive, pure, and gentle, who pleaded for mercy on behalf of less-perfect souls. It was believed that Mary could postpone the death of sinners until they repented, and miracle stories told of her resurrections of the dead, enabling sinners to confess, repent, and then die again, this time in grace. Like those of other saints, Mary's intercessions could transfer souls from the fires of purgatory to the joys of heaven, and her pleas were understood to be especially effective because a good son does not refuse the supplications of his mother. With a greater sympathy for human weakness, and subject herself to flattery, Mary softened the judgments of her son.[48]

The agencies of the church encouraged the worship of Mary as a means of directing religious action toward salvation, as opposed to the devotions to the saints for worldly goals. The mendicant orders, in particular, propagated Mary as a symbol of the universal church, as an alternative to the local saint shrines. The religious elite qualified their support for Mary by the wording of prayers to indicate that she was an intercessor, who could not directly grant requests and could work only through Christ. This qualification made little, if any, impression on the masses who saw Mary as the most efficacious agency with respect to both salvation and terrestrial goals,[49] and in some countries, particularly Italy and Spain, a large number of rituals have focused on Mary with no reference to Christ.[50]

Many devotees, especially women, have turned to Mary as the Virgin, Divine Mother to promote their fertility, to help in childbirth by quickening the birth process and reducing the birth pains, and to help them with sick or injured children.[51] Mary's association with fertility in popular religion is particularly evident where she is worshiped in the form of a black image, as in parts of Italy. Christian iconography associated black with evil, but for peasants it was the color of the fertility of the soil. Black madonnas were also believed to have the power to overcome the plague and to bring justice for peasants against their class oppressors.[52] Popular religion also, however, included representations of Mary as a vengeful goddess who punished those who opposed her wishes or failed to worship her in an appropriate manner. The theme of impious people being severely punished by Mary is found in association with a number of Marian shrines in Italy, and beliefs that, for example, Mary's touch could cause bleeding or other bodily damage are in clear contradiction with the image of Mary conveyed by official Catholicism. Mary's castigations were not limited to the punishment of sin, as defined by the church, but were understood to be motivated by her craving for veneration and her concern that people recognize her position and power.[53] To protect themselves from the potential danger in Mary's power, it was common for Italians to place veils over her images, a practice that was condemned by members of the church elite but accepted by local clergy.[54]

The church elite promoted Mary as a single individual who was the Virgin Mother of Jesus Christ, but these official connotations were rarely evoked in the Marian titles of popular religion, which indicated Mary's dispensation of favors or her association with a particular place or community. Each Mary of popular religion has a separate identity, with her own legends, shrine, distinctive look, and sacred days.[55] Most legends tell how Mary, by an apparition or sign, made known her desire to be worshiped in a particular place in a shrine to be built by the community. The place she chose, whether near water or particular trees or on cliffs or peaks, was often one of significance to the peasant community and provided an alternative to the sacred places of the official church.[56] In Italy, the shrines of the most popular madonnas are located in rural locations, and bonds have developed between a particular Mary and a nearby city, as in the case of Florence and a Madonna located just south of the city.[57]

Catholicism has had a number of female saints apart from Mary, and Mary's mother, Saint Anne, became a popular saint in the later Middle Ages. Like Mary, Saint Anne was believed to promote fertility and to help mothers with their sick and injured children. As the matriarch of a multigenerational holy family, she was called on to authorize the dynastic claims of rulers and to protect the families of aristocrats.[58] Most saints, however, both official and popular, have been male.

At various times the church elite has attempted to promote devotions to Mary and Christ over those to the saints, but it should not be concluded that the saints were a product of popular religion. As in the case of Mary, the forms of religious action focusing on the saints were outcomes of the dynamic relationships between official and popular religion. The development in Christianity of what is commonly called the cult of saints, revolving around shrines, relics, and other paraphernalia, was interpreted in the past as the church's concession to polytheistic populations to facilitate their conversion—and after their conversion as the vulgarized Christianity of the ignorant masses. It is true that saints often took the place of the "pagan" gods in the Christianizing process, but instead of being a grudging accommodation to popular religion, the development of worship centered on saints' shrines was initiated and patronized by bishops in their building of strong ecclesiastical structures linked to political consolidations and economic growth. Economic and political interests were in affinity with religious dispositions: the elite of the church ardently venerated the saints and believed in their miracles.[59]

In comparison with the Christianity of the eastern Mediterranean, where there was more devotion of living saints as intercessors, the Occidental church attempted to resolve the tension between the routinized charisma of office and the personal charisma of living holy people by encouraging the worship of dead saints. Living persons recognized as saints because of their exemplary asceticism and devotions were difficult for the church to control, but once they were dead, the official hagiographies presented them as exemplars of orthodox, official doctrines and practice, and the saints' power was channeled in the church's interests.[60] The saints were commemorated on feast days, typically on the purported anniversaries of their deaths, and their miracles were systematically recorded.[61]

Offerings to saints provided a source of income for monasteries and churches, and as protectors and patrons of those institutions, the saints reinforced the prestige of abbots and bishops, who were the representatives of the saints in this world and possible candidates for sainthood after they passed on to the next. The monasteries were the major context of canonization in the early centuries of the church; episcopal canonization became an established practice in the tenth and eleventh centuries, and papal canonization developed gradually with the growth of papal authority. Episcopal and papal canonization coexisted for some time, but from the late twelfth century, papal commissions were charged with investigating every formal request, and the number of petitions declined as the procedures became more complicated and expensive.[62]

The thirteenth and fourteenth centuries saw some change in emphasis in the type of ecclesiastics adopted as official saints. The monks who renounced the world gave way to bishops who were portrayed as distinguishing themselves by their efforts to save others. Most official saints were clergy, and almost all had occupied positions in the higher ranks of the church; only one parish priest was canonized in the Middle Ages. Saints from the laity, with the exception of a few lay hermits, were generally holders of power, mostly kings and princes. The belief, prevalent in the early medieval period, that noble birth was a precondition of the moral and spiritual perfection of saints continued in northern Europe in later centuries, but in southern Europe the religious values of humility and poverty, promoted by the mendicant orders, reduced the proportion of saints from aristocratic and royal families. Lay saints from modest backgrounds tended to be merchants and artisans; it was exceptional for an official saint to have rural origins. Whatever the official saints' origins, the hagiographic texts and collection of their miracles were the work of educated clerics.[63]

The notion of the saint as intercessor was formulated by the early church, which taught that the martyrs passed immediately into God's presence and that, having accumulated a store of merit, they could protect others and intercede for them. When the notion of sainthood was extended from martyrs to others, such as dead bishops, intercession remained a central belief, and although the church came to be sensitive to criticisms of saints' cults, the Council of Trent in 1563 proclaimed that the saints reigned with Christ and justified seeking their help. The number of papal canonizations were few, however: eight in the fourteenth century, sixteen in the fifteenth, six in the sixteenth, twenty-four in the seventeenth, and twenty-nine in the eighteenth.[64] In the official procedures for canonization established in the early seventeenth century, miraculous intercession after death was one of the three general requirements (the other two were doctrinal purity and heroic virtue) that candidates for sainthood, apart from martyrs, had to satisfy.[65] Theologians taught that the saints' ability to perform miracles stemmed from their exemplary virtues, but the more popular understanding was that the saints' miraculous abilities and their heroic virtues were both manifestations of their supramundane powers.[66]

The various transformations of saints in popular Christianity resulted in considerable differences regarding their meanings and representations among the elite and the lay masses. The incorporation of the lay masses in the worship of official saints was only partially successful, and the number of popular saints multiplied far beyond those canonized by the church. Between 1185 and 1431 there were seventy petitions for canonization, of which half were successful, but there were hundreds of popular saints.

Church leaders contributed to the hagiocentric popular religion by their supply and distribution of saints' relics, which were placed in churches and cathedrals. Relics were objects of devotion long before the spread of saints' images, and ecclesiastics argued that relics were superior to images because they would be part of the resurrection. The popular response was enthusiastic; as concrete objects, relics appeared to afford direct and immediate contact with the sources of supramundane power, and the saints, through their relics, were felt to be forever alive and participating in communities. In encouraging the demand for relics, which gave rise to duplications, thefts, and transfers, ecclesiastics might be seen to have acted in contradiction to their official doctrine of the centrality of God and the Christ, but the provision of saints' relics was an important way by which the church attempted to regulate the consumption of religious items.[67]

The most sought-after relics were the saints' bodily remains, ranging from the whole corpse or skeleton to minute fragments of bone and portions of blood. Other types of relics were items that had been used by the saints, such as clothing and devotional articles, their writings, and pieces of the places where they had resided. The church attempted to limit supply and circulation by opposing previously unknown relics and forbidding that relics be taken out of churches or kept in private homes. Apart from the problem of new relics, however, the possibility of dividing up most relics into small pieces resulted in an elastic supply that was difficult for the church to control. The supply of relics extended to the worship of Mary, although the belief that Mary had ascended body as well as soul into heaven had the effect of limiting her relics to such objects as phials of her milk and her nail parings.[68]

The saints and Mary were called on principally in popular Catholicism for their thaumaturgical powers in achieving this-worldly goals. This involved some displacement of the hierarchy of goals associated with the saints in official Christianity. The elite presented saints as models of holiness who, by rejecting this-worldly pleasures and mortifying the flesh, demonstrated to others the appropriate path to salvation. The masses subordinated the soteriologically linked motifs of the saints to their own everyday concerns: the healing of humans and their animals, recovering stolen objects, arranging marriages, and protecting households from thieves, harmful weather, and evil spirits. Two healing saints, Sebastian and Roche, who provided protection against the plague, were worshiped at one time throughout Catholic Christendom, and there were many other saints who specialized in particular illnesses, such as eye troubles or deafness, or in special protection, such as from insects or fire. Nonspecialized saints, including Mary, were also greatly preoccupied with curing illnesses.[69] Cures and other dispensations were effected by a wide variety of procedures that were seen as providing some contact with the saint: for instance, touching the saints' shrines, images, and relics and drinking the water used to wash them.[70]

In popular religion, saints were bestowed with the emotional attributes typical of humans, and far from being models of mercy and forgiveness, they exacted cruel punishment if they felt slighted or cheated. Saints were subject to humiliation or punishment through their relics and images if it was believed they had refused a request or failed in achieving their devotees' goals; relics were placed in the ground covered with thorns, and images were whipped or pelted with mud and water.[71]

Popular local religion focusing on saints had its own sacred objects, locations, and calendar with its particular feast and fast days that differed from, and occasionally conflicted with, those of the church. The church made attempts to eliminate local practices around the saints, but although the church might succeed in pressuring people to observe a ritual, it was largely unsuccessful in preventing observances. Conflict could occur between a local community and church agencies if the community arranged a celebration around its saint on a day of obligatory rituals in the church calendar, but in general, two pantheons and sacred geographies coexisted and often fused with each other. The generalized devotions propagated by the nonlocated institutions of the church, such as mendicant and teaching orders, missionaries, and the Vatican, were directed to the individual and family and lacked the component of community solidarity and identity of the local shrines. Until recent times, local communities thwarted the attempts of the elite to integrate them within "great tradition" Christianity by appropriating the generalized devotions and focusing them on the shrine.[72]

In contrast to the saints, the angels had never taken human form, and although they occasionally manifested themselves as divine messengers, their incorporeal, timeless natures made them unsuitable as foci of popular shrines and community identities. They were regarded nevertheless as an important category of the powers of good; it was a common belief that each person had a guardian angel who acted as a guide, and their assistance was invoked in worldly matters. The "fallen angels," the rebellious beings who had been cast out of heaven to become Satan and his demons, were represented in more material forms. Ecclesiastics portrayed Satan as the tempter, luring persons into sin and damnation, but popular religion blurred the distinction made by theologians between Satan, the prince of evil, and his servants and followers, the demons. Laypeople concerned themselves with the damage that devils or demons could cause in this world, especially their responsibility for psychological illnesses and their power to possess people against their will.

Terror of demons was cultivated by the religious elite as a means of control, but in popular religion the horrific was sometimes interwoven with the humorous, and the forces of evil were subjected to ridicule. By representing the devil as a buffoon as well as the source of evil, peasants used humor to defuse the threat of a being who had the power to bring them to perdition.[73] Peasants also told stories of demons doing good, and they did not necessarily share the assumption of the church elite that demons had an ulterior evil motive when they assisted people. In general, peasants were less inclined than the elite to accept an absolute distinction between the powers of good and the powers of evil. Just as saints could be maleficent, demons could be beneficent.

The ghosts or souls of the dead who haunted the living were one category of supramundanes that straddled the division of good and evil. Popular beliefs that family members who had died still needed and desired the services of the living, and that without this assistance they returned to trouble the living, were appropriated by the church elite to support their moral teachings and the notion of purgatory. Theologians did not dispute the possibility of ghosts, although some emphasized that it was God alone who permitted the apparitions; the dead could not choose to return to earth, and the living had no means to conjure their return.

Ecclesiastics taught that the dead in heaven and hell could not return but that those who had been consigned to purgatory could be sent back to earth for specific reasons: they might remind the living of such obligations to the church as the payment of tithes; they acted as witnesses to the living of the tortures that awaited them if they did not mend their ways; they sought help from the living to shorten their stay in purgatory, thereby encouraging the practice of saying masses for the dead. One belief was that God let souls remain in purgatory if no masses were said for them, and that the ghosts of these souls visited the living to plead for their help in expiating their sins. Among laypeople, the clergy's explanations for the appearances of ghosts were absorbed into a system of exchange between the living and the dead: the living said prayers and gave offerings for the souls of the dead who, after their entrance into heaven, would intercede on behalf of their benefactors.

The reasons peasants gave for the return of souls were more extensive than those among the church elite, and they did not necessarily have moral connotations. Souls returned as ghosts to take revenge for some hurt done to them, and out of maliciousness or exaggerated notions of what was due to them, they were responsible for illnesses and misfortunes of the living. The popular notion of ghosts included the recently deceased, who sought a companion to take with them to the "other world," and the "untimely dead," those who had died before their time because of accident or foul play. A fusion of official and folk beliefs was evident in the festivals associated with the dead: All Saints' Day, the festival of the deceased who had ascended to heaven, was followed by All Souls' Day, the festival of all the other dead, including those in purgatory and hell.[74]

In addition to supramundanes who were part of the official and popular pantheons, albeit in different guises, were a multitude of supramundanes in the popular religion who had no place in the official religion: nature spirits, leprechauns, dwarves, elves, goblins, sprites, and fairies. The non-official spirits could assist or harm people depending on circumstances of time and place and on their relationships with the humans involved. Elves, for example, were conceived as ambivalent, amoral creatures, invisible or hard to see, whose malicious attacks could be remedied by various means, including charms and Christian liturgy. The church elite condemned such practices as leaving food and drink out for elves or fairies, and the elite absorbed the elves and other such supramundanes within their paradigm of good and evil by categorizing them as demons or as diabolical illusions. Some demons came to take on an elflike appearance as grinning, small, rotund creatures, but in popular religion the elves remained, like other spirits, a distinctive category of supramundanes.[75]

In addition to supramundane beings, the means and conditions of popular religion included objects and processes whose inherent qualities or relationships with one another were deemed relevant to the achievement of this-worldly goals. The evil eye, sometimes with and sometimes without intention, was held to be the cause of many illnesses, misfortunes, and failures in goal attainment. Beliefs in the inherent quality of particular times, such as lucky and unlucky days, were widespread, and although many ecclesiastics opposed such notions, the elite's attribution of symbolic significance to many dates in the year probably reinforced the conception of time as uneven in quality. Church leaders also rejected the widespread beliefs in omens, such as that the appearance or behavior of particular animals was a sign of misfortune to come, but it is doubtful whether their statements led to any reduction in the large number of actions and objects that were thought to bring protection or to cause harm.

The reasons for why some actions and objects rather than others had purported consequences were rarely examined; for example, no one knew or attempted to discover why some days rather than others were unlucky.[76] Astrology was an exception insofar as belief in the influence on earthly events and individuals of the planets, stars, and their constellations rested on theoretical assumptions of the educated concerning the working of an organic universe and the links and correspondences between its different parts. Peasants held beliefs in the influence of certain heavenly bodies, especially the moon, on crops and on human physiology, and there may have been some worshiping of planetary deities, but astrology in the Middle Ages was confined mainly to the courts, aristocracy, and higher church officials.[77]

Environments of Religious Action

Values

Like other world religions, Catholicism has dealt with the tensions between world renunciation and providing the conditions of support for the continuation of the religion. Eastern religions have defused the tension by various forms of differentiation between virtuoso monks, who renounce the world, and professional priests or monk-priests, who perform religious services for laypeople. With some limited exceptions, such as monkhood as a "rite of passage" among young males in some Buddhist countries, the lay masses in the East have remained outside the religious associations of monks and priests. Although popular religion in the East has been greatly influenced by the institutionalized interaction of laypeople with both the priest-type and the virtuoso-type monks, patterns of religious action of monks and laypeople have developed within relatively differentiated institutional complexes. Catholicism, in contrast, has incorporated virtuosos, priests, and the lay masses within a single hierocracy, and it is the structure of the hierocracy that provides the major environmental factor of the differences and interaction between official and nonofficial and between elite and popular religion.

The hierocratic structure and the patterns of religious action are related to the value complex of Catholic universalism. Two aspects of universalism in Catholicism are of relevance in considering the extent to which elites and masses differed in their patterns of religious action. The first was the separation of Christianity from a particular people and social order. After its break from the ethnically Jewish church, the universalist theology of the church and its efforts to convert all peoples to the faith encouraged the development of a hierocracy that would incorporate all believers. The second aspect was the promotion of a soteriological goal, common to all, which limited the development of the dual standards and differentiated patterns of religious action characteristic of Hinduism and Buddhism. Distinctions between virtuosos and ordinary Christians were made with reference to the paths to salvation, but the differences between the virtuoso pattern of renunciation of the world and lay accommodation to the world were not as great as in the Eastern religions.

Within the Catholic Church, renunciation of the world was subordinated to sponsoring and sustaining the hierocracy, and the interpenetration of other-worldly and worldly orientations was expressed in the doctrines of Christ as both man and God and of the church as the "City of God" and "Body of Christ." Among virtuoso monks, the accomplishment of perfection in this world tended to become an end in itself, and an active path of perfectionism developed in addition to the contemplative path. The very notion of renunciation came to be understood as incorporation within the church, because the term *world*, the realm of matter and evil spirits, was regarded as a synonym for all the social institutions outside the church, the City of God.[78] The participation of virtuosos in the social order of the church was not perceived, therefore, as an accommodation to the world but rather as a rejection of the social order outside the church. Thus, the values of universalism and the associated interlinking of worldly and other-worldly orientations limited the differences among the patterns of religious action of virtuosos, priests, and laypeople.

Structure of Religious Organization

More than in any other world religion, the personal charisma of virtuosos in Catholicism was controlled and directed by the hierocratic elite, in order to strengthen the church's supply and distribution of religious benefits to the majority. By providing and supporting monasteries, the hierocracy contained and neutralized the anti-institutional implications of the world-rejecting orientation. Monasticism began as a lay institution, but by the high Middle Ages it had become clericalized, with the monks constituting an estate alongside the "secular" clergy. The concern of world renouncers to reduce their social contacts to a minimum was accommodated within the monasteries by such means as providing cells removed from the proximity of other monks and by regulations that forbade verbal communication among the monks.

Hermits, who lived as recluses outside the monasteries, were worrisome to the church elite. By separating themselves from the institutions of the church, such hermits could attract the devotion of laypeople and possibly become foci of heterodoxy. Ecclesiastics attempted to avoid these possibilities by encouraging those who wished to be solitaries to serve as novitiates before moving into the solitary life, or to make their monastic profession to a bishop and vow to spend their lives in a cell.

At first, monasteries developed somewhat independently of the ecclesiastical hierarchy, but the threat of separate organizations of virtuosos was averted by conferring on bishops the role of visitor or supervisor of the monasteries within their dioceses. Some bishops founded monasteries and encouraged the adoption of particular rules that were expected to govern the organization of the monasteries and the religious action of the monks. Not all monasteries were dependent on the support and protection of the bishops, but the religious orders that maintained a high degree of autonomy from the dioceses in their locations or area of activity were likely to fall under the more direct control of the papacy. New monastic orders submitted their rules for approval to papal authorities, which often required them to make modifications.[79]

Many monks remained segregated from the "secular" clergy and laity, but some orders adopted priestly roles, such as hearing confessions, preaching, and praying on behalf of others, especially the dead, in return for endowments and donations. The adoption of these roles increased the interaction of monks with laypeople, but this interaction was channeled along the lines of role performance approved by the church. By these measures church officials restricted the possibility of laypeople turning to virtuoso monks and treating them as saints who could provide the means to achieve goals independent of the church. Ecclesiastics promoted the worship of dead saints, who were chosen from the ranks of past bishops as well as past monks. Many of the saints worshiped by laypeople were not officially recognized, but the fact that most of them were dead restricted the potential dangers of popular religion to the church.

The distinction between virtuosos and the masses was less central in Catholicism than in the Eastern religions because of the priority of the distinction between clergy and laity.[80] Few monks were virtuosos, but because most virtuosos were monks who had received ordination, the distinction between clergy and laity overlapped in part with the distinction between virtuosos and ordinary Christians. The overlap was a limited one because some laypeople did become virtuosos and were recognized by the church as saints; but more important, most clergy were not virtuosos. In general, the control of virtuosos by the church gave laypeople fewer opportunities than in the East to accommodate the religious action of living virtuosos to the thaumaturgical goals of popular religion, and insofar as laypeople interacted with monks, it was likely to occur when monks acted as priests rather than as virtuosos.

For most laypeople, the major contact with the church was the parish priest rather than the monks. The friars and mendicant monks often preached and performed sacraments for laypeople, especially in the towns, but unlike the parish clergy, they were not the foci of local religious life. The development of the parish system was slow; it was not completed until the eleventh or twelfth century in most European countries, and in the northern and eastern peripheries of Europe the process took longer. The initiative for the formation of most rural parishes came from local residents rather than the church elite, and many parish priests owed their position to local, lay patronage.[81] Once established, however, the church's centrality through the parish in local religious life weakened the possibility that other institutions and organizations, such as the family or village associations, could become alternative religious authorities and suppliers of religious benefits.

Parishes and their priests were the lowest level in a hierarchical organization that became increasingly rationalized and centralized from the eleventh century onward, but until the early modern and modern periods, organizational factors limited the filtering down of the official religion, expounded by the occupants of the higher rungs, to the parish level. A number of parishes formed a diocese, ruled by a bishop; dioceses were grouped together to form provinces, presided over by archbishops; and provinces in turn were grouped under the direction of metropolitan archbishops. Above the metropolitans was the pope in Rome, whose power, accompanied by an increasingly large and complex administration, grew from the middle of the eleventh century.[82] Decisions over church doctrine, which from the early fourth century had been undertaken by the General Council of bishops, came to be reached by agreement between the General Council and the pope who assumed responsibility for convening the council. There was some weakening of the power of the bishops within their dioceses after 1300, and by 1500, bishops no longer had authority over all the clergy in their dioceses.[83]

The gradual centralization of ecclesiastical authority in the papacy had important implications for the higher ranks of the hierarchy but little influence on the majority of parish priests, whose contacts with the bishops and other high ranks continued to be minimal and infrequent. Parish priests were dependent on bishops for their ordination and the consecration of their churches, and the bishops could make their influence felt by visiting parishes and issuing decrees to be read out in parish churches. Although members of the church elite in the Middle Ages expressed opposition to elements in popular religion, few bishops concerned themselves with the reform of religion among peasants or with the discipline of the clergy in their dioceses.

One reason few bishops attempted to influence and build connections with parish priests was that their authority over the priests was restricted by powerful laypeople. Bishops controlled the large churches or minsters that had been established in the urban centers of the Mediterranean region, but many churches in rural districts were founded by landowners who treated the churches as their property and the priests as their tenants. As the church became a more rationalized and powerful hierocracy, property and personnel were increasingly extricated from the hands of lay rulers and landowners, and episcopal ordination became a more crucial factor in the appointment of priests, but lay patronage continued to limit the bishops' authority over both the appointments and the discipline of priests.[84] Parish priests of privately owned churches in subsistence villages had little contact with the clergy of minsters or urban churches, and when they were subject to the competing influences of the ecclesiastical hierarchy and their lay parishioners, their dependence on lay patrons and their socioeconomic position as villeins inclined them to accept the lay demands.[85]

Few priests received a structured training prior to their ordination, and most gained some elementary knowledge, including a minimum of Latin, by a form of apprenticeship with a local priest. In many cases ordinands were sons of priests, and they learned their skills from their fathers. The clergy who were charged by the bishops to examine ordinands were generally satisfied if the candidate could read Latin without necessarily understanding it, showed a familiarity with the church calendar, and knew how to celebrate the sacraments. Few priests had access to the complete text of the Bible, and their knowledge of the Bible was often limited to those parts that were read at Mass. From the thirteenth century on, instructional texts were prepared to aid priests in their roles as preachers, confessors, teachers, and pastors, but the theological ideas discussed in the universities rarely filtered down from the elite to the lower clergy.

Most rural priests were born and socialized in the area of their parishes; they dressed like their parishioners and worked with them in the fields, and there was little to distinguish them economically from other villagers. The priests collected tithes and payments due to the church, but they retained only a small part of these revenues. Church reformers succeeded in eradicating the practice of marriage among priests despite the opposition of rural priests who, like other peasants, worked with their families as economic units. The taking of concubines by clerics remained widespread, and although formally condemned, it was regarded in the church with more tolerance than marriage because it did not constitute a threat to church property.[86]

Religious and Socioeconomic Hierarchies

One factor that affected the degree of incorporation of local religious units and their priests into the wider church was the relationship of the church to the temporal political authorities. As was the case of religion in all traditional societies, Catholicism legitimized political rulers and the social hierarchy, but from a comparative perspective of world religions, it has had a high degree of corporate autonomy from temporal authorities; it was not incorporated into the state, as was Confucianism in China, or encompassed by social strata, as was Hinduism in India, and as a separate ecclesiastical structure, it achieved a far greater independence from temporal authorities than the Buddhist Sangha. Historically, the degree of corporate autonomy of the church has varied considerably. At the beginning of the period under review, the twelfth century, members of the church elite who came to be collectively known as the Gregorian movement succeeded in asserting independent property rights of the church and in wresting from secular authorities the right to invest bishops and priests. These changes served to reduce the influence of the aristocracy over ecclesiastical units and offices, although the kings and a few powerful aristocrats continued to take an important and sometimes decisive part in the appointment of senior church officials.[87]

From the perspective of ecclesiastics, the ideal relationship of church and state was a dual but mutually supportive system of spiritual and temporal governments. In return for the king's support of the church's autonomy, his protection of its religious monopolism, and his generous patronage, the church legitimized and supported his rule. The king's hereditary right was combined with a divine right acquired through his consecration by the church as "God's anointed." Kings with aspirations of spiritual authority were inclined to see their consecration as parallel to that of bishops and to claim a sacred status equal to them. In contrast, ecclesiastics emphasized the differences in the ceremonies of anointing and denied the kings any share in the distribution of divine grace. The kings were not priests and none attempted to celebrate the mass, but their consecration appeared to lift them out of the category of ordinary laypeople, who were entirely subordinate to the clergy in spiritual matters. The status of kings as sacred persons was expressed in belief in their thaumaturgical powers, and for many centuries the claims of the kings of France and England that they could cure people of scrofula simply by their touch were widely accepted.[88]

Belief in the thaumaturgical powers and divine status of kings possibly contributed to conceptions of the heavenly hierarchy as a mirror of the feudal hierarchy, with God as a king surrounded by his court of vassals, the angels and archangels, who gave homage and fealty. The king, like God, was a distant figure whose influence was rarely felt directly by most peasants, who lived their lives within the frame of reference of their villages. Of greater relevance were the local lords, lawgivers, and judges, and it is the relationship of dependence and clientage with these local rulers that has been interpreted as the model for laypeople's relationships with the saints, often the most important supramundanes in the religion of peasants. The decline of secular patronage in postfeudal societies was not, however, accompanied by an equivalent decline in the practices of divine patronage, and the systems of secular patronage vary too widely to account for the common characteristics of the devotion of saints.[89]

The analogies or parallels of relationships with human authorities and with supramundanes are far from exact, and popular conceptions of supramundanes often seem to be reactions against the prevailing relationships with human oppressors.[90] The patron-client relationship appears a more appropriate model for the perspective on saints in official religion, with the emphasis on an asymmetrical exchange implicated in a relationship of unequals, than in popular religion, with its expressions of familiarity with saints. The mutual benefits gained by supplicants and saints in their symmetrical exchange of gifts may be interpreted as expressions of relationships among neighborly peasants, ideally portrayed in terms of community and equality.[91]

A considerable overlap between the religious hierarchy and socioeconomic hierarchy contributed to the differences between the religion of the church elite and the religion of the masses. Throughout the Middle Ages and the early modern period, the majority of high-ranking ecclesiastics, including monks, were recruited from the upper strata of society, especially the aristocracy, and the majority of rural parish priests were recruited from the free peasantry. By channeling a number of their members into monasteries and the high ranks of the church, aristocratic families avoided the fragmentation of their lands, thereby preserving the basis of their wealth and class position. Once primogeniture became the rule, sons who had no prospect of inheriting land were able to continue the aristocratic lifestyle and a high status by becoming abbots in monasteries or bishops, and convents also provided a solution for "surplus" or unmarried daughters. Aristocratic families would commonly give large gifts to the monasteries to which they offered their sons, often at a young age, and when they founded churches with large revenues, the noble lords granted the clerical offices to kinsmen or clients. In the later Middle Ages, the recruitment of monks widened to include the lower nobility and more prosperous peasants and townspeople. The thirteenth-century mendicant orders, in particular, recruited from a wider socioeconomic range, but those from the lower strata entered monasteries as lay brothers, and when they succeeded in becoming monks, they seldom rose to important offices.[92]

Not only were the bishops and other high ranks of the church distanced from the peasants (including rural priests) by estate and class, but the church's extensive land ownership meant that the relationship of the church elite and many peasants was that of lord and peasant. During the Middle Ages, church primates managed their estates like other aristocrats, and high church offices with their attendant property were transferred in much the same way as fiefs.[93]

The aristocratic origins of the church elite and the importance of the church as landowner might appear to support the associations made by a number of authors between the Catholic "great tradition" with the ruling classes and the "little tradition" with the peasantry.[94] The question remains, however, of whether the aristocracy as a whole was influenced by the religion espoused by the church elite, as well as the extent to which aristocrats participated in the popular religion of the peasants. Literacy is a relevant factor here, and apart from a few royal and noble families, most lords during the Middle Ages, like most peasants, were illiterate.[95] Robert Anderson recognizes that it is important not to confuse the aristocracy as a whole with the literate elite, but he argues that the religion of the aristocrats differed substantially from the highly syncretic popular religion of the peasants, and that there was little mutual acculturation between aristocrats and peasants in traditional Europe. He writes that, as early as the tenth century, aristocrats were instructed in monasteries and by chaplains, and that although few aristocrats read much of the Bible, their association with the church elite gave them a superior religious knowledge to that of most peasants.[96]

The social basis of aristocratic culture, to which the peasantry did not have access, was a network of families and circles spread throughout Europe, with cultural centers, notably the courts, whose influence was diffused throughout noble society.[97] The existence of a distinctive aristocratic culture does not mean, however, that aristocrats did not share a popular religion with the peasants. The interests of medieval lords in the activities of the villages within their domains went far beyond the collection of taxes and rents, and they concerned themselves, together with the church, in the regulation of marriage, family, and community.[98] Pieter Spierenburg writes that, whereas the popular culture was the only culture of the majority, the aristocracy was bicultural; in addition to the culture of the courts and patrician mansions, aristocrats participated in various events of the villages, such as the carnival and religious festivals.[99] Thus, although each possessed cultural distinctiveness, there was also cultural overlap between the two, and up to the last decades of the seventeenth century, the aristocracy and peasantry participated together in popular religion.

totalitarianism perhaps comes from total confidence in a particular theory of social life

8

Elite Scholars and Popular Saints

A Brief Excursus on Islam and Judaism

Judaism and Islam have shared with Christianity an exclusivism that requires the building and maintenance of boundaries separating the religion from other traditions. The religious elites of Islam and Judaism referred to clearly delineated canons in promoting their great traditions, and they drew lines between official and unofficial religion. In neither case, however, was there a hierocracy similar to the Catholic Church, whose elite was able to present the institution as the carrier of the great tradition and apply sanctions of the institution, as well as the sanctions of the political regimes that supported it, against non-official religion. The differentiation of political and religious elites in Islamic states that followed on the political-religious fusion of the early Islamic leadership rarely left the *ulema*, the religious elite, with an institutional focus of power independent of the rulers. The largely self-governing Jewish communities that existed in Islamic and Eastern European states into the twentieth century had a number of legal sanctions at their command to exercise social control and maintain religious conformity, but although the more prestigious rabbis could influence decisions and policies, whatever power they exercised was dependent on the governing bodies of lay officials and elders.

Rabbis and ulema were first and foremost scholars and interpreters of the systems of religious law, the *halachah* in Judaism and the *sharia* in Islam, to which all Jews and Muslims were understood to be bound. In both religions the laws contained in the first, or core, texts of the canons, the Pentateuch and the Quran, were greatly expanded on by oral traditions that, when written down, became the basis of further additions and interpretations. The vast compendium of Jewish law known as the Talmud was the focus of commentaries and responses from the rabbis, who also made the law accessible to the majority by writing handbooks, such as the famous *Shulhan Arukh*, which was first published in the sixteenth century. With the elaboration of the Sunna, the examples and statements attributed to the prophet Muhammad as embodied in the *hadith*, or tradition literature, the sharia came to resemble the halachah in its range of jurisdiction and complexity. For the majority of Muslims, conformity to the law was simplified by reference to the "five pillars of Islam": profession of the faith, prayer five times daily, almsgiving, fasting during the month of Ramadan, and pilgrimage to Mecca.[1] In actual practice, the degree of emphasis put on each of the pillars has been highly variable, and beyond minimal formal requirements, there has been considerable diversity of religious behavior among Muslim communities.[2]

The basis of the elite status of the ulema and rabbis was their learning and expertise in the religious law. Some taught in advanced religious schools, and many received honors and recognition of their status in mosques and synagogues, which were often places of study as well as prayer; but unlike Catholic priests, they did not conduct rites, administer sacraments, or assume control over parishes or congregations. There was no clear division between an elite who occupied official positions and serviced laypeople and an elite of virtuosos. The virtuosos were simply those who by virtue of their exceptional scholarship and pious lives were regarded as exemplars of the religious life.

There was no hierarchization of elites and masses in terms of lower and higher soteriological goals, nor was there a higher path to salvation, such as the supererogatory piety of monastic Christianity. The tendencies of religious egalitarianism in Islam and Judaism, albeit confined to males, were particularly evident in traditional Jewish communities, in which the vast majority of males received some formal religious education. The emphasis placed on the value of the study of the Torah for all Jewish men prevented a sharp division between a literate religious elite and an illiterate lay mass. In Judaism as in Islam, however, the vast development of commentaries and interpretations restricted the elucidation of meaning in the sacred texts to a small elite who had acquired specialized training. The scholarship and debates of the rabbinical elite were often remote from the daily life of the Jewish masses, and there were occasions when popular leaders challenged the notion of religious study as the major value of Jewish society. Similarly, the esoteric study of the ulema, many of whom were cut off from the social world of the masses, encouraged popular movements to produce their own men of authority.[3]

The institutional location of ulema within the political and economic frameworks of Islamic societies made for a somewhat greater differentiation from the masses than the location of rabbis within the *kehillot*, the semi-autonomous Jewish communities. In some Sunni countries, the ulema were incorporated into state bureaucracies, primarily as judges and school administrators, and they worked closely with state authorities, providing them with religious legitimation. Income and, in some cases, considerable power were derived from trusts in land and urban property established for the ulema by wealthy donors.[4] Prior to the reforms made from the mid–nineteenth century on, the ulema in the imperial center of Ottoman Turkey were ensconced in the "official" Islam of the empire and incorporated into the political and economic elites. They were given high ranks and titles; they were members of the Imperial Council; and some were part of the stratum of rich merchants and tax farmers. In contrast, in nineteenth-century Morocco, remote from the center and far less bureaucratic than Ottoman Turkey, the notion of official Islam had little meaning, and the ulema were just one of the many sources of religious authority, which included tribal leaders and the heads of Sufi orders.[5]

The ulema provided one of the relatively few avenues of social mobility in traditional Islamic society, and although there were enormous inequalities in opportunity, the ulema were often recruited from a number of classes. They had their own insignia of distinctive turbans and robes, and there was some measure of agreement regarding rules for recruitment, but there was little formal hierarchy and ranking was based predominantly on scholarly achievement, as recognized by other ulema and by local communities.[6] Ulema who received income from the state and administered law in the courts under the authority of secular rulers were often held in contempt by those ulema who pursued their study of religious law while earning their living in other occupations.[7]

Some rabbis of traditional Jewish communities were employed by the kehillot, and although they were recognized as having authority over ritual matters, they were rarely the sole judicial authorities. Only the most famous rabbis could override the decisions of the lay leaders. The salaries of the kehillah rabbis were generally quite low and were exceeded by gratuities for rendering services to individuals, such as answering problems of ritual, performing marriages and divorces, conferring the rabbinic title on qualified candidates, authorizing and examining ritual slaughterers, and performing judicial functions. The performance of rabbinical roles (scholar, teacher, judge, ritualistic adviser) was not dependent on an appointment or office, and kehillah-appointed rabbis often accepted the judgment of other rabbis who supported themselves from fees for their religious services and income from other sources. Like the ulema, the

salvation through conforming behavior to a
sacred pattern (law) is particular to I. + J.?
— perhaps this is important to theocratic potential? why would you
want control of a state if other than keep interest
in controlling behavior?

rabbinate were not part of a formal religious hierarchy and complex bureaucracy, and insofar as a hierarchy was discerned, it was mainly informal, based on recognized scholarship and a pious lifestyle rather than official position.[8]

By their codification, interpretation, and administration of the religious law, by their own pious lives, and by their replies to inquiries concerning the correct forms of behavior according to the law, the ulema
and rabbis of traditional societies were guides and exemplars of behavior
that sacralized the world. Insofar as conformity to the law was believed
to bring about individual and collective salvation, the religious elites
could be seen as contributing indirectly to the soteriological goals of the
masses. The elites were not, however, mediators of salvation, and although some rabbis and ulema gained reputations as miracle makers,
thaumaturgy had never been institutionalized within their roles. Popular
thaumaturges from outside the ulema and rabbinate were common, but
they were rarely figures of high status or foci of religious devotion. The
elites that emerged as alternatives to the ulema and the rabbis were the
saints, who were believed to bring about both the soteriological and the
thaumaturgical goals of their devotees.

The ulema and rabbis have recognized holy men (almost never women),
often from their own ranks, whose exemplary lives in accordance with the
religious values and systems of religious laws are believed to have brought
them closer to God. Visiting saints' tombs was admitted from an early
date in Islamic canonical law, and most of the ulema schools accepted the
miracles of saints. Writing on Morocco, Vincent Cornell states that a significant minority of Islamic saints were legal scholars, and that in the hagiography written by ulema, saints were legitimized by their faithful adherence to the Sunna and by their legal expertise. For the ulema hagiogra-
phers, miracles had to conform to juridical ideals, and they regarded the
manifestation of extraordinary knowledge in the saints' miracles, such as
reading thoughts and uncovering hidden secrets, as more significant than
the saints' efficacy in healing the sick and subduing spirits. Most lay devotees, in contrast, were interested in the saints' thaumaturgical powers,
and the saints with the greatest reputations were those who demonstrated
such powers.[9]

As scholars and interpreters of their respective religious laws, and
being neither priests nor monks, ulema and rabbis were not predisposed
to initiate or support a highly differentiated category of saints to be venerated in official cults. Beliefs that certain persons, alive and dead, were

endowed with a special relation toward God were nevertheless exploited to the full in some forms of popular Judaism and Islam where closeness to God was believed to bring exceptional efficacy.

Saints were more common in Islamic contexts than in Jewish ones. Possible reasons for this difference are the greater emphasis in Judaism on collective than on individual salvation and the absence of a founder whose life could provide a paradigm for saints.[10] Some members of the Islamic religious elite, however, did vehemently oppose sainthood; Ibn Taimiya (d. 1328), a famous scholar, condemned the worship of saints and the veneration of the dead as idolatrous and incompatible with the Quran and the sharia, but after his death, many Muslims visited his tomb to seek his intercession. In the late eighteenth and in the nineteenth century, "purifying" movements attacked the notion of intermediaries, and in the twentieth century, both religious modernists and fundamentalist movements opposed the veneration of saints.[11]

The importance of saints in popular Islam and Judaism has been uneven over geographical areas and periods. In North Africa, where saints were a focal part of popular Islam and Judaism for many centuries, cults of living saints existed side by side with the veneration of dead saints, and both were central to identities of location and ancestry among Muslims and Jews. The living saints of rural and tribal Islam in North Africa were the arbitrators or mediators among tribes in situations where tribal segmentation and competition produced many problems and disputes, with no strong, centralized authority to resolve them. Tribespeople were willing to submit to the saints' rulings on local feuds and other problems because the saints had positions outside tribal alliances and feuds and were believed to be close to God. The saints were central figures in the festivals that marked tribal boundaries and the changing of seasons, and they had followings also among the urban poor, whose devotion, like that of the tribal and rural populations, was expressed in ecstatic rituals featuring music, dance, alcohol, trance, and possession.[12] A few saints had a reputation for efficacy over a wide range of activities, while others developed a reputation for curing specific illnesses. Certain requests, such as help in attracting a loved one, were made only to minor saints. In exchange for their help, the saints received offerings and sacrifices, and bartering over the obligations was not uncommon.[13]

The ability of dead saints to work miracles often surpassed that of live saints, and the shrines of dead saints were focal locations of popular religion among Jews as well as Muslims in North Africa, especially in Morocco and Tunisia. Almost every Jewish community in Morocco had its saint, and, as among the Muslims, the reputations of saints varied from the purely local to those extending over wide areas. Whereas live Muslim saints sometimes became the loci of political power, the significance of the saint among Jews was related to Jewish lack of power: protection from the dangers of non-Jews was one of the major themes of the legends and tales of Jewish saints. There were, however, certain dead saints worshiped by both Jews and Muslims, although they were generally referred to by different names and their festivities were held on different days.[14]

Jewish saints who died and were buried in North Africa made up one of three categories of dead saints that are popular foci of worship among Jews of North African descent in contemporary Israel. The two other categories are those saints from the Talmudic era whose purported graves have been pilgrimage centers from the early Middle Ages and saints who emigrated from North Africa and died in Israel. The two largest pilgrimages, or *hillulot*, of the latter category, drawing thousands of participants, are located in Beersheba, at the tomb of a rabbi from Tunisia who died in 1957, and in the small town of Netivot, at the shrine of a rabbi who died in 1984.[15] In some cases of those saints whose graves are in North Africa, their souls are believed to have relocated to new shrines in Israel. The most successful of these shrines, which draws some fifteen to twenty thousand pilgrims on the day of the saint's anniversary, began in 1973 when a forest worker dedicated a small room in his modest apartment in Safed to a saint buried in the Atlas Mountains. The worker related that the saint had appeared to him in a number of dreams and had indicated a wish to reside in his house.[16]

Participation in the hillulot to saints' shrines grew enormously among Israeli Jews from North Africa in the 1970s and 1980s. During their first years in Israel, after their migration in the 1950s and 1960s, Jews from North Africa appeared to be abandoning the custom. Cut off from the tombs in North Africa, the anniversaries were celebrated by small numbers in homes and neighborhood synagogues. What began as small family gatherings became grand, massive events, with some hillulot drawing thousands who come to pray, to light candles, to eat, drink, and dance, and to seek help from the saints to cure illnesses and overcome infertility.

In addition to the older, first generation, who remember the custom in North Africa, the hillulot have drawn younger Israelis of North African Jewish extraction, many of whom were born in Israel. The popularity of the hillulot is not part of a comprehensive revival of traditional culture of

Jews from North Africa, and it has been suggested that the phenomenon is not so much a reaction to modernization as a consequence of it. After a rise in living standards, and having undergone considerable acculturation to the dominant secular values and patterns of behavior of Israeli society, Jews from North Africa now feel secure enough to assert their specific ethnic identities as Moroccan or Tunisian Jews. As an occasion for the gathering together of considerable numbers in celebration of part of their cultural heritage, the pilgrimage allows North African Jews to express their ethnic identity, solidarity, and power.[17]

The worship of saints in contemporary Israel is not confined to Jews whose geographical history lies in North Africa. Saints are also a focus of the Hasidim, most of whom trace their histories to Eastern Europe. It is interesting to compare Jewish Hasidism with Islamic Sufism, movements that, although historically unconnected, demonstrate remarkable similarities. In both Sufism and Hasidism, groups of mystics with elitist notions, representing alternative religious paths to those of the legalistic traditions of ulema and rabbis, were transformed into saints by phenomenally successful popular movements. Before its popularization, Sufism existed for some centuries as the mysticism of coteries and groups who sought the goal of union with God through asceticism, meditation, and the "annihilation of the self." Over time, relatively informal associations of masters and disciples became formal organizations of orders and lodges, and there developed around the leaders distinctions between inner circles of adepts and outer circles of affiliates and supporters.

Sufism came to be characterized by the veneration of both the current leaders—the living saints—and the dead saints, who were often believed to be the founders of the particular "brotherhoods" or movements. Insofar as the mystical goal of union with God was incorporated into popular Sufism, it was believed to be achieved through the mediumship of the saint, but more important was the belief that the saints' nearness to God or their divine nature enabled them to cure, to make the barren fertile, and to protect against evil beings and powers. With its focus on saint veneration, Sufism was the principal form by which Islam spread in North Africa, Central Asia, and India.[18]

Hasidism began in the 1730s, centuries later than Sufism, in Podolia, an area of the western Ukraine in what was then part of Poland, and it spread rapidly among Eastern European Jews in the last decades of the eighteenth century and first half of the nineteenth century. By the middle of the nineteenth century, Hasidism was the dominant form of Judaism in most Jewish communities in the Ukraine, central Poland, and Galicia; it had a large impact in White Russia and northern Hungary; and it attracted a large minority in Lithuania. The mystical goal of cleaving, in the sense of communion rather than full union with God, was held by some Hasidim to be within the capabilities of all Jews, but the more prevalent notion, from the beginnings of the movement, was that direct accessibility to the divine was possible only for a small number of the spiritually endowed, and that the only path for the masses was through cleaving to the spiritual few, the *zaddikim*, or saints. Devotion and submission to the zaddik, like devotion and submission to the *shaikh* or *pir* in Sufism, was the means to both this-worldly and other-worldly goals.[19]

Unlike Sufism, which incorporated and adapted already-existing saints' cults in such areas as North Africa and India, Hasidism spread among Ashkenazi Jews, whose religion had not been characterized by the veneration of human intermediaries. In Hasidism, as in Sufism, however, notions developed of the cosmic importance of saints. Sufis believed that a hierarchy of saints upheld the order of the universe and that in every epoch there was a saint who was the *qutb* (axis), the perfect human around whom the whole universe revolved. The cosmic role was shared, in some degree, by the higher saints in the hierarchy, and for some believers, who were especially numerous in India, the saints were an integral part of the divine.[20] In Hasidism, the zaddikim were understood to be the "foundation of the world"; God had created the world because of his love for them and expected pleasure from them. The zaddikim contributed to the redemption of the Jewish people and the cosmos by rescuing the divine sparks of God from their captivity within the material and evil world.[21]

The cosmic status and roles of the Sufi and Hasidic saints, together with their immanence and accessibility, made believers confident that a saint's intervention on their behalf would bring about miracles in this world. The combination of the roles of cosmic upholder and redeemer, savior of individual souls, and thaumaturge was powerful and attracted believers even in those contexts where saints' cults had previously been absent, as was the case among Eastern European Jews. Notions that the charisma of the saints was transferred through discipleship or inherited genealogically facilitated the spread of the movements, as did the religious and social services provided by the centers of the living saints or around the shrines of the dead saints. The movements were opposed by the established elites, the ulema and rabbis, who objected to their anti-scholarly tendencies, ecstatic practices, and focus on intermediaries, but as the movements became more moderate and adopted, at least in some branches, the more legalistic traditions, the elites came to accept them.[22]

The vast majority of Hasidim perished in the Holocaust. In the post–World War II period, the zaddikim have remained the foci of the remaining Hasidic groups, but the strengthening of the scholarly and legalistic tendencies among the Hasidim has meant that they are now considered part of the "fundamentalist" or ultra-Orthodox section of the Jewish population. Together with other ultra-Orthodox, or *haredim*, the Hasidim see themselves as carriers of a traditional society, formerly located in Eastern Europe, which they seek to preserve and strengthen in the new locations where they are concentrated, particularly in New York and Israel. In fact, the standards of the contemporary ultra-Orthodox community are more stringent and less compromising than those of the prewar traditional community. The voluntaristic character of the contemporary community, based on members' commitment to the strict religious way of life, means that rabbis no longer have to soften their demands for stringency in order to cater to the less observant, and the tradition of the written law has come to triumph over the more compromising tradition that had been anchored in the daily life of the local traditional community.[23]

Like their Islamic counterparts, Jewish "fundamentalists," or as I prefer to call them, neotraditionalists, assert what they conceive as their authentic tradition against the incursion of the "Western" culture of consumerism, materialism, and immorality. Whereas Jewish neotraditionalists tend to idealize the premodern Jewish communities, however, Islamic neotraditionalists condemn the "folk" religion that is pervasive in traditional Islamic communities. Many Islamic radicals perceive Sufism and saint cults as part of the decadence of the precolonial, traditional Islamic societies that failed to adhere to a "pure" form of Islam and were thereby susceptible to Western conquest and cultural influence. Unlike the Jewish ultra-Orthodox, Islamic radicals do not perceive themselves as part of a historically continuous traditional community but rather as representing a return to the authentic Islam of Muhammad and (for Sunnis) the first caliphs. Thus, the establishment of a truly Islamic state and society, in which the sharia will be the only source of law and custom, requires the purification of Islam from the deviances of popular religion.[24]

The reform of popular religion by agencies that claim to represent an authentic or pure form of their religion is a formidable task. The following account of attempts by Protestants and Catholics shows that, at best, they are likely to achieve only partial change.

9

Protestants, Catholics, and the Reform of Popular Religion

The Protestant Reformation constituted a reformulation of the goals, conditions, and means of Christian religious action. The reformulation had wide-ranging implications for the differentiations that had prevailed in Catholicism between virtuosos and "ordinary" Christians and between clerisy and laypeople. It also had major consequences for the popular religion of the rural masses.

The more radical forms of the Reformation included millenarian movements that expected salvation from the imminent coming of Christ and carried out a variety of actions, including revolts against political regimes, that were intended to hasten Christ's appearance and bring about the messianic kingdom. Among the majority of Protestants, however, the major soteriological goal was no different from that of Catholics: to reside for eternity in paradise. The Protestant abrogation of the idea of purgatory reestablished the stark alternative of Christian soteriology: eternal bliss or eternal damnation.

The dualist conception of heaven and earth involved the disenchantment of the latter; the channels of sacred mediation were greatly reduced, and a radical restatement was made of the polarization between a transcendental God and an immanent world. Protestant theologians debated whether God worked through nature or above it, but until the influence of the mechanical philosophy of the late seventeenth century, few disputed that God could disrupt the course of nature in the form of "special providences." Under the influence of the scientific and philosophical developments from the late seventeenth century, many came to envisage God's providence as an original act of creation, which set in motion a world that henceforth operated in accord with immutable laws. But even before the influence of the new science, the renewed emphasis of Protestants on the transcendentalism of the divine and the disenchantment of the world diminished the perceived capacity of humans to cooperate in the renewal of the seasons or to attain dispensations from the workings of nature.[1]

Protestantism was a religious revolution, not so much in its reformulations of the goals of religious action but in its rejection of the Catholic conditions and means, and the substitution of alternative conditions and means, to achieve those goals. The two sacraments that were retained by the major Protestant movements, communion and baptism, underwent a transformation of meaning that, in most cases, reduced their significance as means of salvation. Martin Luther's substitution of the doctrine of consubstantiation for the Catholic doctrine of transubstantiation still allowed for the divine presence in the wafer, and Lutherans retained a simplified version of the Eucharist as their most frequent service. Luther taught, however, that although the sacraments could serve as an external manifestation of faith, like all forms of works on earth they did not provide the means of attaining salvation. Humans did not earn or deserve salvation; it was a gift of God, and faith rather than works was the essential component.[2]

The Calvinist doctrine was that salvation was entirely dependent on God, who had predestined all humans to either salvation or damnation. In the terminology of the action perspective, Calvin transformed salvation from an end of religious action to a condition; none of the means that were appropriate to the achievement of salvation in other religions (ritual participation, good works, faith in a savior, etc.) could make any difference to the final destination of the person. Humans could not apply their standards to the transcendental God, and to believe that people could influence such a God in the determination of their salvation was absurd. Nevertheless, it was the absolute duty of every human, whether they might be among the saved or not, to observe a religious life, because every person was put on the earth to testify to the glory of God.

Later Calvinist theologians taught that believers were obliged to assume they were among the chosen because any doubt on the matter was a sign of imperfect faith. Believers were then encouraged to prove their election by exhibiting their true faith in their everyday conduct. Although religious actions would not bring about their salvation, they could demonstrate to themselves and to others that they were among the elect. According to Max Weber's famous thesis, the goal substitution of the demonstration of salvation for salvation itself had far-reaching consequences, because the appropriate behavior of demonstration, especially diligence in lawful callings and frugality in consumption, fostered the spirit of capitalism. Weber argued that an emphasis on the proof of salvation continued in the Pietist, Methodist, and Baptist movements even without the doctrine of predestination.[3] He noted, for example, that Methodism revived the Puritan doctrine "that works are not the cause, but only the means of knowing one's state of grace, and even this only when they are performed solely for the glory of God."[4]

The belief that God's grace or a person's true faith was manifested in human conduct in the everyday world undermined the Catholic distinction between the other-worldly path of the virtuoso monks, who acted in accord with a higher morality, and the worldly path of "ordinary" Christians. All Protestant movements, whether they believed in predestination or emphasized free will, whether they were activist or quietist, rejected a dual morality of precepts and the idea that there was a religious way of life, set apart from the world, that was superior to conformity to the moral life in worldly activity. The notion of a religious elite was present in Protestantism, but in place of the distinction between an elite and those who followed a lesser path, the contrast was now between the elite and the unsaved. Weber wrote that Calvinism "substituted for the spiritual aristocracy of monks outside and above the world the spiritual aristocracy of the predestined saints of God within the world."[5] And among those who believed they had demonstrated they were among the chosen, there was "hatred and contempt for others who bore the signs of eternal damnation."[6] The obligation to testify to the glory of God required that the damned be brought, forcibly if necessary, under the auspices of the Protestant church, and Weber noted that the Calvinist "elect," in order to distance themselves from others, set up conventicles within their church. Protestant sects, in comparison, sought an exclusiveness that excluded the damned, and in such cases the distinction was between an elite, which encompassed all members, and outsiders.[7]

In the inclusivist Protestant churches, which brought in the unsaved or as yet unredeemed, it was assumed that the government of the church was in the hands of the elite of the saved, and there was no question that the ordained ministers were among the saved.[8] In general, however, Protestantism weakened the distinction between clerisy and laypeople. The abolition of some sacraments, the modification of others, and the overall reduction of church ritual meant that the Protestant minister could not have the Catholic priest's mystique as a mediator and distributor of sacred power. The desacralization of the Protestant clergy was furthered by the discarding of Catholic vestments, the abolition of celibacy, and the introduction of vernacular liturgies. The Protestant doctrine of "the priesthood of all believers" was supported by the emphasis on the unmediated Bible as the sole standard of doctrine and conduct. Preaching the word became a central part of the Protestant church service, and sermon attendance was understood as a means of salvation. The revelations of the Bible were available, however, without priestly exposition, and preaching was not necessarily confined to the Protestant ministers or pastors.

The undermining of the distinction between clerisy and laypeople was advanced by developments in printing, the appearance of vernacular Bibles and a popular religious literature, and the growth of literacy. A number of Protestant leaders, however, abandoned the notion that the masses were able to understand the Word of God on their own, without the guidance of qualified and trained men. Most Protestant congregations came to have formally ordained, full-time ministers or pastors, and although it was a fundamental tenet among early Protestants that each community had the right to elect its own pastor, the choice generally had to be acceptable to secular authorities and approved by existing ministers. In many cases the appointment of Protestant clergy was taken over by territorial princes or their officials. Hierocratic elites developed that in some churches, such as the Lutheran and the Anglican, took the form of hierocracies of bishops, priests, deacons, and so on. Where laypeople were admitted into the government of the churches, they generally came from among the rich and powerful and were co-opted by the existing church leaderships.[9] The emergent religious elites in the Protestant churches did not claim, however, to have access to a "higher" path of salvation than that available to other believers.

If the Protestant clergy were not mediators of the salvation of laypeople, nor did they provide the supernatural means for laypeople to attain their this-worldly goals. And if laypeople could no longer rely on the intercession of the clergy, nor could they rely on the assistance of supramundane beings and the whole apparatus of religious objects, formulas, and rituals that the Catholic Church had provided to counter evil forces and to prevent and overcome the misfortunes of everyday life. In place of the many supramundane beings who could be entreated, supplicated, or possibly coerced to provide dispensation, the Protestant cosmos was presided over by a God who was of but not in a world that He had created to operate according to impersonal rules.

A significant depopulation of supramundane beings took place: Christ was central and the devil was a very prominent adversary, but the Virgin Mary and the saints were eliminated as intercessors with God. The angels that some Protestants emphasized could not replace the saints because they did not have that combination of the incorporeal and human concreteness that made the saints appear so appropriate for the achievement of worldly ends through supramundane means. Apart from angels, Protestants allowed for a number of supramundane beings to be active in the world, including demons and various kinds of spirits, such as the revenant dead, that were mentioned in the Bible, but many expressed skepticism toward other beings, including ghosts and poltergeists and the various earth spirits, such as fairies and trolls.[10]

Protestant theologians replaced explanations of misfortune in terms of capricious beings with the doctrine of Providence. When people suffered, they were either being punished for their wrongdoing or their faith was being tested. Once the moral defect, the cause of the misfortune, was discovered or made apparent, the only effective response was repentance, moral improvement, and an appeal to God's mercy. Ritual might help people concentrate their thoughts and efforts on their moral reform and their appeal to God, but the churches no longer provided sanctified objects and formulas, such as sacred water and charms, to overcome misfortunes. It was regarded as appropriate, however, for prayers asking for faith and forgiveness of sin to be accompanied by petitions for material blessings. Protestant theologians stressed that petitionary prayers supplemented and did not supersede natural remedies, and that their effectiveness (as well as the effectiveness of the natural remedies) would depend on the moral condition of the petitioner and the suitability of the request. Even if all the appropriate conditions were met, the efficacy of the prayers could not be guaranteed.

In short, the assistance given by official Protestantism in seeking worldly goals was limited and hemmed in by qualifications. Such a religion was unlikely to appeal to the peasant masses who took for granted a religion that provided for nomic and thaumaturgical goals. If membership of a Protestant church was imposed on the peasants, it would not be surprising to find that many peasants sought supernatural relief and help from outside the churches.[11]

Protestantism, Peasants, and Popular Religion

The Reformation has been described as an urban event.[12] Weber suggested an elective affinity between Protestant beliefs and capitalist activities,[13] and although the response of urban groups varied, Protestantism spread most rapidly in the middle and upper strata of many of the larger cities of Europe. Robert Scribner notes that the desire among German urban strata to deprive the clergy of their socioeconomic privileges inclined them to anti-sacerdotalism and made them especially responsive to Protestantism. Radical forms of Protestantism drew support from peasants, but the latter were disillusioned by the failure of Reformation leaders to support their struggle, and their enthusiasm waned after the Peasant War of 1524–25.[14] R. Po-Chia Hsia writes that when Calvinism reached out from its urban centers to the countryside, its appeal was largely restricted to the higher strata, many of whom held state and church offices in the villages.[15]

The spread of Protestantism among the English population has been a subject of some debate. What has been described as a devastating erosion of Catholicism after 1530 left only a minority of committed Catholics by 1570, but the collapse of Catholicism did not mean that the majority of the population had become committed Protestants. As in other European countries, it was the literate and the urban elites who were most responsive to Protestantism, and its spread among the rural masses took several generations.[16] A study of an English village in the seventeenth century shows that the first generation of Puritan villagers was recruited mainly from a new, prosperous stratum of commercial farmers and craftspeople, whose way of life was increasingly removed from the popular culture of the mass of agricultural laborers. As employers, masters, and "pillars of the church," this stratum supported the attempts of parish officers to establish new standards of religious uniformity among the poorer villagers by prosecuting those who did not receive communion or who, on Sunday, worked, played sports, or simply did not come to church. At the end of the century, however, there were few signs that the attempts to enforce religious observances and social discipline had had an impact on the village poor.[17]

The penetration of Protestantism into the English countryside was fostered by the extension of commercialism and capitalism from the towns to the villages and the transformation of farming in response to expanding markets,[18] but in many parts of Europe, Protestantism drew support in rural areas with little urbanization or industry. Rosemary Hopcroft has shown that Protestantism was more likely to be adopted in those rural areas where there were individualized property rights and low levels of community control over agriculture. Highly communal "open fields" regions with strong manorial control were less receptive to the emphasis that Protestant religions placed on individual competency and responsibility in interpreting the Bible and on achieving salvation without the assistance of a clerical intermediary.[19]

Whether Catholicism as official religion was replaced by a Lutheran, Reformed (Calvinist), or other Protestant church did not, of course, depend on the elective affinities, or lack thereof, between those religions and the lives of peasants. The monarchs and princes of the early modern European states adopted one of the "confessions" and used the newly formed "national" churches to consolidate their territorial boundaries and impose social control over their subjects. The imposition of confessional conformity had the advantage of being understood as the implementation of God's work and as a means to strengthen and extend the authority of political regimes. Both Protestant reformers and Catholic defenders allied themselves with centralizing governments, and the bureaucracies of church and state cooperated in endeavors to produce subjects who were both obedient and pious, loyal to both nation-state and national religion.[20] Where rulers replaced Catholicism with Protestantism, the dismantling of the old faith and the imposition of at least nominal adherence to the new faith did not take long, but as part of popular religion, the little traditions of Catholicism continued long after official Catholicism ended.

Protestant reformers found some common ground with popular religion when the latter included elements of anticlericalism, but the Protestant onslaught on Catholic liturgy was bound to extend to popular religion because official Catholicism and popular religion shared patterns of religious action that the Reformers condemned as "magic," "superstition," and "idolatry." The Protestants who denounced the "magical" nature of the sacraments and sacramentals and condemned the "idolatry" that focused on saints and the Virgin Mary could hardly ignore popular practices that used the sacramentals for material goals and directed supplications to local saints and manifestations of the Virgin Mary.[21] In German principalities, Lutheran authorities listed forbidden beliefs and practices, and officials of the state churches were instructed to probe into every parish to seek out and admonish local magicians and witches.[22] As part of the effort to implement a more rational religion and rigorous discipline, Calvinist reformers demonstrated an even greater opposition to "superstitions" than did Lutherans.[23] The Reformers objected in particular to carnival, which they saw as an encouragement to sinful behavior and a focus of non-Christian or anti-Christian magic.[24]

The attempts of Protestant elites to reform popular religion have been deemed by historians to have been unsuccessful in most rural areas, at least during the first century of Protestant reform. As in many Catholic areas, large numbers of nominally Protestant laypeople did not attend church and resented the attempts by ecclesiastics to impose their doctrines and practices. Many villagers refused to become incorporated into the system of moral control by church and state, and they demonstrated a considerable ability to evade that control. When they did attend church, some villagers demonstrated much irreverent and irrelevant activity during the services.[25]

There were Protestant clergy who made concessions to popular religion, such as the ringing of the church bells to ward off bad weather, but they were generally less willing than Catholic priests to compromise. Where Protestant parishioners had access to Catholic priests, some would approach them with requests that their Protestant pastors had refused to accommodate. Otherwise, there remained many popular practitioners who were prepared to use their special knowledge and powers to cure human and animal illnesses, to guard against misfortune, to divine lost or stolen objects, and to perform countermagic against witches.[26]

The socioeconomic gap between Protestant rural clergy and laypeople and the reluctance of Protestant clergy to provide their parishioners with religious means to this-worldly goals resulted in a greater division between official and unofficial religion in Protestant countries than in Catholic ones.[27] Writing on sixteenth- and seventeenth-century England, Keith Thomas expresses doubt as to whether the Anglican Church's official campaign against magic did much to reduce its appeal,[28] and he proceeds to document in considerable detail the popular and non-official religion of most English people in those centuries. The "wise" men and women or village wizards continued to use techniques, including chanting prayers in Latin, that had come down to them from the Middle Ages. Other techniques can be traced to earlier times and have no obvious relationship to Christianity.[29] The magicians plied their trade within an enchanted world that, despite the efforts of Protestant reformers, remained populated by many types of supramundane beings and processes that operated both for and against the human population.

Even in seventeenth-century New England among the Calvinistic Puritans, who mostly came from literate middle strata, the enchanted world was conspicuous. Despite the condemnation of magic by some ministers as blasphemy and the work of the devil, many Puritans saw no contradiction between their faith and the "magical" practices that assisted them in their worldly endeavors. Puritan theology itself may have encouraged turning to protective forms of thaumaturgy. According to Puritan theologians, misfortunes were a consequence of a person's own sins, but their emphasis on a devil who prompted even godly people to sin encouraged believers to externalize the sources of their misfortune, absolve themselves of blame, and seek a countermagic to protect themselves. Divination and astrology were also condemned as blasphemy, but the predestination theology left believers with feelings of uncertainty that led some to seek out the help of fortune-tellers and astrologers.[30]

Thomas writes that, although it is impossible to say how far the disenchantment of official religion by Protestant elites produced an expansion of popular magic, astrology was one area of unofficial religion that expanded and became widely disseminated among the masses. Printing made possible a wide distribution of almanacs in the sixteenth century, and by the beginning of the seventeenth century there existed a popular astrology, with a lower-class clientele, that differed from the cosmological, philosophical, and "scientific" astrology of the educated. The goals sought by the clients of popular astrologers overlapped considerably with those sought with the help of village wise people: appropriate weather for agriculture, fertility, overcoming illness, attracting love objects, recovering lost property, and finding hidden treasures. Protestant clergy were often willing to admit or to tolerate astrological prediction of the weather and its use in agriculture, but they objected to astrological predictions of human behavior, which they saw as incompatible with their doctrines of individual moral responsibility. Astrologers and their clients, by contrast, appear to have had little difficulty in reconciling Protestantism and astrology.[31]

In the eighteenth and nineteenth centuries, the appointment of more educated and higher-status Protestant ministers and priests in rural areas of Europe widened the gap between official religion and popular religion. The distance between clergy and most rural laypeople was particularly great in the nineteenth-century Church of England, in which the priests were set apart from most of their parishioners by their status as "gentlemen" and by their cooperation with the local squire or landlords, who were often the only laypersons whose involvement in the governing of the church they encouraged.[32] This gap was reduced at the end of the eighteenth century and during the first half of the nineteenth century by new Protestant movements, such as Methodism in England, that arose and spread through open-air evangelism in most parts of Protestant Europe.

The popular preachers of Methodism not only reasserted doctrines of the Reformation, such as the unmediated interpretation of the Bible and re-demption by God's grace, but also encouraged belief in the intervention of supramundane beings, including fairies and witches, in daily life. Methodist preachers were attributed with powers to prevent misfortune and to cure, much like those credited to Catholic priests and village wise men and women.[33] Villagers also preferred the noisy, expressive, and egalitarian ser-vices of the Methodist chapels to the decorous and severe tone of Anglican worship.[34] In response to the Methodist challenge, some Anglican priests sought to appeal to their rural parishioners, but although villagers used the church's services for baptism, marriage, and burial, few met the obligation of three communions a year. The only successful innovation of the Angli-can Church among the rural masses in the nineteenth century was a harvest thanksgiving celebrating the creative powers of nature.[35]

In contrast to the parish system of the Church of England, which con-tributed to the division of urban and rural religiosity, the key unit of Methodist organization, the circuit, brought preachers from the towns into the villages, and over time Methodism contributed to stricter and more disciplined forms of religious action among the rural population.[36] Most rural laborers did not, however, make an exclusive commitment to either the Anglican Church or the Methodist chapel, and attendance at both church and chapel, as equally integral parts of the community, was not uncommon. Even where Methodism was regarded as an alternative to the Anglican Church, most rural laborers did not accept everything that its ministers offered, and they added the Methodist ingredients that they selected to the popular mixture of little-tradition Anglicanism and non-Christian elements.[37]

Writing on religion in South Lindsey, a village in Lincolnshire, around the middle of the nineteenth century, James Obelkevich states that al-though the villagers' popular religion provided omens of death, it gave little promise of life after death. It provided a technology rather than a so-teriology, "a way of coping with misfortunes rather than deliverance from them."[38] The Christian elements in the amalgam that was popular reli-gion were directed to "non-Christian ends": Sunday was a lucky day rather than a holy one; the sign of the cross was used to avert bad luck; the Bible was used as a magical means to attract a loved one; and the cru-cifix provided cures. In comparison with Catholicism, the reduction in the Church of England of ritual accoutrements such as rosaries and can-dles, the absence of processions and pilgrimages centered on saintly in-termediaries, and the representational interpretation of the communion provided fewer sources and occasions for the pursuit of this-worldly goals. Many elements of official religion remained, however, and some of these underwent popular transformations. Confirmation was seen as a cure for rheumatism, and the popularity of the ceremony of "churching" or "thanksgiving of women after childbirth" was due not to a pious desire to render thanks to God but rather to a belief that it removed the impurity from tainted women after they had given birth.

The most prominent figure in the official pantheon, Jesus Christ, was virtually absent in the popular religion of South Lindsey, and the Holy Ghost was even less evident. The devil, who was known according to various nicknames, continued to be a salient figure for villagers, even though few clergy now spoke of him. As for non-Christian supramundanes, they had become fewer by the nineteenth century, but beliefs in ghosts and witches remained widespread, and villagers continued to request permission from tree spirits before they chopped the trees down. It would appear that by the mid–nineteenth century, the process of disenchantment among village laborers was far from complete, despite the effects of the Reformation and the influence of science.[39]

Few anthropological studies of popular religion in rural settings in Protestant countries have been conducted in the twentieth century. A study in the 1970s of Straithes, a fishing village in North Yorkshire in which Methodism was the most prominent religion, demonstrated considerable differences between official and popular religion. The continuing importance of local community identity in village Methodism was signified by the rivalry between a Wesleyan chapel and a Primitive Methodist chapel, despite the fact that these Methodist branches had been united for four decades at the national level. The rivalry of the chapels in the village was a matter not of theological or liturgical differences but of family and kin loyalties and community beliefs and practices.

Among the popular rituals in the village were the "purification" rites performed on New Year's Eve for the well-being of the household; dirt was removed from the fire hearth in order that the failings of the past would not be carried on into the new year. Special community services such as the Harvest Festivals, in which the villagers' connection with the sea was emphasized, and Sunday School Anniversaries, in which the strength of the chapel communities was reaffirmed, were far better attended than translocal services, such as those on Easter Sunday. The most important religious times were not when the birth and resurrection of Christ were celebrated but when the communities celebrated the founding of their Sunday schools or the building of their chapels. Unofficial forms of religious action were also prominent in the rituals around birth and death and in the thaumaturgy that related to the occupational hazards of fishing and mining.

The popular, local religion of Straithes deviated not only from the official religion but also from the secularity of the wider society, which many residents perceived to be remote from their way of life. This type of village community, in which popular religion is intricately tied to a strong sense of communal belonging and identity, has become increasingly rare in modern urban and industrialized societies.[40]

Catholicism, Reform, and Popular Religion

The Counter-Reformation was a response, in part, to the Protestant Reformation; the importance of the sacraments as crucial to salvation was reasserted, and non-observation was countered by disciplinary measures and sanctions as well as graphic and detailed depictions of the torments of hell and purgatory. The sacraments, and especially the Eucharist as a focus of contemplation and devotion, were now presented as acts undertaken for personal salvation, rather than as group rituals.[41] In general, the Catholic Church did not attempt such a thorough reform of popular religion as had the major Protestant churches, but as a movement of reform, including the reform of popular religion, the term *Counter-Reformation* has been regarded as a misnomer by some historians who view the changes in the Catholic Church as part of an overall reformation in religion and society.

Like the Protestant Reformation, the Counter-Reformation was very much an urban movement, beginning in the large cities, then spreading to the smaller towns and, finally, the villages.[42] It was supported with enthusiasm by urban strata, but in the countryside religious change, if any, was a slow and uneven process. Most of the rituals that had been subject to popular uses and adaptations in the pre-Reformation period were preserved, and clergy continued to provide a thaumaturgy and to draw the lines between official and unofficial religion, much as they had done in the Middle Ages.

The differences from the past were that ecclesiastics sought to increase lay participation in official religion with an emphasis on frequent communion and confession; they attempted to remove from popular religion elements that had previously been ignored or tolerated; and the campaign against the church's competitors in thaumaturgy was increasingly sustained and severe.[43] In accordance with sharper distinctions between the sacred and the profane, ecclesiastics attempted to prohibit or reform those rituals under church auspices that were occasions for what they considered inappropriate behavior. They objected to wakes because of the overnight mingling of the sexes, and they prohibited the use of churches for dancing, feasting, and other indecorous behavior. A number of popular festivals were condemned, and attempts were made to make religious processions more somber and sober.[44]

Catholic elites also attempted to channel religious devotion away from the saints and toward Jesus and Mary. Italian clerics in particular encouraged the worship of Mary, and as part of their mission among the lay masses, the preaching orders spread the devotion of Mary, especially in the form of the sorrowful Mary near the body of Christ or with Christ's body in her lap. New lay-inspired images of Mary that developed reputations for miracles generally gained quicker acceptance and approval by church authorities than the shrines of popular saints. Although members of the church elite denied that the Marian images were invested with intrinsic supramundane power, they rationalized their acceptance of the popular practices around the images by stating that the veneration of an image was really being offered to the prototype of the image and that the images provided models of piety. Thus, even during the period of Tridentine reforms, the church elite were willing to authorize popular worship organized around allegedly miraculous images, even when they had doubts about the evidence of miracles. The authorities sought to incorporate the images into their devotional models, giving them a Christocentric direction, and to supervise the activities associated with the images and shrines.[45]

Thomas Kselman writes that the Catholic religious elite in the nineteenth century became especially receptive to reports of miracles at Marian shrines because they saw the success of the new shrines, such as the one at Lourdes, as a means of strengthening loyalty to the church against the dangers of intellectual, political, and social changes. In contrast to the small shrines dedicated to local saints, over which the clerical elite had little or no control, the elite made efforts to develop regional and national Marian shrines, where healing rites could be placed in the context of official practices and rituals such as confession and communion.[46] The visions of Bernadette Boubirous at Lourdes were understood to confirm the recently promulgated doctrine of the immaculate conception, and they provided the elite with an opportunity to persuade laypeople to accept papal authority and infallibility.[47] A number of Marian shrines in the nineteenth century became foci of developing nationalism, and by crowning the shrine images in elaborate ceremonies and encouraging pilgrimage to the shrines, the elite sought to demonstrate that the shrines were integrated within the universal church.[48]

Many of the Marian images located in parish churches were promoted by church agencies from outside the community, such as mendicant and missionary orders. They were intended as salvational devotional images to which people would relate as individuals, and their location was considered irrelevant to their characteristics and significance. These efforts by the elite to integrate local communities into the universal community of Christendom were largely frustrated by peasants who appropriated the shrine images as supramundane means of protecting the local community, catering to their requests, and affirming their community identity and boundaries. Writing on peasant communities in Spain in the 1960s, William Christian noted that, although the peasants acknowledged the church teaching that there is one Mary and that all representations of her are interchangeable, in practice they directed their devotions to the village Mary, who was believed to focus her attentions on the village community and its family and individual members. The fiesta days that honored the images were considered necessary for the transitions of the agricultural cycle; the villages as corporate groups turned to the images in times of crisis; and the images were also among the most frequent objects of petition from individual members of the communities. As the processes of modernization have eroded the villages as foci of identity, however, the local village shrines have declined in importance, and regional shrines, associated with wider provincial, diocesan, or cultural identities and approached by individuals and families rather than local collectivities, have expanded.[49]

Whereas ecclesiastics have been willing to accommodate and to encourage little traditions of Marian worship, they have often been critical of unofficial saints. The Counter-Reformation church made fewer canonizations, but in an attempt to regularize the numerous popular saints, the church made beatification a category of canon law in 1635 and went on to pass a large number of beatifications that recognized existing saints' cults that had been approved by local churches and local civil authorities.[50] As a mandatory stage in the process of canonization, the church was able to make a distinction between the "venerable," who had reached this first stage of official recognition, and the fully canonized saints. There remained, of course, many popular saints that ecclesiastics deemed spurious or of diabolical origins.[51] In contrast with the elite representations of the saints as ideal humans who sublimate their own feelings in order to assist others to salvation, the saints in popular Catholicism continued to be thought of as participants in relationships of exchange. Church officials approved the giving of gifts to saints, but in accord with their emphasis on the superiority of the saints over supplicants, they favored gifts that validated and confirmed the power of saints. An asymmetrical relationship was assumed, with an intrinsic difference between the favors given by the saints and the gifts given by supplicants. Although peasants accepted that saints had powers they themselves did not possess, they also expressed feelings of familiarity, especially toward the village or local saints to whom they would turn for help in everyday matters. Peasants were more likely to favor a symmetrical form of reciprocity, in which each partner benefits equally by the exchange.[52]

The reform of popular religion within the Counter-Reformation Catholic Church was accompanied by the persecution of popular religion outside it. The campaigns of ecclesiastics against the non-official elements in popular religion were more systematic and extensive than those of the Middle Ages. The Catholic Church in the sixteenth century followed the Protestant churches in delineating more vigorously than hitherto the boundaries of official religion and persecuting the "superstitions" and "devil-worshiping heresies" that lay beyond those boundaries.[53] Objections were made to the pursuit of "illegitimate" goals, such as the attraction of loved persons through love charms. The theology of the Counter-Reformation taught that people were responsible for their own actions, and a love charm was seen to constitute an attempt to undermine a person's free will and to induce them to sin.[54] Any success in such an endeavor could only be the work of the devil.

It was not, however, so much the specific ends pursued as the auspices under which religious action was taken that continued to provide the basis for the church elite's distinction between religion and "magic" or "superstition." Most priests continued to perform such rituals as ringing the church bells to ward off hail or other dangers to the harvest, and missionaries of the church adopted thaumaturgical action as part of their strategy to strengthen its influence. The Jesuits had their own holy water, Xavier water, which was blessed by a Jesuit or a priest licensed by the

Jesuit General and then distributed as a cure for fevers, blindness, paralysis, and other bodily problems.[55] Yet "magic," beneficent as well as maleficent, performed by persons uncredited by the church was defined by ecclesiastics as diabolical and heretical, and much of the unofficial popular religion that had been tolerated or ignored in the Middle Ages became subject to the demonology of both the Catholic and the Protestant elite. The most prominent expressions of this official demonology were the witch-hunts, trials, and executions that peaked in 1586–91 and 1626–31 and continued sporadically until the early eighteenth century.

Popular religion distinguished between black and white witches: whereas black witches employed their supramundane powers and knowledge to cause harm to others, white witches used their powers and knowledge to heal, find lost objects, supply love potions, and counter black witchcraft. Civil law had made a distinction between white and black magic and had limited punishment to the latter, but the distinction was eroded by canon law, which pronounced that all supernatural power not emanating from the church was demonic. In the fifteenth century, the church elite began to develop the notion of a witch cult, an organized body of witches who met at their sabbath to worship the devil in corporeal, usually animal, form. The witches were accused of having sexual intercourse with demons and feasting on the flesh of babies.

Among the common people, accusations against witches arose after unexpected misfortunes occurred to particular individuals who would then look for the cause, often with the help of the village wise man or woman, among those fellow villagers whom they believed bore a grudge against them. In many cases accusations were made against old women who were known to dabble in magic. The witch-hunts conducted by Catholic and Protestant churchmen in the sixteenth and seventeenth centuries were not organized in response to complaints that witches had used occult means to harm others; such complaints had been a common feature of popular religion for centuries. The elites saw the hunts as a crusade against a devil-worshiping heresy with beliefs and rituals that represented an evil reversal of Christianity.

The masses had understood witchcraft as an activity with the intention of doing harm to others, and not as an organized cult of devil worshipers; but in constructing the ideology of witchcraft, the elites appear to have drawn on elements from popular religion that, in some parts of Europe, included beliefs in human metamorphosis into animals, cannibalistic witches, and other beings who flew or traveled in a supramundane manner at night. Such beliefs were absorbed into the dualistic worldview of the religious elite.[56]

The extent of the impact on popular religion of the religious elites' theologization of witchcraft as a heresy of devil worshipers is difficult to access. The devil, helped by hordes of demons and evil spirits, was a prominent figure in the popular pantheon, and the church officials' accusations of diabolical pacts and rituals were bound to have made an impression of those who knew the accused well. C. Scott Dixon writes that the assimilation of the idea of demonic intervention resulted in even greater recourse to popular magic as protection against witchcraft, but over time the elites' labeling of all popular magic as diabolical did change popular conceptions. The elites' systematization of thought and their emphasis on the rules and logic of inquiry in witchcraft trials influenced the eclectic world of popular belief to become more orderly and to draw clearer boundaries between religion and magic.[57] The effects of the witch-hunts on popular religion should not, however, be exaggerated, and after the end of the witch-hunt period, the notion of witchcraft as malevolence by supernatural means continued among the peasant populations of Europe.

The witch-hunts of the sixteenth and seventeenth centuries were, in part, a by-product of the campaigns for the reform of popular religion, but with regard to Catholic countries, there is little agreement among historians over the extent to which the Counter-Reformation church succeeded in "depaganizing" and "Christianizing" the rural populations. The terms *depaganize* and *Christianize* are those of Jean Delumeau, who wrote that the seventeenth century was the golden age of Christianization, especially in France.[58] Among the historians who are close to this view are Robert Muchembled, who wrote that the efforts to Christianize rural areas in France that began in the sixteenth century became effective in the seventeenth century, when the monarchy as well as the church penetrated into the villages,[59] and Joseph Klaits, who wrote that by the end of the witch-hunting period, the traditional forms of folk religion had either disappeared or been subdued throughout Europe.[60] Somewhat more moderate in their evaluations of the evidence are Robert Scribner[61] and Christina Larner,[62] who wrote of the only partial success of the Counter-Reformation Catholic Church to change peasant religion, and Philip Hoffman, who noted that although there were signs of a shift in piety in the seventeenth century, ecclesiastics did not succeed in suppressing popular festivals, which continued into the nineteenth century and beyond.[63] More forceful in this view is Timothy Tackett, who wrote that most efforts in eighteenth-century France to purify religion from "folkloric" elements were largely unsuccessful, and many such elements continued into the nineteenth century and the early twentieth century.[64]

The portrayal of a unified Catholic elite attempting to reform and impose limits on popular religion has been questioned by Marc R. Forster in his study of villages in the seventeenth century in the bishopric of Speyer, located in the middle Rhine Valley. Aristocratic in origin, the upper clergy in Speyer viewed the reforms of Tridentine Catholicism as a threat to their autonomy and privileges, and most were tolerant of, and even supportive of, popular religion. Without the pressures of the local religious elite, the rural communes were able to resist the wider reform tendencies and continued to shape their popular Catholicism. Priests were obliged to continue to bless crops and animals and to tolerate the carnivals in which people drank heavily and engaged in uninhibited sexual behavior. The continuing fusion of official and popular religion, as in the Corpus Christi processions, when the Host was carried through the village, strengthened the Speyer villagers' attachment to the church and explains the absence of widespread anticlericalism and religious indifference that came to characterize much of the French peasantry in the eighteenth century. Thus, there was greater adherence to the church among the rural populations where Tridentine Catholicism appeared in a diluted form and popular religion remained strong.

Forster points to two major conditions for the lack of reform and the continuing popularity of the church in Speyer. One condition was the absence of a strong episcopal structure. The fragmentation and decentralization of the church in the Speyer area enabled the local elite to modify the reforms that the religious orders had initiated. It also allowed the parish priests and village communes to organize their religious life, especially the processions and festivals, without interference. The other condition was the absence of a strong state or nation-building political elite. This absence, which existed in much of southern and western Germany, was in contrast with the Calvinist Palatinate, Lutheran Württemberg, or Catholic Bavaria, where strong political elites called on the cooperation of reformed churches to discipline the populations. Villagers in Speyer continued to perceive their village churches as local institutions rather than as organs of the state or as units of an interfering church.

After 1650 there was a dramatic change in the education of rural parish priests and in their commitment to reform, but in Speyer, the absence of a strong state and ecclesiastical structures enabled villages to resist the efforts of the more reform-minded priests to force villagers to confess more frequently, behave more morally, and give up their popular practices.[65] In other areas, where reformist priests were part of the cooperative endeavors of strong states and episcopal administrations, their influence may have been greater, but the response of peasants to the attempts to "civilize" and discipline them were by no means uniformly positive. Many peasants resented the interference of priests whose socioeconomic status, unlike that of the parish priests in the Middle Ages, was higher than that of most peasants.

In the Catholic countries of eighteenth-century Europe, the men who filled the higher ranks of the church hierarchy—the cardinals, archbishops, bishops, and cathedral canons—came from the wealthiest and most prestigious strata. This was especially evident in France, where the higher positions recruited from the nobility and the upper bourgeoisie and the rural parish priesthood from the less poor section of the peasantry. In comparison with the Middle Ages, a position in the lower clergy during the eighteenth century had become a professional option with greater economic and social advantages, and although the majority of parish priests came from the lower strata, they tended to come from the wealthier families of their hometowns or villages and to have received an education in secondary schools and seminaries. Unlike the bishops, who often moved to more lucrative and prestigious posts, most priests did not change parishes during their professional lives, but the priests were set apart from the majority of their parishioners by their education, title, clothing, lifestyle, and higher income and status.[66]

In the eighteenth century the Catholic Church was still a prominent landowner and tithe gatherer, but there were differences among countries, and among regions in particular countries, with respect to the importance of the church in the economy of rural society. The church had less influence over the peasants where it was a large landowner, as in southern Iberia and Italy, and more influence where its property was less substantial and peasant ownership was more important, as in northern Portugal, the Basque Provinces, and Brittany.[67]

Whatever the effects on the majority of peasants, the reforms of the Counter-Reformation church began the process of drawing parish priests closer to, and making them exponents of, official religion. The Counter-Reformation period saw the beginnings of sustained efforts by the elite to differentiate the lower clergy from laypeople and to make them effective agents of the church. The soutane, or cassock, was made obligatory for priests, and bishops applied sanctions to overcome the reluctance of priests to accept it.

Rural priests continued to drink, gamble, and participate in village dances and games, and Hoffman writes that, in France, the village clergy remained largely untouched by the Counter-Reformation before 1615. The reform of the rural clergy was a slow process, but closer supervision and demands by the bishops that priests behave in a more austere and decorous manner gradually began to take effect. By the end of the seventeenth century, priests had become less familiar in their contacts with laypeople.

Within newly formed seminaries and other educational institutions, ordinands were socialized into the official and more elitist forms of the religion, and after their training, priests sought to diffuse and inculcate what they had been taught through their sermons, parish schools, and catechism classes. The attempts by some priests to suppress popular customs and their refusals to carry out what they considered "superstitious" or "magical" practices brought them into conflict with their parishioners, who resented the interference and challenge to their traditional religion.[68] These tensions continued into the twentieth century, when many parish priests in rural areas came to be seen as outsiders to the community and as representatives of a church that sought to interfere with traditional religion. Even where the priests came from the same rural milieu as their parishioners, their training in mostly urban seminaries, in which they acquired an elitist form of the religion, placed them apart from their rural congregations.

Regional differences in the organization of the Catholic Church have affected the extent to which rural priests have become an integral part of the hierocracy and exponents of official religion. There are, for example, considerable differences in this respect between northern and southern Italy. Whereas priests in northern Italy have been subject to their bishops in both religious and financial matters, thereby enabling reforming bishops to exercise influence, the churches in southern Italy have been administered collegially by groups of priests, each priest receiving a share in the revenues generated by the property. The priests in northern Italy have been instrumental in expunging thaumaturgical devices, promoting the observance of sacraments, and making Christ a more central figure in religious worship. Priests in southern Italy have continued to participate with laypeople in thaumaturgical patterns of religious action at variance with official Counter-Reformation religion.[69]

Differences between priests and rural laypeople were intensified in many areas of Catholic Europe by the reforms of Vatican II in the early 1960s, and tension has arisen between the official religion of the "modern" priests and the popular religion of rural laypeople, especially in

Mediterranean countries. Not all Catholic countries have experienced this tension. The anticlericalism linked to popular religion that exists in Portugal, Spain, and Italy is rare in Ireland, which differs from the Mediterranean countries in that during the nineteenth century, popular religion came to be penetrated by official religious practices, especially weekly attendance at Mass, and the authority of the clergy.[70]

The attempt by post–Vatican II priests in rural areas to redirect the religious action of their parishioners away from nomic and thaumaturgical goals and toward a greater concern with individual salvation has involved centering the religion more on God and Christ and reducing the religious activities around the saints. Throughout Europe, saint processions have been a target of reform by progressive priests who have objected to the devotion to images and the "profane" actions, such as music and dancing, that are part of the festivities that surround the saints. These actions have strengthened anticlericalism among many rural residents, who, in addition to voicing the long-established complaints that priests charge too highly for their services and that they are hypocritical, especially in sexual matters, now object to their interference in popular religious practices.

The emphasis of the priests on individual salvation has made little impression on laypeople, who have become increasingly skeptical toward the promise of an afterlife. Many take a practical "just in case" attitude toward personal salvation, and they continue to attend Mass and to express concern that they receive the last rites before dying. But conceptions of an existence after death have become increasingly vague, and few envisage the possibility of retribution in hell or purgatory. Saints remain important among many rural laypeople for the assistance they give in this life, their identity with the local communities, and the recreational opportunities provided by their festivities. Priests have met lay opposition when they have attempted to remove the images of saints from the churches or to change the arrangement of images, putting Mary or Jesus in the place of a saint. Some laypeople have become "pious anticlerics" and have asserted that it is the laypeople and not the priests who are now the carriers of the eternally valid religion.[71]

The Decline of Popular Religion

The process of withdrawal by the aristocracy and urban bourgeoisie from popular culture began in the seventeenth century, and in the eighteenth century, the upper strata came to consider popular culture as vulgar and superstitious. For example, astrology, which had been part of the popular religion of all classes and, in its "high" form, had enjoyed scientific status, retained widespread popularity among the lower strata but was rejected in the eighteenth century by the educated classes, who came to perceive it as a belief of the ignorant.[72] In general, a concern with decorum, restraint, and conformity to official religion was demonstrated by the upper strata, who distanced themselves from a popular religion that some sought to transform or suppress.[73]

In rural areas, the distancing of nonpeasant strata from popular religion was related not only to educational developments and the diffusion of urban culture but also to fundamental socioeconomic changes that dissolved the traditional village community. England was the first country in which there was a transformation of the rural economy from the peasant, smallholding, largely subsistence, and local-market agriculture to a capitalist agriculture, with large farms employing landless laborers and producing for a extensive market. Capitalist agriculture was established in England by the eighteenth century, but the social transformation did not cover all rural strata until the second half of the nineteenth century.

The withdrawal of the class of large landowners from popular religion began in the seventeenth century, and they were followed by the "farmers," or smaller landowners and lessees, who emerged as a self-conscious class in the eighteenth and in the first half of the nineteenth century. As the upper and middle strata turned from the village community to lives focused more on their families and classes, the landless laborers were the last to preserve a popular religion, including its communal festivals, albeit in somewhat truncated forms. In the last decades of the nineteenth century, the laborers also abandoned many community customs for a more family-oriented existence.

The decline of popular religion among English farm workers was related to the development of a class consciousness that emerged around the middle of the nineteenth century, together with literacy, greater individualism, and self-discipline. The 1860s saw the growth of trade-union organization among farm workers, followed in 1872 and 1873 by the formation of two nationwide organizations of agricultural workers and a series of strikes. The support of many Anglican clergy for the landowners and employers meant that the laborers' abandonment of popular religion was likely to be accompanied by even less participation in the Church of England. The decline in rural attendance of Anglican churches in this period was also the consequence of the decline of the "closed" parishes, in which powerful squires cooperated with the parsons, and of the appearance of a new type of squire, who recognized no special tie with the villagers under his auspices and made no attempt to influence attendance at church. The decline of specifically rural cultures was accelerated by emigration to the towns, and by World War I, little remained of the traditional community and its popular religion.[74]

In other European societies similar declines in popular religion occurred, beginning among the most educated urban strata and continuing in rural areas down through the classes. Writing on France, Muchembled describes a clear division, becoming evident around 1660, between the culture of the court, aristocracy, and various bourgeoisie and the culture of the masses. The development of schools and greater literacy within the towns accentuated the contrast between the urban areas and the rural areas, where the customs and festivals of popular religion persisted more openly. In the eighteenth century, divisions also emerged in rural areas between the priests and wealthier villagers, who belittled popular culture, and the poorer peasants, whose "mentalities evolved slowly until the middle of the nineteenth century."[75] Historical studies of the religion of peasants in the nineteenth century have found a very similar popular religion to that of the Middle Ages,[76] but the increase in literacy and socioeconomic change in the second half of the century was accompanied by a weakening of the "ritual reveries" and the disappearance of the "excesses" of popular culture. Popular religion as a coherent cultural system was replaced by a more loosely fashioned religion of stricter Christianity and various "superstitions."[77]

Eugen Weber states that the assimilation of the rural masses in France to the dominant French culture, the transformation of peasants into "Frenchmen," occurred only from the last decades of the nineteenth century onward. The development of roads, railways, and wider markets brought hitherto remote rural populations into contact with urban, cosmopolitan populations, and the language and values of the dominant culture were taught in the new schools and spread by printed matter.[78] As we move closer to the present day, examples in Europe of rural communities with the characteristic features of "traditional European" popular religions become more restricted to certain regions of Spain, Portugal, and southern Italy. The erosion of these features has accelerated since the 1960s,[79] and at the end of the twentieth century, anthropologists in search of popular religion in a Catholic or possibly Protestant context were likely to carry out their investigations in Central and South America.[80]

By the end of the nineteenth century, the religious divergence that had emerged from the middle of the seventeenth century between the educated strata and the rural masses had narrowed considerably,[81] but the same socioeconomic forces that were conducive to the penetration of official religion were also favorable to secularization and the diffusion of ideologies that opposed the church. The efforts of the Catholic Church in the second half of the nineteenth century to draw the masses closer to official religion met with considerable success in some countries and areas and with failure in others. The outcomes of the endeavors of church agencies were a consequence of the constellations of economic and political divisions both within nations and between them. There was, for example, a considerable difference between Ireland, where the success of the church was related to the fusion of Catholic and Irish nationalist identities against a Protestant, colonial oppressor, and France, which was divided internally between politically conservative forces supported by the church and politically liberal forces with secularist identities and ideologies. In France, the Catholic Church was successful in some areas but not in others, where it met considerable anticlericalism.[82]

National and area differences with respect to the influence of the church continued in the twentieth century, but since the 1960s, the trend in the rural areas of most European Catholic countries has been a decline in religious beliefs and practice. The church no longer encounters either a popular religion with strong non-official elements or secularist ideologies; instead, it encounters a general indifference toward religion. In most Catholic countries and areas, it is doubtful whether the rural masses were ever extensively incorporated into official religion. By the time the non-official elements in popular religion began to give way to a stronger penetration of official religion, the forces of secularization in Europe were already well under way.

A Different Historical Trajectory: The Popularization of Church Religion in the United States

Peasants were the principal carriers of the community forms of popular religion in "traditional" Europe, and the dwindling of the peasant class in Europe has inevitably been accompanied by the decline of community-based popular religion. In most European societies, the institutional religion of the churches has not gained by these changes; church affiliations and attendances shrank during the twentieth century, and although in even the most unchurched societies only small minorities pronounce themselves atheists, the majority do not subscribe to major tenets of Christianity, such as the existence of the devil and life after death. Far higher percentages of affiliation, attendance, and beliefs are to be found in the United States. The debate over the differences between Europe and the United States with respect to the populations' levels of institutional religious adherence is a complex one, outside the compass of this work,[83] but I suggest the relevance of differences regarding the relationships of elite and popular religion.

One reason the United States differed from Europe is that it never had a massive class of peasants comparable to those in Europe and Asia. In 1800, 94 percent of Americans lived on farms, and in 1890 almost three-quarters of the population lived in rural areas or in towns with fewer than eight thousand people. The rural population continued to grow in absolute numbers up to the 1940s, but only the black sharecroppers in the post–Civil War South could be considered a class of peasants. The social pattern of rural life in the United States, which was especially prominent in the vast Midwest, was of small, independent farming families who, unlike European peasants living together in villages, tended to reside in individual farmsteads some distance from one another.[84] If rural churches were hard to sustain because of the distances, there was also little social basis for the development of unofficial forms of popular religion anchored in small, closely knit communities.

The absence of clearly differentiated religious elites in American Protestantism was another factor that distinguished religion in the United States from religion in Europe. Even in the colonial period, when religious and civil authority were highly integrated, a strict division between clerisy elites and laypeople was less common than in Europe. In the New England settlements, Calvinist theology encouraged the notion that it was the whole community of believers, laypeople and ministers alike, who constituted the elite. As the number of ethnic groups grew, the increase in religious groups undermined the claims to an exclusive authority by religious elites.

What tendencies there were in the colonial period for elite/lay distinctions were weakened by the First Amendment to the Constitution of the new republic, which provided for the separation of church and state, and by the removal of financial support for churches by states in the first decades of the nineteenth century. State churches and governmental support for religious regulation, which continued in various forms and degrees in other Christian societies, were replaced in the United States by the principle of voluntarism and a religious free market where the success of religious movements depended on their attracting and evangelizing the population.

Without governmental aid, churches had to depend on the resources of local populations, which led to congregational self-government becoming the predominant form of church organization. Among the churches influenced by Calvinist theology, elitist notions gave way to the belief in the possibility of universal salvation, so that practically all Protestant groups became proselytizing movements. Even the episcopal elite of the Episcopalian Church, the Anglican Church in America, realized they were now a voluntary association who had to reach out for members and involve the laity in the church government.[85] The educated clergies of the Episcopalian, Congregationalist, and Presbyterian churches, however, which had been the dominant churches in the colonial period, were at a disadvantage in the rural areas compared with the Methodist and Baptist preachers, who, with their little education and farming backgrounds, were far closer to the largely unchurched rural population. The preachers' coarse language and earthy humor, their acceptance of supramundane involvement in everyday life, and their encouragement of emotional display appealed to the common people. They warned of sin and hellfire, but they extolled the virtues of ordinary people and did not subject popular religion to the scrutiny of an official orthodoxy.

The Methodists and Baptists organized revivalist camp meetings for widely distributed rural families, who often traveled long distances for socializing and recreation as well as religion. Despite the strict moral codes of the Methodist and Baptist churches, the early camp meetings were similar in some ways to the religious festivals and carnivals in Europe: in the heightened emotionalism fueled by music and alcohol; in the loosening of constraints, especially of sexual behavior; and in the role reversals that included males submitting to the religious ministrations of women and children. In contrast with the leaders of British Methodism, who disapproved of the unlicensed preaching and popular enthusiasms of camp meetings and were willing to accept fewer recruits in order to preserve discipline, American Methodist leaders promoted the camp meetings as a major instrument of recruitment. The respectability of the camp meetings did, however, become a matter of concern among the American leaders, and by the mid–nineteenth century they had achieved a fair level of regulation by their expulsion of disruptive elements and their spatial organization of participants and scheduling of activities.[86]

Influenced by developments in the commercial theater, revivalist preachers became adept in the stage management of camp meetings and in the provision of recreational activities. The skilled, emotionally charged performances of the preachers and the ecstatic displays of the cured and the saved also provided entertainment value for those whose participation in camp meetings was mainly one of spectatorship. Urban revivals with their large choirs provided spectacles of singing, healing, and salvation on an even bigger scale. The success of the evangelicals in their marketing of religion with a popular appeal has continued until this day, as evidenced by the gospel music industry, book publishing, and televangelists, who portray a beneficent God who heals illnesses, solves personal problems, and saves the souls of spectators.[87]

The combination of soteriology and thaumaturgy, socializing and entertainment, provided in the camp and revival meetings continued when congregations were established with professional ministers. Unlike the religious elites typical of the state and national churches in Europe, whose legal privileges and financial support relieved them of the need to market popular forms of religion, American ministers have depended on their congregations for their living, and they have had fewer opportunities to develop patterns of religious action that differentiate them from the populace.

The professionalism of ministers did not necessarily make them any the less oriented to the market, but it does appear to have reduced the appeal of those movements that had grown rapidly with a populist clerisy. The Methodists were by far the fastest-growing movement in the first half of the nineteenth century and remained the largest movement into the twentieth century, but when their clergy became professionalized, the movement's growth rate was overtaken by the Baptists, whose largely autonomous congregations continued to be served by less-educated farmer preachers. In the twentieth century, the constellations of groups that came to be known as Fundamentalism, the Holiness movement, and Pentecostalism provided leaders who eschewed college education and professional certifications and encouraged popular styles of religious action, including ecstatic demonstrations and enthusiastic chanting and singing.[88]

The market for Protestant religion was a highly competitive one in the United States, but the market mentality was not absent from the Catholic Church, which has had greater success in promoting affiliation and attendance than most of the state-supported Catholic churches of Europe and

Latin America. Although the Catholic Church was not in the business of conversion, its clergy's appreciation of the implications of voluntarism and religious competition led them to conduct parish mission movements that were in some ways the Catholic counterpart to the revivalism of Protestants. The parish missions established devotional societies for laypeople, and these provided similar forms of contact with patron saints and Madonnas to those available in the numerous European shrines and pilgrimages, which were rare in the United States.[89]

Traditional forms of popular religion were brought to the United States by immigrants from peasant backgrounds, especially those from Catholic southern Europe and, more recently, from Latin America. In the urban ethnic enclaves of late-nineteenth-century and early-twentieth-century America, Catholic immigrants re-created shrines of community Madonnas and saints, including many outside ecclesiastical control. In the streets of ethnic neighborhoods, feast days were held when the residents came together to worship their local holy figures.

The immigrants confronted a Catholic Church dominated by the Irish, an earlier wave of immigrants, who filled the positions of a fully developed episcopal structure. The Irish had Americanized the church by their partial adoption of voluntarism and their encouragement of lay participation, but they looked askance at the popular Catholicism of the new immigrants, especially the Italians, who worshiped their saints and Madonnas in their homes and in the streets rather than in the churches. The Italian immigrants attended the churches for baptism and weddings but rarely for Sunday mass.[90]

Like its counterpart in Europe in the nineteenth century, the American Catholic hierarchy encouraged Marian worship and tried to bring popular expressions of that worship under its auspices. Churches, schools, and seminaries were named after various titles of Mary, and the hierarchy sought to regulate the import and distribution within the United States of the "healing" water from Lourdes.[91] It took time, however, for the elite to establish its authority over the worship of popular Madonnas among the immigrants. When a large area of Harlem became an Italian ghetto, an important Madonna of southern Italy, the Madonna of Mount Carmel, became the focus of an annual festival on 115th Street, and for some time popular devotion to the Madonna overwhelmed the official Catholicism of the parish. Only after the church officially recognized the neighborhood Madonna was it able to assert its authority. When the Italians began to leave Harlem, the parish clergy introduced changes in the devotions to the Madonna, emphasizing decorum and the importance of going to confession and communion during the festival.[92]

The locally based popular Catholicism brought by immigrants from southern Europe declined with the migration of white Catholic groups from the inner cities to ethnically heterogenous outlying urban areas and middle-class suburbs, where the second and third generations came increasingly to identify with American Catholics from Europe as a whole. Supramundane assistance to overcome illnesses, misfortunes, and family crises was still sought, and it was during this period of the crystallization of American Catholic identity that the church established shrines to appeal to American Catholics who lived far beyond the neighborhoods in which the shrines were located. Particularly prominent was the shrine of Saint Jude, founded by a religious order in 1926, which gained devotees throughout the United States.

The shrine of Saint Jude was not situated in an ethnic enclave or thought of as a place to be visited but was rather a national shrine to which all American Catholics could direct their supplications for the saint's protection. The clergy and lay associates who managed Saint Jude's shrine developed many devices, included associations for reducing time in purgatory and receiving perpetual masses, to attract and sustain the loyalty and donations of their national clientele. The shrine directed a devotional pitch in 1939 to those who had "any difficult case to be solved quickly, any trouble for which help is needed. . . . If you wish his visible and speedy help, join and be a fervent promoter of St. Jude's League."[93] The shrine marketed numerous items, such as blessed oil, medallions, and different sorts of rosaries, and by their adoption of modern methods of advertising, the organizers helped Saint Jude become a holy figure to whom large numbers of American Catholics turned when they sought the means to overcome their worldly problems.

Saint Jude's popularity grew considerably during the Great Depression and war years, and unlike a number of the local neighborhood shrines, its popularity did not decline in the postwar years. The promoters of Saint Jude were not alone among the American Catholic clergy of the time in recognizing that popular devotions were a formidable source of revenue. In the postwar years, saints were promoted as good investments by many clergy, who were competing with one another to provide buildings and raise funds among the relocating American Catholic population. The clergy's encouragement of popular practices seeking the miraculous came to an end, however, when it was opposed by the ethos of the Second

Vatican Council, which reemphasized the notion of the saints as models of moral life rather than as intercessory beings with extraordinary power. Saint Jude's shrine ceased its supply of holy oil, but although its spokespeople affirmed a disinterested love of the saint, they reassured the devotees that they could still call on the saint to help them with their everyday problems.[94]

Up to the 1960s, the Catholic Church in the United States appeared to have been successful in its incorporation of Americanized Catholics, but although levels of affiliation and attendance have remained high compared with most European and Latin American Catholic countries, in recent decades there has been a decline in these measures of institutional religious adherence. Moreover, the incorporation of Hispanic Catholics who came to the United States with a popular Catholicism similar to that of the earlier Italian immigrants has been less successful than earlier incorporations, and many have defected to Protestant sects.

The American Catholic Church is no longer providing the combined formula of soteriology and thaumaturgy that attracted so many in the past. Many of the middle-class descendants of European immigrants share the distaste of the liberally educated clerisy for the popular devotions to saints and Madonnas, but the religion that is now promoted by many of the new religious elite, emphasizing social morality and a depersonalized supramundane, fails to retain levels of high commitment and participation among laypeople. When immigrants from Latin America seek salvation and healing, they often find it in the Pentecostal churches rather than in their parishes.[95]

Popular religion in the United States, which is conveyed through the mass media and consumed in privatized fashion by individuals and families, has supplemented rather than provided an alternative to church religion. It is often supplied by professionals who occupy positions in churches. An example of one such churchman is Norman Vincent Peale, a Presbyterian minister, whose book *The Power of Positive Thinking* has sold millions of copies since its first edition in 1952 and is still regularly printed. Peale's book is an example of "inspirational" religious literature, which is characterized by a lack of concern with salvation in an afterlife and a strong focus on this-worldly goals of health, occupational achievement, power, successful living, and "peace of mind." During the years of economic depression, inspirational books emphasized the goal of wealth, but since the 1930s, psychotherapeutic aid to alleviate emotional suffering has become a more important theme. The appropriate means are not

participation in rituals and belief in dogmas but rather appropriate subjective states, a "positive thinking" that discounts feelings of anxiety and
fear as simply instances of wrong or bad thinking. To assist the right kind
of thinking are devices such as standard prayers that provide the "spiritual technology" for success. As Peale wrote: "Learn to pray correctly, scientifically. Employ tested and proven methods."[96]

Inspirational literature is one of many religious activities and media
that have contributed to what Charles H. Lippy calls "popular religiosity"
in the United States. Popular religiosity, in Lippy's formulation, is the creation and maintaining by individuals of their worlds of meaning, and it is
because it is an inner, personal experience of the individual that Lippy
prefers the term *popular religiosity* to *popular religion*. In popular religiosity, there is the assumption that nature and everyday life are pervaded by
the supernatural, which is accessible without the mediation of official
representatives of religious institutions; but unlike the popular religion
that has been the focus of this work, popular religiosity is not anchored in
a local community or, indeed, in any group whatsoever. Lippy's history of
popular religiosity in the United States is a chronology of religious phenomena, many of which were promoted by denominations and movements, that perpetuated, reinforced, or intensified personal religious experiences: the evangelical revivals; the Holiness movement; the Catholic
mission movement; religious newspapers, periodicals, and novels; nineteenth-century movements such as Christian Science, New Thought, and
Theosophy; Vatican II; religious movements from Asia; the occult and the
New Age; and Christian rock music.[97]

Lippy's formulation highlights the relative absence in the United States
of a popular religion that is not only differentiated from the religion of
elites but also includes elements that are in tension with official religion.
Working in an open, competitive religious market and seeking to appeal
to widely distributed and mobile populations, religious organizations
have churched America by popularizing religion. In the second half of the
twentieth century, the popularization of religion, especially by the evangelicals, increasingly meant the adoption and adaption of a popular culture shaped in large part by the mass media.

10

Comparisons

The framework of religious action, and in particular the typology of religious goals (nomic, transformative, thaumaturgical, extrinsic), provides the conceptual framework for comparisons of religious elites, popular religions, and the relationships between the two in the world religions. The reasons why religious elites and peasant masses are likely to differ in their religious actions were considered in the first chapter. Similarities among elite patterns and among popular patterns are noted in this chapter, but the emphasis here is on the differences, which are interpreted in relation to the world religions' values, organizations, and societal contexts.

The comparisons are of societies where religious elites hold status and authority and where the popular religion of the masses is embedded in local communities. These conditions no longer prevail in urban, industrial societies, and in the less-developed societies, even remote rural communities have been affected by the processes of modernity (commercialization, industrialization, urbanization, literacy) and by the processes of advanced communications and information technologies that are said to characterize "high modernity" or "postmodernity."

The weakening of the boundaries and identities of local communities in societies undergoing rapid social change does not necessarily result in the disappearance of popular religion, which can take on more organized forms as religious movements that attract members across whole societies. Many of the new religious movements that emerged in Japan after World War II incorporated traditional forms of popular religion, and in Latin America the thaumaturgy and emotional, festive rituals of Pentecostalism, which has spread rapidly since the 1950s, are similar to popular Catholicism. There remain, however, in some of the most populous contemporary societies, vast peasant populations whose popular religion has not yet been eroded or fundamentally transformed by their partial incorporation into the global village. India is perhaps the most prominent example, and in China, popular religion has revived after the loosening of restrictions on religious activities.

Elites

Religious elites have differed both among and within the world religions with respect to the extent that they have focused on certain goals of religious action or sought to encompass them all. One source of differentiation among elites is the tension between, on the one hand, goals of affirmation and continuity (nomic) and dispensation within the world (thaumaturgical) and, on the other hand, transformation. Some elites have specialized in nomic religious action (calendar rites and rites of passage), whereas others have sought to bring about transformation, either by sacralizing the world or seeking salvation from it. Thaumaturgical goals might then be left to non-official religious specialists (village magicians, shamans, etc.), but it is rare for such a strict division of labor to occur. In many cases, official elites have combined nomic and thaumaturgical, transformative and thaumaturgical, or all three types of religious action. Extrinsic goals, such as a cynical manipulation of religion to support the status quo, may also be present, but whether such goals, which are rarely acknowledged, are regarded as uncommon or ubiquitous, their analysis is unlikely to contribute to the tracing of differences among elites.

A distinction between nomic and transformative action has not been clear-cut, especially where transformationism has taken the form of sacralization of the world rather than soteriology. In Confucianism, the goal of the renewal of or harmony with the Tao could take a nomic direction when the Tao was identified with the existential present and a transformative direction when its achievement was seen to require the sacralization of an imperfect or damaged world. Literati who felt an acute tension between the goal of harmony through sacralization and the existent state of affairs may not have sought bureaucratic office, but the nature of their goal was unlikely to lead them to a radical renunciation of the world. Although "quiet sitting" was perhaps a mild form of other-worldly meditation, the major means for both the nomic and transformative types was accumulation of merit through worldly actions of correct ceremony and ethical behavior. The occupation of or aspirations to official office of most literati limited any transformative tendency.

Sacralization of the world, achieved by study and conformity to divine law, was the major transformative goal of the scholarly elites of Judaism and Islam, who would often leave the bulk of thaumaturgical action to non-official religious specialists. In comparison with Confucianism, sacralization of the world in Judaism and Islam was related to soteriology, both of the messianic and paradisiacal varieties, and alternative elites to the scholars emerged when the transformative goal of mystical virtuosos took the form of uniting with or cleaving to the divine. In some areas, in certain periods, a distinction emerged in Islam and Judaism between two, sometimes competing elites: an elite of scholars, seeking the sacralization of the world through divine law, and an elite of mystagogues, including some who renounced the world and practiced meditation and other mystical techniques. Although the combination of scholarship, extreme piety, and an ascetic lifestyle could result in the attribution of sainthood, it was the mystic saints or mystagogues who drew devotees requesting their help in the attainment of soteriological and thaumaturgical goals.

The differentiation of elites within Judaism and Islam was not a distinction of virtuosos and organizational specialists; there were virtuosos among the scholars as well as among the mystagogues, and many of the scholars did not occupy official positions in religious institutions. Moreover, as interpreters of the religious law, the religious elites of Islam and Judaism were not priests, and when religious services were conducted or led by religious specialists, these were not considered priests in the sense of mediators with deities.

A more stable, long-lasting division of religious elites, between virtuosos who renounced the world and priests who were mediators or channels of grace for laypeople, emerged in religions with either a hierarchically conceived soteriology or a higher path to a common soteriological goal. A two-tier soteriology has prevailed in Hinduism and Buddhism: the ultimate salvations of moksha and nirvana as distinct from the proximate salvation of a good rebirth, which is considered by many as a very distant stage from ultimate salvation. Each soteriological goal has its appropriate means; the ultimate salvation requires meditation and renunciation of the world, whereas a good rebirth requires accumulation of merit by ritual and ethical action within the world.

In Hinduism there is a distinction between sadhus, who focus on their individual salvation, and priests, who perform religious actions designed to achieve good rebirths and nomic and thaumaturgical goals. The interrelationship of rebirth and nomic goals is frequently evident, especially in the case of funeral rites performed by funeral priests, who are often Brahmans. Apart from the specialization of temple, domestic, and funeral priests, at a more general level of goal orientation there is some differentiation between Brahmanic priests, who deal more with nomic goals, and non-Brahmanic priests, who deal more with thaumaturgical goals.

The two-tier soteriology in Theravada Buddhism is a basis for the division within the Sangha, between a minority of virtuoso monks who seek nirvana through the path of meditation and the majority of priest-monks who seek a good rebirth for both themselves and the laypeople whom they serve by teaching, holding prayer sessions, and performing pastoral activities. Forest-dwelling virtuosos restrict their interaction with laypeople, but like village and town-dwelling monks, they provide a "field of merit" for laypeople who provide them with their material needs. Virtuosos are believed to have extraordinary powers, acquired on their paths to ultimate salvation, and many respond to lay requests to use those powers to achieve thaumaturgical goals. Among the services of Buddhist priests for laypeople is the performance of funeral ceremonies, a service that is especially prominent among the Buddhist priests in China and Japan, where Buddhism is closer to the Mahayana stream with an emphasis on the successful transfer of the deceased to paradise rather than on nirvana or rebirth.

The basis for the division within the Catholic religious elite has been a two-tier path rather than a two-tier soteriology. There have been elements of hierarchy within the single soteriology: paradise was conceived hierarchically, and a division existed between those who went straight to heaven after death and those whose unremitted sins had to be purged through tortures in purgatory before they could enter heaven. Although the taking of sacraments was a necessary, though not sufficient, means to salvation for all persons, it is likely that many monks and priests in the higher ranks believed they had an advantage over laypeople with respect to their chances to bypass purgatory and arrive at a high position in heaven.

Priests did not necessarily agree with monks regarding the position each sector of the elite could expect in heaven, but for some time it was commonly acknowledged that renunciation of the world in monasteries was the higher path to salvation. Monks were believed to contribute disproportionately to the "treasure of merit" from which those with greater involvement in the world could draw for absolution of their sins. Unlike the Buddhist monks' field of merit, the treasure of merit did not require contact between monks and laypeople, for unlike Buddhism, Christian renunciation did not prohibit the monks' involvement in economic activities and require their material dependence on laypeople. As part of the hierocracy, however, Christian monks were drawn into priestly roles, and in contrast with the somewhat passive provision by Buddhist monks of a field of merit for laypeople, the involvement of Christian monks in the church's distribution of religious facilities took activist directions, including the reform of popular religion. Thus, although the division between two elites in Catholicism was given clear institutional expression within the hierocracy, a division in terms of distinct patterns of religion action was less stable in Catholicism than in Hinduism and Buddhism.

The Protestant emphases on salvation as a gift of God, individual faith, and a single morality in worldly activity were not conducive to a distinction between a virtuoso elite and a clerisy. There were differences among the Protestant movements with respect to whether salvation was achieved, at least in part—as in Lutheranism—or fully ascribed—as in Calvinism—but in every movement a single soteriology and a common path were appropriate for all believers. The one, all-important distinction was between the saved, who either had accepted God's redemptive gift or had been chosen, and the unsaved, who either had fallen from grace or had been damned from the beginning. There was no purgatory to allow for the expiation of sins, and there were no saintly mediators to assist weaker and less-worthy believers. In many Protestant movements, however, there emerged "charismatics" who were recognized as being anointed by the divine, which gave them the thaumaturgical powers to assist other believers.

Popular Religions

The religious breakthroughs of the world religions were not confined to elites. The changes associated with the world religions and indicated by the term *transcendentalism* may have taken considerable time to encompass the peasant masses, and in many cases we do not have sufficient historical data on popular religion to trace the historical contours of the change. The labels used to describe transcendentalism in popular religion (superficial or basic, minor or extensive) depend on one's frame of reference, but enough has been written to show that to label popular religion as "just magic" is a distortion. Accounts of popular religion have demonstrated that the religions of the masses included conceptions of transcendent supramundanes, goals of transformation, and religious identities that extended beyond the local units in which the economic and social lives of the majority in traditional societies were largely confined.

There was no society in which the religious patterns of elites and masses did not overlap considerably, but a number of tentative generalizations concerning the differences between religious elites and the masses are possible. No clear difference presents itself with respect to the engagement of elites and masses in nomic goals, but elites, and particularly virtuosos, have devoted more time to transformative action. When transformationism took the form of soteriology, the material conditions of the masses and their battle for day-to-day survival pushed the notion of other-worldly salvation and its appropriate action into the background, behind that of thaumaturgical action.

A related difference was that the religious action of the masses was oriented less to the "higher," or more transcendental, gods than was the religious action of the elite. Elites and masses have generally placed the same gods at the apex of pantheons, but the masses recognized that the distant, high gods were unlikely to help them in achieving mundane, worldly goals. Superior placement in the pantheon did not necessarily imply that the supramundane was a powerful force on earth. High gods were generally benevolent, but as timeless deities, unbound to particular groups, and little concerned with what they could receive from humans, they were unlikely to concern themselves with the specific problems of ordinary people. Lower gods, in contrast, were identified with particular groups and were dependent on the worship and offerings of humans; they were close to daily life and were likely to provide specific remedies for specific ills.

Elites were more likely to emphasize transcendental identities; in many cases they were tied to organizations, such as orders of monks or associations of priests, with branches and members over extensive areas. Peasants were rarely incorporated into such organizations, and although they were influenced by them, their religious lives remained largely embedded in their local communities. Only in the case of Christianity were the masses incorporated into a translocal, transnational organization, but for most peasants in "traditional" Catholic Europe, the local parish was the major focus of religious identity. Wider religious identities among the lay masses were more typical of Protestantism, which appealed to urban, especially bourgeois strata and to those rural populations where individualized property rights and the growth of commercial agriculture weakened communal ties.

World religions differ as much at the popular levels as at the elite levels with respect to transformative goals, pantheons, and means. A judgment regarding the relative emphases on transformative goals is difficult to make, although popular religion in China and Japan, like much of elite religion in those countries, was especially worldly, with relatively weak forms of transformationism. Differences among popular religions are clearer with respect to the forms of, rather than the emphases on, soteriology: rebirth in Hinduism and Theravada Buddhism in contrast with paradise in Judaism, Christianity, and Islam. Messianic soteriology was the focus of many movements in Judaism, Christianity, Islam, and, to a lesser extent, Buddhism; but either most messianic movements have been of short duration, or their soteriology has lost its messianic tension and has been replaced by paradise after death. In popular Hinduism and Buddhism, paradises (and hells) are frequently understood as temporary locations before rebirth, while in a number of other cases, particularly in certain streams of Mahayana Buddhism, paradise is understood as the final destination or of such long duration as to make consideration of what comes afterward of little interest.

In the popular forms of all the world religions, soteriology has been overshadowed by thaumaturgy, but the distinction between worldly goals and salvation has rarely been emphasized at the popular level. Soteriology and thaumaturgy have been linked in at least two ways. First, particular means are purported to bring about both worldly and other-worldly benefits. For example, Hindus and Buddhists expect that the change in their karma as a consequence of meritorious deeds will both improve their condition in this life and bring about a good rebirth, and Catholics expect that their participation in the sacraments will result in worldly advantages as well as increase their chances of reaching heaven and reducing their time in purgatory after death. Second, thaumaturgical and soteriological goals are understood to be interdependent. In all popular religions, the participation of the living in funeral rituals is intended to assist the deceased in achieving salvation and is also expected to pay dividends for the living, because once the dead are appropriately located, they will be able to protect the living and provide them with material benefits.

The gods at the apex of the pantheons, who tend to be represented in abstract ways—such as T'ien, Brahman, and God the Father—are rarely appealed to in religious action, whatever the nature of the goals. The somewhat less abstract high gods, such as the Jade Emperor, Shiva and Vishnu in their highest forms, the gods closest to the Buddha, and Christ, are linked to nomic and soteriological goals, but they are generally less relevant than lower deities in the achievement of people's thaumaturgical goals. In Eastern religions, impersonal supramundane principles, karma in particular, are relevant to religious action, but the impersonal nature of karma does not mean that it is abstractly conceived; in fact, the discourse of karma focuses on individuals, and popular religion tends to conceptualize the workings of karma in highly concrete terms. Karma is linked to rebirth and general worldly welfare, but specific worldly misfortunes and their solutions are more commonly linked to personalized supramundanes in the lower strata of the pantheon.

The popular pantheons of "monotheistic" and "polytheistic" religions have differed less with respect to the relative prominence of the highest god in religious action than they have with respect to the extent of differentiation made between deities and humans. This differentiation has been least evident in the pantheons of Chinese and Japanese religion, where a large number of deities were believed to have been humans and where ancestors are an especially prominent category of supramundanes. The greatest differentiation has been made in the monotheistic religions, especially Judaism and Islam. Nevertheless, in all popular religions, it is the deities who are conceived to be closest to humans in their purported characteristics that have been most important in patterns of religious action.

Two prominent categories of supramundanes in popular religions are goddesses and saints. The importance of goddesses varies significantly among popular religions: they are most prominent in Hinduism; they represent one of the major non-official and nonbureaucratic categories in Chinese religion; they are found more in Mahayana than in Theravada Buddhism; and they are of least importance in Judaism and Islam. Perhaps the most interesting comparison is between Hinduism and Catholicism. In both cases a distinction can be made between the universal form of the goddess (Devi or Shakti, the universal Mary) and the particularistic forms, which are foci of local identities and frequently associated with fertility and protection from or curing of illnesses. Hindu goddesses span a wide range of representations, from the most protective, ideal wife and mother to the most dangerous of deities. The manifestations of Mary are more consistently beneficent, but representations such as the black Madonnas include elements of danger. Women often take a leading role in the worship of goddesses, and women frequently represent and worship the goddesses in ways different from those of men.

Of the generally beneficent categories of supramundanes, saints have been prominent in all the popular forms of religion considered in this work. As humans or former humans, they are purported to understand and to sympathize or empathize with people's desires and wishes, and as supramundanes, they have the power to bring about the realization of those desires and wishes. In some popular religions the most important saints are alive; in others they are dead; but in all cases they are believed to be highly efficacious in achieving both the soteriological and thaumaturgical goals of their devotees.

With respect to the lower categories of supramundanes, there are striking similarities among popular religions in their conceptions of ghosts or spirits of the dead. The belief that ghosts are unhappy spirits, who haunt and cause harm to the living because of the nature of their deaths or because their kin have not carried out the appropriate rituals to settle them in the afterlife (possibly they had no kin), is common to almost all popular religions. Community rituals are carried out for the benefit of, and for protection against, the "hungry ghosts" who have not been cared for by kin.

Ghosts are only one of many maleficent forces that are common in all popular pantheons. The Eastern religions have a greater number of ambiguous supramundanes, who can work both good and evil. The status of supramundanes in Hinduism and Buddhism also tends to be more fluid than in other world religions, and humans are able to transform the characteristics of deities and move them from one level of the pantheon to another.

In all popular religions, the types of transactions with and the nature of offerings to supramundanes vary in accord with their positions in the pantheons. In general, transactions with higher gods are conceived as asymmetrical; offerings to them are frequently understood as symbolic, and reciprocal favors in exchange for worship and devotions are not seen to be guaranteed. Reciprocity is expected from lower gods, with whom hard negotiations may be conducted.

Elites and Popular Religion

Distinctions have been made among a number of orientations of elites (toleration, superimposition, repression) and lay masses (indifference, appropriation, resistance) toward each other's religious actions. The religious goals of virtuosos and their path of renunciation have often distanced them from lay religious patterns, toward which they have displayed an indifferent toleration. Some virtuoso mystagogues and saints have gained lay followings, and the virtuosos have been influenced in turn by lay devotees who have encouraged them to perform thaumaturgical acts. A common dilemma of virtuosos with lay followings has been between the desire to remove themselves from worldly pursuits and contacts and the wish to meet the demands of laypeople from whom they receive material and other benefits.

The strategies of elites who occupy the higher ranks of religious organizations are commonly influenced by two sets of interests that are in tension with each other: (1) their status interests to maintain or increase distinctions (including religious action) between themselves and the lay masses and (2) their material, political, organizational, and ideological interests to monopolize and control the distribution of religious benefits among the total population. Status interests may induce members of the elite to emphasize the religious distance between themselves and the masses; other interests may induce them to impose their religious patterns on the masses.

It was rare for an elite to operate a consistent strategy over a long period toward the lay masses: they sought both to diffuse the great tradition among the masses and to draw religious boundaries between themselves and the masses. The elite propagated what they regarded as the most elementary notions and behaviors of the great tradition, but they limited direct access to the canon, the purported core of the great tradition, and up to the period of large-scale printing, the few copies of the sacred writings were in the hands of the religious elite and a small number of powerful laypeople. Even when there were no formal restrictions on lay access to the canon, most laypeople were unable to read, and of those who were able to read the vernacular, there were few who could read the sacred language.

Elites differed, however, in the extent to which they emphasized diffusion and boundary maintenance, in their methods of diffusion, and in their policies toward unofficial forms of popular religion. Elites varied in their strategies with respect to both the supramundanes and the religious specialists (the wise people, shamans and shamanesses, etc.) of popular religion. With respect to the deities, one strategy of the elites was to superimpose their deities on those of popular religion; this involved changes in the names, iconography, and forms of worship of the deities. Another strategy was the incorporation of the popular supramundanes, with little or no change in identities and characteristics, into the lower ranks of the official pantheon. Popular deities who remained outside or were excluded from the official pantheon were either tolerated by elites as part of the culture of the "uncivilized" masses or repressed as purported threats to official religion. Likewise, religious specialists from among the masses who performed their roles outside the hierocracies or organizations of monks and priests were either tolerated or persecuted by the elite. An elite seeking to monopolize the distribution of religious benefits might incorporate popular deities into its pantheon and attempt to exclude popular religious specialists as mediators or organizers of the gods' worship.

In all cases, both values and structural dimensions have constituted the bases of the divisions between religious elites and lay masses, but the relative importance of values and structures has varied. In Hinduism and Theravada Buddhism, two-tier soteriologies have comprised the most important value that has distinguished between elites, especially virtuosos, and the masses. The bases of priestly elites have also depended on the caste system in Hinduism and the Sangha in Buddhism. The structural bases of the elite/lay mass distinction were more important in China, where soteriology was absent from Confucianism, the dominant elite religion, and in Europe, where Catholicism emphasized a single soteriology (albeit with some hierarchical elements). It was in China and in Christian countries that the notion of official religion came to the fore: elite religion was an integral part of the institutional apparatus of the Chinese patrimonial state, and in Catholicism, the structural basis of official religion was a strong hierocracy supported by regimes.

In accord with the Chinese state's goal of hierarchical order, the religious elite from the literati superimposed state deities on a number of local, popular deities, who were thereby incorporated into the highly bureaucratized official pantheon. As members of the highest status group of the society, however, the elite of the state religion sought to strengthen their status claims through religious differentiation and made no sustained effort to incorporate the masses into official religion. Most popular supramundanes remained outside official religion, and non-official temples with their own priests were allowed to operate side by side with official temples, the two sets catering to differentiated but overlapping populations. For the most part, the persecution of popular religion was limited to sectarian or transregional religious movements, which were regarded as political threats. The Buddhist and Taoist elites, who remained largely outside official religion, also combined strategies of superimposition with the drawing of boundaries between their religions and popular religion, but the absence of strong religious institutions made these boundaries porous.

The Catholic elite superimposed its supramundanes, particularly Mary and the saints, on goddesses of fertility and other popular deities, and in contrast with China, the unincorporated supramundanes and their human mediators were condemned as belonging to the powers of evil, in rebellion against God and God's representative on earth, the church. The Catholic elite were recruited from the higher social strata, but unlike the religious elite from the Chinese literati, the status of bishops was derived not from their membership in a status group composed of mostly laypeople but from their high positions within the hierocracy. The status and power of the Catholic elite were linked to their success in establishing and maintaining their organization's monopolistic distribution of religious benefits, a monopolism driven also by the belief that the church was the only valid vehicle of the true religion. Although unofficial, popular religion was consistently condemned by members of the elite, it was nevertheless rarely persecuted by them until the early modern period. As part of the Reformation and the Counter-Reformation, more sustained campaigns to reform popular religion included the repression of popular practices such as indecorous festivals and the diabolization and persecution of individuals who were purported to worship the supramundane enemies of Christianity.

Neither basis of official religion—strong patrimonial state or hierocracy—was present in India and the Theravada countries of Southeast Asia. Hindu and Buddhist rulers supported the religions with endowments; Brahmans were, on occasion, incorporated into civil administrations; and some Buddhist kings supported the unification and hierarchization of the Sangha; but political regimes lacked the continuity of the Chinese state and its complex bureaucratic structure. The religious elites of Hinduism and Buddhism legitimized political regimes in India and Southeast Asia, but kings were rarely dependent on the support of religious elites, whose political influence tended to be limited. In contrast with Europe, there was no Hindu or Buddhist hierocracy to put pressure on rulers or the lay masses. The religious organizations of the elites do not encompass laypeople (the temporary monasticism of a large proportion of males in some Buddhist countries might be considered a partial exception), and the elites are themselves divided by separate orders, by the gods they serve, and, in India, by caste or subcaste. The links among temples and monasteries are loose, and there is only a minimal hierarchy of the priestly offices and monks' positions.

The material support of Brahman priests and the purchase of their services required that sections of the population accept the elite's "Brahmanism" or Hinduism, and this involved the Brahmans in some "Sanskritization" of local, popular deities. Rather than being mandated from above, however, Sanskritization was often initiated from below by castes who wished to improve their position. The caste status of the Brahmans depended on the maintenance of religious differences, and they did not therefore seek to homogenize religious action among the population. As long as their exclusive rights as priests of the highest supramundanes were recognized, the Brahman elite did not oppose popular forms of religion served by non-Brahmanic priests.

The Buddhist elite have incorporated some popular deities into the Buddhist cosmology, but a prominent tendency in Theravada Buddhism has been to differentiate between Buddhism, which provides the path to salvation (both proximate and ultimate), and the spirit cults, which deal only with worldly problems and goals. Buddhism also provides a thaumaturgy, but its superiority over the spirit cults is attributed to its soteriology. Although monks are more likely than laypeople to clarify this differentiation, the general recognition of the superiority of Buddhism over spirit worship has enabled the Buddhist elite to tolerate popular religious specialists, such as mediums who deal with spirits.

Judaism and Islam have shared with Christianity an exclusivity from other religious traditions and a concern to monopolize the distribution of religious benefits among the respective populations. Unlike the Catholic elite, the Jewish and Muslim religious elites are interpreters of the law rather than priests, and without hierocracies and political power, they have generally been tolerant toward popular religion. The focus of rabbis and ulema on the interpretation of the law left a niche for popular practitioners of thaumaturgy, and the elites were unable to prevent the development and spread of popular movements around alternative elites of saints, who offered their followers both soteriology and thaumaturgy.

Elites vary greatly in the extent to which they have sought to change popular religion or remain content to tolerate it. When elites have attempted to transform popular religion, the masses have responded by appropriation or resistance or a combination of the two. Peasants have often accepted the superimposition of deities and have come to worship, for example, the Virgin Mary or one of the consorts of Shiva in place of a local fertility goddess; but the peasants have appropriated such deities in ways that correspond to their own goals and representations of deities. Thus, although local gods might have their names changed or, as occurred in China, come to be known by both official and popular names, there was often little essential change with respect to their attributes and to the goals sought through their agency. In China, local officials masked the minimal changes in popular religion by representing popular deities to their superiors in ways that conformed to official expectations. In India, high Sanskritic gods were parochialized, and in Catholic Europe, local Madonnas were viewed as quite separate from the Madonnas of other villages. Whereas elites regarded saints as exemplars who had reached the highest form of salvation, laypeople entered into hard negotiations with saints in order to achieve their worldly goals. In some cases, the appropriation of deities by the masses resulted in major transformations, as in the case of the bodhisattvas, who lost their Buddhist attributes and became popular gods and goddess in China and Japan.

In most societies, peasants continued to worship deities that were outside official religion or the great traditions of the elites. Various categories of popular gods in China, particularly the goddesses, the comic gods, and martial heroes, remained quite separate from the bureaucratized pantheon of official religion. A large number of supramundanes in India have not been connected to the Sanskritic deities, and lower castes do not always accept the elites' hierarchizations of the deities. Although the powers of Buddhism are invoked in Theravada countries to bring the spirits under control, the worship of spirits is often carried on quite separately from the rituals of Buddhism. In many of these cases, elites have acknowledged the existence of the popular supramundanes while emphasizing their inferior nature and refraining from participating in their worship. Similarly, the existence, in Islamic countries, of *djinn*, believed to be composed of vapor or smokeless flame, and in Jewish communities, of *dybbukim*, devils believed to possess people, has been acknowledged by the respective elites, who have nevertheless condemned their worship. Condemnation has rarely been acted on, and with the exception of the Catholics, religious elites have generally not interfered with the worship of popular deities.

Peasants are often critical of religious elites. The sincerity of Hindu and Buddhist renouncers has often been questioned, and some laypeople criticize the "selfishness" of renouncers who are concerned only with their own salvation. Priests are often criticized for their inappropriate materialism and hypocrisy, and in those cases where celibacy is expected, their sexual behavior is sometimes questioned. Examples of popular ridicule of elite religion occurred in China, where rituals involving the comic deities made fun of the pomp and decorum of officialdom and their religion, and in Catholic Europe, where carnivals "turned the world upside down," reversing the hierarchies and offering laughter in place of the solemnity of official religion. Although such ceremonies and festivals could provide the spark for rebellion, this was unusual, and a common argument has been that rituals of reversal were safety valves, occasions for letting off steam, that enabled the hierarchies to continue. Whatever the effects of such rituals, in Europe the Protestant and Counter-Reformation elites disapproved of what they saw as an illegitimate mixing of the sacred and profane, and they contributed to the "civilizing process" of popular festivals.

Commodification, Popular Culture, and Popular Religion in the West

The Christian religious elites who sought to reform popular festivals found allies among capitalists, both in agriculture and in industry, who opposed the festivals as hindrances to disciplined labor and production. Viewed as occasions of idleness and disorderly behavior, the religious festivals were incongruent with rational time scheduling and work regimens. Workers opposed interferences with their traditional festivities, but they were unable to withstand religious reform after it gained the support of the economically dominant classes. The number of holy days declined, and the carnivalesque role-reversal components were muffled and restrained.

The growth of the modern, consumer-based economy in the nineteenth and twentieth centuries brought changes in the economic ramifications of festive holidays. By the end of the nineteenth century, holidays in Western societies were no longer seen as impediments to rational economic production but as important occasions for consumption and profit. The Christmas season, which had been reduced to Christmas Eve and Christmas Day for the sake of industrial efficiency and urban order, became the grand festival of consumption. The commodities sold at Christmas include religious items such as manufactured creches, cards with religious messages, and recorded sacred music, but most Christmas presents and paraphernalia have no Christian meanings, and the development of the modern Christmas has taken place with little involvement of the churches.

The churches took a more important role in the growth of consumerism around Easter. In the United States in the 1880s, the afternoon promenade of Easter churchgoers became the Easter Parade, the great fashion show of the year; church music and decorations turned into the interior displays of department stores; and religious symbols such as crosses and church replicas were sold in large numbers. The reinvention of festivals by consumerism is particularly evident in the case of Saint Valentine, who from a thaumaturgical saint in the medieval world and an intercessor between young men and women in later centuries became, in the nineteenth century, the nominal reason for the exchange of mass-produced greetings.

From community celebrations in the streets, fields, and churchyards, religious festivals became foci of personal relationships, especially reciprocal exchanges within the family and among relatives and friends. The critics of the consumerism that now propels the festivals have included religious professionals who bewail the loss of religious meanings, especially of Christmas and Easter. The criticisms may be viewed as an attack on popular culture and as a modern form of the attacks on popular religion by the religious elites in the past, but the extent to which festivals driven by commercial interests are a form of popular culture is also subject to controversy.[1] Even if we grant that the holiday observances are "popular" in crucial ways, because consumption is always having an effect on production, the holidays include little in the way of popular *religion*. Insofar as the festivals include invocations of supramundane beings, these occur within the religious institutions. Christmas and Easter are the only days of the year when many churches in Europe have large congregations.

The religious festivals are only one example, albeit a prominent one, of the commodification of religion in modern societies. The marketing of religious items was not absent in preindustrial societies, but with the general expansion of the marketplace of culture in the nineteenth and twentieth centuries, there has been an enormous increase in the buying and selling of religious items and services. Nowhere is this more evident than in the United States, where the separation of church and state, religious pluralism, and consequent high competition were conducive to the marketing and popularizing of religion both by the churches and by independent entrepreneurs. Religious professionals adopted the merchants' techniques of publicity, and from the early decades of the twentieth century on, churchgoing was advertised as a popular thing to do, with an emphasis on the benefits of companionship and comfort as well as on salvation. Reading material, which was almost the sole religious commodity in the early stages of the development of the cultural mass market, has retained its importance, with an increasing number of religious books appearing on the best-seller nonfiction list. Books that have sold in the millions include those that provide religious formulas for success, such as *The Power of Positive Thinking*, by Norman Vincent Peale, and those that predict the millennium, of which the most prominent example is *The Late, Great Planet Earth*, by Hal Lindsey. From the 1980s into the twenty-first century, books for "conservative" or evangelical Christians have included diet books, love-making manuals, jogging and exercise books, and the Christian equivalents of Harlequin romances. Religious commodities in the cultural market have diversified considerably since World War II, and in addition to books, the Christian bookshops, of which there are about six thousand in the United States, sell videos, rock music, bumper stickers, T-shirts, coffee mugs, and frisbees, all with Christian messages.

Salesmanship was an important component of religious radio stations, from the 1920s on, and, after 1950, of the televangelists, who in some cases expanded their corporations to include spectacular temple complexes and religious theme parks. Outside the specifically Christian market, a highly diversified range of religious products are marketed under the "New Age" tag that became popular in the 1980s. There are numerous New Age businesses, including publishers of books and magazines, radio stations, music companies, hotels, restaurants, holistic health-care centers, and training courses that range from self-improvement to "transcendental awareness." New Age products include items to assist meditation and prayer, such as cushions, yoga mats, incense, and crystals, and to produce health and longevity, such as health foods, natural vitamins, and microbiotic cookware.[2]

Little remains of rural, community-based popular religion in Western societies, but it can be argued that the commodification of religion, together with the deregulation of the established churches and the declining relevance of official religions, has made room for a popular religion that is based not on local communities but rather on a loosely structured network of groups, amorphous organizations, and businesses, especially those involved in the mass media. At this point my discussion links up with those sociologists of Western religion who, while admitting the decline of mainstream churches and denominations and the fall in the levels of belief in the central doctrines of official religion, point to a relatively uninstitutional-ized, decentralized religious culture that has been termed a *cultic milieu*.[3] The fuzziness of the boundaries of this alternative religious culture, over-lapping as it does with all kinds of alternative therapies, medicines, health foods, quasi- or pseudoscience, environmentalism, and vegetarianism, makes any estimation of the proportion of the populations involved im-possible to calculate, but the numbers involved would appear to be suffi-cient to justify the use of the term *popular religion*.

Many of the new religious movements that were established or grew rapidly in the late 1960s and the 1970s have been linked to the cultic mi-lieu. Although some of the new movements drew on the Judeo-Christian tradition, others represented Western adaptations of Eastern religions or provided quasi-religious therapies. The membership of the new religious movements remained, however, a tiny proportion of the populations, and it is the less-organized forms, the audience cults and the client cults, that have assembled the bulk of the alternative patterns of religion.

Client cults consist of consultants and their fee-paying clients, and al-though those offering the cult service may be organized, there is little or no organization of clients, whose involvement is partial and who are often members of churches unconnected to the cult service. Even more diffusely organized are the audience cults, whose consumers may have some contact with cult lecturers or workshop leaders but who otherwise consume the cult beliefs through newspapers, magazines, books, radio, television, and the Internet.[4] In contrast with the local community con-text of traditional popular religion, whose "wise people" performed ser-vices for their fellow residents in face-to-face relationships, the modern cult purveyors are unlikely to know their clients outside the service rela-tionships and often communicate with them through relatively imper-sonal media and places, such as bookshops, lecture halls, conventions, and festivals.

In the 1980s the term *New Age* came to be used to refer to a large part of the cultic milieu. Most participants in the New Age are involved as an audience, and involvement is frequently restricted to only one or two of the many activities that have come to be associated with the label. *New Age* encompasses alternative medicines, ecological issues, herbal-ism, meditation exercises, and Eastern religions, as well as a wide range of items that were previously categorized as part of the occult: astrol-ogy, telepathy, ESP (extrasensory perception), clairvoyance, graphology, palmistry, and beliefs in ghosts, UFOs (unidentified flying objects), lost civilizations, and reincarnation. Among the activities that have had phases of popularity under the "New Age" label are use of crystals in healing and divination, shamanism, and "channeling," which refers to communications from non-ordinary consciousnesses such as the spirits of dead pop stars and space commanders from other planets.[5]

Some of the more committed New Agers join their beliefs to criticisms of modern societies and point to "premodern" societies, such as those of the Native Americans, the Inuit, and the Tibetans, as superior. The belief among some New Agers that it is possible to receive revelations from the spirits of plants may be seen as a return to animism, although in general, few New Agers emphasize their links with the popular religion of the peasants of past Western societies. The neopagan, witchcraft groups, who believe they are practicing a traditional folk religion, tend to dissociate themselves from beliefs and activities that label themselves "new."[6]

New Age activities have been categorized on a continuum from world-rejecting to world-accepting. The world-rejecting stance is that involvement in modern capitalist society damages the self, but it is the world-affirming stance, with its promises of inner spirituality together with the benefits of modern capitalist society, that has become the dominant trend in the New Age. Many New Age services, as well as new religious movements such as est (Erhard Seminar Training), Scientology, TM (Transcendental Meditation), and Nichiren Shoshu, provide means that are purported to allow their clients or members both to sacralize their selves and to succeed in capitalism. In some versions, inner spirituality becomes merely the means to the ends of prosperity and power.[7]

The this-worldly orientations of the New Age are shared by the most successful new religious movements. Whereas earlier sectarian movements, as variants of the dominant Christian tradition, emphasized other-worldly salvation, to be attained by ascetic forms of religious action, the goals of new movements are those of health, wealth, happiness, and positive life experiences, to be attained by relatively undemanding techniques such as short meditation sessions and chanting mantras. Christian sects in the past often drew their members from lower-middle and lower social strata, whose desire for salvation has often been interpreted as a response to their relative deprivation in this world. The new religious movements draw most of their members and participants from materially secure, educated strata who seek religions that offer to meet their rising expectations of this-worldly benefits.[8] Changes in popular religion are also to be expected when its major carriers are no longer peasants, living hard and often short lives, but economic classes who have high standards of living and expect high levels of enjoyment over lengthy life spans.

Nomic goals have become secularized in the sense that, whereas in the past the concern was to conserve and renew the natural order by sacrifice to or identity with supramundane beings, the concern today is to conserve the environment and prevent further damage by this-worldly techniques of limitation, conservation, and renewal of natural resources. There is, however, a New Age environmentalism that conceives the planet as an animate object, a self-regulating superorganism that demands the respect due to a superior being.[9]

As in popular religion in general, the most prominent goals of most New Age participants are thaumaturgical. There is also an extrinsic goal among many participants in the sense that the New Age or cultic activities are a form of entertainment, a nonserious, playful activity for casual dabbling that treats supramundane agents and forces, once fearful and threatening, as attractive and amusing. For a minority of the more highly involved, there is a transformational goal insofar as the Age of Aquarius, replacing that of Pisces, is believed to represent a radically changed planet—an age that, according to some, has already begun, while according to others, it is coming in the near future. Quasi-religious forms of environmentalism link saving the planet with self-development, but the prominent form of transformationism in the New Age is the transformation of the self and not of the natural and social orders. The self, as potentially or actually perfect, is both the major supramundane condition of New Age religious action and its principal goal: the New Age is manifested when people overcome their false levels of consciousness and come to achieve or to experience their essential, perfect selves. A wide variety of techniques are available to liberate the self from the false levels of consciousness and to help it achieve its true nature. This self-transformation is, for the most part, a transformation that is expected to occur in this world.[10]

For large proportions of the populations in Western societies, the goals of avoiding hell, limiting one's time in purgatory, or gaining a place in paradise have receded as the existence of such other-worldly places has lost its credibility. Hope has been transferred from heaven to earth; recent surveys in a number of Western societies have found that, whereas no more than one-quarter of the populations believe in hell, and between one-third and one-half believe in heaven, between one-fifth and one-quarter now believe in reincarnation. Reincarnation is one of a number of non-official popular beliefs (astrology is another) that, while associated by New Agers with the New Age, is found among many people, including members of Christian churches, who take little interest in or may never have heard of the New Age. Some conceive of reincarnation from one life to another as spiritual progress, but they do not consider reincarnation as a goal that requires special religious behavior or a practical morality.[11]

In their thaumaturgical focus, past and contemporary popular religions are similar; but whereas, in the past, one important focus of popular religion was protection against those evil forces believed to bring ill fortune, illness, and death, popular religion today focuses on the achievement of greater health, more success, an even longer life, as well as less tangible goals such as creativity and autonomy. Defensive goals have largely been displaced by goals signifying optimism, self-esteem, and success. The supramundanes, which in traditional popular religions included many threatening and fearful beings, are now predominantly good-natured and exist only to assist humans in their goals of self-improvement. Some groups conceive certain energy fields as polluting or see the self as subject to elements, possibly from previous lives, that hinder its improvement, but for the most part, the universe is conceived of as a benign place in which the self can achieve the good that is inherent within it.

In those Western Catholic societies where the majority no longer regularly attend church services, many nominal Catholics construct their personalized forms of religion by drawing principally on a stock of Christian symbols, without the mediation of a regulating institution. We may continue in such cases to refer to little traditions, although they are now little traditions of individuals or families rather than of whole communities. In more religiously pluralistic settings, individuals draw on a wide range of religious sources, including several world religions as well as Western occult traditions, to construct a religious *bricolage* of the conditions and means of religious action. It may be that in societies of advanced modernity or postmodernity, where religious elites have been left with little power or influence and where official religion has lost its meaning, the major forms of religious action will be those of individualized popular religion.

Notes

NOTES TO CHAPTER 1

1. Karl Jaspers, *The Origin and Goal of History* (London: Routledge & Kegan Paul, 1953); S. N. Eisenstadt, "The Axial Age Breakthroughs—Their Characteristics and Origins," in S. N. Eisenstadt, ed., *The Origins and Diversity of Axial Age Civilizations* (Albany: State University of New York Press, 1986), pp. 1–25.

2. Michael Mann, *The Sources of Social Power*, vol. 1: *A History of Power from the Beginning to A.D. 1760* (Cambridge: Cambridge University Press, 1986), pp. 301–2, 363.

3. Robert N. Bellah, "Religious Evolution," *American Sociological Review* 29 (1964):358–74.

4. Benjamin I. Schwartz, "Wisdom, Revelation and Doubt: Perspectives on the First Millennium BC," *Daedalus* 104 (Spring 1975):1.

5. Jaspers, *Origin and Goal of History*, p. 1.

6. Ernest Gellner, *Plough, Sword and Book: The Structure of Human History* (London: Collins Harvill, 1988), p. 91.

7. Max Weber, *The Methodology of the Social Sciences* (New York: Free Press, 1949), p. 52.

8. Max Weber, "The Social Psychology of the World Religions," in H. H. Gerth and C. Wright Mills, eds., *From Max Weber: Essays in Sociology* (London: Routledge & Kegan Paul, 1948), p. 267.

9. Ibid.

10. See, for example, Chaturvedi Badrinath, "Max Weber's Wrong Understanding of Indian Civilization," in Detlef Kantowsky, ed., *Recent Research on Max Weber's Studies of Hinduism* (Munich: Weltforum Verlag, 1986), pp. 45–58.

11. Max Weber, *Economy and Society* (New York: Bedminster Press, 1968), pp. 407–19, 437–38, 519–21; Max Weber, "Science as a Vocation," in Gerth and Mills, eds., pp. 148–49; Max Weber, *The Protestant Ethic and the Spirit of Capitalism* (London: George Allen & Unwin, 1930), pp. 117–18.

12. The term *supramundane* to refer to beings such as deities, spirits, saints, demons, etc. and to cosmic processes such as the Tao and karma is preferred here to *supernatural*. Such beings and processes are not necessarily viewed by people as above or apart from nature.

13. Bellah, "Religious Evolution."

14. Eisenstadt, "Axial Age Breakthroughs," pp. 2–3.

15. Peter L. Berger, *The Sacred Canopy* (Garden City, N.Y.: Doubleday, 1967), pp. 34–35, 113–18.

16. Steven Collins, *Nirvana and Other Buddhist Felicities* (Cambridge: Cambridge University Press, 1998), pp. 104, 176–77.

17. Bellah, "Religious Evolution"; Gananath Obeyesekere, "Theodicy, Sin and Salvation in a Sociology of Buddhism," in E. R. Leach, ed., *Dialectic in Practical Religion* (Cambridge: Cambridge University Press, 1968), pp. 12–18; S. N. Eisenstadt, "The Axial Age: The Emergence of Transcendental Visions and the Rise of Clerics," *Archives Europeennes de Sociologie* 23 (1982):294–314.

18. Eisenstadt has distinguished the types of salvation in the world religions as this-worldly, as in Confucianism; other-worldly, as in Hinduism and Buddhism; and a combination of this- and other-worldly themes, as in the monotheistic religions. Eisenstadt, "Axial Age Breakthroughs," p. 16. A this-worldly salvation may be seen as a contradiction in terms, and Weber, for one, denied that Confucianism was a salvationist religion. Max Weber, *The Religion of China: Confucianism and Taoism* (New York: Macmillan, 1964), pp. 156, 228. Most contemporary scholars of Confucianism argue that Confucianism included transcendental elements.

19. Obeyesekere, "Theodicy, Sin and Salvation," pp. 14–18.

20. Timothy Fitzgerald, "Hinduism and the 'World Religion' Fallacy," *Religion* 20 (1990):101–18.

21. These definitions are modifications of those made by Vilfredo Pareto, the classical theorist of elites. See T. B. Bottomore, *Elites and Society* (London: C. A. Watts, 1964), pp. 1–3; Anthony Giddens, *The Class Structure of the Advanced Societies* (London: Hutchinson, 1973), pp. 119–20.

22. Weber, "Social Psychology of the World Religions," pp. 287–88.

23. Weber, *Economy and Society*, pp. 1166–73.

24. Ibid., pp. 54, 56.

25. Ibid., pp. 560, 1166–68.

26. Ibid., pp. 472, 479, 481–82, 1160, 1177–78, 1180–81.

27. R. W. Scribner, "Interpreting Religion in Early Modern Europe," *European Studies Review* 13 (1983):89–105; H. C. Erik Midelfort, "Sin, Melancholy, Obsession: Insanity and Culture in Sixteenth Century Germany," in Steven L. Kaplan, ed., *Understanding Popular Culture: Europe from the Middle Ages to the Nineteenth Century* (Berlin: Mouton, 1984), p. 113; Roger Chartier, *Cultural History: Between Practices and Representations* (Cambridge: Polity Press, 1988), pp. 38–39; Ellen Badone, "Introduction," in Ellen Badone, ed., *Religious Orthodoxy and Popular Faith in European Society* (Princeton, N.J.: Princeton University Press, 1990), pp. 4–8; C. Scott Dixon, "Popular Beliefs and the Reformation in Brandenburg-Ansbach," in Bob Scribner and Trevor Johnson, eds., *Popular Religion in Germany*

and Central Europe, 1400–1800 (London: Macmillan, 1996), pp. 119–39; Nancy Caciola, "Wraiths, Revenants and Ritual in Medieval Culture," *Past and Present* 152 (1996):5–6.

28. Natalie Zemon Davis, "Some Tasks and Themes in the Study of Popular Religion," in Charles Trinkaus and Heiko A. Oberman, eds., *The Pursuit of Holiness in Late Medieval and Renaissance Religion* (Leiden: E. J. Brill, 1974), pp. 308–9.

29. Peter Brown, *The Cult of the Saints: Its Rise and Function in Latin Christianity* (Chicago: University of Chicago Press, 1981), pp. 13–20; Peter Brown, *Society and the Holy in Late Antiquity* (London: Faber & Faber, 1982), pp. 8–13; Scribner, "Interpreting Religion in Early Modern Europe"; Bob Scribner, "Introduction," in Scribner and Johnson, eds., *Popular Religion*, pp. 1–15; David Hall, "Introduction," in Kaplan, ed., *Understanding Popular Culture*, pp. 5–18; Davis, "Some Tasks and Themes"; Aron Gurevich, *Medieval Popular Culture: Problems of Belief and Perception* (Cambridge: Cambridge University Press, 1988), pp. xiv–xv.

30. Enzo Pace, "The Debate on Popular Religion in Italy," *Sociological Analysis* 40 (1979):71–75.

31. This is William Christian's point about popular religion when he writes about sixteenth-century Spain. He prefers to use the term *local religion* and writes that only few kinds of people, such as certain humanists and mystics, did not think in local terms. William A. Christian Jr., *Local Religion in Sixteenth-Century Spain* (Princeton, N.J.: Princeton University Press, 1981), pp. 178–79.

32. Karen Louise Jolly, *Popular Religion in Late Saxon England: Elf Charms in Context* (Chapel Hill: University of North Carolina Press, 1996), pp. 18–21, 89–97, 173–74.

33. Conflations of intellectual levels, social carriers, and social contexts were made by anthropologists who distinguished between great and little traditions. See, for example, Robert Redfield, *Peasant Society and Culture: An Anthropological Approach to Civilization* (Chicago: University of Chicago Press, 1956); McKim Marriott, "Little Communities in an Indigenous Civilization," in McKim Marriott, ed., *Village India: Studies in the Little Community* (Chicago: University of Chicago Press, 1955), pp. 171–222.

34. Jack Goody, *The Logic of Writing and the Organization of Society* (Cambridge: Cambridge University Press, 1985), pp. 1–26. Certain qualifications should be made here. Collins notes that the transcendentalism of both the Upanishads and early Buddhism emerged before the introduction of writing, or at least before the use of writing for cultural materials, and that the subsequent traditions continued to be oral in many senses of the word (Collins, *Nirvana and Other Buddhist Felicities*, p. 23). King writes that Hinduism was handed down orally through many generations from gurus to specially initiated disciples who belonged to the upper castes of the "twice born" (Ursula King, "Some Reflections on Sociological Approaches to the Study of Modern Hinduism," *Numen* 36 (1989):81).

35. Jean-Claude Schmitt, *The Holy Greyhound: Guinefort, Healer of Children since the Thirteenth Century* (Cambridge: Cambridge University Press, 1983), p. 1. See also Jacques Le Goff, *Time, Work, and Culture in the Middle Ages* (Chicago: University of Chicago Press, 1980), pp. 156–58, 327; Robert Muchembled, *Popular Culture and Elite Culture in France 1400–1750* (Baton Rouge: Louisiana State University Press, 1985), p. 28; R. Manselli, *La Religion populaire au moyen âge: Problèmes de méthode et d'histoire* (Montreal: Institute d'Etudes Mediévales Albert-le-Grand, 1975), p. 191.

36. Brian Stock, *The Implications of Literacy: Written Language and Models of Interpretations in the Eleventh and Twelfth Centuries* (Princeton, N.J.: Princeton University Press, 1983), pp. 99–100, 522–23.

37. Bryan Wilson, *Religion in Sociological Perspective* (Oxford: Oxford University Press, 1982), pp. 173–74.

38. Keith Thomas, *Religion and the Decline of Magic* (Harmondsworth: Penguin, 1973), pp. 5–20; Muchembled, *Popular Culture and Elite Culture in France*, pp. 16–24.

39. Karl Marx and Frederick Engels, *On Religion* (Moscow: Foreign Languages Publishing House, 1955), p. 42.

40. Ibid., pp. 135–36.

41. A qualification made by Weber to this comparison was that a religious lay intellectualism was not important during the medieval period in Occidental Christianity. Weber, *Economy and Society*, pp. 500–513.

42. Ibid., pp. 468–70.

NOTES TO CHAPTER 2

1. Max Weber, *Economy and Society* (New York: Bedminster Press, 1968), p. 4.

2. Ibid., pp. 24–26.

3. Ibid., pp. 399–400, 527–28.

4. Ibid., pp. 423–24.

5. Ibid., p. 403.

6. Ibid., pp. 400–417, 428–31.

7. Ibid., pp. 422–24, 431.

8. Ibid., p. 424.

9. Colin Campbell, *The Myth of Social Action* (Cambridge: Cambridge University Press, 1996), pp. 115, 118, 131.

10. Ibid., p. 57.

11. Ibid., p. 160.

12. David G. Mandelbaum, "Transcendental and Pragmatic Aspects of Religion," *American Anthropologist* 68 (1966):1174–91.

13. Bryan Wilson, *Religion in Sociological Perspective* (Oxford: Oxford University Press, 1982), pp. 27–30.

14. Steven Collins, *Nirvana and Other Buddhist Felicities* (Cambridge: Cambridge University Press, 1998), p. 105.

15. See especially Bryan Wilson, *Magic and the Millennium* (London: Heinemann Educational Books, 1973).

16. Wilson, *Religion in Sociological Perspective*, pp. 30–31.

17. Religiously inspired goals of social transformation by communal action were only briefly mentioned by Weber. Even in his writings on charismatic domination, which Weber presented as a revolutionary force in history, he gave little attention to religious movements that sought to restructure society. Weber noted that social reform was not a central part of the messages or calls for change of the ethical religious prophets, such as the Israelite prophets, Zoroaster, and Muhammad, who provided the most prominent examples of charismatic leadership. Weber, *Economy and Society*, pp. 443–44, 1115–17.

18. Emile Durkheim, *The Elementary Forms of the Religious Life* (New York: Collier Books, 1961 [1912]), p. 403.

19. Ibid., pp. 474–75.

20. Ibid., p. 414.

21. Ibid., pp. 337–65.

22. Ibid., pp. 337–433.

23. Ibid., pp. 434–61.

24. See W. S. F. Pickering, *Durkheim's Sociology of Religion: Themes and Theories* (London: Routledge & Kegan Paul, 1984).

25. Karl Marx and Frederick Engels, *On Religion* (Moscow: Foreign Languages Publishing House, 1955), pp. 127–34, 303.

26. Robert K. Merton, *Social Theory and Social Structure* (New York: Free Press, 1968), pp. 96–99.

27. Peter L. Berger, *The Sacred Canopy* (Garden City, N.Y.: Doubleday, 1967).

28. J. Milton Yinger, *The Scientific Study of Religion* (London: Macmillan, 1970).

29. J. H. M. Beattie, "On Understanding Ritual," in Bryan R. Wilson, ed., *Rationality* (Oxford: Basil Blackwell, 1970), pp. 240–68. For a critical account, see John Skorupski, *Symbol and Theory* (Cambridge: Cambridge University Press, 1976).

30. Skorupski, *Symbol and Theory.*

31. Talcott Parsons, *The Structure of Social Action*, 2 vols. (New York: Free Press, 1949 [1937]), pp. 210–11, 256–63, 432–33, 657.

32. Stanley Jeyaraja Tambiah, *Magic, Science, Religion, and the Scope of Rationality* (Cambridge: Cambridge University Press, 1990), pp. 71–73, 80–83, 136.

33. R. L. Stirrat, *Power and Religiosity in a Post-Colonial Setting* (Cambridge: Cambridge University Press, 1992), pp. 159–68.

34. Most theoretical discussions of religion in anthropology are remote from a Weberian action framework, but elements of an action perspective are to be found in the works of anthropologists whose main concern has been to present

an ethnography and analysis of religion in a particular society. See, for example, David N. Gellner, *Monk, Householder, and Tantric Priest* (Cambridge: Cambridge University Press, 1992); William A. Christian Jr., *Person and God in a Spanish Valley* (New York: Seminar Press, 1972), pp. 114–27; João De Pina-Cabral, *Sons of Adam, Daughters of Eve: The Peasant Worldview of the Alto Minho* (Oxford: Clarendon Press, 1988), pp. 164–73.

NOTES TO CHAPTER 3

1. Max Weber, *The Religion of China: Confucianism and Taoism* (New York: Macmillan, 1964), p. 228.

2. Ibid., 177–90, 206, 227–29.

3. Max Weber, *Economy and Society* (New York: Bedminster Press, 1968), p. 625; Wolfgang Schluchter, *Rationalism, Religion, and Domination: A Weberian Perspective* (Berkeley: University of California Press, 1989), p. 120.

4. Weber, *Economy and Society*, p. 611; Max Weber, *Ancient Judaism* (New York: Free Press, 1952), pp. 313–17, 395, 397.

5. Max Weber, *The Religion of India* (New York: Free Press, 1958), pp. 22–23, 119–20, 152, 166–69, 175, 207–8, 213–14, 330–33.

6. Weber, *Economy and Society*, p. 526.

7. Max Weber, "The Social Psychology of the World Religions," in H. H. Gerth and C. Wright Mills, eds., *From Max Weber: Essays in Sociology* (London: Routledge & Kegan Paul, 1948), p. 277.

8. Weber, *Economy and Society*, 1167.

9. Weber, "Social Psychology of the World Religions," p. 288.

10. Weber, *Economy and Society*, pp. 1166–73.

11. Weber, *Religion of China*, pp. 20–32.

12. Weber, *Religion of India*, pp. 168, 173, 187.

13. Weber, *Ancient Judaism*, p. 223.

14. Weber, *Economy and Society*, pp. 413–16, 419.

15. Weber, *Ancient Judaism*, pp. 224–27, 308–11; Schluchter, *Rationalism, Religion, and Domination*, pp. 182–85.

16. Weber, *Ancient Judaism*, pp. 118–38.

17. Ibid., pp. 195, 303–11.

18. Weber, *Economy and Society*, pp. 447–48.

19. Ibid., pp. 529–39, 557–76. There are indications of a somewhat esoteric belief in predestination in the classical Confucian texts, but it was not developed. Weber, *Religion of China*, pp. 206–7.

20. Weber, *Religion of China*, pp. 142, 144–45, 152–57, 177–90, 206, 227–29, 235–36.

21. Weber, *Religion of India*, pp. 22–23, 119–20, 144, 152–58, 163–69, 175, 182–89, 206–15, 218, 222, 330–33.

22. Weber, *Economy and Society*, p. 611; Weber, *Ancient Judaism*, pp. 396–97.

23. Weber, *Economy and Society*, pp. 531–34, 573–75.

24. Weber, *Religion of India*, pp. 120–21.

25. Ibid., pp. 163–65.

26. Weber, *Ancient Judaism*, p. 4.

27. Ibid., pp. 343–45, 417.

28. Ibid., p. 5; Weber, *Economy and Society*, pp. 498.

29. Schluchter, *Rationalism, Religion, and Domination*, pp. 228–30, 240–45.

30. Weber, *Ancient Judaism*, p. 394.

31. Ibid., pp. 222–23.

32. Ibid., pp. 221–22, 394.

33. Max Weber, *The Protestant Ethic and the Spirit of Capitalism* (London: George Allen & Unwin, 1930), pp. 105, 117; Weber, *Religion of China*, pp. 226–27.

34. Weber, *Religion of China*, pp. 128, 155, 194, 200, 229.

35. Weber, *Religion of India*, pp. 138–39, 149–50.

36. Weber, "Social Psychology of the World Religions," pp. 287–88.

37. Weber, *Economy and Society*, pp. 457–63.

38. Weber, "Social Psychology of the World Religions," pp. 287–90.

39. Weber, *Protestant Ethic*, pp. 109–11, 226–27.

40. Weber, "Social Psychology of the World Religions," pp. 276, 287–88.

41. Weber, *Religion of China*, pp. 143–44, 173–74, 177, 230, 233.

42. Weber, *Religion of India*, p. 192.

43. Ibid., pp. 327–28, 334–36, 342.

44. Ibid., pp. 295–319.

45. Ibid., pp. 228–29, 236–55.

46. Weber, *Ancient Judaism*, pp. 223–24, 303–5, 314–15, 397–400, 412–13.

47. Weber, *Economy and Society*, p. 447; Weber, *Religion of China*, pp. 20–32.

48. Weber, *Religion of China*, pp. 20–32.

49. Weber, *Ancient Judaism*, pp. 79, 81, 83.

50. Ibid., pp. 303–11.

51. Ibid., pp. 278–84.

52. Ibid., p. 414.

53. Ibid., p. 419; Weber, *Economy and Society*, pp. 617, 630.

54. Weber, "Social Psychology of the World Religions," p. 276.

55. Weber, *Religion of China*, pp. 13–20; Weber, *Religion of India*, pp. 90, 127–31, 337–38.

56. Weber, *Religion of China*, pp. 42–47, 107–38, 152–57, 227–29; Weber, *Economy and Society*, pp. 1049–50.

57. Weber, *Religion of China*, pp. 138–39, 194, 196.

58. Weber, *Religion of India*, pp. 16–19, 39–43, 57–65, 177.

59. Ibid., pp. 181–84.

60. Ibid., pp. 200–202.

61. Ibid., pp. 202, 206, 215–16, 226–27.

62. Weber, *Economy and Society*, pp. 469–70, 482–86.

63. Ibid., pp. 1158–62, 1170–71, 1174–76.

64. Ibid., pp. 455–56.

65. Ibid., p. 482.

66. Ibid., p. 1164.

67. Weber, *Religion of China*, pp. 142, 177, 194, 201.

68. Weber, *Religion of India*, pp. 156–57, 292–93.

69. Weber, *Economy and Society*, pp. 1123–24.

70. Ibid., pp. 1167–68, 1173.

71. Weber, "Social Psychology of the World Religions," p. 289.

72. Weber, *Economy and Society*, pp. 502–3, 507–8, 513, 1180–81.

73. Ibid., pp. 455–56, 1123–24, 1171–73.

74. Fredrich H. Tenbruck, "The Problem of Thematic Unity in the Works of Max Weber," *British Journal of Sociology* 31 (1980):316–35.

75. Talcott Parsons, "Introduction to Max Weber's 'The Sociology of Religion,'" in Talcott Parsons, *Sociological Theory and Modern Society* (New York: Free Press, 1967), pp. 57–58.

76. Jürgen Habermas, *The Theory of Communicative Action*, vol 1: *Reason and the Rationalization of Society* (Boston: Beacon Press, 1984), pp. 202–3.

77. Ibid., pp. 209–10.

78. Wolfgang Schluchter, *The Rise of Western Rationalism: Max Weber's Developmental History* (Berkeley: University of California Press, 1981), pp. 157–58.

79. Schluchter, *Rationalism, Religion, and Domination*, p. 140.

80. On the utilitarian scheme in Marxism, see David Lockwood, *Solidarity and Schism: "The Problem of Disorder" in Durkheimian and Marxist Sociology* (Oxford: Clarendon Press, 1992), pp. 170–71, 209–10, 292–93, 357.

81. Antonio Gramsci, *Selections from Prison Notebooks* (London: Lawrence & Wishart, 1971), pp. 328, 332.

82. Ibid., p. 7.

83. Joseph V. Femia, *Gramsci's Political Thought: Hegemony, Consciousness and the Revolutionary Process* (Oxford: Clarendon Press, 1981), p. 132.

84. Paul Ransome, *Antonio Gramsci: A New Introduction* (New York: Harvester Wheatsheaf, 1992), pp. 132–39, 142–43.

85. Gramsci, *Selections from Prison Notebooks*, p. 332.

86. Lockwood, *Solidarity and Schism*, pp. 47–48; Femia, *Gramsci's Political Thought*, p. 276.

87. Gramsci, *Selections from Prison Notebooks*, p. 396.

88. Leonardo Salamini, *The Sociology of Political Praxis: An Introduction to Gramsci's Theory* (London: Routledge & Kegan Paul, 1981), pp. 55–60, 89–91; Alberto Maria Cirese, "Gramsci's Observations on Folklore," in Anne Showstack Sassoon, ed., *Approaches to Gramsci* (London: Writers and Readers Publishing

Cooperative Society, 1982), pp. 212–47; Femia, *Gramsci's Political Thought*, pp. 56–57.

89. Nicholas Abercrombie, Stephen Hill, and Bryan S. Turner, *The Dominant Ideology Thesis* (London: George Allen & Unwin, 1980), esp. chaps. 3, 4.

90. Otto Maduro, *Religion and Social Conflicts* (Maryknoll, N.Y.: Orbis Books, 1982), pp. 122–26.

91. Roger N. Lancaster, *Thanks to God and the Revolution: Popular Religion and Class Consciousness in the New Nicaragua* (New York: Columbia University Press, 1988). See also James C. Scott, "Protest and Profanation: Agrarian Revolt and the Little Tradition, Part 1," *Theory and Society* 4 (1977):1–38; David Lehmann, *Struggle for the Spirit: Religious Transformation and Popular Culture in Brazil and Latin America* (Cambridge: Polity Press, 1996).

92. Maduro, *Religion and Social Conflicts*, pp. 86–87.

NOTES TO CHAPTER 4

1. Sectarian religious movements have been characterized by the same syncretistic tendencies as characterize the milieu from which they emerge. Daniel L. Overmyer, *Folk Buddhist Religion: Dissenting Sects in Late Traditional China* (Cambridge, Mass.: Harvard University Press, 1976); David K. Jordan and Daniel L. Overmyer, *The Flying Phoenix: Aspects of Chinese Sectarianism in Taiwan* (Princeton, N.J.: Princeton University Press, 1986); Kenneth Dean, *Lord of the Three in One: The Spread of a Cult in Southeast China* (Princeton, N.J.: Princeton University Press, 1998).

2. Arthur P. Wolf, "Introduction," in Arthur P. Wolf, ed., *Religion and Ritual in Chinese Society* (Stanford: Stanford University Press, 1974), pp. 9, 17; James L. Watson, "Anthropological Analyses of Chinese Religion," *China Quarterly* 66 (1976):355–64.

3. Marcel Granet, *The Religion of the Chinese People* (Oxford: Basil Blackwell, 1975 [1922]); C. K. Yang, *Religion in Chinese Society* (Berkeley: University of California Press, 1967); Maurice Freedman, "On the Sociological Study of Chinese Religion," in Wolf, ed., *Religion and Ritual in Chinese Society*, pp. 351–69.

4. Daniel L. Overmyer, "Dualism and Conflict in Chinese Popular Religion," in Frank E. Reynolds and Theodore M. Ludwig, eds., *Transitions and Transformations in the History of Religions* (Leiden: E. J. Brill, 1980), p. 154; Michael Saso, *Blue Dragon, White Tiger: Taoist Rites of Passage* (Washington, D.C.: The Taoist Center, 1990), pp. 2–16, 161; Meir Shahar and Robert P. Weller, "Introduction," in Meir Shahar and Robert P. Weller, eds., *Unruly Gods: Divinity and Society in China* (Honolulu: University of Hawaii Press, 1996), pp. 2–3.

5. Thomas A. Wilson, *Genealogy of the Way: The Construction and Uses of the Confucian Tradition in Late Imperial China* (Stanford: Stanford University Press, 1995), pp. 6, 23–25; Kai-wing Chow, *The Rise of Confucian Ritualism in Late*

Imperial China: Ethics, Classics, and Lineage Discourse (Stanford: Stanford University Press, 1994), pp. 8–9, 224.

6. Stephan Feuchtwang, "School-Temple and City God," in G. William Skinner, ed., *The City in Late Imperial China* (Stanford: Stanford University Press, 1977), p. 581; Romeyn Taylor, "Official and Popular Religion and the Political Organization of Chinese Society in the Ming," in Kwang-Ching Liu, ed., *Orthodoxy in Late Imperial China* (Berkeley: University of California Press, 1990), pp. 126–57; Richard J. Smith, "Ritual in Ch'ing Culture," in Liu, ed., *Orthodoxy in Late Imperial China*, pp. 281–310; James L. Watson, "Standardizing the Gods: The Promotion of T'ien Hou ('Empress of Heaven') Along the South China Coast, 960–1960," in David Johnson, Andrew J. Nathan, and Evelyn S. Rawski, eds., *Popular Culture in Late Imperial China* (Berkeley: University of California Press, 1985), pp. 292–323; C. K. Yang, *Religion in Chinese Society* (Berkeley: University of California Press, 1967), pp. 187–92.

7. Yang, *Religion in Chinese Society*, pp. 181–83; Stephan Feuchtwang, *The Imperial Metaphor: Popular Religion in China* (London: Routledge, 1992), pp. 9–10, 43–44.

8. Yang, *Religion in Chinese Society*, pp. 183–85; Taylor, "Official and Popular Religion," p. 133.

9. Taylor, "Official and Popular Religion," pp. 132–33, 143–45; Feuchtwang, "School-Temple and City God," pp. 593–94; Feuchtwang, *Imperial Metaphor*, pp. 64, 195–96; Smith, "Ritual in Ch'ing Culture," pp. 288, 291.

10. Shahar and Weller, "Introduction," p. 4.

11. Angela R. Zito, "City Gods and Their Magistrates," in Donald S. Lopez Jr., ed., *Religions of China in Practice* (Princeton, N.J.: Princeton University Press, 1996), pp. 72–81; A. R. Zito, "City Gods, Filiality, and Hegemony in Late Imperial China," *Modern China* 13 (1987):333–71.

12. Wm. Theodore de Bary, *The Trouble with Confucianism* (Cambridge, Mass.: Harvard University Press, 1991).

13. Thomas A. Metzger, *Escape from Predicament: Neo-Confucianism and China's Evolving Political Culture* (New York: Columbia University Press, 1977), pp. 67–68, 198–202.

14. Metzger, *Escape from Predicament*, pp. 60–68, 81, 110–11, 203–4; Wm. Theodore de Bary, "Introduction," in Wm. Theodore de Bary, ed., *The Unfolding of Neo-Confucianism* (New York: Columbia University Press, 1975), pp. 17–21; Wm. Theodore de Bary, "Neo-Confucian Cultivation and the Seventeenth-Century 'Enlightenment,'" in de Bary, ed., *Unfolding of Neo-Confucianism*, pp. 170–71; Julia Ching, "What Is Confucian Spirituality," in Irene Eber, ed., *Confucianism: The Dynamics of Tradition* (New York: Macmillan, 1986), pp. 70–74, 79.

15. Lawrence G. Thompson, *Chinese Religion: An Introduction* (Encino, Calif.: Dickenson Publishing, 1975), pp. 5–6; Joseph Needham, *Science and Civilization in China*, vol. 2: *History of Scientific Thought* (Cambridge: Cambridge University

Press, 1956), pp. 8–9; Benjamin I. Schwartz, "Transcendence in Ancient China," *Daedalus* 104 (Spring 1975):60, 65–67.

16. Yang, *Religion in Chinese Society*, pp. 248–49, 272–74; Kwang-Ching Liu, "Socioethics as Orthodoxy: A Perspective," in Liu, ed., *Orthodoxy in Late Imperial China*, pp. 54–55; Feuchtwang, "School-Temple and City God," p. 595; Schwartz, "Transcendence in Ancient China," pp. 59, 62, 64; Mark Elvin, "Was There a Transcendental Breakthrough in China?" in S. N. Eisenstadt, ed., *The Origins and Diversity of Axial Age Civilizations* (Albany: State University New York Press, 1986), pp. 328, 333–38; Jacques Gernet, *China and the Christian Impact: A Conflict of Cultures* (Cambridge: Cambridge University Press, 1985), pp. 37, 195, 204, 211–12, 246; Ching, "What Is Confucian Spirituality," p. 69.

17. Thompson, *Chinese Religion*, p. 3; Evelyn S. Rawski, "A Historian's Approach to Chinese Death Ritual," in James L. Watson and Evelyn S. Rawski, eds., *Death Ritual in Late Imperial and Modern China* (Berkeley: University of California Press, 1988), pp. 24–25; Stuart E. Thompson, "Death, Food, and Fertility," in Watson and Rawski, eds., p. 108; Overmyer, "Dualism and Conflict," pp. 154, 157; Smith, "Ritual in Ch'ing Culture," p. 287.

18. Metzger, *Escape from Predicament*; de Bary, *Trouble with Confucianism*; Sarit Helman, "Turning Classic Models into Utopias: The Neo-Confucianist Critique," *International Journal of Comparative Sociology* 29 (1988):93–110.

19. Cynthia J. Brokaw, *The Ledgers of Merit and Demerit: Social Change and Moral Order in Late Imperial China* (Princeton, N.J.: Princeton University Press, 1991).

20. Patricia Ebrey, *Confucianism and Family Rituals in Imperial China: A Social History of Writing about Rites* (Princeton, N.J.: Princeton University Press, 1991), pp. 207, 212–15.

21. Thompson, *Chinese Religion*, p. 101; Herrlee G. Creel, *What Is Taoism? and Other Studies in Chinese Cultural History* (Chicago: University of Chicago Press, 1970), pp. 2–20, 39–43; Stephen Bokenkamp, "The Purification Ritual of the Luminous Perfected," in Lopez, ed., *Religions of China in Practice*, pp. 268–77.

22. Thompson, *Chinese Religion*, p. 95; Thomas Boehmer, "Taoist Alchemy: A Sympathetic Approach through Symbols," in Michael Saso and David W. Chappell, eds., *Buddhist and Taoist Studies* (Honolulu: University of Hawaii Press, 1977), pp. 55–56.

23. Thompson, *Chinese Religion*, pp. 96–100; Boehmer, "Taoist Alchemy," pp. 63–69.

24. Holmes Welch, *The Parting of the Way: Lao Tzu and the Taoist Movement* (Boston: Beacon Press, 1957), p. 112; Creel, *What Is Taoism?* pp. 7–20.

25. Kenneth Dean, *Taoist Ritual and Popular Cults of Southeast China* (Princeton, N.J.: Princeton University Press, 1993), pp. 6, 24; Kristofer M. Schipper, "The Written Memorial in Taoist Ceremonies," in Wolf, ed., *Religion and Ritual in Chinese Society*, pp. 309–12.

26. Michael R. Saso, *Taoism and the Rite of Cosmic Renewal* (Seattle: Washington State University Press, 1972); Saso, *Blue Dragon, White Tiger*, pp. 183–88; P. Steven Sangren, *History and Magical Power in a Chinese Community* (Stanford: Stanford University Press, 1987), p. 170; Dean, *Taoist Ritual*, p. 15.

27. Sangren, *History and Magical Power*, pp. 79–81.

28. Robert P. Weller, *Unities and Diversities in Chinese Religion* (Seattle: University of Washington State, 1987), pp. 146, 163.

29. Ibid., p. 95.

30. Michael Saso, "Orthodoxy and Heterodoxy in Taoist Ritual," in Wolf, ed., *Religion and Ritual in Chinese Society*, p. 335.

31. Dean, *Taoist Ritual*, p. 182.

32. Schipper, "Written Memorial in Taoist Ceremonies," pp. 309–11.

33. Arthur F. Wright, *Buddhism in Chinese History* (Stanford: Stanford University Press, 1959), p. 103.

34. Lewis R. Lancaster, "Buddhism and Family in East Asia," in George A. DeVos and Takao Sotue, eds., *Religion and the Family in East Asia* (Berkeley: University of California Press, 1986), pp. 139–51.

35. Thompson, *Chinese Religion*, p. 91

36. Ibid., pp. 91–94.

37. Saso, *Blue Dragon, White Tiger*, pp. 22, 55, 73, 76, 94, 99.

38. Yang, *Religion in Chinese Society*, p. 155.

39. Arthur P. Wolf, "Gods, Ghosts, and Ancestors," in Arthur P. Wolf, ed., *Studies in Chinese Society* (Stanford: Stanford University Press, 1978), pp. 131–82; Weller, *Unities and Diversities*, pp. 37–49; Emily Martin Ahern, *Chinese Ritual and Politics* (Cambridge: Cambridge University Press, 1981).

40. Wolf, "Gods, Ghosts, and Ancestors," pp. 134–44; Ahern, *Chinese Ritual and Politics*, pp. 29, 81–82, 92–101; Myron L. Cohen, "Souls and Salvation: Conflicting Themes in Chinese Popular Religion," in Watson and Rawski, eds., *Death Ritual*, pp. 180–202; Weller, *Unities and Diversities*, pp. 47–49, 97; Sangren, *History and Magical Power*, pp. 51–52, 127–31, 138–39; Feuchtwang, *Imperial Metaphor*, pp. 92, 18–19, 41–43.

41. Wolf, "Gods, Ghosts, and Ancestors," pp. 176–79; Ahern, *Chinese Ritual and Politics*, pp. 38–39, 93; Emily M. Ahern, *The Cult of the Dead in a Chinese Village* (Stanford: Stanford University Press, 1973), pp. 167–70; Sangren, *History and Magical Power*, pp. 53–56, 61–63.

42. Meir Shahar, "Vernacular Fiction and the Transmission of Gods' Cults in Late Imperial China," in Shahar and Weller, eds., *Unruly Gods*, pp. 97–99; Brigette Baptandier, "The Lady Linshui: How a Woman Became a Goddess," in Shahar and Weller, eds., *Unruly Gods*, pp. 104–49; Chun-Fang Yu, "A Sutra Promoting the White-Robed Guanyin as Giver of Sons," in Lopez, ed., *Religions of China in Practice*, pp. 97–105; Weller, *Unities and Diversities*, pp. 50–51; Sangren, *History and Magical Power*, pp. 73–74; P. Steven Sangren, "Female Gender

in Chinese Religious Symbols: Kuan Yin, Ma Tsu, and the 'Eternal Mother,'" *Signs* 9 (1983):4–25.

43. Watson, "Standardizing the Gods," pp. 292–324.

44. Sangren, *History and Magical Power*, pp. 87–92, 194–96.

45. Shahar, "Vernacular Fiction," pp. 184–85, 199–202.

46. Paul R. Katz, *Demon Hordes and Burning Boats: The Cult of Marshall Wen in Late Imperial China* (Albany: State University of New York Press, 1995), pp. 59–60, 62–75.

47. Yang, *Religion in Chinese Society*, pp. 168–73.

48. Maurice Freedman, "Ritual Aspects of Chinese Kinship and Marriage," in *The Study of Chinese Society: Essays by Maurice Freedman* (Stanford: Stanford University Press, 1979), pp. 273–95; Maurice Freedman, "Ancestor Worship: Two Facets of the Chinese Case," in *Study of Chinese Society*, pp. 296–312; Wolf, "Gods, Ghosts, and Ancestors," pp. 162–68; Ahern, *Cult of the Dead*, pp. 161, 261–62; Yang, *Religion in Chinese Society*, pp. 35–52; Weller, *Unities and Diversities*, pp. 24–26.

49. Wolf, "Gods, Ghosts, and Ancestors," pp. 169–73; David K. Jordan, *Gods, Ghosts, and Ancestors: The Folk Religion of a Taiwanese Village* (Berkeley: University of California Press, 1972), pp. 139–70; Stevan Harrell, "The Concept of Soul in Chinese Folk Religion," *Journal of Asian Studies* 38 (1979):519–20; Weller, *Unities and Diversities*, pp. 60–66.

50. Wolf, "Gods, Ghosts, and Ancestors," pp. 145–59, 169–70; Jordan, *Gods, Ghosts, and Ancestors*, pp. 140–41, 169–70; Duane Pang, "The P'u-tu Ritual: A Celebration of the Chinese Community of Honolulu," in Saso and Chappell, eds., *Buddhist and Taoist Studies*, pp. 95–122; James L. Watson, "The Structure of Chinese Funerary Rites: Elementary Forms, Ritual Sequence and the Primacy of Performance," in Watson and Rawski, eds., *Death Ritual*, pp. 3–19; Weller, *Unities and Diversities*, pp. 60–66, 119–23; Sangren, *History and Magical Power*, pp. 81–82, 144–48; Saso, *Blue Dragon, White Tiger*, pp. 58–59, 91, 141; Philip A. Kuhn, *Soulstealers: The Chinese Sorcery Scare of 1768* (Cambridge, Mass.: Harvard University Press, 1990), pp. 97–98, 114.

51. Max Weber, *The Religion of China: Confucianism and Taoism* (New York: Macmillan, 1964), pp. 173–74.

52. Freedman, "On the Sociological Study of Chinese Religion," p. 355; See also Weller, *Unities and Diversities*, p. 89; Evelyn S. Rawski, "Popular Culture in China," in Ching-I Tu, ed., *Tradition and Creativity: Essays on East Asian Civilization* (New Brunswick: Transaction Books, 1987), pp. 41–42; Sangren, *History and Magical Power*, pp. 1–3.

53. Feuchtwang, "School-Temple and City God," p. 582.

54. Yang, *Religion in Chinese Society*, pp. 48–53, 244–59, 267–76, 276; Anthony C. Yu, "Religion and Literature of China: The 'Obscure Way' of the Journey to the West," in Tu, ed., *Tradition and Creativity*, pp. 110–13; Thompson, *Chinese*

Religion, pp. 77–78; Feuchtwang, "School-Temple and City God," p. 607; Smith, "Ritual in Ch'ing Culture," pp. 307–9.

55. Maurice Freedman, "Geomancy," in *Study of Chinese Society*, p. 325; Feuchtwang, *Imperial Metaphor*, pp. 38–39.

56. Thompson, *Chinese Religion*, pp. 9–11; Jordan, *Gods, Ghosts, and Ancestors*, pp. 31–32; Freedman, "Ancestor Worship," p. 297.

57. Weller, *Unities and Diversities*, pp. 138–39; Sangren, *History and Magical Power*, pp. 162, 164, 197.

58. Overmyer, "Dualism and Conflict," pp. 153–84.

59. Yang, *Religion in Chinese Society*, pp. 275–77.

60. Watson, "Standardizing the Gods"; Prasenjit Duara, "Superscribing Symbols: The Myth of Guandi, the Chinese God of War," *Journal of Asian Studies* 47 (1988):778–95.

61. Shahar and Weller, "Introduction," pp. 3, 15, 20, 26, 28; Shahar, "Vernacular Fiction," pp. 184–85, 204; Robert P. Weller, "Matricidal Magistrates and Gambling Gods: Weak States and Strong Spirits in China," in Shahar and Weller, eds., *Unruly Gods*, pp. 264–65; Katz, *Demon Hordes and Burning Boats*, pp. 113–15.

62. Taylor, "Official and Popular Religion," p. 148.

63. Feuchtwang, "School-Temple and City God," pp. 588–89; Taylor, "Official and Popular Religion," pp. 156–58.

64. Michael Szonyi, "The Illusion of Standardizing the Gods: The Cult of the Five Emperors in Late Imperial China," *Journal of Asian Studies* 56 (1997): 113–35.

65. Feuchtwang, "School-Temple and City God," pp. 588–91.

66. Jordan, *Gods, Ghosts, and Ancestors*, pp. 38–39; Philip C. Baity, "The Ranking of Gods in Chinese Folk Religion," *Asian Folklore Studies* 35 (1977):77–84; Yang, *Religion in Chinese Society*, pp. 57–59.

67. Taylor, "Official and Popular Religion," p. 129; Feuchtwang, "School-Temple and City God," pp. 597–98, 607.

68. Dean, *Taoist Ritual*, pp. 13–18, 32, 175–84; Saso, *Blue Dragon, White Tiger*, pp. 22–23.

69. Dean, *Taoist Ritual*, pp. 14, 37, 131–71, 175, 179, 184.

70. Katz, *Demon Hordes and Burning Boats*, pp. 106–18, 138–40, 173.

71. Weller, *Unities and Diversities*, pp. 97, 113–14, 119–23.

72. Ibid., pp. 119–23.

73. Wright, *Buddhism in Chinese History*, pp. 97–98; P. Steven Sangren, "Great Tradition and Little Traditions Reconsidered: The Question of Cultural Integration in China," *Journal of Chinese Studies* 1 (1984):10–11.

74. Taylor, "Official and Popular Religion," p. 130; Dean, *Taoist Ritual*, p. 37.

75. Ebrey, *Confucianism and Family Rituals*, pp. 216–24.

76. Alexander Woodside, "State, Scholars, and Orthodoxy: The Ch'ing Academics 1736–1839," in Liu, ed., *Orthodoxy in Late Imperial China*, pp. 160–62.

77. Feuchtwang, "School-Temple and City God," pp. 590, 597; Stephan Feuchtwang, "City Temples in Taipei under Three Regimes," in Mark Elvin and G. William Skinner, eds., *The Chinese City between Two Worlds* (Stanford: Stanford University Press, 1974), p. 281; Thompson, *Chinese Religion*, p. 71; Thomas A. Wilson, "The Ritual Formation of Confucian Orthodoxy and the Descendants of the Sage," *Journal of Asian Studies* 55 (1996):563–64; Barrington Moore Jr., *Social Origins of Dictatorship and Democracy: Lord and Peasant in the Making of the Modern World* (London: Allen Lane, The Penguin Press, 1967), p. 206.

78. Wilson, "Ritual Formation of Confucian Orthodoxy," pp. 559–84.

79. Wm. Theodore de Bary, "Some Common Tendencies in Neo-Confucianism," in David S. Nivison and Arthur F. Wright. eds., *Confucianism in Action* (Stanford: Stanford University Press, 1959), pp. 28–29.

80. Ebrey, *Confucianism and Family Rituals*, p. 7.

81. Lauren Pfister, "Reassessing Max Weber's Evaluation of the Confucian Classics," in Jon Davies and Isabel Wollaston, eds., *The Sociology of Sacred Texts* (Sheffield: Sheffield Academic Press, 1993), pp. 99–110.

82. Smith, "Ritual in Ch'ing Culture," p. 303; Woodside, "State, Scholars, and Orthodoxy," p. 164.

83. Yang, *Religion in Chinese Society*, pp. 187–203; Taylor, "Official and Popular Religion," pp. 149–53; Smith, "Ritual in Ch'ing Culture," p. 304.

84. Yang, *Religion in Chinese Society*, pp. 194, 197, 204–9.

85. Ibid., pp. 214–15.

86. See articles in Shahar and Weller, eds., *Unruly Gods*.

87. Theda Skocpol, *States and Social Revolutions* (Cambridge: Cambridge University Press, 1979), pp. 70–71.

88. Romeyn Taylor, "Chinese Hierarchy in Comparative Perspective," *Journal of Asian Studies* 48 (1989):502–3; Ahern, *Chinese Ritual and Politics*, pp. 84–85; Szonyi, "Illusion of Standardizing the Gods," pp. 130–31.

89. Barbara E. Ward, "Readers and Audiences: An Exploration of the Spread of Traditional Chinese Culture," in Ravindra K. Jain, ed., *Text and Context: The Social Anthropology of Tradition* (Philadelphia: Institute for the Study of Human Issues, 1977), pp. 189–90; David Johnson, "Communication, Class, and Consciousness in Late Imperial China," in Johnson, Nathan, and Rawski, eds., *Popular Culture in Late Imperial China*, pp. 56, 64; Ebrey, *Confucianism and Family Rituals*, pp. 205–6.

90. Saso, *Blue Dragon, White Tiger*, p. 22.

91. Rolf A. Stein, "Religious Taoism and Popular Religion from the Second to Seventh Centuries," in Holmes Welch and Anna Seidel, eds., *Facets of Taoism: Essays in Chinese Religion* (New Haven: Yale University Press, 1979), pp. 53–81; Welch, *Parting of the Way*, pp. 107, 135; Creel, *What Is Taoism?* pp. 8–10.

92. R. Ransdorp, "Official and Popular Religion in the Chinese Empire," in Pieter Hendrik Vrijhof and Jacques Waardenburg, eds., *Official and Popular*

Religion: Analysis of a Theme for Religious Studies (The Hague: Mouton Publishers, 1979), pp. 387–426; Yang, *Religion in Chinese Society*, pp. 24–25, 115–23, 301–39; Edwin O. Reischauer and John K. Fairbank, *East Asia: The Great Tradition* (London: George Allen & Unwin, 1960), pp. 175–76. In contemporary Taiwan, Buddhist monks and priests are more organized and centralized than their Taoist counterparts, who have not had a monastic tradition on the island. Weller, *Unities and Diversities*, p. 110.

93. Saso, *Blue Dragon, White Tiger*, pp. 55–56, 90–91, 99.

94. Weber, *Religion of China*, pp. 173–74.

95. Moore, *Social Origins of Dictatorship and Democracy*, pp. 163–75; Skocpol, *States and Social Revolutions*, pp. 70–72.

96. Joseph R. Levenson, *Confucian China and Its Modern Fate*, vol. 2: *The Problem of Monarchical Decay* (London: Routledge & Kegan Paul, 1964), pp. 25–51; Joseph R. Levenson, "The Suggestiveness of Vestiges: Confucianism and Monarchy at the Last," in Nivison and Wright, eds., *Confucianism in Action*, pp. 252–59; Chow, *Rise of Confucian Ritualism*, pp. 8–9, 204, 214, 224–27.

97. Moore, *Social Origins of Dictatorship and Democracy*, pp. 165–73, 206–13.

98. R. David Arkush, "Orthodoxy and Heterodoxy in Twentieth-Century Chinese Peasant Proverbs," in Liu, ed., *Orthodoxy in Late Imperial China*, pp. 312–13.

99. Elizabeth J. Perry, "Taipings and Triads: The Role of Religion in Inter-Rebel Relations," in Janos M. Bak and Gerhard Benecke, eds., *Religion and Rural Revolt* (Manchester: Manchester University Press, 1984), pp. 342–44.

100. J. J. M. de Groot, *The Religious System of China*, 6 vols. (Leiden: E. J. Brill, 1892–1910); Dean, *Taoist Ritual*, pp. 3–6; Prasenjit Duara, "Knowledge and Power in the Discourse of Modernity: The Campaigns against Popular Religion in Early Twentieth-Century China," *Journal of Asian Studies* 50 (1991):67–83.

101. *New York Times*, April 27, July 30, and December 27, 1999.

NOTES TO CHAPTER 5

1. Murry Milner Jr., *Status and Sacredness* (New York: Oxford University Press, 1994), pp. 46–47.

2. The original meaning of the Persian word *Hindu*, which derives from *Sindu*, a Sanskrit name for the river Indus, was a native of India, the land around and beyond the Indus. *Hinduism* is a term that became current in English in the nineteenth century to refer to the "indigenous" religion of the people of India, or that religious civilization that was seen to have gradually evolved from the ancient Vedic religion of the Indo-European peoples who settled in India in the last centuries of the second millennium B.C.E. C. J. Fuller, *The Camphor Flame* (Princeton, N.J.: Princeton University Press, 1992), pp. 10–11; Ursula King, "Some Reflections on Sociological Approaches to the Study of Modern Hin-

duism," *Numen* 36 (1989):73–76; Arvind Sharma, "Some Misunderstandings of the Hindu Approach to Religious Plurality," *Religion* 8 (1978):133–54.

3. Frank Whaling, "The Hindu Tradition in Today's World," in Frank Whaling, ed., *Religion in Today's World* (Edinburgh: T. & T. Clark, 1987), pp. 129–31; Robert C. Lester, "Hinduism: Veda and Sacred Texts," in Frederick M. Denny and Rodney L. Taylor, eds., *The Holy Book in Comparative Perspective* (Columbia: University of South Carolina Press, 1985), pp. 126–47; Madeleine Biardeau, *Hinduism: The Anthropology of a Civilization* (Delhi: Oxford University Press, 1989); K. M. Sen, *Hinduism* (Harmondsworth: Penguin, 1961).

4. Milner, *Status and Sacredness*, pp. 46–47, 77–78; Andre Beteille, *Caste, Class, and Power: Changing Patterns of Social Stratification in a Tanjore Village* (Berkeley: University of California Press, 1965) pp. 44, 189; Richard Gombrich, *Theravada Buddhism: A Social History from Ancient Benares to Modern Colombo* (London: Routledge & Kegan Paul, 1988), p. 39; Stanley Jeyaraja Tambiah, "From Varna to Caste through Mixed Unions," in *Culture, Thought and Social Action: An Anthropological Perspective* (Cambridge, Mass.: Harvard University Press, 1985), pp. 214–18.

5. Cynthia Keppley Mahmood, "Hinduism in Context: Approaching a Religious Tradition through External Sources," in Stephen D. Glazier, ed., *Anthropology of Religion: A Handbook* (Westport, Conn.: Greenwood Press, 1997), pp. 305–18.

6. Jonathan Parry, "The Brahmanical Tradition and the Technology of the Intellect," in Joanna Overing, ed., *Reason and Morality* (London: Tavistock, 1985), pp. 204–5; Fuller, *Camphor Flame*, p. 27.

7. David R. Kinsley, *Hinduism: A Cultural Perspective* (Englewood Cliffs: Prentice-Hall, 1982), pp. 16, 83–84; C. J. Fuller, *Servants of the Goddess: The Priests of a South Indian Temple* (Cambridge: Cambridge University Press, 1984), p. 64.

8. Louis Dumont, "World Renunciation in Indian Religions," appendix in *Homo Hierarchicus: The Caste System and Its Implications* (Chicago: University of Chicago Press, 1980), pp. 271–72; Biardeau, *Hinduism*, pp. 53–55; Charles Malamoud, "On the Rhetoric and Semantics of Purusartha," in T. N. Madan, ed., *Way of Life: King, Householder, Renouncer* (New Delhi: Vikas Publishing House, 1982), pp. 39, 43–46; Ronald Inden, "Hierarchies of Kings in Early Medieval India," in Madan, ed., *Way of Life*, p. 101.

9. Fuller, *Servants of the Goddess*, pp. 12–16, 23–35.

10. Ibid., pp. 10–11, 21; George Michell, *The Hindu Temple: An Introduction to Its Meaning and Forms* (London: Paul Elek, 1977), pp. 63–65; Carl Gustav Diehl, *Instrument and Purpose: Studies on Rites and Rituals in South India* (Lund: C. W. K. Gleerup, 1956), p. 356.

11. Lawrence A. Babb, *The Divine Hierarchy: Popular Hinduism in Central India* (New York: Columbia University Press, 1975), pp. 180–81; Vinay Kumar

Srivastava, *Religious Renunciation of a Pastoral People* (Delhi: Oxford University Press, 1997), pp. 99–103.

12. J. Gabriel Campbell, *Saints and Householders: A Study of Hindu Ritual and Myth among the Kangra Rajputs* (Kathmandu: Ratna Pustak Bhandar, 1976), pp. 105, 111–14.

13. Jonathan P. Parry, *Death in Banaras* (Cambridge: Cambridge University Press, 1994), pp. 30–32, 112, 158.

14. Kinsley, *Hinduism*, pp. 82, 87; Biardeau, *Hinduism*, pp. 21–29; Agehananda Bharati, "The Self in Hindu Thought and Action," in Anthony J. Marsella, George DeVos, and Francis L. K. Hsu, eds., *Culture and Self: Asian and Western Perspectives* (New York: Tavistock, 1985), p. 187; J. P. Parry, "Death and Cosmogony in Kashi," in Madan, ed., *Way of Life*, p. 352; Lynn Bennett, *Dangerous Wives and Sacred Sisters: Social and Symbolic Roles of High-Caste Women in Nepal* (New York: Columbia University Press, 1983), pp. 35–36.

15. S. J. Tambiah, "Purity and Auspiciousness at the Edge of the Hindu Context," in John B. Carman and Frederique A. Marglin, eds., *Purity and Auspiciousness in Indian Society* (Leiden: E. J. Brill, 1985), p. 105; Kinsley, *Hinduism*, pp. 7–9, 82–91; Biardeau, *Hinduism*, pp. 26–29, 42; Romila Thapar, "The Householder and the Renouncer in the Brahmanical and Buddhist Traditions," in Madan, ed., *Way of Life*, pp. 274–75.

16. Richard Burghart, "Renunciation in the Religious Traditions of South Asia," *Man* (n.s.) 18 (1983):635–53; Richard Burghart, "Wandering Ascetics of the Ramanandi Sect," *History of Religions* 22 (1983):361–80. Female renouncers are few. According to various calculations, one-tenth or fewer of the ascetics in Banaras are female. Srivastava, *Religious Renunciation*, p. 228.

17. Edward Shils, "Some Observations on the Place of Intellectuals in Max Weber's Sociology, with Special Reference to Hinduism," in S. N. Eisenstadt, ed., *The Origin and Diversity of Axial Age Civilizations* (Albany: State University of New York Press, 1986), pp. 437–40; Kinsley, *Hinduism*, pp. 87–90; Biardeau, *Hinduism*, pp. 26–27; John B. Carman, "Conclusion: Axes of Sacred Values in Hindu Society," in Carman and Marglin, eds., *Purity and Auspiciousness*, p. 116; Richard Waterstone, *India* (London: Duncan Baird, 1995), pp. 70–71, 84–101.

18. Fuller, *Camphor Flame*, pp. 32–36; Srivastava, *Religious Renunciation*, pp. 84, 146.

19. Waterstone, *India*, p. 70.

20. Ibid., pp. 90–91. On the cults of gurus and god-men, see Lawrence A. Babb, *Redemptive Encounters: Three Modern Styles in the Hindu Tradition* (Berkeley: University of California Press, 1986); and D. A. Swallow, "Ashes and Powers: Myth, Rite and Miracle in an Indian God-Man's Cult," *Modern Asian Studies* 16 (1982):123–58.

21. Babb, *Divine Hierarchy*, pp. 91–92.

22. D. F. Pocock, *Mind, Body and Wealth: A Study of Belief and Practice in an*

Indian Village (Oxford: Basil Blackwell, 1973), pp. 37–38; Parry, "Death and Cosmogony in Kashi," p. 352.

23. Bennett, *Dangerous Wives and Sacred Sisters*, p. 40.

24. Susan Snow Wadley, *Shakti: Power in the Conceptual Structure of Karimpur Religion* (Chicago: Department of Anthropology, University of Chicago, 1975), pp. 102–4.

25. E. Alan Morinis, *Pilgrimage in the Hindu Tradition: A Case Study of West Bengal* (Delhi: Oxford University Press, 1984), pp. 267–70.

26. A. M. Abraham Ayrookuzhiel, *The Sacred in Popular Hinduism* (Madras: The Christian Institute for the Study of Religion and Society, 1983), pp. 133–34, 142.

27. Bennett, *Dangerous Wives and Sacred Sisters*, pp. 47–48.

28. Pauline Mahar Kolenda, "Religious Anxiety and Hindu Fate," *Journal of Asian Studies* 23 (1964):71–81; See the collection of articles in Charles F. Keyes and E. Valentine Daniel, eds., *Karma: An Anthropological Inquiry* (Berkeley: University of California Press, 1983).

29. Ayrookuzhiel, *The Sacred in Popular Hinduism*, pp. 133–34, 142–43.

30. Susan S. Wadley and Bruce W. Berr, "Eating Sins in Karimpur," in McKim Marriott, ed., *India through Hindu Categories* (New Delhi: Sage, 1990), p. 140.

31. Paul G. Hiebert, "Karma and Other Explanation Traditions in a South Indian Village," in Keyes and Daniel, eds., *Karma*, pp. 119–30.

32. Charles F. Keyes, "Introduction: The Study of Popular Ideas of Karma," in Keyes and Daniel, eds., *Karma*, p. 6; Lawrence A. Babb, "Destiny and Responsibility: Karma in Popular Hinduism," in Keyes and Daniel, eds., *Karma*, p. 168.

33. Wendy Doniger O'Flaherty, "Karma and Rebirth in the Vedas and Puranas," in W. D. O'Flaherty, ed., *Karma and Rebirth in Classical Indian Traditions* (Berkeley: University of California Press, 1980), pp. 3–37.

34. J. Bruce Long, "The Concepts of Human Action and Rebirth in the Mahabharata," in O'Flaherty, ed., *Karma and Rebirth*, pp. 38–60.

35. Hiebert, "Karma and Other Explanation Traditions"; Sheryl B. Daniel, "The Tool Box Approach of the Tamil to the Issues of Moral Responsibility and Human Destiny," in Keyes and Daniel, eds., *Karma*, pp. 27–62.

36. Keyes, "Introduction," pp. 14–21; Babb, "Destiny and Responsibility," pp. 167–68.

37. Judy F. Pugh, "Astrology and Fate: The Hindu and Muslim Experiences," in Keyes and Daniel, eds., *Karma*, pp. 131–46.

38. Ayrookuzhiel, *The Sacred in Popular Hinduism*, pp. 128, 137.

39. Michael Moffatt, *An Untouchable Community in South India: Structure and Consensus* (Princeton, N.J.: Princeton University Press, 1979), p. 216; Bennett, *Dangerous Wives and Sacred Sisters*, p. 48.

40. Ayrookuzhiel, *The Sacred in Popular Hinduism*, pp. 30–40, 161–62.

41. Babb, *Divine Hierarchy*, p. 216.

42. Ayrookuzhiel, *The Sacred in Popular Hinduism*, p. 30; Wadley, *Shakti*, pp. 116–18.

43. Pocock, *Mind, Body and Wealth*, pp. 87–88; Michell, *Hindu Temple*, pp. 23–24.

44. Babb, *Divine Hierarchy*, p. 195. Other "high" important gods are Surya, the sun god, and Agni, the fire god. Michell, *Hindu Temple*, p. 31; Bennett, *Dangerous Wives and Sacred Sisters*, p. 49.

45. Babb, *Divine Hierarchy*, p. 240; Srivastava, *Religious Renunciation*, pp. 79–84.

46. Babb, *Divine Hierarchy*, p. 242.

47. For a description of a Shiva temple complex, see Buddhadeb Chaudhuri, *The Bakreshwar Temple* (Delhi: Inter-India Publications, 1981).

48. Fuller, *Camphor Flame*, pp. 38–40; Waterstone, *India*, pp. 76–77.

49. Fuller, *Camphor Flame*, pp. 32–36.

50. Ibid., pp. 36–44.

51. Babb, *Divine Hierarchy*, pp. 222–29; William S. Sax, *Mountain Goddess: Gender and Politics in a Himalayan Pilgrimage* (New York: Oxford University Press, 1991), pp. 30–33.

52. Fuller, *Camphor Flame*, pp. 44–48.

53. Ibid., pp. 48–50; Srivastava, *Religious Renunciation*, pp. 66–67.

54. Fuller, *Camphor Flame*, pp. 30–1, 166–77; Daniel Gold, *The Lord as Guru: Hindi Sants in North Indian Tradition* (New York: Oxford University Press, 1987), pp. 3–8.

55. Swallow, "Ashes and Powers"; Babb, *Redemptive Encounters*, pp. 160–212.

56. Babb, *Divine Hierarchy*, pp. 76, 92, 243–44; Susan Bayly, *Saints, Goddesses and Kings: Muslims and Christians in South Indian Society 1700–1900* (Cambridge: Cambridge University Press, 1989) pp. 32–33; Ayrookuzhiel, *The Sacred in Popular Hinduism*, p. 145; Michell, *Hindu Temple*, pp. 33, 36; Tom Selwyn, "Adharma," in Madan, ed., *Way of Life*, p. 388.

57. Waterstone, *India*, pp. 68–69, 162–63; Campbell, *Saints and Householders*, p. 31; Fuller, *Camphor Flame*, pp. 58–59; Babb, *Divine Hierarchy*, p. 107; Ayrookuzhiel, *The Sacred in Popular Hinduism*, pp. 43–44, 54–58.

58. James J. Preston, "Creation of the Sacred Image: Apotheosis and Destruction in Hinduism," in Joanne Punzo Waghorne and Norman Cutler, eds., *Gods of Flesh, Gods of Stone: The Embodiment of Divinity in India* (Chambersburg, Pa.: Anima, 1985), pp. 9–10, 26, 29–30; Fuller, *Servants of the Goddess*, pp. 14–5; Fuller, *Camphor Flame*, pp. 59–62.

59. Babb, *Divine Hierarchy*, pp. 48–50.

60. Moffatt, *Untouchable Community in South India*, pp. 250–67.

61. Babb, *Divine Hierarchy*, pp. 54–59; Milner, *Status and Sacredness*, pp. 175–81.

62. Diana L. Eck, *Banaras, City of Light* (London: Routledge & Kegan Paul, 1983), p. 20; Diehl, *Instrument and Purpose*, pp. 154, 167.

63. Fuller, *Camphor Flame*, pp. 69–72.

64. Ibid., pp. 69–72; Moffatt, *Untouchable Community in South India*, p. 238; Babb, *Divine Hierarchy*, p. 241.

65. Robert Redfield, *Peasant Society and Culture: An Anthropological Approach to Civilization* (Chicago: University of Chicago Press, 1956).

66. McKim Marriott, "Little Communities in an Indigenous Civilization," in McKim Marriott, ed., *Village India: Studies in the Little Community* (Chicago: University of Chicago Press, 1969 [1955]), pp. 171–222.

67. Fuller, *Camphor Flame*, pp. 54–56.

68. Ibid., pp. 24–28; Milner, *Status and Sacredness*, pp. 185–86.

69. Babb, *Divine Hierarchy*, pp. 177–214.

70. Louis Dumont, "A Folk Deity of Tamil Nad: Aiyanar, the Lord," in T. N. Madan, ed., *Religion in India* (Delhi: Oxford University Press, 1991), pp. 20–32.

71. M. N. Srinivas, "Sanskritization and Westernization," in Norman Birnbaum and Gertrud Lenzer, eds., *Sociology of Religion: A Book of Readings* (Englewood Cliffs: Prentice-Hall, 1969), pp. 373–81.

72. Dumont, *Homo Hierarchicus*, pp. 36–37, 44–45, 54–55, 74–76, 108.

73. David G. Mandelbaum, *Society in India,* vol. 1: *Continuity and Change* (Berkeley: University of California Press, 1970), p. 223; Andre Beteille, *Society and Politics in India: Essays in Comparative Perspective* (London: Athlone Press, 1991), pp. 41, 122–39.

74. Richard Burghart, "Hierarchical Models of the Hindu Social System," *Man* 13 (1978):519–36.

75. Peter Van Der Veer, *Gods on Earth: The Management of Religious Experience and Identity in a North Indian Pilgrimage Center* (London: Athlone Press, 1988), pp. 261–62; Nicholas B. Dirks, *The Hollow Crown: Ethnohistory of an Indian Kingdom* (Cambridge: Cambridge University Press, 1987), p. 28.

76. Bayly, *Saints, Goddesses and Kings*, pp. 65–69; Burghart, "Hierarchical Models"; J. Duncan M. Derrett, "Rajadharma," *Journal of Asian Studies* 35 (1976):597–609.

77. Srivastava, *Religious Renunciation*, pp. 266–67.

78. Dirks, *Hollow Crown*, pp. 283–84.

79. J. C. Heesterman, "Power, Priesthood, and Authority," in *The Inner Conflict of Tradition: Essays in Indian Ritual, Kingship, and Society* (Chicago: University of Chicago Press, 1985), p. 142.

80. Van Der Veer, *Gods on Earth*, pp. 261–62.

81. Arjun Appadurai, *Worship and Conflict under Colonial Rule: A South Indian Case* (Cambridge: Cambridge University Press, 1981), pp. 20–22; James J. Preston, *Cult of the Goddess: Social and Religious Change in a Hindu Temple* (New Delhi: Vikas Publishing House, 1980), pp. 55–56; Michell, *Hindu Temple*, p. 63; Fuller, *Servants of the Goddess*, p. 14.

82. Barrington Moore Jr., *Social Origins of Dictatorship and Democracy: Lord*

and Peasant in the Making of the Modern World (London: Allen Lane, The Penguin Press, 1967), pp. 335–36.

83. Ibid., p. 335.

84. Fuller, *Camphor Flame*, pp. 255–56.

85. Milner, *Status and Sacredness*, pp. 48–49, 53–70.

86. Fuller, *Camphor Flame*, pp. 18–19.

87. Wadley, *Shakti*, pp. 81–82, 182.

88. Beteille, *Caste, Class and Power*, pp. 3–7, 191–99; Beteille, *Society and Politics in India*, p. 124.

89. Burghart, "Hierarchical Models."

90. John A. Hall, *Powers and Liberties: The Causes and Consequences of the Rise of the West* (Harmondsworth: Penguin, 1986), pp. 71–72, 76–77.

91. Moore, *Social Origins*, pp. 315–29, 339–40.

92. Bayly, *Saints, Goddesses and Kings*, pp. 49–51; Dirks, *Hollow Crown*, pp. 29–30, 53; Nicholas B. Dirks, "The Original Caste: Power, History and Hierarchy in South Asia," in Marriott, ed., *India through Hindu Categories*, p. 66.

93. Fuller, *Camphor Flame*, p. 106.

94. Michael Mann, *The Sources of Social Power*, vol 1: *A History of Power from the Beginning to A.D. 1760* (Cambridge: Cambridge University Press, 1986), pp. 360–61; David Shulman, "Asvatthaman and Brhannada: Brahmin and Kingly Paradigms in the Sanskrit Epics," in Eisenstadt, ed., *Origins and Diversity*, pp. 424–25.

95. David M. Miller and Dorothy C. Wertz, *Hindu Monastic Life and the Monks and Monasteries of Bhubaneswar* (Montreal: McGill-Queen's University Press, 1976), pp. 4, 129–31, 135–36, 154, 190–91, 195.

96. Diehl, *Instrument and Purpose*, pp. 153–54; Miller and Wertz, *Hindu Monastic Life*, pp. 155–56, 160, 174–86; Pocock, *Mind, Body and Wealth*, pp. 98–100; Van Der Veer, *Gods on Earth*, pp. 71–72, 75–76, 107–8, 283.

NOTES TO CHAPTER 6

1. Richard Gombrich, *Theravada Buddhism: A Social History from Ancient Benares to Modern Colombo* (London: Routledge & Kegan Paul, 1988), pp. 4, 127–32, 137; Gananath Obeyesekere, *The Cult of the Goddess Pattini* (Chicago: University of Chicago Press, 1984), pp. 517–20; Uma Chakravarti, *The Social Dimensions of Early Buddhism* (Delhi: Oxford University Press, 1987), pp. 171–73; Jane Bunnag, "The Way of the Monk and the Way of the World: Buddhism in Thailand, Laos and Cambodia," in Heinz Bechert and Richard Gombrich, eds., *The World of Buddhism* (London: Thames and Hudson, 1984), pp. 160–61.

2. Steven Collins, *Nirvana and Other Buddhist Felicities* (Cambridge: Cambridge University Press, 1998), pp. 18, 565–67.

3. For accounts of the four fundamental truths and the eightfold path, attrib-

uted to the Buddha, see Richard F. Gombrich, *Precept and Practice: Traditional Buddhism in the Rural Highlands of Ceylon* (Oxford: Clarendon Press, 1971), pp. 69–71; Melford P. Spiro, *Buddhism and Society* (Berkeley: University of California Press, 1982), chap. 2; Etienne Lamotte, "The Buddha, His Teachings and His Sangha," in Bechert and Gombrich, eds., *The World of Buddhism*, pp. 41–58.

4. Richard Gombrich, "Introduction: The Buddhist Way," in Bechert and Gombrich, eds., *World of Buddhism*, p. 12. Statements about the Buddha's beliefs and teachings are, in fact, statements about what is attributed to the Buddha in writings some centuries after his death. We have no direct knowledge of Buddhism prior to the reign of Asoka, ca. 268–239 B.C.E. Collins, *Nirvana and Other Buddhist Felicities*, pp. 53–57.

5. Ilana Friedrich Silber, *Virtuosity, Charisma, and Social Order: A Comparative Sociological Study of Monasticism in Theravada Buddhism and Medieval Catholicism* (Cambridge: Cambridge University Press, 1995), p. 80.

6. Ibid., pp. 91–93.

7. Richard F. Gombrich, "The Evolution of the Sangha," in Bechert and Gombrich, eds., *World of Buddhism*, p. 77.

8. Gombrich, *Theravada Buddhism*, p. 71.

9. Charles F. Keyes, "Merit Transference in the Karmic Theory of Popular Theravada Buddhism," in Charles F. Keyes and E. Valentine Daniel, eds., *Karma: An Anthropological Inquiry* (Berkeley: University of California Press, 1983), p. 272.

10. Gombrich, "Introduction," p. 13.

11. Silber, *Virtuosity, Charisma, and Social Order*, pp. 62–63.

12. Ibid., p. 69.

13. Tom Lowenstein, *The Vision of the Buddha* (London: Duncan Baird, 1996), p. 60; Silber, *Virtuosity, Charisma, and Social Order*, pp. 66, 71–72.

14. Robert C. Lester, *Theravada Buddhism in Southeast Asia* (Ann Arbor: University of Michigan Press, 1973), pp. 76–78; Silber, *Virtuosity, Charisma, and Social Order*, pp. 62–63.

15. Lester, *Theravada Buddhism in Southeast Asia*, p. 77.

16. B. J. Terwiel, *Monks and Magic: An Analysis of Religious Ceremonies in Central Thailand* (London: Curzon Press, 1979), p. 22.

17. Michael B. Carrithers, "They Will Be Lords upon the Island: Buddhism in Sri Lanka," in Bechert and Gombrich, eds., *World of Buddhism*, pp. 143–44; Silber, *Virtuosity, Charisma, and Social Order*, p. 105.

18. Lamotte, "The Buddha," pp. 51–52; Hajime Nakamura, "The Basic Teachings of Buddhism," in Heinrich Dumoulin and John C. Maraldo, eds., *Buddhism in the Modern World* (New York: Collier Books, 1976), pp. 17–21; Gombrich, "Introduction," p. 9; Lester, *Theravada Buddhism in Southeast Asia*, p. 31; Collins, *Nirvana and Other Buddhist Felicities*, pp. 96–99, 152–57.

19. Gombrich, *Theravada Buddhism*, pp. 62, 64; Richard Gombrich and Gananath Obeyesekere, *Buddhism Transformed: Religious Change in Sri Lanka*

(Princeton, N.J.: Princeton University Press, 1988), p. 26; Stanley Jeyaraja Tambiah, *The Buddhist Saints of the Forest and the Cults of Amulets: A Study of Charisma, Hagiography, Sectarianism and Millennial Buddhism* (Cambridge: Cambridge University Press, 1984), pp. 28, 38.

20. Spiro, *Buddhism and Society*, chap. 2; Gananath Obeyesekere, "The Buddhist Pantheon in Ceylon and Its Extensions," in Manning Nash, ed., *Anthropological Studies in Theravada Buddhism* (New Haven: Southeast Asia Studies, Yale University, 1966), pp. 12–13; Stanley Jeyaraja Tambiah, "A Thai Cult of Healing through Meditation," in *Culture, Thought and Social Action: An Anthropological Perspective* (Cambridge, Mass.: Harvard University Press, 1985), pp. 110–11.

21. Tambiah, *Buddhist Saints of the Forest*, pp. 45–47, 135–39, 296; Tambiah, "Thai Cult of Healing," pp. 107–9.

22. Gombrich, *Precept and Practice*, p. 322; Bunnag, "Way of the Monk," p. 162.

23. Manning Nash, *The Golden Road to Modernity* (Chicago: University of Chicago Press, 1973), p. 303; Bunnag, "Way of the Monk," pp. 161, 165; Heinz Bechert, "To Be a Burmese Is to Be a Buddhist," in Bechert and Gombrich, eds., *World of Buddhism*, p. 155; Keyes, "Merit Transference," p. 274.

24. Silber, *Virtuosity, Charisma, and Social Order*, p. 94; Jasper Ingersoll, "The Priest Role in Central Village Thailand," in Nash, ed., *Anthropological Studies in Theravada Buddhism*, p. 73.

25. Jane Bunnag, *Buddhist Monk, Buddhist Layman: A Study of Urban Monastic Organization in Central Thailand* (Cambridge: Cambridge University Press, 1973), p. 36; Lester, *Theravada Buddhism in Southeast Asia*, p. 88.

26. Yoneo Ishii, *Sangha, State, and Society: Thai Buddhism in History* (Honolulu: University of Hawaii Press, 1986), p. 19; Terwiel, *Monks and Magic*, p. 20; Bunnag, *Buddhist Monk, Buddhist Layman*, p. 36; Bechert, "To Be a Burmese," pp. 154–55; Keyes, "Merit Transference," p. 279; Lester, *Theravada Buddhism in Southeast Asia*, pp. 84–91.

27. Gombrich, *Theravada Buddhism*, p. 88; S. J. Tambiah, "The Renouncer: His Individuality and His Community," in T. N. Madan, ed., *Way of Life: King, Householder, Renouncer* (New Delhi: Vikas Publishing House, 1982), pp. 306–7.

28. Michael Carrithers, *The Forest Monks of Sri Lanka: An Anthropological and Historical Study* (Delhi: Oxford University Press, 1983), pp. 280–81.

29. It may be said that offerings are made to the Buddha precisely because he is not present; his absence from the cycle of rebirths is inextricably linked with his discovery and teaching of the path to nirvana. Kevin Trainor, *Relics, Ritual, and Representation in Buddhism: Rematerializing the Sri Lankan Theravada Tradition* (Cambridge: Cambridge University Press, 1997), pp. 30–31, 143–44, 158–66, 189–90.

30. Keyes, "Merit Transference," pp. 273, 283; Gombrich, *Theravada Buddhism*, pp. 124–25; Lester, *Theravada Buddhism in Southeast Asia*, pp. 110–12.

31. Ingersoll, "Priest Role," p. 59; Bunnag, "Way of the Monk," p. 168.

32. Tambiah, *Buddhist Saints of the Forest*, p. 146; Carrithers, "They Will Be Lords," p. 134.

33. Ingersoll, "Priest Role," pp. 60–61.

34. Tambiah, *Buddhist Saints of the Forest*, pp. 278, 336; David E. Pfanner, "The Buddhist Monk in Rural Burmese Society," in Nash, ed., *Anthropological Studies in Theravada Buddhism*, pp. 86–87; Bunnag, "Way of the Monk," pp. 168–69.

35. Martin Southwold, *Buddhism in Life: The Anthropological Study of Religion and the Sinhalese Practice of Buddhism* (Manchester: Manchester University Press, 1983), pp. 104–9; Martin Southwold, "True Buddhism and Village Buddhism in Sri Lanka," in J. Davis, ed., *Religious Organization and Religious Experience* (New York: Academic Press, 1982), pp. 141–43; Bunnag, "Way of the Monk," p. 162; Ingersoll, "Priest Role," p. 61; Fred R. von der Mehden, *Religion and Modernization in Southeast Asia* (Syracuse, N.Y.: Syracuse University Press, 1986), p. 82; Lester, *Theravada Buddhism in Southeast Asia*, pp. 118–29.

36. Lester, *Theravada Buddhism in Southeast Asia*, p. 57.

37. Nash, *Golden Road to Modernity*, pp. 106–7, 303.

38. Terwiel, *Monks and Magic*, pp. 246–48.

39. Martin Southwold, "Buddhism and Evil," in David Parkin, ed., *The Anthropology of Evil* (Oxford: Basil Blackwell, 1985), pp. 134–35, 138.

40. Southwold, "True Buddhism and Village Buddhism," pp. 141–43.

41. On the bodhisattva, see David N. Gellner, *Monk, Householder, and Tantric Priest* (Cambridge: Cambridge University Press, 1992), pp. 109–11.

42. Nash, *Golden Road to Modernity*, pp. 105–7, 184–86; S. J. Tambiah, "The Ideology of Merit and the Social Correlates of Buddhism in a Thai Village," in E. R. Leach, ed., *Dialectic in Practical Religion* (Cambridge: Cambridge University Press, 1968), pp. 51–52; Spiro, *Buddhism and Society*, pp. 155–57; Gombrich and Obeyesekere, *Buddhism Transformed*, p. 22; Keyes, "Merit Transference," pp. 265–71.

43. von der Mehden, *Religion and Modernization*, pp. 67–69; Nash, *Golden Road to Modernity*, pp. 114, 296–97, 299.

44. Gananath Obeyesekere, "Theodicy, Sin and Salvation in a Sociology of Buddhism," in Leach, ed., *Dialectic in Practical Religion*, pp. 26–27; Gombrich and Obeyesekere, *Buddhism Transformed*, p. 28.

45. Gombrich, *Theravada Buddhism*, pp. 66–67, 124–25, 147; Nash, *Golden Road to Modernity*, pp. 115–37; Tambiah, "Ideology of Merit," pp. 66–68.

46. Lester, *Theravada Buddhism in Southeast Asia*, pp. 59, 141.

47. Ibid., pp. 15–16; Lowenstein, *Vision of the Buddha*, p. 23.

48. Trainor, *Relics, Ritual, and Representation*, pp. 193–94.

49. Gombrich, *Precept and Practice*, pp. 103–17, 139–41; Gombrich, *Theravada Buddhism*, pp. 123–24, 146; Bruce Kapferer, *A Celebration of Demons: Exorcism and the Aesthetics of Healing in Sri Lanka* (Providence: Berg Publishers, 1991), p. 43.

50. Obeyesekere, *Cult of the Goddess Pattini*, pp. 58–59; Obeyesekere, "Buddhist Pantheon in Ceylon," pp. 2–8, 12–13; Gombrich, *Precept and Practice*, pp. 139–41.

51. Kapferer, *Celebration of Demons*, pp. 52, 174–75; R. L. Stirrat, *Power and Religiosity in a Post-Colonial Setting* (Cambridge: Cambridge University Press, 1992), pp. 29–30; Gombrich and Obeyesekere, *Buddhism Transformed*, p. 30.

52. Gombrich, *Precept and Practice*, pp. 181–82; Gombrich and Obeyesekere, *Buddhism Transformed*, pp. 16, 22–23.

53. Obeyesekere, *Cult of the Goddess Pattini*, p. 60.

54. Gombrich and Obeyesekere, *Buddhism Transformed*, pp. 33–34, 99–100.

55. Obeyesekere, *Cult of the Goddess Pattini*, pp. 54–55, 427, 444–45.

56. Gombrich and Obeyesekere, *Buddhism Transformed*, p. 34.

57. S. J. Tambiah, *World Conqueror and World Renouncer: A Study of Buddhism and Polity in Thailand against a Historical Background* (Cambridge: Cambridge University Press, 1976), p. 520; David Joel Steinberg, ed., *In Search of Southeast Asia* (New York: Praeger, 1971), pp. 63–64; Hans-Dieter Evers, *Monks, Priests and Peasants: A Study of Buddhism and Social Structure in Central Ceylon* (Leiden: E. J. Brill, 1972), pp. 98–99, 102–5.

58. Gombrich, *Theravada Buddhism*, p. 146; Trainor, *Relics, Ritual, and Representation*, p. 31.

59. Nash, *Golden Road to Modernity*, pp. 167–71; Jane C. Nash, "Living with Nats: An Analysis of Animism in Burman Village Social Relations," in Nash, ed., *Anthropological Studies in Theravada Buddhism*, pp. 117–36; Melford P. Spiro, *Burmese Supernaturalism* (Englewood Cliffs: Prentice-Hall, 1967); Bechert, "To Be a Burmese," p. 155; Obeyesekere, *Cult of the Goddess Pattini*, p. 62; Kapferer, *Celebration of Demons*, p. 161; Stirrat, *Power and Religiosity*, p. 86.

60. Obeyesekere, *Cult of the Goddess Pattini*, p. 54.

61. Philip J. Hughes, "The Assimilation of Christianity in the Thai Culture," *Religion* 14 (1984):320, 323.

62. Stirrat, *Power and Religiosity*, pp. 172–73.

63. Obeyesekere, *Cult of the Goddess Pattini*, pp. 65–69; Kapferer, *Celebration of Demons*, pp. 164–65, 172–73; Gombrich and Obeyesekere, *Buddhism Transformed*, p. 31; Stirrat, *Power and Religiosity*, p. 85.

64. Kapferer, *Celebration of Demons*, p. 164; Obeyesekere, *Cult of the Goddess Pattini*, p. 53.

65. Southwold, *Buddhism in Life*, pp. 163–64, 169; Evers, *Monks, Priests and Peasants*, pp. 67–68.

66. Obeyesekere, "Buddhist Pantheon in Ceylon," p. 12; Obeyesekere, *Cult of the Goddess Pattini*, p. 60; Gombrich and Obeyesekere, *Buddhism Transformed*, p. 18.

67. Obeyesekere, *Cult of the Goddess Pattini*, pp. 64–66.

68. Kapferer, *Celebration of Demons*, pp. 172–77, 320; Obeyesekere, *Cult of the Goddess Pattini*, pp. 56, 67; Gombrich and Obeyesekere, *Buddhism Transformed*, p. 19.

69. Southwold, *Buddhism in Life*, pp. 2–4; Trevor Ling, "Sinhalese Buddhism in Recent Anthropological Writing: Some Implications," *Religion* 1 (1971):50–51.

70. Gombrich, *Precept and Practice*, pp. 49, 68.

71. Heinz Bechert, "Contradictions in Sinhalese Buddhism," in Bardwell L. Smith, ed., *Tradition and Change in Theravada Buddhism: Essays on Ceylon and Thailand in the Nineteenth and Twentieth Centuries* (Leiden: E. J. Brill, 1973), pp. 14–15.

72. Southwold, *Buddhism in Life*, pp. 119–26; Southwold, "True Buddhism and Village Buddhism," p. 146; Gombrich, *Theravada Buddhism*, pp. 20, 71, 155; Nash, *Golden Road to Modernity*, pp. 105, 293; Keyes, "Merit Transference," pp. 272–73.

73. Gombrich, *Precept and Practice*, pp. 151–52.

74. Southwold, *Buddhism in Life*, pp. 163–64.

75. Michael M. Ames, "Magical-Animism and Buddhism: A Structural Analysis of the Sinhalese System," *Journal of Asian Studies* 23 (1964):40–42; Michael M. Ames, "Ritual Prestations and the Structure of the Sinhalese Pantheon," in Nash, ed., *Anthropological Studies in Theravada Buddhism*, pp. 42–45.

76. A. Thomas Kirsch, "Complexity in the Thai Religious System: An Interpretation," *Journal of Asian Studies* 36 (1977):258–62.

77. Spiro, *Burmese Supernaturalism*, pp. 257–67.

78. Ibid., pp. 254–55.

79. Bunnag, "Way of the Monk," p. 162.

80. Ames, "Magical-Animism and Buddhism"; Gananath Obeyesekere, "The Great Tradition and the Little in the Perspective of Sinhalese Buddhism," *Journal of Asian Studies* 22 (1963):139–53; Bechert, "Contradictions in Sinhalese Buddhism."

81. Ames, "Magical-Animism and Buddhism."

82. Spiro, *Buddhism and Society*, pp. 143, 159–61.

83. S. J. Tambiah, *Buddhism and the Spirit Cults in North-East Thailand* (Cambridge: Cambridge University Press, 1970), pp. 41–42, 55–56, 340–42, 346; See also Kapferer, *Celebration of Demons*, p. 43.

84. B. J. Terwiel, "A Model for the Study of Thai Buddhism," *Journal of Asian Studies* 35 (1976):402–3; Terwiel, *Monks and Magic*, pp. 1–4.

85. Kapferer, *Celebration of Demons*, pp. 44–45, 321–22.

86. Southwold, *Buddhism in Life*, pp. 164–66.

87. Gombrich, *Theravada Buddhism*, pp. 95–96; Silber, *Virtuosity, Charisma, and Social Order*, pp. 63–71, 106–16; Tambiah, "The Renouncer," p. 306; Tambiah, *Buddhist Saints of the Forest*, pp. 135–36, 175.

88. Southwold, *Buddhism in Life*, pp. 104–9; Silber, *Virtuosity, Charisma, and Social Order*, pp. 108–9.

89. Gombrich, *Theravada Buddhism*, pp. 4, 71–72, 90, 155–56, 184.

90. Ibid., pp. 73–74, 87–89; Tambiah, "The Renouncer," pp. 304–5; Tambiah, *World Conqueror and World Renouncer*, pp. 519–20; Steven Piker, "Buddhism and

Modernization in Contemporary Thailand," in Smith, ed., *Tradition and Change in Theravada Buddhism*, pp. 54–55.

91. Southwold, *Buddhism in Life*, pp. 104–9.

92. Gombrich, *Theravada Buddhism*, pp. 162–63; Carrithers, *Forest Monks of Sri Lanka*, pp. 140–42; Silber, *Virtuosity, Charisma, and Social Order*, pp. 86–88.

93. Gombrich, *Precept and Practice*, p. 317; Silber, *Virtuosity, Charisma and Social Order*, pp. 80–82.

94. Tambiah, *Buddhist Saints of the Forest*, pp. 133–35; Gananath Obeyesekere, "Religion and Polity in Theravada Buddhism: Continuity and Change in a Great Tradition," *Comparative Studies in Society and History* 21 (1979):626–39.

95. E. Michael Mendelson, *Sangha and State in Burma: A Study of Monastic Sectarianism and Leadership* (Ithaca: Cornell University Press, 1975), pp. 58, 162–72; Tambiah, *Buddhist Saints of the Forest*, pp. 53–59; Obeyesekere, "Religion and Polity."

96. Nash, *Golden Road to Modernity*, pp. 143–45; Southwold, "True Buddhism and Village Buddhism," p. 140.

97. Obeyesekere, "Religion and Polity"; Heinz Bechert, "Theravada Buddhist Sangha: Some General Observations on Historical and Political Factors in Its Development," *Journal of Asian Studies* 29 (1970):769; Silber, *Virtuosity, Charisma, and Social Order*, pp. 98–99.

98. Bunnag, "Way of the Monk," p. 167; Tambiah, *Buddhist Saints of the Forest*, pp. 145–48, 333; Gombrich, *Theravada Buddhism*, pp. 105–6; Silber, *Virtuosity, Charisma, and Social Order*, pp. 83–85; Mendelson, *Sangha and State in Burma*, pp. 162–72.

99. Tambiah, *Buddhist Saints of the Forest*, p. 73; Carrithers, *Forest Monks of Sri Lanka*, pp. 140–42.

100. Gombrich, *Precept and Practice*, p. 313.

101. Tambiah, *World Conqueror and World Renouncer*, pp. 125–26; Tambiah, *Buddhist Saints of the Forest*, p. 241; Steinberg, ed., *In Search of Southeast Asia*, pp. 169–70; Mendelson, *Sangha and State in Burma*, p. 32.

102. Mendelson, *Sangha and State in Burma*, p. 57.

103. Gombrich, *Theravada Buddhism*, p. 69; Tambiah, *Buddhist Saints of the Forest*, pp. 76–77.

104. Steinberg, ed., *In Search of Southeast Asia*, pp. 23–29, 40–42.

105. Silber, *Virtuosity, Charisma, and Social Order*, pp. 103–4.

106. Lowenstein, *Vision of the Buddha*, pp. 52, 60–63, 89, 92.

107. On the interaction of Mahayana Buddhism and Hinduism in Nepal, see Gellner, *Monk, Householder, and Tantric Priest*.

108. H. Byron Earhart, *Japanese Religion: Unity and Diversity* (Encino, Calif.: Dickenson, 1994), pp. 94–96, 99–102, 120; J. H. Kamstra, "The Complexity of Japanese Religion," in Pieter Hendrik Vrijhof and Jacques Waardenburg, eds., *Official and Popular Religion: Analysis of a Theme for Religious Studies* (The Hague: Mouton, 1979), pp. 446–48.

109. Ian Reader, *Religion in Contemporary Japan* (Honolulu: University of Hawaii Press, 1991), pp. 38–39.

110. Ibid., pp. 80–82, 88; John K. Nelson, "Warden + Virtuoso + Salaryman = Priest: Paradigms within Japanese Shinto for Religious Specialists and Institutions," *Journal of Asian Studies* 56 (1997):681, 688.

111. Reader, *Religion in Contemporary Japan*, pp. 31, 113–28; H. Byron Earhart, *A Religious Study of the Mount Haguro Sect of Shugendo: An Example of Japanese Mountain Religion* (Tokyo: Sophia University, 1970), pp. 2–3, 152.

112. Ichiro Hori, *Folk Religion in Japan: Continuity and Change* (Chicago: University of Chicago Press, 1968) pp. 199–200; Shimazono Susuma, "The Living Kami Idea in the New Religions of Japan," *Japanese Journal of Religious Studies* 6 (1979):389–412.

113. Reader, *Religion in Contemporary Japan*, pp. 56, 60–69; Ian Reader, "Shinto," in Ian Reader, ed., *Japanese Religions: Past and Present* (Sandgate, Folkestone, Kent: Japan Library, 1993), pp. 64–65; Winston Davis, *Japanese Religion and Society: Paradigms of Structure and Change* (Albany: State University of New York Press, 1992), pp. 77–78; Earhart, *Japanese Religion*, pp. 21–22.

114. Earhart, *Japanese Religion*, pp. 61–64; Hori, *Folk Religion in Japan*, pp. 85, 93, 120–22.

115. Reader, *Religion in Contemporary Japan*, pp. 40–44, 48–49, 90–92, 96–101; Ian Reader, "Folk Religion," in Reader, ed., *Japanese Religions*, pp. 52–53, 56; Hori, *Folk Religion in Japan*, pp. 72–73, 116–17, 122–24, 133, 138–39; Robert J. Smith, *Ancestor Worship in Contemporary Japan* (Stanford: Stanford University Press, 1974), pp. 11–12, 15, 40–48, 54–55, 66, 123–24, 127–29, 133–41, 145–46, 218–19; Carmen Blacker, "Rethinking the Study of Religion in Japan," in Adriana Boscaro, Franco Gatti, and Massimo Raveri, eds., *Rethinking Japan*, vol. 2 (Sandgate, Folkestone, Kent: Japan Library, 1990), p. 246.

116. Reader, *Religion in Contemporary Japan*, p. 38; Noboru Miyata, "Popular Beliefs in Contemporary Japan," in Boscaro, Gatti, and Raveri, eds., *Rethinking Japan*, vol. 2, p. 243.

117. Earhart, *Japanese Religion*, pp. 28, 39, 46, 72–73; Esben Andreasen, "Japanese Religions: An Introduction," in Reader, ed., *Japanese Religions*, p. 42; Ichiro Hori, ed., *Japanese Religion: A Survey by the Agency for Cultural Affairs* (Tokyo: Kodansha International, 1972), p. 18.

118. Andreasen, "Japanese Religions," p. 43; Reader, *Religion in Contemporary Japan*, pp. 50–51.

NOTES TO CHAPTER 7

1. William A. Christian Jr., *Person and God in a Spanish Valley* (New York: Seminar Press, 1972); Ellen Badone, *The Appointed Hour: Death, Worldview, and Social Change in Brittany* (Berkeley: University of California Press, 1989). See also

articles collected in Ellen Badone, ed., *Religious Orthodoxy and Popular Faith in European Society* (Princeton, N.J.: Princeton University Press, 1990).

2. Robert T. Anderson, *Traditional Europe: A Study in Anthropology and History* (Belmont, Calif.: Wadsworth, 1971).

3. Ibid., pp. 89, 92, 154; Donald A. Nielsen, "The Inquisition, Rationalization, and Sociocultural Change in Medieval Europe," in William H. Swatos Jr., ed., *Time, Place, and Circumstance: Neo-Weberian Studies in Comparative Religious History* (New York: Greenwood Press, 1990), pp. 110–17; Susan Reynolds, *Kingdoms and Communities in Western Europe, 900–1300* (Oxford: Clarendon Press, 1984), pp. 79–81, 89.

4. Gary Macy, "Was There a 'The Church' in the Middle Ages?" in R. Swanson, ed., *Unity and Diversity in the Church* (Oxford: Blackwell, 1996), pp. 107–16.

5. Karen Louise Jolly, *Popular Religion in Late Saxon England: Elf Charms in Context* (Chapel Hill: University of North Carolina Press, 1996), pp. 9–11, 19–22, 116, 123.

6. Anderson, *Traditional Europe*, pp. 12, 143–44.

7. Ibid., pp. 12, 79, 87, 95, 124, 143–44.

8. David Gentilcore, *From Bishop to Witch: The System of the Sacred in Early Modern Terra d'Otrando* (Manchester: Manchester University Press, 1992), p. 32; Miri Rubin, "Religious Culture in Town and Country: Reflections on a Great Divide," in David Abulafia, Michael Franklin, and Miri Rubin, eds., *Church and City 1000–1500: Essays in Honour of Christopher Brooke* (Cambridge: Cambridge University Press, 1992), pp. 3–22.

9. Michael P. Carroll, *Madonnas That Maim: Popular Catholicism in Italy since the Fifteenth Century* (Baltimore: Johns Hopkins University Press, 1992), pp. 8–12.

10. Max Weber, *Economy and Society* (New York: Bedminster Press, 1968), pp. 1166–68.

11. Norman Cohn, *The Pursuit of the Millennium* (London: Paladin, 1970 [1957]), pp. 13, 29; Yonina Talmon, "Millenarian Movements," *Archives europeennes de sociologie* 7 (1966):159, 162–63; Ernest Lee Tuveson, *Millennium and Utopia* (New York: Harper & Row, 1964), pp. 14–17.

12. Marjorie Reeves, *The Influence of Prophecy in the Later Middle Ages* (Oxford: Oxford University Press, 1969), pp. 242, 303–6.

13. Cohn, *Pursuit of the Millennium*, pp. 52–59, 80–81, 85, 281–85.

14. Ludo J. R. Mills, *Angelic Monks and Earthly Men: Monasticism and Its Meaning to Medieval Society* (Woodbridge, Suffolk: Boydell Press, 1992), p. 139; Gerd Tellenbach, *Church, State and Christian Society at the Time of the Investiture Contest* (Oxford: Basil Blackwell, 1966), pp. 47, 50.

15. Jean Delumeau, *Sin and Fear: The Emergence of a Western Guilt Culture, Thirteenth–Eighteenth Centuries* (New York: St. Martin's Press, 1990), p. 402; Aron Gurevich, *Medieval Popular Culture: Problems of Belief and Perception* (Cambridge: Cambridge University Press, 1988), p. 115.

16. Gurevich, *Medieval Popular Culture*, pp. 105, 115, 119–22, 137–45; Philippe Aries, *Western Attitudes toward Death, from the Middle Ages to the Present* (Baltimore: Johns Hopkins University Press, 1974), pp. 29–31; Jacques Le Goff, *The Birth of Purgatory* (Chicago: University of Chicago Press, 1984), p. 231; Caroline Walker Bynum, *The Resurrection of the Body in Western Christianity, 200–1336* (New York: Columbia University Press, 1995), p. 14; Delumeau, *Sin and Fear*, pp. 90–91. Gurevich questions Aries's statements that the Last Judgment became popular only in the twelfth century and that the idea of individual judgment after death appeared only at the end of the Middle Ages. Gurevich, *Medieval Popular Culture*, pp. 120–21, 138–39.

17. Delumeau, *Sin and Fear*, pp. 285–87.

18. Le Goff, *Birth of Purgatory*; Gurevich, *Medieval Popular Culture*, pp. 148–49. Gurevich criticizes Le Goff's analysis of the development of purgatory in terms of intellectual history and emphasizes instead the pressure on the clergy by the masses who were concerned with making paradise a realistic option for "sinners." A. J. Gurevich, "Popular and Scholarly Medieval Cultural Traditions: Notes in the Margin of Jacques Le Goff's Book," *Journal of Medieval History* 9 (1983): 71–90. Carroll questions Le Goff's argument that folkloric traditions shaped the notion of purgatory. He writes that the evidence in Italy suggests purgatory did not become an important part of popular religion until the seventeenth century, after the suggestion by theologians in the sixteenth century that the souls in purgatory could help the living. Michael P. Carroll, *Veiled Threats: The Logic of Popular Catholicism in Italy* (Baltimore: Johns Hopkins University Press, 1996), pp. 120–25, 130–34.

19. Philippe Aries, *The Hour of Our Death* (New York: Alfred A. Knopf, 1981), pp. 24, 267–68, 277; Badone, *The Appointed Hour*, p. 132.

20. Badone, *The Appointed Hour*, p. 56.

21. See, for example, Gurevich, *Medieval Popular Culture*, pp. 81–82, 89; Mary O'Neil, "Magical Healing, Love Magic and the Inquisition in Late Sixteenth-Century Modena," in Stephen Haliezer, ed., *Inquisition and Society in Early Modern Europe* (London: Croom Helm, 1987), pp. 99–104; William A. Christian Jr., *Local Religion in Sixteenth-Century Spain* (Princeton, N.J.: Princeton University Press, 1981), pp. 23–28; C. Scott Dixon, "Popular Beliefs and the Reformation in Brandenburg-Ansbach," in Bob Scribner and Trevor Johnson, eds., *Popular Religion in Germany and Central Europe, 1400–1800* (London: Macmillan, 1996), p. 123.

22. Christian, *Local Religion in Sixteenth-Century Spain*, pp. 142–43, 147.

23. Bernard Hamilton, *Religion in the Medieval West* (London: Edward Arnold, 1986), pp. 43–45; Gerd Tellenbach, *The Church in Western Europe from the Tenth to the Early Twelfth Century* (Cambridge: Cambridge University Press, 1993), pp. 94, 98; R. N. Swanson, *Religion and Devotion in Europe c.1215–c.1515* (Cambridge: Cambridge University Press, 1995), pp. 236–37; John L. McKenzie, S.J., *The Roman Catholic Church* (London: Weidenfeld and Nicholson, 1969), pp. 141–54.

24. Tellenbach, *Church, State and Christian Society*, pp. 53–57.

25. Ibid., p. 50.

26. Hamilton, *Religion in the Medieval West*, pp. 32–33; Tellenbach, *Church in Western Europe*, p. 103; R. W. Southern, *Western Society and the Church in the Middle Ages* (Harmondsworth: Penguin, 1970), pp. 228–30; Henrietta Leyser, *Hermits and the New Monasticism: A Study of Religious Communities in Western Europe, 1000–1150* (London: Macmillan, 1984).

27. Tellenbach, *Church in Western Europe*, pp. 105–6, 128; Southern, *Western Society and the Church*, pp. 224–28; Hamilton, *Religion in the Medieval West*, pp. 26–27; Ilana Friedrich Silber, *Virtuosity, Charisma, and Social Order: A Comparative Sociological Study of Monasticism in Theravada Buddhism and Medieval Catholicism* (Cambridge: Cambridge University Press, 1995), pp. 127–28.

28. Silber, *Virtuosity, Charisma, and Social Order*, pp. 146–48.

29. Hamilton, *Religion in the Medieval West*, p. 56.

30. Ibid., pp. 70–71, 107–8; Caroline Walker Bynum, *Jesus as Mother: Studies in the Spirituality of the High Middle Ages* (Berkeley: University of California Press, 1982), p. 31.

31. Hamilton, *Religion in the Medieval West*, pp. 72, 109–10.

32. Swanson, *Religion and Devotion in Europe*, pp. 183–84.

33. Ibid., pp. 30–33; Hamilton, *Religion in the Medieval West*, pp. 116–17, 138; Miri Rubin, *Corpus Christi: The Eucharist in Late Medieval Culture* (Cambridge: Cambridge University Press, 1991), pp. 55, 73, 347–48; Rubin, "Religious Culture in Town and Country," p. 13; Gabor Klaniczay, *The Uses of Supernatural Power: The Transformation of Popular Religion in Medieval and Early-Modern Europe* (Princeton, N.J.: Princeton University Press, 1990), pp. 51, 63–64; McKenzie, *Roman Catholic Church*, pp. 140–54.

34. Keith Thomas, *Religion and the Decline of Magic* (Harmondsworth: Penguin, 1973), pp. 36–38; Richard Kieckhefer, *Magic in the Middle Ages* (Cambridge: Cambridge University Press, 1989), p. 79; Gentilcore, *From Bishop to Witch*, p. 7.

35. Robert W. Scribner, "The Reformation, Popular Magic, and the 'Disenchantment of the World,'" *Journal of Interdisciplinary History* 23 (1993):478–80; Gentilcore, *From Bishop to Witch*, pp. 94–95.

36. Gentilcore, *From Bishop to Witch*, pp. 7, 98.

37. Robert Muchembled, *Popular Culture and Elite Culture in France 1400–1750* (Baton Rouge: Louisiana State University Press, 1985), pp. 83–92; Patrick Curry, *Prophecy and Power: Astrology in Early Modern England* (Cambridge: Polity Press, 1989), p. 102; Dixon, "Popular Beliefs and the Reformation," pp. 120–21; Richard A. Horsley, "Further Reflection on Witchcraft and European Folk Religion," *History of Religions* 19 (1979):78; Thomas, *Religion and the Decline of Magic*, pp. 210, 317.

38. Thomas, *Religion and the Decline of Magic*, pp. 31–34, 46–56, 210–27, 252–64, 278–91, 318; O'Neil, "Magical Healing, Love Magic and the Inquisition," p.

91; Christina Larner, *Enemies of God: The Witch-Hunt in Scotland* (Oxford: Basil Blackwell, 1983), p. 140; Scribner, "The Reformation," pp. 480–82; Jolly, *Popular Religion in Late Saxon England*, pp. 27, 90–94, 170–71; Kieckhefer, *Magic in the Middle Ages*, pp. 67–78; Gentilcore, *From Bishop to Witch*, pp. 102–3, 107–18.

39. Robert W. Scribner, "Elements of Popular Belief," in Thomas A. Brady Jr., Heiko A. Oberman, James D. Tracy, eds., *Handbook of European History 1400–1600: Late Middle Ages, Renaissance and Reformation*, vol 1: *Structures and Assertions* (Leiden: E. J. Brill, 1994), pp. 238–42.

40. Hamilton, *Religion in the Medieval West*, pp. 40, 87, 104, 106; Maureen Flynn, *Sacred Charity: Confraternities and Social Welfare in Spain, 1400–1700* (Ithaca: Cornell University Press, 1989), p. 30.

41. Hamilton, *Religion in the Medieval West*, pp. 40–41, 104; Carroll, *Madonnas That Maim*, pp. 14–17.

42. Michael P. Carroll, *The Cult of the Virgin Mary: Psychological Origins* (Princeton, N.J.: Princeton University Press, 1986), pp. 4–5; Hamilton, *Religion in the Medieval West*, pp. 104–5.

43. Carroll, *Cult of the Virgin Mary*, pp. 219–22; Thomas A. Kselman, *Miracles and Prophecies in Nineteenth-Century France* (New Brunswick, N.J.: Rutgers University Press, 1983), p. 33; Christian, *Local Religion in Sixteenth-Century Spain*, p. 206.

44. Mary Lee Nolan and Sidney Nolan, *Christian Pilgrimage in Modern Western Europe* (Chapel Hill: University of North Carolina Press, 1989), p. 116.

45. Marina Warner, *Alone of All Her Sex: The Myth and the Cult of the Virgin Mary* (London: Pan Books, 1985 [1976]), pp. xxii, 104–5, 130–47, 182–85, 191, 286, 336.

46. Ibid., pp. 236–54; Kathleen Ashley and Pamela Sheingorn, *Interpreting Cultural Symbols: Saint Anne in Late Medieval Society* (Athens: University of Georgia Press, 1990), p. 13; Andrea Dahlberg, "The Body as a Principle of Holism: Three Pilgrimages to Lourdes," in John Eade and Michael J. Sallnow, eds., *Contesting the Sacred: The Anthropology of Christian Pilgrimage* (London: Routledge, 1991), pp. 33–34.

47. Warner, *Alone of All Her Sex*, pp. 82–89, 94; Victor Turner and Edith Turner, *Image and Pilgrimage in Christian Culture* (New York: Columbia University Press, 1978), p. 154.

48. Warner, *Alone of All Her Sex*, pp. 315–25; Christian, *Person and God in a Spanish Valley*, p. 175; Flynn, *Sacred Charity*, pp. 27–29.

49. Warner, *Alone of All Her Sex*, pp. 289, 323.

50. Carroll, *Cult of the Virgin Mary*, p. 20; Carroll, *Veiled Threats*, p. 17.

51. Warner, *Alone of All Her Sex*, pp. 273–78; Christian, *Local Religion in Sixteenth-Century Spain*, p. 98.

52. Lucia Chiavola Birnbaum, *Black Madonnas: Feminism, Religion, and Politics in Italy* (Boston: Northeastern University Press, 1993).

53. Carroll, *Madonnas That Maim*, pp. 67–75, 87.

54. Carroll, *Veiled Threats*, pp. 19–22.

55. Carroll, *Madonnas That Maim*, pp. 27, 59–66.

56. Christian, *Local Religion in Sixteenth-Century Spain*, pp. 82, 91.

57. Carroll, *Madonnas That Maim*, p. 27.

58. Ashley and Sheingorn, *Interpreting Cultural Symbols*.

59. Peter Brown, *The Cult of the Saints: Its Rise and Function in Latin Christianity* (Chicago: University of Chicago Press, 1981); R. Van Den Broek, "Popular Religious Practices and Ecclesiastical Policies in the Early Church," in Peter Hendrik Vrijhuf and Jacques Waardenburg, eds., *Official and Popular Religion: Analysis of a Theme for Religious Studies* (The Hague: Mouton, 1979), pp. 30–32; Barbara Abou-El-Haj, *The Medieval Cult of Saints: Formations and Transformations* (Cambridge: Cambridge University Press, 1994), pp. 7–8.

60. Brown, *Cult of the Saints*; Peter Brown, *Society and the Holy in Late Antiquity* (London: Faber and Faber, 1982); Joyce E. Salisbury, *Iberian Popular Religion 600 B.C. to 700 A.D.: Celts, Romans and Visigoths* (New York: Edwin Mellen Press, 1985) pp. 131–63; Swanson, *Religion and Devotion in Europe*, pp. 152–54.

61. Richard Kieckhefer, "Imitators of Christ: Sainthood in the Christian Tradition," in Richard Kieckhefer and George D. Bond, eds., *Sainthood: Its Manifestations in World Religions* (Berkeley: University of California Press, 1988), pp. 4–5.

62. Adriaan H. Bredero, *Christendom and Christianity in the Middle Ages* (Grand Rapids, Mich.: Wm. B. Erdmans, 1994), pp. 160–75; Andre Vauchez, "The Saint," in Jacques Le Goff, ed., *The Medieval World* (London: Collins and Brown, 1990), pp. 325–26; Patrick J. Geary, *Furta Sacra: Thefts of Relics in the Central Middle Ages* (Princeton, N.J.: Princeton University Press, 1978), pp. 21–26.

63. Gurevich, *Medieval Popular Culture*, pp. 59–60; Vauchez, "The Saint," pp. 320, 327; Andre Vauchez, *The Laity in the Middle Ages: Religious Beliefs and Devotional Practices* (Notre Dame: University of Notre Dame Press, 1993), pp. 51–72, 99–101; Klaniczay, *Uses of Supernatural Power*, pp. 98–108, 111–28; Donald Weinstein and Rudolph M. Bell, *Saints and Society: The Two Worlds of Western Christendom, 1000–1700* (Chicago: University of Chicago Press, 1982), pp. 196–202.

64. Turner and Turner, *Image and Pilgrimage*, pp. 156–58; Peter Burke, "How to Be a Counter-Reformation Saint," in Kasper von Greyerz, ed., *Religion and Society in Early Modern Europe 1500–1800* (London: George Allen & Unwin, 1984), pp. 45–46; Weinstein and Bell, *Saints and Society*, pp. 168–69.

65. Weinstein and Bell, *Saints and Society*, pp. 141–43.

66. Gentilcore, *From Bishop to Witch*, p. 169.

67. Salisbury, *Iberian Popular Religion*, pp. 232–33; Christian, *Local Religion in Sixteenth-Century Spain*, pp. 126–28; Geary, *Furta Sacra*, pp. 4, 35–39, 152–59.

68. Warner, *Alone of All Her Sex*, pp. 82, 95, 200; Rosalind Brooke and Christopher Brooke, *Popular Religion in the Middle Ages, Western Europe 1000–1300* (London: Thames and Hudson, 1984), pp. 195–99; Geary, *Furta Sacra*, pp. 27–29; Gentilcore, *From Bishop to Witch*, pp. 187–91.

69. Gurevich, *Medieval Popular Culture*, pp. 43–48; Judith Devlin, *The Superstitious Mind: French Peasants and the Supernatural in the Nineteenth Century* (New Haven: Yale University Press, 1987), pp. 11–13, 151; A. N. Galpern, *The Religions of the People in Sixteenth-Century Champagne* (Cambridge, Mass.: Harvard University Press, 1976), p. 53.

70. Steven Wilson, "Introduction," in Steven Wilson, ed., *Saints and Their Cults: Studies in Religion, Sociology, Folklore, and History* (Cambridge: Cambridge University Press, 1983), p. 19.

71. Gurevich, *Medieval Popular Culture*, pp. 43–48; Devlin, *Superstitious Mind*, pp. 15–17, 54.

72. Christian, *Local Religion in Sixteenth-Century Spain*, pp. 174–77; Christian, *Person and God in a Spanish Valley*, pp. 45–47.

73. Jeffrey Burton Russell, *Lucifer: The Devil in the Middle Ages* (Ithaca: Cornell University Press, 1984), pp. 63, 65, 259; Hamilton, *Religion in the Medieval West*, pp. 87–88; Gurevich, *Medieval Popular Culture*, pp. 165, 193–94; Scribner, "Elements of Popular Belief," pp. 236–37.

74. Le Goff, *Birth of Purgatory*, pp. 293–94; Gurevich, "Popular and Scholarly Medieval Cultural Traditions," pp. 74, 79; Thomas, *Religion and the Decline of Magic*, pp. 701–21; Pieter Spierenburg, *The Broken Spell: A Cultural and Anthropological History of Preindustrial Europe* (New Brunswick: Rutgers University Press, 1991), pp. 134–36; Valerie I. J. Flint, *The Rise of Magic in Early Medieval Europe* (Princeton, N.J.: Princeton University Press, 1991), pp. 213–14; Jean Delumeau, *Catholicism between Luther and Voltaire: A New View of the Counter-Reformation* (London: Burns & Oates, 1977), p. 167; Scribner, "Elements of Popular Belief," p. 238; Muchembled, *Popular Culture and Elite Culture*, pp. 61–64; Carroll, *Veiled Threats*, pp. 139–56.

75. Russell, *Lucifer*, p. 78; Hamilton, *Religion in the Medieval West*, p. 102; Gurevich, *Medieval Popular Culture*, p. 191; Jolly, *Popular Religion in Late Saxon England*, pp. 132–38.

76. Thomas, *Religion and the Decline of Magic*, pp. 735–47.

77. Kieckhefer, *Magic in the Middle Ages*, pp. 127–30.

78. Cf. Ernst Troeltsch, *The Social Teaching of the Christian Churches* (New York: Harper & Row, 1960 [1911]).

79. Hamilton, *Religion in the Medieval West*, pp. 26–27, 181–85; Tellenbach, *Church in Western Europe*, pp. 123–24, 294; Swanson, *Religion and Devotion in Europe*, pp. 6–7; Michael Hill, *The Religious Order: A Study of Virtuoso Religion and Its Legitimation in the Nineteenth-Century Church of England* (London: Heinemann, 1973), pp. 24–25.

80. Silber, *Virtuosity, Charisma, and Social Order*, p. 122.

81. Hamilton, *Religion in the Medieval West*, p. 17; John Van Engen, "The Christian Middle Ages as an Historiographical Problem," *American Historical Review* 91 (1986):542.

82. Swanson, *Religion and Devotion in Europe*, pp. 43–50; Hamilton, *Religion in the Medieval West*, pp. 15–25.

83. Hamilton, *Religion in the Medieval West*, pp. 23–25.

84. Tellenbach, *Church in Western Europe*, pp. 29, 176, 290; Swanson, *Religion and Devotion in Europe*, p. 53.

85. Jolly, *Popular Religion in Late Saxon England*, pp. 46–47, 51–53, 69–70.

86. Swanson, *Religion and Devotion in Europe*, pp. 43–59; Hamilton, *Religion in the Medieval West*, pp. 16–17, 23–25, 62, 68–69; Tellenbach, *Church in Western Europe*, pp. 32–33, 161–67; Anderson, *Traditional Europe*, pp. 155–56.

87. Hamilton, *Religion in the Medieval West*, pp. 19–21; Tellenbach, *Church in Western Europe*, pp. 178, 290; Bynum, *Jesus as Mother*, pp. 9–11; Marc Bloch, *Feudal Society* (London: Routledge & Kegan Paul, 1962), pp. 348–52.

88. Marc Bloch, *The Royal Touch: Sacred Monarchy and Scrofula in England and France* (London: Routledge & Kegan Paul, 1973); Tellenbach, *Church, State and Christian Society*, pp. 57–69.

89. João De Pina-Cabral, *Sons of Adam, Daughters of Eve: The Peasant Worldview of the Alto Minho* (Oxford: Clarendon Press, 1988), p. 163.

90. Scribner, "Elements of Popular Belief," p. 244; David Nichols, *Deity and Domination: Images of God and the State in the Nineteenth and Twentieth Centuries* (London: Routledge, 1989), pp. 233–34.

91. Pina-Cabral, *Sons of Adam*, pp. 165–66.

92. Hamilton, *Religion in the Medieval West*, pp. 29, 32–33; Tellenbach, *Church in Western Europe*, p. 103; Southern, *Western Society and the Church*, pp. 224, 228–30; Mills, *Angelic Monks and Earthly Men*, pp. 64–66.

93. Anderson, *Traditional Europe*, p. 88.

94. James C. Scott, "Protest and Profanation: Agrarian Revolt and the Little Tradition, Part 1," *Theory and Society* 4 (1977):1–38; Roger N. Lancaster, *Thanks to God and the Revolution: Popular Religion and Class Consciousness in the New Nicaragua* (New York: Columbia University Press, 1988).

95. Bloch, *Feudal Society*, p. 80.

96. Anderson, *Traditional Europe*, pp. 11–13, 17–18, 35–41, 161–62.

97. Ibid., pp. 78–79.

98. Ibid., pp. 143–45.

99. Spierenburg, *Broken Spell*, pp. 51–53.

NOTES TO CHAPTER 8

1. Daniel Pipes, *In the Path of God: Islam and Political Power* (New York: Basic Books, 1983), pp. 30–39; Mervin F. Verbit, "The Political Character of Judaism and Islam: Some Comparisons," in Michael Curtis, ed., *Religion and Politics in the Middle East* (Boulder, Colo.: Westview Press, 1981), pp. 69–76.

2. Ladislav Holy, *Religion and Custom in a Muslim Society: The Berti of Sudan* (Cambridge: Cambridge University Press, 1991), p. 1.

3. Stephen Sharot, *Messianism, Mysticism, and Magic: A Sociological Analysis of Jewish Religious Movements* (Chapel Hill: University of North Carolina Press, 1982), pp. 28, 135, 141, 147; Michael Gilsenan, *Recognizing Islam: Religion and Society in the Modern Arab World* (New York: Pantheon Books, 1982), p. 33.

4. Daniel Bates and Amal Rassam, *Peoples and Cultures of the Middle East* (Englewood Cliffs: Prentice-Hall, 1983), pp. 54–56; Stephen Sharot, *Judaism: A Sociology* (Newton Abbot: David & Charles, 1976), pp. 15–17.

5. Gilsenan, *Recognizing Islam*, pp. 37–54.

6. Bates and Rassam, *Peoples and Cultures*, pp. 54–55. In Shi'a countries the religious elite were more hierarchical and centralized than in Sunni countries; see pp. 65–67.

7. Bryan S. Turner, *Weber and Islam* (London: Routledge & Kegan Paul, 1974), pp. 115–16.

8. Sharot, *Judaism*, p. 30.

9. Vincent J. Cornell, *Realm of the Saint: Power and Authority in Moroccan Sufism* (Austin: University of Texas Press, 1998), pp. 3–4, 7, 113, 116–19, 275–76.

10. Dale F. Eickelman, *Moroccan Islam: Tradition and Society in a Pilgrimage Center* (Austin: University of Texas Press, 1976), pp. 158–60; Robert L. Cohn, "Sainthood on the Periphery: The Case of Judaism," in Richard Kieckhefer and George D. Bond, eds., *Sainthood: Its Manifestations in World Religions* (Berkeley: University of California Press, 1988), pp. 43–68.

11. Ignaz Goldziher, *Muslim Studies*, vol. 2 (London: George Allen & Unwin, 1971), pp. 259, 262–64, 335–37; Vincent Crapanzano, *The Hamadsha: A Study of Moroccan Ethnopsychiatry* (Berkeley: University of California Press, 1973), pp. 13–17; Emanuel Marx, "Communal and Individual Pilgrimage: The Region of Saints' Tombs in South Sinai," in R. P. Werbner, ed., *Regional Cults* (London: Academic Press, 1977), pp. 29–30; Eickelman, *Moroccan Islam*, pp. 11, 60–62; J. D. J. Waardenburg, "Official and Popular Religion as a Problem in Islamic Studies," in Pieter Hendrik Vrijhof and Jacques Waardenburg, eds., *Official and Popular Religion: Analysis of a Theme for Religious Studies* (The Hague: Mouton, 1979), pp. 240–42; William M. Brinner, "Prophet and Saint: The Two Exemplars of Islam," in John Stratton Hawley, ed., *Saints and Virtues* (Berkeley: University of California Press, 1987), pp. 45, 55; Frederick M. Denny, "'God's Friends': The Sanctity of Persons in Islam," in Kieckhefer and Bond, eds., *Sainthood*, pp. 6–7.

12. Ernest Gellner, *Muslim Society* (Cambridge: Cambridge University Press, 1981), pp. 40–53. Gellner contrasted the personalized, ecstatic, and unscriptural Islam around the saints in rural and tribal areas with the scriptural, scholarly, unitarian, puritanical Islam of the urban religious elite and bourgeois. Cornell questions this oppositional pairing and writes that although the greatest Moroccan

saints were rural in origin and usually remained in the countryside, their approach to religious doctrine was "orthodox," and an urban ethos pervaded Moroccan sainthood. Cornell, *Realm of the Saint*, pp. xxvii, 93–95, 118–20.

13. Eickelman, *Moroccan Islam*, pp. 162, 178–79.

14. Issachar Ben-Ami, "Folk-Veneration of Saints among the Moroccan Jews," in Shelomo Morag, Issachar Ben-Ami, and Norman A. Stillman, eds., *Studies in Judaism and Islam* (Jerusalem: Magnes Press, 1981), pp. 283–344; Alex Weingrod, *The Saint of Beersheba* (Albany: State University of New York Press, 1990); Harvey E. Goldberg, "Potential Politics: Jewish Saints in the Moroccan Countryside and in Israel," in Mart Bax, Peter Kloos, and Adrianus Koster, eds., *Faith and Polity: Essays on Religion and Politics* (Amsterdam: VU University Press, 1992), pp. 235–50.

15. Eyal Ben-Ari and Yoram Bilu, "Saints' Sanctuaries in Israeli Development Towns: On a Mechanism of Urban Transformation," *Urban Anthropology* 16 (1987):244–72; Weingrod, *Saint of Beersheba*.

16. Yoram Bilu, "Dreams and the Wishes of the Saints," in Harvey E. Goldberg, ed., *Judaism Viewed from Within and from Without* (Albany: State University of New York Press, 1987), pp. 285–313.

17. Weingrod, *Saint of Beersheba*, pp. 81–85, 104–6.

18. J. Spencer Trimingham, *The Sufi Orders in Islam* (Oxford: Clarendon Press, 1971); Marshall G. S. Hodgson, *The Venture of Islam*, vol. 2 (Chicago: University of Chicago Press, 1974), pp. 203–28; Ira M. Lapidus, *A History of Islamic Societies* (Cambridge: Cambridge University Press, 1988), pp. 168–71, 443–69; Michael Gilsenan, *Saint and Sufi in Modern Egypt: An Essay in the Sociology of Religion* (Oxford: Clarendon Press, 1973), pp. 2–12, 21, 43–44; Crapanzano, *The Hamadsha*, pp. 2–4, 17–19, 135, 170; Susan Bayly, *Saints, Goddesses and Kings: Muslims and Christians in South Indian Society 1700–1900* (Cambridge: Cambridge University Press, 1989), pp. 14–16, 110–12; Valerie J. Hoffman, *Sufism, Mystics, and Saints in Modern Egypt* (Columbia: University of South Carolina Press, 1995), pp. 90–92, 98–101.

19. Sharot, *Messianism, Mysticism, and Magic*, pp. 139–44; Ada Rapoport-Albert, "God and the Zaddik as the Two Focal Points of Hasidic Worship," *History of Religions* 18 (1979):296–325; Gershom Scholem, *Major Trends in Jewish Mysticism* (New York: Schocken Books, 1961), pp. 325–50; Ada Rapoport-Albert, "Hasidism after 1772: Structural Continuity and Change," in Ada Rapoport-Albert, ed., *Hasidism Reappraised* (London: Littman Library of Jewish Civilization, 1996), pp. 126–28.

20. Hodgson, *Venture of Islam*, p. 228; Trimingham, *Sufi Orders in Islam*, pp. 133–34; Bayly, *Saints, Goddesses and Kings*, p. 95; Crapanzano, *The Hamadsha*, pp. 15–17; Hoffman, *Sufism, Mystics and Saints*, pp. 93–94.

21. Sharot, *Messianism, Mysticism, and Magic*, pp. 159–61.

22. Trimingham, *Sufi Orders in Islam*, pp. 104, 149, 173–74; Lapidus, *History*

of Islamic Societies, pp. 168–69; Hoffman, *Sufism, Mystics and Saints*, pp. 128–29, 203–5; Sharot, *Messianism, Mysticism, and Magic*, pp. 162–88; Rapoport Albert, "Hasidism after 1772," pp. 103, 137–38.

23. Menachem Friedman, "Life Tradition and Book Tradition in the Development of Ultraorthodox Judaism," in Goldberg, ed., *Judaism Viewed from Within and from Without*, pp. 235–55.

24. Stephen Sharot, "Religious Fundamentalism: Neo-Traditionalism in Modern Societies," in Bryan Wilson, ed., *Religion: Contemporary Issues* (London: Bellew Publishing, 1992), pp. 30–32; Hoffman, *Sufism, Mystics and Saints*, pp. 118–21.

NOTES TO CHAPTER 9

1. Keith Thomas, *Religion and the Decline of Magic* (Harmondsworth: Penguin, 1973), pp. 92–93; David Zaret, *The Heavenly Contract: Ideology and Organization in Pre-Revolutionary Puritanism* (Chicago: University of Chicago Press, 1985), p. 42.

2. The Eucharist was also performed frequently by Anglicans and on special occasions or monthly by Presbyterians and radical Protestant movements. Edward Muir, *Ritual in Early Modern Europe* (Cambridge: Cambridge University Press, 1997), pp. 170–72; Pamela Johnston and Bob Scribner, *The Reformation in Germany and Switzerland* (Cambridge: Cambridge University Press, 1993), pp. 88–89; Richard Godbeer, *The Devil's Dominion: Magic and Religion in Early New England* (Cambridge: Cambridge University Press, 1992), pp. 25–30.

3. Max Weber, *The Protestant Ethic and the Spirit of Capitalism* (London: George Allen & Unwin, 1930), pp. 137–41.

4. Ibid., p. 141.

5. Ibid., p. 121.

6. Ibid., p. 122.

7. Ibid., pp. 122, 131.

8. Ibid., p. 122.

9. William Monter, *Ritual, Myth and Magic in Early Modern Europe* (Athens: Ohio University Press, 1984), pp. 23–24; Zaret, *Heavenly Contract*, pp. 12, 15, 24–28, 34–40; Johnston and Scribner, *Reformation in Germany and Switzerland*, pp. 58, 128–29; Michael Walzer, *The Revolution of the Saints: A Study in the Origins of Radical Politics* (Cambridge, Mass.: Harvard University Press, 1965), pp. 52–54, 115.

10. Monter, *Ritual, Myth and Magic*, p. 23; Zaret, *Heavenly Contract*, p. 41; Jane Schneider, "Spirits and the Spirit of Capitalism," in Ellen Badone, ed., *Religious Orthodoxy and Popular Faith in European Society* (Princeton, N.J.: Princeton University Press, 1990), pp. 42–43; Jurgen Beyer, "A Lubeck Prophet in Local and Lutheran Context," in Bob Scribner and Trevor Johnson, eds., *Popular Religion in*

Germany and Central Europe, 1400–1800 (London: Macmillan, 1996), pp. 168, 173; Robert W. Scribner, "The Reformation, Popular Magic, and the 'Disenchantment of the World,'" *Journal of Interdisciplinary History* 23 (1993):482, 486–87.

11. Thomas, *Religion and the Decline of Magic*, pp. 60–79, 87–103, 132–37, 146; Godbeer, *Devil's Dominion*, pp. 25–30, 77–78.

12. Robert W. Scribner, "Religion, Society and Culture: Reorienting the Reformation," *History Workshop* 14 (1982):5.

13. Weber, *Protestant Ethic*, p. 26.

14. Scribner, "Religion, Society and Culture," pp. 4–9; Marc R. Forster, *The Counter-Reformation in the Villages: Religion and Reform in the Bishopric of Speyer, 1560–1720* (Ithaca: Cornell University Press, 1992), p. 13.

15. R. Po-Chia Hsia, *Social Discipline in the Reformation: Central Europe 1550–1750* (London: Routledge, 1989), pp. 154, 165, 176–79.

16. Robert Whiting, *The Blind Devotion of the People: Popular Religion and the English Reformation* (Cambridge: Cambridge University Press, 1989), pp. 145–46, 151, 259–60, 266–68; Eamon Duffy, *The Stripping of the Altars: Traditional Religion in England, c.1400–c.1580* (New Haven: Yale University Press, 1992). Calvinism reached into the poorer strata in England, and in the relatively rustic environment of Scotland, Calvinism replaced Catholicism. Margaret Spufford, "The Importance of Religion in the Sixteenth and Seventeenth Centuries," in Margaret Spufford, ed., *The World of Rural Dissenters 1520–1725* (Cambridge: Cambridge University Press, 1995), pp. 1–18; Monter, *Ritual, Myth and Magic*, p. 52.

17. Keith Wrightson and David Levine, *Poverty and Piety in an English Village, Terling, 1525–1700* (New York: Academic Press, 1979), pp. 156–81.

18. Zaret, *Heavenly Contract*, pp. 48–51.

19. Rosemary L. Hopcroft, "Rural Organization and Receptivity to Protestantism," *Journal for the Scientific Study of Religion* 36 (1997):158–81.

20. Hsia, *Social Discipline in the Reformation*, pp. 1–3, 18–19, 143, 176–77; Gunther Lottes, "Popular Culture and the Early Modern State in Sixteenth Century Germany," in Steven L. Kaplan, ed., *Understanding Popular Culture: Europe from the Middle Ages to the Nineteenth Century* (Berlin: Mouton, 1984), pp. 173–74.

21. Johnston and Scribner, *Reformation in Germany and Switzerland*, p. 81; Godbeer, *Devil's Dominion*, pp. 11–13.

22. C. Scott Dixon, "Popular Beliefs and the Reformation in Brandenburg-Ansbach," in Scribner and Johnson, eds., *Popular Religion*, p. 125; Gerald Strauss, *Luther's House of Learning: Indoctrination of the Young in the German Reformation* (Baltimore: Johns Hopkins University Press, 1978), pp. 302–5.

23. Hsia, *Social Discipline in the Reformation*, pp. 26–27; Monter, *Ritual, Myth and Magic*, pp. 43–44.

24. Muir, *Ritual in Early Modern Europe*, p. 140.

25. Strauss, *Luther's House of Learning*, pp. 299, 302; Hsia, *Social Discipline in*

the Reformation, pp. 136–37; Thomas, *Religion and the Decline of Magic*, pp. 189–97.

26. Scribner, "The Reformation," pp. 482–84, 488.

27. R. J. W. Evans, *The Making of the Habsburg Monarchy* (Oxford: Clarendon Press, 1979), pp. 263–65, 269–70, 275; Stuart Clark, "Protestant Demonology: Sin, Superstition and Society (c.1520–c.1630)," in Bengt Ankarloo and Gustav Henningsen, eds., *Early Modern European Witchcraft Centres and Peripheries* (Oxford: Clarendon Press, 1990), pp. 72–79; Lottes, "Popular Culture," pp. 177–79; Dixon, "Popular Beliefs and the Reformation," pp. 123–25; Monter, *Ritual, Myth and Magic*, pp. 26–28, 46–47; Scribner, "Religion, Society and Culture," p. 11; Strauss, *Luther's House of Learning*, pp. 303–4.

28. Thomas, *Religion and the Decline of Magic*, p. 330.

29. Ibid., pp. 210–11, 221, 271.

30. Godbeer, *Devil's Dominion*, pp. 59–60, 64–65, 69, 77–78, 119–20, 125–26; Jon Butler, "Magic, Astrology, and the Early American Religious Heritage, 1600–1760," *American Historical Review* 84 (1979):325–34; Charles H. Lippy, *Being Religious, American Style: A History of Popular Religiosity in the United States* (Westport, Conn.: Greenwood Press, 1994), pp. 23–43.

31. Thomas, *Religion and the Decline of Magic*, pp. 346–78, 425–58; Patrick Curry, *Prophecy and Power: Astrology in Early Modern England* (Cambridge: Polity Press, 1989), pp. 110, 113–15.

32. James Obelkevich, *Religion and Rural Society: South Lindsey 1825–1875* (Oxford: Clarendon Press, 1976), pp. 120–24, 174–77.

33. Hugh McLeod, *Religion and the People of Western Europe, 1789–1970* (Oxford: Oxford University Press, 1981), pp. 34, 37–40; David Clark, *Between Pulpit and Pew: Folk Religion in a North Yorkshire Fishing Village* (Cambridge: Cambridge University Press, 1982), pp. 64–65.

34. Obelkevich, *Religion and Rural Society*, p. 145.

35. Ibid., pp. 137–43, 152–60.

36. Ibid., pp. 5–6; McLeod, *Religion and the People of Western Europe*, p. 40.

37. Obelkevich, *Religion and Rural Society*, pp. 318–20; Clark, *Between Pulpit and Pew*, p. 66.

38. Obelkevich, *Religion and Rural Society*, p. 308.

39. Ibid., pp. 259–312.

40. Clark, *Between Pulpit and Pew*.

41. Jean Delumeau, *Sin and Fear: The Emergence of a Western Guilt Culture, Thirteenth–Eighteenth Centuries* (New York: St. Martin's Press, 1990); Ellen Badone, *The Appointed Hour: Death, Worldview, and Social Change in Brittany* (Berkeley: University of California Press, 1989), pp. 174–76, 188–91; Philip T. Hoffman, *Church and Community in the Diocese of Lyon 1500–1789* (New Haven: Yale University Press, 1984), pp. 84, 123; Christina Larner, *Enemies of God: The Witch-Hunt in Scotland* (Oxford: Basil Blackwell, 1983), pp. 157, 193.

42. Hoffman, *Church and Community*, pp. 169–79.

43. Robert Muchembled, *Popular Culture and Elite Culture in France 1400–1750* (Baton Rouge: Louisiana State University Press, 1985), pp. 4, 105; Hoffman, *Church and Community*, p. 91; Dixon, "Popular Beliefs and the Reformation," p. 125.

44. Hoffman, *Church and Community*, pp. 87, 131–36; Ronald Hutton, *The Rise and Fall of Merry England: The Ritual Year 1400–1700* (Oxford: Oxford University Press, 1994), pp. 70–72; Muchembled, *Popular Culture and Elite Culture*, pp. 160–80; Forster, *Counter-Reformation in the Villages*, p. 94.

45. David Gentilcore, *From Bishop to Witch: The System of the Sacred in Early Modern Terra d'Otrando* (Manchester: Manchester University Press, 1992), pp. 194–95; Michael P. Carroll, *Veiled Threats: The Logic of Popular Catholicism in Italy* (Baltimore: Johns Hopkins University Press, 1996), pp. 50–76, 92–93.

46. Thomas A. Kselman, *Miracles and Prophecies in Nineteenth-Century France* (New Brunswick, N.J.: Rutgers University Press, 1983), pp. 17–33, 37, 57–59, 192–200.

47. John Eade and Michael J. Sallnow, "Introduction," in John Eade and Michael J. Sallnow, eds., *Contesting the Sacred: The Anthropology of Christian Pilgrimage* (London: Routledge, 1991), pp. 16, 19; Andrea Dahlberg, "The Body as a Principle of Holism: Three Pilgrimages to Lourdes," in Eade and Sallnow, eds., *Contesting the Sacred*, pp. 30–50.

48. Victor Turner and Edith Turner, *Image and Pilgrimage in Christian Culture* (New York: Columbia University Press, 1978), pp. 63–65.

49. William A. Christian Jr., *Person and God in a Spanish Valley* (New York: Seminar Press, 1972), pp. 45–71.

50. Adriaan H. Bredero, *Christendom and Christianity in the Middle Ages* (Grand Rapids, Mich.: Wm. B. Eerdmans, 1994), p. 178.

51. Gentilcore, *From Bishop to Witch*, pp. 163–64.

52. João De Pina-Cabral, *Sons of Adam, Daughters of Eve: The Peasant Worldview of the Alto Minho* (Oxford: Clarendon Press, 1986), pp. 165–71.

53. Jean Delumeau, *Catholicism between Luther and Voltaire: A New View of the Counter-Reformation* (London: Burns & Oates, 1977); R. W. Scribner, "Interpreting Religion in Early Modern Europe," *European Studies Review* 13 (1983): 89–105; Mary R. O'Neil, "Magical Healing, Love Magic and the Inquisition in Late Sixteenth-Century Modena," in Stephen Haliezer, ed., *Inquisition and Society in Early Modern Europe* (London: Croom Helm, 1987), pp. 88–114.

54. O'Neil, "Magical Healing," in Haliezer, ed., *Inquisition and Society*, pp. 97–99; Gentilcore, *From Bishop to Witch*, pp. 7, 211–14.

55. Trevor Johnson, "Blood, Tears and Xavier-Water: Jesuit Missionaries and Popular Religion in the Eighteenth-Century Upper Paltinate," in Scribner and Johnson, eds., *Popular Religion*, pp. 184–85, 195–98.

56. Norman Cohn, *Europe's Inner Demons* (New York: Basic Books, 1975);

Nachman Ben-Yehuda, *Deviance and Moral Boundaries: Witchcraft, the Occult, Science Fiction, Deviant Sciences and Scientists* (Chicago: University of Chicago Press, 1985), pp. 27–70; Thomas, *Religion and the Decline of Magic*, pp. 517–698; Christina Larner, *Witchcraft and Religion: The Politics of Popular Belief* (Oxford: Basil Blackwell, 1984); Gentilcore, *From Bishop to Witch*, pp. 13–14, 238–55.

57. Dixon, "Popular Beliefs and the Reformation," pp. 138–39.

58. Delumeau, *Catholicism between Luther and Voltaire*, p. 190.

59. Muchembled, *Popular Culture and Elite Culture*, p. 43.

60. Joseph Klaits, *Servants of Satan: The Age of the Witch Hunts* (Bloomington: Indiana University Press, 1985), p. 83.

61. R. W. Scribner, "Introduction," in Scribner and Johnson, eds., *Popular Religion*, pp. 11–12.

62. Larner, *Witchcraft and Religion*, p. 122.

63. Hoffman, *Church and Community*, p. 137.

64. Timothy Tackett, *Priest and Parish in Eighteenth-Century France: A Social and Political Study of the Cures in a Diocese of Dauphine 1750–1791* (Princeton, N.J.: Princeton University Press, 1977), p. 215.

65. Forster, *Counter-Reformation in the Villages*.

66. William J. Callahan and David Higgs, "Introduction," in William J. Callahan and David Higgs, eds., *Church and Society in Catholic Europe of the Eighteenth Century* (Cambridge: Cambridge University Press, 1979), pp. 2–4; Olwen Hufton, "The French Church," in Callahan and Higgs, eds., *Church and Society*, pp. 16–24; Tackett, *Priest and Parish*, pp. 30–31, 63–65, 101, 110, 117–18, 151–55, 165–66.

67. Callahan and Higgs, "Introduction," pp. 2–3, 5–6.

68. Hoffman, *Church and Community*, pp. 50–52, 57, 70–73, 81–83, 98–118, 128–66; Delumeau, *Catholicism between Luther and Voltaire*, pp. 180–83, 187; Tackett, *Priest and Parish*, pp. 154–55; Gentilcore, *From Bishop to Witch*, pp. 42–59, Forster, *Counter-Reformation in the Villages*, pp. 6–7, 21–23, 59, 89–93, 101, 106.

69. Michael P. Carroll, "Religion, Ricettizie, and the Immunity of Southern Italy to the Reformation," *Journal for the Scientific Study of Religion* 31 (1992): 247–60.

70. Pina-Cabral, *Sons of Adam*, pp. 197–200; Ellen Badone, "Introduction," in Ellen Badone, ed., *Religious Orthodoxy and Popular Faith in European Society* (Princeton, N.J.: Princeton University Press, 1990), p. 11; Caroline B. Brettell, "The Priest and His People: The Contractual Basis for Religious Practice in Rural Portugal," in Badone, ed., *Religious Orthodoxy and Popular Faith*, pp. 55–75; Ruth Behar, "The Struggle for the Church: Popular Anticlericalism and Religiosity in Post-Franco Spain," in Badone, ed., *Religious Orthodoxy and Popular Faith*, pp. 76–112; Lawrence J. Taylor, "Stories of Power, Powerful Stories: The Drunken Priest in Donegal," in Badone, ed., *Religious Orthodoxy and Popular Faith*, pp. 163–84.

71. Badone, "Introduction," pp. 8–12; Brettell, "Priest and His People"; Behar, "Struggle for the Church"; Stanley Brandes, "Conclusion: Reflections on the Study of Religious Orthodoxy and Popular Faith in Europe," in Badone, ed., *Religious Orthodoxy and Popular Faith*, p. 190; Joyce Riegelhaupt, "Popular Anti-Clericalism and Religiosity in Pre-1974 Portugal," in Eric R. Wolf, ed., *Religion, Power and Protest in Local Communities* (Berlin: Mouton, 1984), pp. 93–115; Pina-Cabral, *Sons of Adam*, pp. 131, 142, 204–10.

72. Curry, *Prophecy and Power*.

73. Peter Burke, *Popular Culture in Early Modern Europe* (London: Temple Smith, 1978); Hutton, *Rise and Fall of Merry England*; Pieter Spierenburg, *The Broken Spell: A Cultural and Anthropological History of Preindustrial Europe* (New Brunswick: Rutgers University Press, 1991); Klaits, *Servants of Satan*, pp. 76–77.

74. Obelkevich, *Religion and Rural Society*, pp. 23–27, 57, 61, 78, 81, 90, 97, 310–14; Hugh McLeod, *Religion and Society in England 1850–1914* (London: Macmillan, 1996), pp. 112, 202–5.

75. Muchembled, *Popular Culture and Elite Culture*, p. 308.

76. Judith Devlin, *The Superstitious Mind: French Peasants and the Supernatural in the Nineteenth Century* (New Haven: Yale University Press, 1987); Evans, *Making of the Habsburg Monarchy*, pp. 267–68.

77. Muchembled, *Popular Culture and Elite Culture*, pp. 279–311.

78. Eugen Weber, *Peasants into Frenchmen: The Modernization of Rural France 1870–1914* (London: Chatto & Windus, 1979), pp. 485–88, 494.

79. Christian, *Person and God in a Spanish Valley*; Badone, *Appointed Hour*.

80. Roger N. Lancaster, *Thanks to God and the Revolution: Popular Religion and Class Consciousness in the New Nicaragua* (New York: Columbia University Press, 1988); David Lehmann, *Struggle for the Spirit: Religious Transformation and Popular Culture in Brazil and Latin America* (Cambridge: Polity Press, 1996).

81. Weber, *Peasants into Frenchmen*.

82. David Martin, *A General Theory of Secularization* (Oxford: Basil Blackwell, 1978); Jonathan Sperber, *Popular Catholicism in Nineteenth-Century Germany* (Princeton, N.J.: Princeton University Press, 1984).

83. For a recent discussion, see Steve Bruce, *Religion in the Modern World: From Cathedrals to Cults* (Oxford: Oxford University Press, 1996), pp. 29–35, 129–43.

84. Barrington Moore Jr., *Social Origins of Dictatorship and Democracy: Lord and Peasant in the Making of the Modern World* (London: Allen Lane, The Penguin Press, 1967), pp. 111, 127–28; Roger Finke and Rodney Stark, *The Churching of America, 1776–1990* (New Brunswick: Rutgers University Press, 1992), pp. 94, 96, 208.

85. Seymour Martin Lipset, *The First New Nation: The United States in Historical and Comparative Perspective* (New York: Anchor Books, 1967), pp. 181–85; L. Laurence Moore, *Selling God: American Religion in the Marketplace of Culture*

(New York: Oxford University Press, 1994), pp. 7–11, 64–67; Stephen R. Warner, "Work in Progress toward a New Paradigm for the Sociological Study of Religion in the United States," *American Journal of Sociology* 98 (1993):1044–93.

86. Finke and Stark, *Churching of America*, pp. 54–96; Moore, *Selling God*, pp. 44–49, 77–78, 164–65; Nathan O. Hatch, *The Democratization of American Christianity* (New Haven: Yale University Press, 1989), pp. 8–12, 50–52, 55, 132–38, 150–53, 204–5.

87. Moore, *Selling God*, pp. 51–55, 149–55, 184–87, 245–50; Lippy, *Being Religious*, p. 200.

88. Finke and Stark, *Churching of America*, pp. 145–76; Hatch, *Democratization of American Christianity*, pp. 214–19.

89. Lippy, *Being Religious*, pp. 88, 115–20.

90. Peter W. Williams, *Popular Religion in America: Symbolic Change and the Modernization Process in Historical Perspective* (Englewood Cliffs: Prentice-Hall, 1980), pp. 76–78; Robert Anthony Orsi, *The Madonna of 115th Street: Faith and Community in Italian Harlem, 1880–1950* (New Haven: Yale University Press, 1985), pp. xv–xvii, 55, 61–64; Robert A. Orsi, *Thank You, St. Jude: Women's Devotion to the Patron Saint of Hopeless Causes* (New Haven: Yale University Press, 1996), pp. 27–28.

91. Collen McDannell, *Material Christianity: Religion and Popular Culture in America* (New Haven: Yale University Press, 1995), pp. 132–37, 149.

92. Orsi, *Madonna of 115th Street*, pp. 60–64, 69, 72–74, 169–70.

93. Quoted in Orsi, *Thank You, St. Jude*, p. 16.

94. Ibid., pp. 15–37.

95. Finke and Stark, *Churching of America*, pp. 256–72.

96. Louis Schneider and Sanford M. Dornbusch, *Popular Religion: Inspirational Books in America* (Chicago: University of Chicago Press, 1958), quotes of Peale on p. 63.

97. Lippy, *Being Religious*. In his work on popular religion in America, Williams dealt primarily with religious movements, including sects and cults, that exist apart from and in tension with the established or mainstream religious organizations. Williams, *Popular Religion in America*.

NOTES TO CHAPTER 10

1. Leigh Eric Schmidt, *Consumer Rites: The Buying and Selling of American Holidays* (Princeton, N.J.: Princeton University Press, 1995); L. Laurence Moore, *Selling God: American Religion in the Marketplace of Culture* (New York: Oxford University Press, 1994), pp. 205–6.

2. Moore, *Selling God*, pp. 213–18, 239–63; Charles H. Lippy, *Being Religious, American Style: A History of Popular Religiosity in the United States* (Westport, Conn.: Greenwood Press, 1994), pp. 224–29.

3. Colin Campbell, "The Cult, the Cultic Milieu and Secularization," *A Sociological Yearbook of Religion in Britain* 5 (1972):119–36.

4. Rodney Stark and William Sims Bainbridge, *The Future of Religion* (Berkeley: University of California Press, 1985), pp. 26–30, 208–33.

5. For a useful summary of the New Age, see Steve Bruce, *Religion in the Modern World: From Cathedrals to Cults* (Oxford: Oxford University Press, 1996), pp. 196–229. For a collection of articles on the New Age, see James R. Lewis and J. Gordon Melton, eds., *Perspectives on the New Age* (Albany: State University of New York Press, 1992). For a collection of readings and articles on the occult before the term *New Age* became popular, see Edward A. Tiryakian, ed., *On the Margin of the Visible: Sociology, the Esoteric, and the Occult* (New York: John Wiley & Sons, 1974).

6. Aidan A. Kelly, "An Update on Neopagan Witchcraft in America," in Lewis and Melton, eds., *Perspectives on the New Age*, pp. 136–51.

7. Paul Heelas, "Prosperity and the New Age Movement: The Efficacy of Spiritual Economics," in Bryan Wilson and Jamie Cresswell, eds., *New Religious Movements: Challenge and Response* (London: Routledge, 1999), pp. 51–77.

8. Bryan Wilson, "Introduction," in Wilson and Cresswell, eds., *New Religious Movements*, pp. 1–11.

9. Colin Campbell, "The Easternisation of the West," in Wilson and Cresswell, eds., *New Religious Movements*, p. 40; Bruce, *Religion in the Modern World*, p. 211.

10. Heelas, "Prosperity and the New Age Movement," pp. 51–77; Bruce, *Religion in the Modern World*, pp. 179–81.

11. Tony Walter and Helen Waterhouse, "A Very Private Belief: Reincarnation in Contemporary England," *Sociology of Religion* 60 (1999):187–97; Tony Walter, *The Eclipse of Eternity: A Sociology of the Afterlife* (London: Macmillan, 1996), pp. 24, 34, 47.

Bibliography

Abercrombie, Nicholas, Stephen Hill, and Bryan S. Turner. *The Dominant Ideology Thesis*. London: George Allen & Unwin, 1980.

Abou-El-Haj, Barbara. *The Medieval Cult of Saints: Formations and Transformations*. Cambridge: Cambridge University Press, 1994.

Ahern, Emily M. *The Cult of the Dead in a Chinese Village*. Stanford: Stanford University Press, 1973.

————. *Chinese Ritual and Politics*. Cambridge: Cambridge University Press, 1981.

Ames, Michael M. "Magical-Animism and Buddhism: A Structural Analysis of the Sinhalese System." *Journal of Asian Studies* 23 (1964):21–52.

————. "Ritual Prestations and the Structure of the Sinhalese Pantheon." In Manning Nash, ed., *Anthropological Studies in Theravada Buddhism*, pp. 27–50. New Haven: Southeast Asia Studies, Yale University, 1966.

Anderson, Robert T. *Traditional Europe: A Study in Anthropology and History*. Belmont, Calif.: Wadsworth, 1971.

Andreasen, Esben. "Japanese Religions: An Introduction." In Ian Reader, ed., *Japanese Religions: Past and Present*, pp. 33–43. Sandgate, Folkestone, Kent: Japan Library, 1993.

Appadurai, Arjun. *Worship and Conflict under Colonial Rule: A South Indian Case*. Cambridge: Cambridge University Press, 1981.

Aries, Philippe. *Western Attitudes toward Death, from the Middle Ages to the Present*. Baltimore: Johns Hopkins University Press, 1974.

————. *The Hour of Our Death*. New York: Alfred A. Knopf, 1981.

Arkush, R. David. "Orthodoxy and Heterodoxy in Twentieth-Century Chinese Peasant Proverbs." In Kwang-Ching Liu, ed., *Orthodoxy in Late Imperial China*, pp. 311–31. Berkeley: University of California Press, 1990.

Ashley, Kathleen, and Pamela Sheingorn. *Interpreting Cultural Symbols: Saint Anne in Late Medieval Society*. Athens: University of Georgia Press, 1990.

Ayrookuzhiel, A. M. Abraham. *The Sacred in Popular Hinduism*. Madras: The Christian Institute for the Study of Religion and Society, 1983.

Babb, Lawrence A. *The Divine Hierarchy: Popular Hinduism in Central India*. New York: Columbia University Press, 1975.

————. "Destiny and Responsibility: Karma in Popular Hinduism." In Charles F.

Keyes and E. Valentine Daniel, eds., *Karma: An Anthropological Inquiry*, pp. 163–81. Berkeley: University of California Press, 1983.

Babb, Lawrence A. *Redemptive Encounters: Three Modern Styles in the Hindu Tradition*. Berkeley: University of California Press, 1986.

Badone, Ellen. *The Appointed Hour: Death, Worldview, and Social Change in Brittany*. Berkeley: University of California Press, 1989.

———. "Introduction." In Ellen Badone, ed., *Religious Orthodoxy and Popular Faith in European Society*, pp. 3–22. Princeton, N.J.: Princeton University Press, 1990.

Badrinath, Chaturvedi. "Max Weber's Wrong Understanding of Indian Civilization." In Detlef Kantowsky, ed., *Recent Research on Max Weber's Studies of Hinduism*, pp. 45–58. Munich: Weltfoum Verlag, 1986.

Baity, Philip C. "The Ranking of Gods in Chinese Folk Religion." *Asian Folklore Studies* 35 (1977):77–84.

Baptandier, Brigette. "The Lady Linshui: How a Woman Became a Goddess." In Meir Shahar and Robert P. Weller, eds., *Unruly Gods: Divinity and Society in China*, pp. 105–49. Honolulu: University of Hawaii Press, 1996.

Bates, Daniel, and Amal Rassam. *Peoples and Cultures of the Middle East*. Englewood Cliffs: Prentice-Hall, 1983.

Bayley, Susan. *Saints, Goddesses and Kings: Muslims and Christians in South Indian Society 1700–1900*. Cambridge: Cambridge University Press, 1989.

Beattie, J. H. M. "On Understanding Ritual." In Bryan R. Wilson, ed., *Rationality*, pp. 240–68. Oxford: Basil Blackwell, 1970.

Bechert, Heinz. "Theravada Buddhist Sangha: Some General Observations on Historical and Political Factors in Its Development." *Journal of Asian Studies* 29 (1970):761–78.

———. "Contradictions in Sinhalese Buddhism." In Bardwell L. Smith, ed., *Tradition and Change in Theravada Buddhism: Essays on Ceylon and Thailand in the Nineteenth and Twentieth Centuries*, pp. 7–17. Leiden: E. J. Brill, 1973.

———. "To Be a Burmese Is to Be a Buddhist." In Heinz Bechert and Richard Gombrich, eds., *The World of Buddhism*, pp. 147–58. London: Thames and Hudson, 1984.

Behar, Ruth. "The Struggle for the Church: Popular Anticlericalism and Religiosity in Post-Franco Spain." In Ellen Badone, ed., *Religious Orthodoxy and Popular Faith in European Society*, pp. 76–112. Princeton, N.J.: Princeton University Press, 1990.

Bellah, Robert N. "Religious Evolution." *American Sociological Review* 29 (1964): 358–74.

Ben-Ami, Issachar. "Folk-Veneration of Saints among the Moroccan Jews." In Shelomo Morag, Issachar Ben-Ami, and Norman A. Stillman, eds., *Studies in Judaism and Islam*, pp. 283–344. Jerusalem: Magnes Press, 1981.

Ben-Ari, Eyal, and Yoram Bilu. "Saints' Sanctuaries in Israeli Development

Towns: On a Mechanism of Urban Transformation." *Urban Anthropology* 16 (1987):244–72.

Bennett, Lynn. *Dangerous Wives and Sacred Sisters: Social and Symbolic Roles of High-Caste Women in Nepal.* New York: Columbia University Press, 1983.

Ben-Yehuda, Nachman. *Deviance and Moral Boundaries: Witchcraft, the Occult, Science Fiction, Deviant Sciences and Scientists.* Chicago: University of Chicago Press, 1985.

Berger, Peter L. *The Sacred Canopy.* Garden City, N.Y.: Doubleday, 1967.

Beteille, Andre. *Caste, Class, and Power: Changing Patterns of Social Stratification in a Tanjore Village.* Berkeley: University of California Press, 1965.

———. *Society and Politics in India: Essays in Comparative Perspective.* London: Athlone Press, 1991.

Beyer, Jurgen. "A Lubeck Prophet in Local and Lutheran Context." In Bob Scribner and Trevor Johnson, eds., *Popular Religion in Germany and Central Europe, 1400–1800,* pp. 166–82. London: Macmillan, 1996.

Bharati, Agehananda. "The Self in Hindu Thought and Action." In Anthony J. Marsella, George DeVos, and Francis L. K. Hsu, eds., *Culture and Self: Asian and Western Perspectives,* pp. 185–230. New York: Tavistock, 1985.

Biardeau, Madeleine. *Hinduism: The Anthropology of a Civilization.* Delhi: Oxford University Press, 1989.

Bilu, Yoram. "Dreams and the Wishes of the Saints." In Harvey E. Goldberg, ed., *Judaism Viewed from Within and from Without,* pp. 285–313. Albany: State University of New York Press, 1987.

Birnbaum, Lucia Chiavola. *Black Madonnas: Feminism, Religion, and Politics in Italy.* Boston: Northeastern University Press, 1993.

Blacker, Carmen. "Rethinking the Study of Religion in Japan." In Adriana Boscaro, Franco Gatti, and Massimo Raveri, eds., *Rethinking Japan,* vol. 2, pp. 237–41. Sandgate, Folkestone, Kent: Japan Library, 1990.

Bloch, Marc. *Feudal Society.* London: Routledge & Kegan Paul, 1962.

———. *The Royal Touch: Sacred Monarchy and Scrofula in England and France.* London: Routledge & Kegan Paul, 1973.

Boehmer, Thomas. "Taoist Alchemy: A Sympathetic Approach through Symbols." In Michael Saso and David W. Chappell, eds., *Buddhist and Taoist Studies,* pp. 55–78. Honolulu: University of Hawaii Press, 1977.

Bokenkamp, Stephen. "The Purification Ritual of the Luminous Perfected." In Donald S. Lopez Jr., ed., *Religions of China in Practice,* pp. 268–77. Princeton, N.J.: Princeton University Press, 1996.

Bottomore, T. B. *Elites and Society.* London: C. A. Watts, 1964.

Brandes, Stanley. "Conclusion: Reflections on the Study of Religious Orthodoxy and Popular Faith in Europe." In Ellen Badone, ed., *Religious Orthodoxy and Popular Faith in European Society,* pp. 185–200. Princeton, N.J.: Princeton University Press, 1990.

Bredero, Adriaan H. *Christendom and Christianity in the Middle Ages*. Grand Rapids, Mich.: Wm. B. Eerdmans, 1994.

Brettell, Caroline B. "The Priest and His People: The Contractual Basis for Religious Practice in Rural Portugal." In Ellen Badone, ed., *Religious Orthodoxy and Popular Faith in European Society*, pp. 55–75. Princeton, N.J.: Princeton University Press, 1990.

Brinner, William M. "Prophet and Saint: The Two Exemplars of Islam." In John Stratton Hawley, ed., *Saints and Virtues*, pp. 36–51. Berkeley: University of California Press, 1987.

Brokaw, Cynthia J. *The Ledgers of Merit and Demerit: Social Change and Moral Order in Late Imperial China*. Princeton, N.J.: Princeton University Press, 1991.

Brooke, Rosalind, and Christopher Brooke. *Popular Religion in the Middle Ages, Western Europe 1000–1300*. London: Thames and Hudson, 1984.

Brown, Peter. *The Cult of the Saints: Its Rise and Function in Latin Christianity*. Chicago: University of Chicago Press, 1981.

———. *Society and the Holy in Late Antiquity*. London: Faber and Faber, 1982.

Bruce, Steve. *Religion in the Modern World: From Cathedrals to Cults*. Oxford: Oxford University Press, 1996.

Bunnag, Jane. *Buddhist Monk, Buddhist Layman: A Study of Urban Monastic Organization in Central Thailand*. Cambridge: Cambridge University Press, 1973.

———. "The Way of the Monk and the Way of the World: Buddhism in Thailand, Laos and Cambodia." In Heinz Bechert and Richard Gombrich, eds., *The World of Buddhism*, pp. 159–70. London: Thames and Hudson, 1984.

Burghart, Richard. "Hierarchical Models of the Hindu Social System." *Man* 13 (1978):519–36.

———. "Wandering Ascetics of the Ramanandi Sect." *History of Religions* 22 (1983):361–80.

———. "Renunciation in the Religious Traditions of South Asia." *Man* 18 (1983): 635–53.

Burke, Peter. *Popular Culture in Early Modern Europe*. London: Temple Smith, 1978.

———. "How to Be a Counter-Reformation Saint." In Kasper von Greyerz, ed., *Religion and Society in Early Modern Europe 1500–1800*, pp. 45–55. London: George Allen & Unwin, 1984.

Butler, Jon. "Magic, Astrology, and the Early American Religious Heritage, 1600–1760." *American Historical Review* 84 (1979):317–46.

Bynum, Caroline Walker. *Jesus as Mother: Studies in the Spirituality of the High Middle Ages*. Berkeley: University of California Press, 1982.

———. *The Resurrection of the Body in Western Christianity, 200–1336*. New York: Columbia University Press, 1995.

Caciola, Nancy. "Wraiths, Revenants and Ritual in Medieval Culture." *Past and Present* 152 (1996):3–45.

Callahan, William J., and David Higgs. "Introduction." In William J. Callahan and David Higgs, eds., *Church and Society in Catholic Europe of the Eighteenth Century*, pp. 1–12. Cambridge: Cambridge University Press, 1979.

Campbell, Colin. "The Cult, the Cultic Milieu and Secularization." *A Sociological Yearbook of Religion in Britain* 5 (1972):119–36.

———. *The Myth of Social Action*. Cambridge: Cambridge University Press, 1996.

———. "The Easternisation of the West." In Bryan Wilson and Jamie Cresswell, eds., *New Religious Movements: Challenge and Response*, pp. 35–48. London: Routledge, 1999.

Campbell, J. Gabriel. *Saints and Householders: A Study of Hindu Ritual and Myth among the Kangra Rajputs*. Kathmandu: Ratna Pustak Bhandar, 1976.

Carman, John B. "Conclusion: Axes of Sacred Value in Hindu Society." In John B. Carman and Frederique Apffel Marglin, eds., *Purity and Auspiciousness in Indian Society*, pp. 109–20. Leiden: E. J. Brill, 1985.

Carrithers, Michael. *The Forest Monks of Sri Lanka: An Anthropological and Historical Study*. Delhi: Oxford University Press, 1983.

———. "They Will Be Lords upon the Island: Buddhism in Sri Lanka." In Heinz Bechert and Richard Gombrich, eds., *The World of Buddhism*, pp. 133–46. London: Thames and Hudson, 1984.

Carroll, Michael P. *The Cult of the Virgin Mary: Psychological Origins*. Princeton, N.J.: Princeton University Press, 1986.

———. *Madonnas That Maim: Popular Catholicism in Italy since the Fifteenth Century*. Baltimore: Johns Hopkins University Press, 1992.

———. "Religion, Ricettizie, and the Immunity of Southern Italy to the Reformation." *Journal for the Scientific Study of Religion* 31 (1992):247–60.

———. *Veiled Threats: The Logic of Popular Catholicism in Italy*. Baltimore: Johns Hopkins University Press, 1996.

Chakravarti, Uma. *The Social Dimensions of Early Buddhism*. Delhi: Oxford University Press, 1987.

Chartier, Roger. *Cultural History: Between Practices and Representations*. Cambridge: Polity Press, 1988.

Chaudhuri, Buddhadeb. *The Bakreshwar Temple*. Delhi: Inter-India Publications, 1981.

Ching, Julia. "What Is Confucian Spirituality." In Irene Eber, ed., *Confucianism: The Dynamics of Tradition*, pp. 63–80. New York: Macmillan, 1986.

Chow, Kai-wing. *The Rise of Confucian Ritualism in Late Imperial China: Ethics, Classics, and Lineage Discourse*. Stanford: Stanford University Press, 1994.

Christian, William A. Jr. *Person and God in a Spanish Valley*. New York: Seminar Press, 1972.

———. *Local Religion in Sixteenth-Century Spain*. Princeton, N.J.: Princeton University Press, 1981.

Cirese, Alberto Maria. "Gramsci's Observations on Folklore." In Anne Showstack Sassoon, ed., *Approaches to Gramsci*, pp. 212–47. London: Writers and Readers Publishing Cooperative Society, 1982.

Clark, David. *Between Pulpit and Pew: Folk Religion in a North Yorkshire Fishing Village*. Cambridge: Cambridge University Press, 1982.

Clark, Stuart. "Protestant Demonology: Sin, Superstition and Society (c.1520–c.1630)." In Bengt Ankarloo and Gustav Henningsen, eds., *Early Modern European Witchcraft Centres and Peripheries*, pp. 45–81. Oxford: Clarendon Press, 1990.

Cohen, Myron L. "Souls and Salvation: Conflicting Themes in Chinese Popular Religion." In James L. Watson and Evelyn S. Rawski, eds., *Death Ritual in Late Imperial and Modern China*, pp. 180–202. Berkeley: University of California Press, 1988.

Cohn, Norman. *The Pursuit of the Millennium*. London: Paladin, 1970 [1957].

———. *Europe's Inner Demons*. New York: Basic Books, 1975.

Cohn, Robert L. "Sainthood on the Periphery: The Case of Judaism." In Richard Kieckhefer and George D. Bond, eds., *Sainthood: Its Manifestations in World Religions*, pp. 43–68. Berkeley: University of California Press, 1988.

Collins, Steven. *Nirvana and Other Buddhist Felicities*. Cambridge: Cambridge University Press, 1998.

Cornell, Vincent J. *Realm of the Saint: Power and Authority in Moroccan Sufism*. Austin: University of Texas Press, 1998.

Crapanzano, Vincent. *The Hamadsha: A Study of Moroccan Ethnopsychiatry*. Berkeley: University of California Press, 1973.

Creel, Herrlee G. *What Is Taoism? and Other Studies in Chinese Cultural History*. Chicago: University of Chicago Press, 1970.

Curry, Patrick. *Prophecy and Power: Astrology in Early Modern England*. Cambridge: Polity Press, 1989.

Dahlberg, Andrea. "The Body as a Principle of Holism: Three Pilgrimages to Lourdes." In John Eade and Michael J. Sallnow, eds., *Contesting the Sacred: The Anthropology of Christian Pilgrimage*, pp. 30–50. London: Routledge, 1991.

Daniel, Sheryl B. "The Tool Box Approach of the Tamil to the Issues of Moral Responsibility and Human Destiny." In Charles F. Keyes and E. Valentine Daniel, eds., *Karma: An Anthropological Inquiry*, pp. 27–62. Berkeley: University of California Press, 1983.

Davis, Natalie Zemon. "Some Tasks and Themes in the Study of Popular Religion." In Charles Trinkaus and Heiko A. Oberman, eds., *The Pursuit of Holiness in Late Medieval and Renaissance Religion*, pp. 307–36. Leiden: E. J. Brill, 1974.

Davis, Winston. *Japanese Religion and Society: Paradigms of Structures and Change*. Albany: State University of New York Press, 1992.

Dean, Kenneth. *Taoist Ritual and Popular Cults in Southeast China*. Princeton, N.J.: Princeton University Press, 1993.

———. *Lord of the Three in One: The Spread of a Cult in Southeast China*. Princeton, N.J.: Princeton University Press, 1998.

de Bary, Wm. Theodore. "Some Common Tendencies in Neo-Confucianism." In David S. Nivison and Arthur F. Wright, eds., *Confucianism in Action*, pp. 25–49. Stanford: Stanford University Press, 1959.

———. "Introduction." In Wm. Theodore de Bary, ed., *The Unfolding of Neo-Confucianism*, pp. 1–36. New York: Columbia University Press, 1975.

———. "Neo-Confucian Cultivation and the Seventeenth-Century 'Enlightenment.'" In Wm. Theodore de Bary, ed., *The Unfolding of Neo-Confucianism*, pp. 141–216. New York: Columbia University Press, 1975.

———. *The Trouble with Confucianism*. Cambridge, Mass.: Harvard University Press, 1991.

de Groot, J. J. M. *The Religious System of China*. 6 vols. Leiden: E. J. Brill, 1892–1910.

Delumeau, Jean. *Catholicism between Luther and Voltaire: A New View of the Counter-Reformation*. London: Burns & Oates, 1977.

———. *Sin and Fear: The Emergence of a Western Guilt Culture, Thirteenth–Eighteenth Centuries*. New York: St. Martin's Press, 1990.

Denny, Frederick M. "'God's Friends': The Sanctity of Persons in Islam." In Richard Kieckhefer and George D. Bond, eds., *Sainthood: Its Manifestations in World Religions*, pp. 69–97. Berkeley: University of California Press, 1988.

Derrett, J. Duncan M. "Rajadharma." *Journal of Asian Studies* 35 (1976):597–609.

Devlin, Judith. *The Superstitious Mind: French Peasants and the Supernatural in the Nineteenth Century*. New Haven: Yale University Press, 1987.

Diehl, Carl Gustav. *Instrument and Purpose: Studies on Rites and Rituals in South India*. Lund: C. W. K. Gleerup, 1956.

Dirks, Nicholas B. *The Hollow Crown: Ethnohistory of an Indian Kingdom*. Cambridge: Cambridge University Press, 1987.

———. "The Original Caste: Power, History and Hierarchy in South Asia." In McKim Marriott, ed., *India through Hindu Categories*, pp. 59–77. New Delhi: Sage, 1990.

Dixon, C. Scott. "Popular Beliefs and the Reformation in Brandenburg-Ansbach." In Bob Scribner and Trevor Johnson, eds., *Popular Religion in Germany and Central Europe, 1400–1800*, pp. 119–39. London: Macmillan, 1996.

Duara, Prasenjit. "Superscribing Symbols: The Myth of Guandi, the Chinese God of War." *Journal of Asian Studies* 47 (1988):778–95.

———. "Knowledge and Power in the Discourse of Modernity: The Campaigns against Popular Religion in Early Twentieth-Century China." *Journal of Asian Studies* 50 (1991):67–83.

Duffy, Eamon. *The Stripping of the Altars: Traditional Religion in England, c.1400–c.1580*. New Haven: Yale University Press, 1992.

Dumont, Louis. *Homo Hierarchicus: The Caste System and Its Implications*. Chicago: University of Chicago Press, 1980 [1970].

———. "A Folk Deity of Tamil Nad: Aiyanar, the Lord." In T. N. Madan, ed., *Religion in India*, pp. 20–32. Delhi: Oxford University Press, 1991.

Durkheim, Emile. *The Elementary Forms of the Religious Life*. New York: Collier Books, 1961 [1912].

Eade, John, and Michael J. Sallnow. "Introduction." In John Eade and Michael J. Sallnow, eds., *Contesting the Sacred: The Anthropology of Christian Pilgrimage*, pp. 1–29. London: Routledge, 1991.

Earhart, H. Byron. *A Religious Study of the Mount Haguro Sect of Shugendo: An Example of Japanese Mountain Religion*. Tokyo: Sophia University, 1970.

———. *Japanese Religion: Unity and Diversity*. Encino, Calif.: Dickenson, 1994.

Ebrey, Patricia. *Confucianism and Family Rituals in Imperial China: A Social History of Writing about Rites*. Princeton, N.J.: Princeton University Press, 1991.

Eck, Diana L. *Banaras, City of Light*. London: Routledge & Kegan Paul, 1983.

Eickelman, Dale F. *Moroccan Islam: Tradition and Society in a Pilgrimage Center*. Austin: University of Texas Press, 1976.

Eisenstadt, S. N. "The Axial Age: The Emergence of Transcendental Visions and the Rise of Clerics." *Archives Europeennes de Sociologie* 23 (1982):294–314.

———. "The Axial Age Breakthroughs—Their Characteristics and Origins." In S. N. Eisenstadt, ed., *The Origins and Diversity of Axial Age Civilizations*, pp. 1–25. Albany: State University of New York Press, 1986.

Elvin, Mark. "Was There a Transcendental Breakthrough in China?" In S. N. Eisenstadt, ed., *The Origins and Diversity of Axial Age Civilizations*, pp. 325–59. Albany: State University of New York Press, 1986.

Evans, R. J. W. *The Making of the Habsburg Monarchy*. Oxford: Clarendon Press, 1979.

Evers, Hans-Dieter. *Monks, Priests and Peasants: A Study of Buddhism and Social Structure in Central Ceylon*. Leiden: E. J. Brill, 1972.

Femia, Joseph V. *Gramsci's Political Thought: Hegemony, Consciousness and the Revolutionary Process*. Oxford: Clarendon Press, 1981.

Feuchtwang, Stephan. "City Temples in Taipei under Three Regimes." In Mark Elvin and G. William Skinner, eds., *The Chinese City between Two Worlds*, pp. 263–301. Stanford: Stanford University Press, 1974.

———. "School-Temple and City God." In G. William Skinner, ed., *The City in Late Imperial China*, pp. 581–608. Stanford: Stanford University Press, 1977.

———. *The Imperial Metaphor: Popular Religion in China*. London: Routledge, 1992.

Finke, Roger, and Rodney Stark. *The Churching of America, 1776–1990.* New Brunswick: Rutgers University Press, 1992.

Fitzgerald, Timothy. "Hinduism and the 'World Religion' Fallacy." *Religion* 20 (1990):101–18.

Flint, Valerie I. J. *The Rise of Magic in Early Medieval Europe.* Princeton, N.J.: Princeton University Press, 1991.

Flynn, Maureen. *Sacred Charity: Confraternities and Social Welfare in Spain, 1400–1700.* Ithaca: Cornell University Press, 1989.

Forster, Marc R. *The Counter-Reformation in the Villages: Religion and Reform in the Bishopric of Speyer, 1560–1720.* Ithaca: Cornell University Press, 1992.

Freedman, Maurice. "Ancestor Worship: Two Facets of the Chinese Case." In *The Study of Chinese Society: Essays by Maurice Freedman,* pp. 296–312. Stanford: Stanford University Press, 1979.

———. "Geomancy." In *The Study of Chinese Society: Essays by Maurice Freedman,* pp. 313–33. Stanford: Stanford University Press, 1979.

———. "On the Sociological Study of Chinese Religion." In Arthur P. Wolf, ed., *Religion and Ritual in Chinese Society,* pp. 351–69. Stanford: Stanford University Press, 1974.

———. "Ritual Aspects of Chinese Kinship and Marriage." In *The Study of Chinese Society: Essays by Maurice Freedman,* pp. 273–95. Stanford: Stanford University Press, 1979.

Friedman, Menachem. "Life Tradition and Book Tradition in the Development of Ultraorthodox Judaism." In Harvey E. Goldberg, ed., *Judaism Viewed from Within and from Without,* pp. 235–55. Albany: State University of New York Press, 1987.

Fuller, C. J. *Servants of the Goddess: The Priests of a South Indian Temple.* Cambridge: Cambridge University Press, 1984.

———. *The Camphor Flame.* Princeton, N.J.: Princeton University Press, 1992.

Galpern, A. N. *The Religions of the People in Sixteenth-Century Champagne.* Cambridge, Mass.: Harvard University Press, 1976.

Geary, Patrick J. *Furta Sacra: Thefts of Relics in the Central Middle Ages.* Princeton, N.J.: Princeton University Press, 1978.

Gellner, David N. *Monk, Householder, and Tantric Priest.* Cambridge: Cambridge University Press, 1992.

Gellner, Ernest. *Muslim Society.* Cambridge: Cambridge University Press, 1981.

———. *Plough, Sword and Book: The Structure of Human History.* London: Collins Harvill, 1988.

Gentilcore, David. *From Bishop to Witch: The System of the Sacred in Early Modern Terra d'Otrando.* Manchester: Manchester University Press, 1992.

Gernet, Jacques. *China and the Christian Impact: A Conflict of Cultures.* Cambridge: Cambridge University Press, 1985.

Giddens, Anthony. *The Class Structure of the Advanced Societies*. London: Hutchinson, 1973.

Gilsenan, Michael. *Saint and Sufi in Modern Egypt: An Essay in the Sociology of Religion*. Oxford: Clarendon Press, 1973.

———. *Recognizing Islam: Religion and Society in the Modern Arab World*. New York: Pantheon Books, 1982.

Godbeer, Richard. *The Devil's Dominion: Magic and Religion in Early New England*. Cambridge: Cambridge University Press, 1992.

Gold, Daniel. *The Lord as Guru: Hindi Sants in North Indian Tradition*. New York: Oxford University Press, 1987.

Goldberg, Harvey E. "Potential Politics: Jewish Saints in the Moroccan Countryside and in Israel." In Mart Bax, Peter Kloos, and Adrianus Koster, eds., *Faith and Polity: Essays on Religion and Politics*, pp. 235–50. Amsterdam: VU University Press, 1992.

Goldziher, Ignaz. *Muslim Studies*. Vol. 2. London: George Allen & Unwin, 1971.

Gombrich, Richard F. *Precept and Practice: Traditional Buddhism in the Rural Highlands of Ceylon*. Oxford: Clarendon Press, 1971.

———. "The Evolution of the Sangha." In Heinz Bechert and Richard Gombrich, eds., *The World of Buddhism*, pp. 77–89. London: Thames and Hudson, 1984.

———. "Introduction: The Buddhist Way." In Heinz Bechert and Richard Gombrich, eds., *The World of Buddhism*, pp. 9–14. London: Thames and Hudson, 1984.

———. *Theravada Buddhism: A Social History from Ancient Benares to Modern Colombo*. London: Routledge & Kegan Paul, 1988.

Gombrich, Richard, and Gananath Obeyesekere. *Buddhism Transformed: Religious Change in Sri Lanka*. Princeton, N.J.: Princeton University Press, 1988.

Goody, Jack. *The Logic of Writing and the Organization of Society*. Cambridge: Cambridge University Press, 1985.

Gramsci, Antonio. *Selections from Prison Notebooks*. London: Lawrence & Wishart, 1971.

Granet, Marcel. *The Religion of the Chinese People*. Oxford: Basil Blackwell, 1975 [1922].

Gurevich, Aron. "Popular and Scholarly Medieval Cultural Traditions: Notes in the Margin of Jacques Le Goff's Book." *Journal of Medieval History* 9 (1983): 71–90.

———. *Medieval Popular Culture: Problems of Belief and Perception*. Cambridge: Cambridge University Press, 1988.

Habermas, Jürgen. *The Theory of Communicative Action*. Vol. 1, *Reason and the Rationalization of Society*. Boston: Beacon Press, 1984.

Hall, David. "Introduction." In Steven L. Kaplan, ed., *Understanding Popular Culture: Europe from the Middle Ages to the Nineteenth Century*, pp. 5–18. Berlin: Mouton, 1984.

Hall, John A. *Powers and Liberties: The Causes and Consequences of the Rise of the West*. Harmondsworth: Penguin, 1986.

Hamilton, Bernard. *Religion in the Medieval West*. London: Edward Arnold, 1986.

Harrell, Stevan. "The Concept of Soul in Chinese Folk Religion." *Journal of Asian Studies* 38 (1979):519–28.

Hatch, Nathan O. *The Democratization of American Christianity*. New Haven: Yale University Press, 1989.

Heelas, Paul. "Prosperity and the New Age Movement: The Efficacy of Spiritual Economics." In Bryan Wilson and Jamie Cresswell, eds., *New Religious Movements: Challenge and Response*, pp. 51–77. London: Routledge, 1999.

Heesterman, J. C. "Power, Priesthood, and Authority." In *The Inner Conflict of Tradition: Essays in Indian Ritual, Kingship, and Society*, pp. 141–57. Chicago: University of Chicago Press, 1985.

Helman, Sarit. "Turning Classic Models into Utopias: The Neo-Confucianist Critique." *International Journal of Comparative Sociology* 29 (1988):93–110.

Hiebert, Paul G. "Karma and Other Explanation Traditions in a South Indian Village." In Charles F. Keyes and E. Valentine Daniel, eds., *Karma: An Anthropological Inquiry*, pp. 119–30. Berkeley: University of California Press, 1983.

Hill, Michael. *The Religious Order: A Study of Virtuoso Religion and Its Legitimation in the Nineteenth-Century Church of England*. London: Heinemann, 1973.

Hodgson, Marshall G. S. *The Venture of Islam*. Vol. 2. Chicago: University of Chicago Press, 1974.

Hoffman, Philip T. *Church and Community in the Diocese of Lyon 1500–1789*. New Haven: Yale University Press, 1984.

Hoffman, Valerie J. *Sufism, Mystics, and Saints in Modern Egypt*. Columbia: University of South Carolina Press, 1995.

Holy, Ladislav. *Religion and Custom in a Muslim Society: The Berti of Sudan*. Cambridge: Cambridge University Press, 1991.

Hopcroft, Rosemary L. "Rural Organization and Receptivity to Protestantism." *Journal for the Scientific Study of Religion* 36 (1997):158–81.

Hori, Ichiro. *Folk Religion in Japan: Continuity and Change*. Chicago: University of Chicago Press, 1968.

———, ed. *Japanese Religion: A Survey by the Agency for Cultural Affairs*. Tokyo: Kodanshu International, 1972.

Horsley, Richard A. "Further Reflection on Witchcraft and European Folk Religion." *History of Religions* 19 (1979):71–95.

Hsia, R. Po-Chia. *Social Discipline in the Reformation: Central Europe, 1550–1750*. London: Routledge, 1989.

Hufton, Olwen. "The French Church." In William J. Callahan and David Higgs, eds., *Church and Society in Catholic Europe of the Eighteenth Century*, pp. 13–33. Cambridge: Cambridge University Press, 1979.

Hughes, Philip J. "The Assimilation of Christianity in the Thai Culture." *Religion* 14 (1984):313–36.

Hutton, Ronald. *The Rise and Fall of Merry England: The Ritual Year 1400–1700.* Oxford: Oxford University Press, 1994.

Inden, Ronald. "Hierarchies of Kings in Early Medieval India." In T. N. Madan, ed., *Way of Life: King, Householder, Renouncer,* pp. 99–125. New Delhi: Vikas Publishing House, 1982.

Ingersoll, Jasper. "The Priest Role in Central Village Thailand." In Manning Nash, ed., *Anthropological Studies in Theravada Buddhism,* pp. 51–76. New Haven: Southeast Asia Studies, Yale University, 1966.

Ishii, Yoneo. *Sangha, State, and Society: Thai Buddhism in History.* Honolulu: University of Hawaii Press, 1986.

Jaspers, Karl. *The Origin and Goal of History.* London: Routledge & Kegan Paul, 1953.

Johnson, David. "Communication, Class, and Consciousness in Late Imperial China." In David Johnson, Andrew J. Nathan, and Evelyn S. Rawski, eds., *Popular Culture in Late Imperial China,* pp. 34–72. Berkeley: University of California Press, 1985.

Johnson, Trevor. "Blood, Tears and Xavier-Water: Jesuit Missionaries and Popular Religion in the Eighteenth-Century Upper Paltinate." In Bob Scribner and Trevor Johnson, eds., *Popular Religion in Germany and Central Europe, 1400–1800,* pp. 183–202. London: Macmillan, 1996.

Johnston, Pamela, and Bob Scribner. *The Reformation in Germany and Switzerland.* Cambridge: Cambridge University Press, 1993.

Jolly, Karen Louise. *Popular Religion in Late Saxon England: Elf Charms in Context.* Chapel Hill: University of North Carolina Press, 1996.

Jordan, David K. *Gods, Ghosts, and Ancestors: The Folk Religion of a Taiwanese Village.* Berkeley: University of California Press, 1972.

Jordan, David K., and Daniel L. Overmyer. *The Flying Phoenix: Aspects of Chinese Sectarianism in Taiwan.* Princeton, N.J.: Princeton University Press, 1986.

Kamstra, J. H. "The Complexity of Japanese Religion." In Pieter Hendrik Vrijhof and Jacques Waardenburg, eds., *Official and Popular Religion: Analysis of a Theme for Religious Studies,* pp. 427–61. The Hague: Mouton, 1979.

Kapferer, Bruce. *A Celebration of Demons: Exorcism and the Aesthetics of Healing in Sri Lanka.* Providence: Berg Publishers, 1991.

Katz, Paul R. *Demon Hordes and Burning Boats: The Cult of Marshall Wen in Late Imperial China.* Albany: State University of New York Press, 1995.

Kelly, Aidan A. "An Update on Neopagan Witchcraft in America." In James R. Lewis and J. Gordon Melton, eds., *Perspectives on the New Age,* pp. 136–51. Albany: State University of New York Press, 1992.

Keyes, Charles F. "Introduction: The Study of Popular Ideas of Karma." In

Charles F. Keyes and E. Valentine Daniel, eds., *Karma: An Anthropological Inquiry*, pp. 1–24. Berkeley: University of California Press, 1983.

———. "Merit Transference in the Karmic Theory of Popular Theravada Buddhism." In Charles F. Keyes and E. Valentine Daniel, eds., *Karma: An Anthropological Inquiry*, pp. 261–86. Berkeley: University of California Press, 1983.

Kieckhefer, Richard. "Imitators of Christ: Sainthood in the Christian Tradition." In Richard Kieckhefer and George D. Bond, eds., *Sainthood: Its Manifestations in World Religions*, pp. 1–42. Berkeley: University of California Press, 1988.

———. *Magic in the Middle Ages*. Cambridge: Cambridge University Press, 1989.

King, Ursula. "Some Reflections on Sociological Approaches to the Study of Modern Hinduism." *Numen* 36 (1989):72–97.

Kinsley, David R. *Hinduism: A Cultural Perspective*. Englewood Cliffs: Prentice-Hall, 1982.

Kirsch, A. Thomas. "Complexity in the Thai Religious System: An Interpretation." *Journal of Asian Studies* 36 (1977):241–66.

Klaits, Joseph. *Servants of Satan: The Age of the Witch Hunts*. Bloomington: Indiana University Press, 1985.

Klaniczay, Gabor. *The Uses of Supernatural Power: The Transformation of Popular Religion in Medieval and Early-Modern Europe*. Princeton, N.J.: Princeton University Press, 1990.

Kolenda, Pauline Mahar. "Religious Anxiety and Hindu Fate." *Journal of Asian Studies* 23 (1964):71–81.

Kselman, Thomas A. *Miracles and Prophecies in Nineteenth-Century France*. New Brunswick, N.J.: Rutgers University Press, 1983.

Kuhn, Philip A. *Soulstealers: The Chinese Sorcery Scare of 1768*. Cambridge, Mass: Harvard University Press, 1990.

Lamotte, Etienne. "The Buddha, His Teachings and His Sangha." In Heinz Bechert and Richard Gombrich, eds., *The World of Buddhism*, pp. 41–58. London: Thames and Hudson, 1984.

Lancaster, Lewis R. "Buddhism and Family in East Asia." In George A. DeVos and Takao Sotue, eds., *Religion and the Family in East Asia*, pp. 139–51. Berkeley: University of California Press, 1986.

Lancaster, Roger N. *Thanks to God and the Revolution: Popular Religion and Class Consciousness in the New Nicaragua*. New York: Columbia University Press, 1988.

Lapidus, Ira M. *A History of Islamic Societies*. Cambridge: Cambridge University Press, 1988.

Larner, Christina. *Enemies of God: The Witch-Hunt in Scotland*. Oxford: Basil Blackwell, 1983.

———. *Witchcraft and Religion: The Politics of Popular Belief*. Oxford: Basil Blackwell, 1984.

Le Goff, Jacques. *Time, Work, and Culture in the Middle Ages.* Chicago: University of Chicago Press, 1980.

———. *The Birth of Purgatory.* Chicago: University of Chicago Press, 1984.

Lehmann, David. *Struggle for the Spirit: Religious Transformation and Popular Culture in Brazil and Latin America.* Cambridge: Polity Press, 1996.

Lester, Robert C. *Theravada Budddhism in Southeast Asia.* Ann Arbor: University of Michigan Press, 1973.

———. "Hinduism: Veda and Sacred Texts." In Frederick M. Denny and Rodney L. Taylor, eds., *The Holy Book in Comparative Perspective,* pp. 126–47. Columbia: University of South Carolina Press, 1985.

Levenson, Joseph R. "The Suggestiveness of Vestiges: Confucianism and Monarchy at the Last." In David S. Nivison and Arthur F. Wright, eds., *Confucianism in Action,* pp. 244–67. Stanford: Stanford University Press, 1959.

———. *Confucian China and Its Modern Fate.* Vol. 2: *The Problem of Monarchical Decay.* London: Routledge & Kegan Paul, 1964.

Lewis, James R., and J. Gordon Melton, eds. *Perspectives on the New Age.* Albany: State University of New York Press, 1992.

Leyser, Henrietta. *Hermits and the New Monasticism: A Study of Religious Communities in Western Europe, 1000–1150.* London: Macmillan, 1984.

Ling, Trevor. "Sinhalese Buddhism in Recent Anthropological Writing: Some Implications." *Religion* 1 (1971):49–59.

Lippy, Charles H. *Being Religious, American Style: A History of Popular Religiosity in the United States.* Westport, Conn.: Greenwood Press, 1994.

Lipset, Seymour Martin. *The First New Nation: The United States in Historical and Comparative Perspective.* New York: Anchor Books, 1967.

Liu, Kwang-Ching. "Socioethics as Orthodoxy: A Perspective." In Kwan-Ching Liu, ed., *Orthodoxy in Late Imperial China,* pp. 53–100. Berkeley: University of California Press, 1990.

Lockwood, David. *Solidarity and Schism: "The Problem of Disorder" in Durkeimian and Marxist Sociology.* Oxford: Clarendon Press, 1992.

Long, J. Bruce. "The Concepts of Human Action and Rebirth in the Mahabharata." In W. D. O'Flaherty, ed., *Karma and Rebirth in Classical Indian Traditions,* pp. 38–60. Berkeley: University of California Press, 1980.

Lottes, Gunther. "Popular Culture and the Early Modern State in Sixteenth Century Germany." In Steven L. Kaplan, ed., *Understanding Popular Culture: Europe from the Middle Ages to the Nineteenth Century,* pp. 147–88. Berlin: Mouton, 1984.

Lowenstein, Tom. *The Vision of the Buddha.* London: Duncan Baird, 1996.

Macy, Gary. "Was There a 'The Church' in the Middle Ages?" In R. Swanson, ed., *Unity and Diversity of the Church,* pp. 107–16. Oxford: Blackwell, 1996.

Madan, G. R. *Western Sociologists on Indian Society: Marx, Spencer, Weber, Durkheim, Pareto.* London: Routledge & Kegan Paul, 1979.

Maduro, Otto. *Religion and Social Conflicts.* Maryknoll, N.Y.: Orbis Books, 1982.

Mahmood, Cynthia Keppley. "Hinduism in Context: Approaching a Religious Tradition through External Sources." In Stephen D. Glazier, ed., *Anthropology of Religion: A Handbook,* pp. 305–18. Westport, Conn.: Greenwood Press, 1997.

Malamoud, Charles. "On the Rhetoric and Semantics of Purusartha." In T. N. Madan, ed., *Way of Life: King, Householder, Renouncer,* pp. 35–54. New Delhi: Vikas Publishing House, 1982.

Mandelbaum, David G. "Transcendental and Pragmatic Aspects of Religion." *American Anthropologist* 68 (1966):1174–91.

———. *Society in India.* Vol. 1: *Continuity and Change.* Berkeley: University of California Press, 1970.

Mann, Michael. *The Sources of Social Power.* Vol. 1: *A History of Power from the Beginning to A.D. 1760.* Cambridge: Cambridge University Press, 1986.

Manselli, R. *La Religion populaire au moyen âge: Problèmes de méthode et de d'histoire.* Montreal: Institute d'Etudes Mediévales Albert-le-Grand, 1975.

Marriott, McKim. "Little Communities in an Indigenous Civilization." In McKim Marriott, ed., *Village India: Studies in the Little Community,* pp. 171–222. Chicago: University of Chicago Press, 1969 [1955].

Martin, David. *A General Theory of Secularization.* Oxford: Basil Blackwell, 1978.

Marx, Emanuel. "Communal and Individual Pilgrimage: The Region of Saints' Tombs in South Sinai." In R. P. Werbner, ed., *Regional Cults,* pp. 29–51. London: Academic Press, 1977.

Marx, Karl, and Frederick Engels. *On Religion.* Moscow: Foreign Languages Publishing House, 1955.

McDannell, Collen. *Material Christianity: Religion and Popular Culture in America.* New Haven: Yale University Press, 1995.

McKenzie, John L., S. J. *The Roman Catholic Church.* London: Weidenfeld and Nicholson, 1969.

McLellan, David. *Marxism and Religion.* London: Macmillan, 1987.

McLeod, Hugh. *Religion and the People of Western Europe, 1789–1970.* Oxford: Oxford University Press, 1981.

———. *Religion and Society in England 1850–1914.* London: Macmillan, 1996.

Mendelson, E. Michael. *Sangha and State in Burma: A Study of Monastic Sectarianism and Leadership.* Ithaca: Cornell University Press, 1975.

Merton, Robert K. *Social Theory and Social Structure.* New York: Free Press, 1968 [1949].

Metzger, Thomas A. *Escape from Predicament: Neo-Confucianism and China's Evolving Political Culture.* New York: Columbia University Press, 1977.

Michell, George. *The Hindu Temple: An Introduction to Its Meaning and Forms.* London: Paul Elek, 1977.

Midelfort, H. C. Erik. "Sin, Melancholy, Obsession: Insanity and Culture in

Sixteenth Century Germany." In Steven L. Kaplan, ed., *Understanding Popular Culture: Europe from the Middle Ages to the Nineteenth Century*, pp. 113–45. Berlin: Mouton, 1984.

Miller, David M., and Dorothy C. Wertz. *Hindu Monastic Life and the Monks and Monasteries of Bhubaneswar*. Montreal: McGill-Queen's University Press, 1976.

Mills, Ludo J. R. *Angelic Monks and Earthly Men: Monasticism and Its Meaning to Medieval Society*. Woodbridge, Suffolk: Boydell Press, 1992.

Milner, Murry Jr. *Status and Sacredness*. New York: Oxford University Press, 1994.

Miyata, Noboru. "Popular Beliefs in Contemporary Japan." In Adriana Boscaro, Franco Gatti, and Massimo Raveri, eds., *Rethinking Japan*, vol. 2, pp. 242–49. Sandgate, Folkestone, Kent: Japan Library, 1990.

Moffatt, Michael. *An Untouchable Community in South India: Structure and Consensus*. Princeton, N.J.: Princeton University Press, 1979.

Monter, William. *Ritual, Myth and Magic in Early Modern Europe*. Athens: Ohio University Press, 1984.

Moore, Barrington, Jr. *Social Origins of Dictatorship and Democracy: Lord and Peasant in the Making of the Modern World*. London: Allen Lane, Penguin Press, 1967.

Moore, L. Laurence. *Selling God: American Religion in the Marketplace of Culture*. New York: Oxford University Press, 1994.

Morinis, E. Alan. *Pilgrimage in the Hindu Tradition: A Case Study of West Bengal*. Delhi: Oxford University Press, 1984.

Muchembled, Robert. *Popular Culture and Elite Culture in France 1400–1750*. Baton Rouge: Louisiana State University Press, 1985.

Muir, Edward. *Ritual in Early Modern Europe*. Cambridge: Cambridge University Press, 1997.

Nakamura, Hajime. "The Basic Teachings of Buddhism." In Heinrich Dumoulin and John C. Maraldo, eds., *Buddhism in the Modern World*, pp. 3–31. New York: Collier Books, 1976.

Nash, Jane C. "Living with Nats: An Analysis of Animism in Burman Village Social Relations." In Manning Nash, ed., *Anthropological Studies in Theravada Buddhism*, pp. 117–36. New Haven: Southeast Asia Studies, Yale University, 1966.

Nash, Manning. *The Golden Road to Modernity*. Chicago: University of Chicago Press, 1973.

Needham, Joseph. *Science and Civilization in China*. Vol. 2: *History of Scientific Thought*. Cambridge: Cambridge University Press, 1956.

Nelson, John K. "Warden + Virtuoso + Salaryman = Priest: Paradigms within Japanese Shinto for Religious Specialists and Institutions." *Journal of Asian Studies* 56 (1997):678–707.

Nichols, David. *Deity and Domination: Images of God and the State in the Nineteenth and Twentieth Centuries*. London: Routledge, 1989.

Nielsen, Donald A. "The Inquisition, Rationalization, and Sociocultural Change in Medieval Europe." In William H. Swatos Jr., ed., *Time, Place, and Circumstance: Neo-Weberian Studies in Comparative Religious History*, pp. 107–22. New York: Greenwood Press, 1990.

Nolan, Mary Lee, and Sidney Nolan. *Christian Pilgrimage in Modern Western Europe*. Chapel Hill: University of North Carolina Press, 1989.

Obelkevich, James. *Religion and Rural Society: South Lindsey 1825–1875*. Oxford: Clarendon Press, 1976.

Obeyesekere, Gananath. "The Great Tradition and the Little in the Perspective of Sinhalese Buddhism." *Journal of Asian Studies* 22 (1963):139–53.

———. "The Buddhist Pantheon in Ceylon and Its Extensions." In Manning Nash, ed., *Anthropological Studies in Theravada Buddhism*, pp. 1–26. New Haven: Southeast Asia Studies, Yale University, 1966.

———. "Theodicy, Sin and Salvation in a Sociology of Buddhism." In E. R. Leach, ed., *Dialectic in Practical Religion*, pp. 7–40. Cambridge: Cambridge University Press, 1968.

———. "Religion and Polity in Theravada Buddhism: Continuity and Change in a Great Tradition." *Comparative Studies in Society and History* 21 (1979): 626–39.

———. *The Cult of the Goddess Pattini*. Chicago: University of Chicago Press, 1984.

O'Flaherty, Wendy Doniger. "Karma and Rebirth in the Vedas and Puranas." In W. D. O'Flaherty, ed., *Karma and Rebirth in Classical Indian Traditions*, pp. 3–37. Berkeley: University of California Press, 1980.

O'Neil, Mary R. "Magical Healing, Love Magic and the Inquisition in Late Sixteenth-Century Modena." In Stephen Haliezer, ed., *Inquisition and Society in Early Modern Europe*, pp. 88–114. London: Croom Helm, 1987.

Orsi, Robert Anthony. *The Madonna of 115th Street: Faith and Community in Italian Harlem, 1880–1950*. New Haven: Yale University Press, 1985.

———. *Thank You, St. Jude: Women's Devotion to the Patron Saint of Hopeless Causes*. New Haven: Yale University Press, 1996.

Overmyer, Daniel L. *Folk Buddhist Religion: Dissenting Sects in Late Traditional China*. Cambridge, Mass.: Harvard University Press, 1976.

———. "Dualism and Conflict in Chinese Popular Religion." In Frank E. Reynolds and Theodore M. Ludwig, eds., *Transitions and Transformations in the History of Religions*, pp. 153–81. Leiden: E. J. Brill, 1980.

Pace, Enzo. "The Debate on Popular Religion in Italy." *Sociological Analysis* 40 (1979):71–75.

Pang, Duane. "The P'u-tu Ritual: A Celebration of the Chinese Community of Honolulu." In Michael Saso and David W. Chappell, eds., *Buddhist and Taoist Studies*, pp. 95–122. Honolulu: University Press of Hawaii, 1977.

Parry, Jonathan P. "Death and Cosmogony in Kashi." In T. N. Madan, ed., *Way of*

Life: King, Householder, Renouncer, pp. 337–65. New Delhi: Vikas Publishing House, 1982.

Parry, Jonathan P. "The Brahmanical Tradition and the Technology of the Intellect." In Joanna Overing, ed., *Reason and Morality*, pp. 200–25. London: Tavistock, 1985.

———. *Death in Banaras*. Cambridge: Cambridge University Press, 1994.

Parsons, Talcott. *The Structure of Social Action*. 2 vols. New York: Free Press, 1949 [1937].

———. "Introduction to Max Weber's 'The Sociology of Religion.'" In Talcott Parsons, *Sociological Theory and Modern Society*, pp. 35–78. New York: Free Press, 1967.

Perry, Elizabeth J. "Taipings and Triads: The Role of Religion in Inter-Rebel Relations." In Janos M. Bak and Gerhard Benecke, eds., *Religion and Rural Revolt*, pp. 342–53. Manchester: Manchester University Press, 1984.

Pfanner, David E. "The Buddhist Monk in Rural Burmese Societies." In Manning Nash, ed., *Anthropological Studies in Theravada Buddhism*, pp. 77–96. New Haven: Southeast Asia Studies, Yale University, 1966.

Pfister, Lauren. "Reassessing Max Weber's Evaluation of the Confucian Classics." In Jon Davies and Isabel Wollaston, eds., *The Sociology of Sacred Texts*, pp. 99–110. Sheffield: Sheffield Academic Press, 1993.

Pickering, W. S. F. *Durkheim's Sociology of Religion: Themes and Theories*. London: Routledge & Kegan Paul, 1984.

Piker, Steven. "Buddhism and Modernization in Contemporary Thailand." In Bardwell Smith, ed., *Tradition and Change in Theravada Buddhism: Essays on Ceylon and Thailand in the 19th and 20th Centuries*, pp. 51–67. Leiden: E. J. Brill, 1973.

Pina-Cabral, João De. *Sons of Adam, Daughters of Eve: The Peasant Worldview of the Alto Minho*. Oxford: Clarendon Press, 1988.

Pipes, Daniel. *In the Path of God: Islam and Political Power*. New York: Basic Books, 1983.

Pocock, D. F. *Mind, Body and Wealth: A Study of Belief and Practice in an Indian Village*. Oxford: Basil Blackwell, 1973.

Preston, James J. *Cult of the Goddess: Social and Religious Change in a Hindu Temple*. New Delhi: Vikas Publishing House, 1980.

———. "Creation of the Sacred Image: Apotheosis and Destruction in Hinduism." In Joanne Punzo Waghorne and Norman Cutler, eds., *Gods of Flesh, Gods of Stone: The Embodiment of Divinity in India*, pp. 9–30. Chambersburg, Pa.: Anima, 1985.

Pugh, Judy F. "Astrology and Fate: The Hindu and Muslim Experiences." In Charles F. Keyes and E. Valentine Daniel, eds., *Karma: An Anthropological Inquiry*, pp. 131–46. Berkeley: University of California Press, 1983.

Ransdorp, R. "Official and Popular Religion in the Chinese Empire." In Pieter Hendrik Vrijhof and Jacques Waardenburg, eds., *Official and Popular Religion:*

Analysis of a Theme for Religious Studies, pp. 387–426. The Hague: Mouton Publishers, 1979.

Ransome, Paul. *Antonio Gramsci: A New Introduction*. New York: Harvester Wheatsheaf, 1992.

Rapoport-Albert, Ada. "God and the Zaddik as the Two Focal Points of Hasidic Worship." *History of Religions* 18 (1979):296–325.

———. "Hasidism after 1772: Structural Continuity and Change." In Ada Rapoport-Albert, ed., *Hasidism Reappraised*, pp. 76–140. London: Littman Library of Jewish Civilization, 1996.

Rawski, Evelyn S. "Popular Culture in China." In Ching-I Tu, ed., *Tradition and Creativity: Essays on East Asian Civilization*, pp. 41–65. New Brunswick: Transaction Books, 1987.

———. "A Historian's Approach to Chinese Death Ritual." In James L. Watson and Evelyn S. Rawski, eds., *Death Ritual in Late Imperial and Modern China*, pp. 20–34. Berkeley: University of California Press, 1988.

Reader, Ian. *Religion in Contemporary Japan*. Honolulu: University of Hawaii Press, 1991.

———. "Folk Religion." In Ian Reader, ed., *Japanese Religions: Past and Present*, pp. 44–59. Sandgate, Folkestone, Kent: Japan Library, 1993.

———. "Shinto." In Ian Reader, ed., *Japanese Religions: Past and Present*, pp. 64–92. Sandgate, Folkestone, Kent: Japan Library, 1993.

Redfield, Robert. *Peasant Society and Culture: An Anthropological Approach to Civilization*. Chicago: University of Chicago Press, 1956.

Reeves, Marjorie. *The Influence of Prophecy in the Later Middle Ages*. Oxford: Oxford University Press, 1969.

Reischauer, Edwin O., and John K. Fairbank. *East Asia: The Great Tradition*. London: George Allen & Unwin, 1960.

Reynolds, Susan. *Kingdoms and Communities in Western Europe, 900–1300*. Oxford: Clarendon Press, 1984.

Riegelhaupt, Joyce. "Popular Anti-Clericalism and Religiosity in Pre-1974 Portugal." In Eric R. Wolf, ed., *Religion, Power and Protest in Local Communities*, pp. 93–115. Berlin: Mouton, 1984.

Rubin, Miri. *Corpus Christi: The Eucharist in Late Medieval Culture*. Cambridge: Cambridge University Press, 1991.

———. "Religious Culture in Town and Country: Reflections on a Great Divide." In David Abulafia, Michael Franklin, and Miri Rubin, eds., *Church and City 1000–1500: Essays in Honour of Christopher Brooke*, pp. 3–22. Cambridge: Cambridge University Press, 1992.

Russell, Jeffrey Burton. *Lucifer: The Devil in the Middle Ages*. Ithaca: Cornell University Press, 1984.

Salamini, Leonardo. *The Sociology of Political Praxis: An Introduction to Gramsci's Theory*. London: Routledge & Kegan Paul, 1981.

Salisbury, Joyce E. *Iberian Popular Religion 600 B.C. to 700 A.D.: Celts, Romans and Visigoths*. New York: Edwin Mellen Press, 1985.

Sangren, P. Steven. "Female Gender in Chinese Religious Symbols: Kuan Yin, Ma Tsu, and the 'Eternal Mother.'" *Signs* 9 (1983):4–25.

———. "Great Tradition and Little Traditions Reconsidered: The Question of Cultural Integration in China." *Journal of Chinese Studies* 1 (1984):1–24.

———. *History and Magical Power in a Chinese Community*. Stanford: Stanford University Press, 1987.

Saso, Michael. *Taoism and the Rite of Cosmic Renewal*. Seattle: Washington State University Press, 1972.

———. "Orthodoxy and Heterodoxy in Taoist Ritual." In Arthur P. Wolf, ed., *Religion and Ritual in Chinese Society*, pp. 325–36. Stanford: Stanford University Press, 1974.

———. *Blue Dragon, White Tiger: Taoist Rites of Passage*. Washington, D.C.: The Taoist Center, 1990.

Sax, William S. *Mountain Goddess: Gender and Politics in a Himalayan Pilgrimage*. New York: Oxford University Press, 1991.

Schipper, Kristofer M. "The Written Memorial in Taoist Ceremonies." In Arthur P. Wolf, ed., *Religion and Ritual in Chinese Society*, pp. 309–24. Stanford: Stanford University Press, 1974.

Schluchter, Wolfgang. *The Rise of Western Rationalism: Max Weber's Developmental History*. Berkeley: University of California Press, 1981.

———. *Rationalism, Religion, and Domination: A Weberian Perspective*. Berkeley: University of California Press, 1989.

Schmidt, Leigh Eric. *Consumer Rites: The Buying and Selling of American Holidays*. Princeton, N.J.: Princeton University Press, 1995.

Schmitt, Jean-Claude. *The Holy Greyhound: Guinefort, Healer of Children since the Thirteenth Century*. Cambridge: Cambridge University Press, 1983.

Schneider, Jane. "Spirits and the Spirit of Capitalism." In Ellen Badone, ed., *Religious Orthodoxy and Popular Faith in European Society*, pp. 24–53. Princeton, N.J.: Princeton University Press, 1990.

Schneider, Louis, and Sanford M. Dornbusch. *Popular Religion: Inspirational Books in America*. Chicago: University of Chicago Press, 1958.

Scholem, Gershom. *Major Trends in Jewish Mysticism*. New York: Schocken Books, 1961.

Schwartz, Benjamin I. "Transcendence in Ancient China." *Daedalus* 104 (Spring 1975): 57–68.

———. "Wisdom, Revelation and Doubt: Perspectives on the First Millennium BC." *Daedalus* 104 (Spring 1975):1–8.

Scott, James C. "Protest and Profanation: Agrarian Revolt and the Little Tradition," Part 1. *Theory and Society* 4 (1977):1–38.

Scribner, Robert W. "Religion, Society and Culture: Reorienting the Reformation." *History Workshop* 14 (1982):2–22.

———. "Interpreting Religion in Early Modern Europe." *European Studies Review* 13 (1983):89–105.

———. "The Reformation, Popular Magic, and the 'Disenchantment of the World.'" *Journal of Interdisciplinary History* 23 (1993):475–94.

———. "Elements of Popular Belief." In Thomas A. Brady Jr., Heiko A. Oberman, and James D. Tracy, eds., *Handbook of European History 1400–1600: Late Middle Ages, Renaissance and Reformation*, vol 1: *Structures and Assertions*, pp. 231–62. Leiden: E. J. Brill, 1994.

———. "Introduction." In Bob Scribner and Trevor Johnson, eds., *Popular Religion in Germany and Central Europe, 1400–1800*, pp. 1–15. London: Macmillan, 1996.

Selwyn, Tom. "Adharma." In T. N. Madan, ed., *Way of Life: King, Householder, Renouncer*, pp. 381–401. New Delhi: Vikas Publishing House, 1982.

Sen, K. M. *Hinduism*. Harmondsworth: Penguin, 1961.

Shahar, Meir. "Vernacular Fiction and the Transmission of Gods' Cults in Late Imperial China." In Meir Shahar and Robert P. Weller, eds., *Unruly Gods: Divinity and Society China*, pp. 184–211. Honolulu: University of Hawaii Press, 1996.

Shahar, Meir, and Robert P. Weller. "Introduction." In Meir Shahar and Robert P. Weller, eds., *Unruly Gods: Divinity and Society in China*, pp. 1–36. Honolulu: University of Hawaii Press, 1996.

Sharma, Arvind. "Some Misunderstandings of the Hindu Approach to Religious Plurality." *Religion* 8 (1978):133–54.

Sharot, Stephen. *Judaism: A Sociology*. Newton Abbot: David & Charles, 1976.

———. *Messianism, Mysticism, and Magic: A Sociological Analysis of Jewish Religious Movements*. Chapel Hill: University of North Carolina Press, 1982.

———. "Religious Fundamentalism: Neo-Traditionalism in Modern Societies." In Bryan Wilson, ed., *Religion: Contemporary Issues*, pp. 24–45. London: Bellew Publishing, 1992.

Shils, Edward. "Some Observations on the Place of Intellectuals in Max Weber's Sociology, with Special Reference to Hinduism." In S. N. Eisenstadt, ed., *The Origin and Diversity of Axial Age Civilizations*, pp. 427–52. Albany: State University of New York Press, 1986.

Shulman, David. "Asvatthaman and Brhannada: Brahmin and Kingly Paradigms in the Sanskrit Epics." In S. N. Eisenstadt, ed., *The Origins and Diversity of Axial Age Civilizations*, pp. 407–26. Albany: State University of New York Press, 1986.

Silber, Ilana Friedrich. *Virtuosity, Charisma, and Social Order: A Comparative Sociological Study of Monasticism in Theravada Buddhism and Medieval Catholicism*. Cambridge: Cambridge University Press, 1995.

Skocpol, Theda. *States and Social Revolutions*. Cambridge: Cambridge University Press, 1979.

Skorupski, John. *Symbol and Theory*. Cambridge: Cambridge University Press, 1976.

Smith, Richard J. "Ritual in Ch'ing Culture." In Kwang-Ching Liu, ed., *Orthodoxy in Late Imperial China*, pp. 281–310. Berkeley: University of California Press, 1990.

Smith, Robert J. *Ancestor Worship in Contemporary Japan*. Stanford: Stanford University Press, 1974.

Southern, R. W. *Western Society and the Church in the Middle Ages*. Harmondsworth: Penguin, 1970.

Southwold, Martin. "True Buddhism and Village Buddhism in Sri Lanka." In J. Davis, ed., *Religious Organization and Religious Experience*, pp. 137–52. New York: Academic Press, 1982.

———. *Buddhism in Life: The Anthropological Study of Religion and the Sinhalese Practice of Buddhism*. Manchester: Manchester University Press, 1983.

———. "Buddhism and Evil." In David Parkin, ed., *The Anthropology of Evil*, pp. 128–41. Oxford: Basil Blackwell, 1985.

Sperber, Jonathan. *Popular Catholicism in Nineteenth-Century Germany*. Princeton, N.J.: Princeton University Press, 1984.

Spierenburg, Pieter. *The Broken Spell: A Cultural and Anthropological History of Preindustrial Europe*. New Brunswick: Rutgers University Press, 1991.

Spiro, Melford P. *Burmese Supernaturalism*. Englewood Cliffs: Prentice-Hall, 1967.

———. *Buddhism and Society*. Berkeley: University of California Press, 1982 [1970].

Spufford, Margaret. "The Importance of Religion in the Sixteenth and Seventeenth Centuries." In Margaret Spufford, ed., *The World of Rural Dissenters 1520–1725*, pp. 1–18. Cambridge: Cambridge University Press, 1995.

Srinivas, M. N. "Sanskritization and Westernization." In Norman Birnbaum and Gertrud Lenzer, eds., *Sociology of Religion: A Book of Readings*, pp. 373–81. Englewood Cliffs: Prentice-Hall, 1969.

Srivastava, Vinay Kumar. *Religious Renunciation of a Pastoral People*. Delhi: Oxford University Press, 1997.

Stark, Rodney, and William Sims Bainbridge. *The Future of Religion*. Berkeley: University of California Press, 1985.

Stein, Rolf A. "Religious Taoism and Popular Religion from the Second to Seventh Centuries." In Holmes Welch and Anna Seidel, eds., *Facets of Taoism: Essays in Chinese Religion*, pp. 53–81. New Haven: Yale University Press, 1979.

Steinberg, David Joel, ed. *In Search of Southeast Asia*. New York: Praeger, 1971.

Stirrat, R. L. *Power and Religiosity in a Post-Colonial Setting*. Cambridge: Cambridge University Press, 1992.

Stock, Brian. *The Implications of Literacy: Written Language and Models of Inter-*

pretations in the Eleventh and Twelfth Centuries. Princeton, N.J.: Princeton University Press, 1983.

Strauss, Gerald. *Luther's House of Learning: Indoctrination of the Young in the German Reformation*. Baltimore: John Hopkins University Press, 1978.

Susuma, Shimazono. "The Living Kami Idea in the New Religions of Japan." *Japanese Journal of Religious Studies* 6 (1979):389–412.

Swallow, D. A. "Ashes and Powers: Myth, Rite and Miracle in an Indian God-Man's Cult." *Modern Asian Studies* 16 (1982):123–58.

Swanson, R. N. *Religion and Devotion in Europe c.1215–c.1515*. Cambridge: Cambridge University Press, 1995.

Szonyi, Michael. "The Illusion of Standardizing the Gods: The Cult of the Five Emperors in Late Imperial China." *Journal of Asian Studies* 56 (1997):113–35.

Tackett, Timothy. *Priest and Parish in Eighteenth-Century France: A Social and Political Study of the Cures in a Diocese of Dauphine 1750–1791*. Princeton, N.J.: Princeton University Press, 1977.

Talmon, Yonina. "Millenarian Movements." *Archives europeennes de sociologie* 7 (1966):159–200.

Tambiah, Stanley Jeyaraja. "The Ideology of Merit and the Social Correlates of Buddhism in a Thai Village." In E. R. Leach, ed., *Dialectic in Practical Religion*, pp. 41–121. Cambridge: Cambridge University Press, 1968.

———. *Buddhism and the Spirit Cults in North-East Thailand*. Cambridge: Cambridge University Press, 1970.

———. *World Conqueror and World Renouncer: A Study of Buddhism and Polity in Thailand against a Historical Background*. Cambridge: Cambridge University Press, 1976.

———. "The Renouncer: His Individuality and His Community." In T. N. Madan, ed., *Way of Life: King, Householder, Renouncer*, pp. 299–320. New Delhi: Vikas Publishing House, 1982.

———. *The Buddhist Saints of the Forest and the Cults of Amulets: A Study of Charisma, Hagiography, Sectarianism and Millennial Buddhism*. Cambridge: Cambridge University Press, 1984.

———. "From Varna to Caste through Mixed Unions." In *Culture, Thought and Social Action: An Anthropological Perspective*, pp. 212–51. Cambridge, Mass.: Harvard University Press, 1985.

———. "Purity and Auspiciousness at the Edge of the Hindu Context." In John B. Carman and Frederique Apffel Marglin, eds., *Purity and Auspiciousness in Indian Society*, pp. 94–108. Leiden: E. J. Brill, 1985.

———. "A Thai Cult of Healing through Meditation." In *Culture, Thought and Social Action: An Anthropological Perspective*, pp. 87–122. Cambridge, Mass.: Harvard University Press, 1985.

———. *Magic, Science, Religion, and the Scope of Rationality*. Cambridge: Cambridge University Press, 1990.

Taylor, Lawrence J. "Stories of Power, Powerful Stories: The Drunken Priest in Donegal." In Ellen Badone, ed., *Religious Orthodoxy and Popular Faith in European Society*, pp. 163–84. Princeton, N.J.: Princeton University Press, 1990.

Taylor, Romeyn. "Chinese Hierarchy in Comparative Perspective." *Journal of Asian Studies* 48 (1989):490–511.

———. "Official and Popular Religion and the Political Organization of Chinese Society in the Ming." In Kwang-Ching Liu, ed., *Orthodoxy in Late Imperial China*, pp. 126–57. Berkeley: University of California Press, 1990.

Tellenbach, Gerd. *Church, State and Christian Society at the Time of the Investiture Contest*. Oxford: Basil Blackwell, 1966.

———. *The Church in Western Europe from the Tenth to the Early Twelfth Century*. Cambridge: Cambridge University Press, 1993.

Tenbruck, Fredrich H. "The Problem of Thematic Unity in the Works of Max Weber." *British Journal of Sociology* 31 (1980):316–35.

Terwiel, B. J. "A Model for the Study of Thai Buddhism." *Journal of Asian Studies* 35 (1976):319–403.

———. *Monks and Magic: An Analysis of Religious Ceremonies in Central Thailand*. London: Curzon Press, 1979.

Thapar, Romila. "The Householder and the Renouncer in the Brahmanical and Buddhist Traditions." In T. N. Madan, ed., *Way of Life: King, Householder, Renouncer*, pp. 273–98. New Delhi: Vikas Publishing House, 1982.

Thomas, Keith. *Religion and the Decline of Magic*. Harmondsworth: Penguin, 1973.

Thompson, Lawrence G. *Chinese Religion: An Introduction*. Encino, Calif.: Dickenson Publishing, 1975.

Thompson, Stuart E. "Death, Food, and Fertility." In James L. Watson and Evelyn S. Rawski, eds., *Death Ritual in Late Imperial and Modern China*, pp. 71–108. Berkeley: University of California Press, 1988.

Tiryakian, Edward A., ed. *On the Margin of the Visible: Sociology, the Esoteric, and the Occult*. New York: John Wiley & Sons, 1974.

Trainor, Kevin. *Relics, Ritual, and Representation in Buddhism: Rematerializing the Sri Lankan Theravada Tradition*. Cambridge: Cambridge University Press, 1997.

Trimingham, J. Spencer. *The Sufi Orders in Islam*. Oxford: Clarendon Press, 1971.

Troeltsch, Ernst. *The Social Teaching of the Christian Churches*. New York: Harper & Row, 1960.

Turner, Bryan S. *Weber and Islam*. London: Routledge & Kegan Paul, 1974.

Turner, Victor, and Edith Turner. *Image and Pilgrimage in Christian Culture*. New York: Columbia University Press, 1978.

Tuveson, Ernest Lee. *Millennium and Utopia*. New York: Harper & Row, 1964.

Van Den Broek, R. "Popular Religious Practices and Ecclesiastical Policies in the Early Church." In Peter Hendrik Vrijhuf and Jacques Waardenburg, eds., *Offi-*

cial and Popular Religion: Analysis of a Theme for Religious Studies, pp. 11–54. The Hague: Mouton, 1979.

Van Der Veer, Peter. *Gods on Earth: The Management of Religious Experience and Identity in a North Indian Pilgrimage Center*. London: Athlone Press, 1988.

Van Engen, John. "The Christian Middle Ages as an Historiographical Problem." *American Historical Review* 91 (1986):519–52.

Vauchez, Andre. "The Saint." In Jacques Le Goff, ed., *The Medieval World*, pp. 313–45. London: Collins and Brown, 1990.

———. *The Laity in the Middle Ages: Religious Beliefs and Devotional Practices*. Notre Dame: University of Notre Dame Press, 1993.

Verbit, Mervin F. "The Political Character of Judaism and Islam: Some Comparisons." In Michael Curtis, ed., *Religion and Politics in the Middle East*, pp. 69–76. Boulder, Colo.: Westview Press, 1981.

von der Mehden, Fred R. *Religion and Modernization in Southeast Asia*. Syracuse, N.Y.: Syracuse University Press, 1986.

Waardenburg, J. D. J. "Official and Popular Religion as a Problem in Islamic Studies." In Pieter Hendrik Vrijhof and Jacques Waardenburg, eds., *Official and Popular Religion: Analysis of a Theme for Religious Studies*, pp. 340–86. The Hague: Mouton, 1979.

Wadley, Susan Snow. *Shakti: Power in the Conceptual Structure of Karimpur Religion*. Chicago: Department of Anthropology, University of Chicago, 1975.

Wadley, Susan S., and Bruce W. Berr. "Eating Sins in Karimpur." In McKim Marriott, ed., *India through Hindu Categories*, pp. 131–48. New Delhi: Sage, 1990.

Walter, Tony. *The Eclipse of Eternity: A Sociology of the Afterlife*. London: Macmillan, 1996.

Walter, Tony, and Helen Waterhouse. "A Very Private Belief: Reincarnation in Contemporary England." *Sociology of Religion* 60 (1999):187–97.

Walzer, Michael. *The Revolution of the Saints: A Study in the Origins of Radical Politics*. Cambridge, Mass.: Harvard University Press, 1965.

Ward, Barbara E. "Readers and Audiences: An Exploration of the Spread of Traditional Chinese Culture." In Ravindra K. Jain, ed., *Text and Context: The Social Anthropology of Tradition*, pp. 181–203. Philadelphia: Institute for the Study of Human Issues, 1977.

Warner, Marina. *Alone of All Her Sex: The Myth and the Cult of the Virgin Mary*. London: Pan Books, 1985 [1976].

Warner, Stephen R. "Work in Progress toward a New Paradigm for the Sociological Study of Religion in the United States." *American Journal of Sociology* 98 (1993):1044–93.

Waterstone, Richard. *India*. London: Duncan Baird, 1995.

Watson, James L. "Anthropological Analyses of Chinese Religion." *China Quarterly* 66 (1976):355–64.

———. "Standardizing the Gods: The Promotion of T'ien Hou ('Empress of

Heaven') Along the South China Coast, 960–1960." In David Johnson, Andrew J. Nathan, and Evelyn S. Rawski, eds., *Popular Culture in Late Imperial China*, pp. 292–323. Berkeley: University of California Press, 1985.

Watson, James L. "The Structure of Chinese Funerary Rites: Elementary Forms, Ritual Sequence and the Primacy of Performance." In James L. Watson and Evelyn S. Rawski, eds., *Death Ritual in Late Imperial and Modern China*, pp. 3–19. Berkeley: University of California Press, 1988.

Weber, Eugen. *Peasants into Frenchmen: The Modernization of Rural France 1870–1914*. London: Chatto & Windus, 1979.

Weber, Max. *The Protestant Ethic and the Spirit of Capitalism*. London: George Allen & Unwin, 1930.

———. "Science as a Vocation." In H. H. Gerth and C. Wright Mills, eds., *From Max Weber: Essays in Sociology*, pp. 129–56. London: Routledge & Kegan Paul, 1948.

———. "The Social Psychology of the World Religions." In H. H. Gerth and C. Wright Mills, eds., *From Max Weber: Essays in Sociology*, pp. 267–301. London: Routledge and Kegan Paul, 1948.

———. *The Methodology of the Social Sciences*. New York: Free Press, 1949.

———. *Ancient Judaism*. New York: Free Press, 1952.

———. *The Religion of India*. New York: Free Press, 1958.

———. *The Religion of China: Confucianism and Taoism*. New York: Macmillan, 1964.

———. *Economy and Society*. New York: Bedminster Press, 1968.

Weingrod, Alex. *The Saint of Beersheba*. Albany: State University of New York Press, 1990.

Weinstein, Donald, and Rudolph M. Bell. *Saints and Society: The Two Worlds of Western Christendom 1000–1700*. Chicago: University of Chicago Press, 1982.

Welch, Holmes. *The Parting of the Way: Lao Tzu and the Taoist Movement*. Boston: Beacon Press, 1957.

Weller, Robert P. *Unities and Diversities in Chinese Religion*. Seattle: University of Washington State, 1987.

———. "Matricidal Magistrates and Gambling Gods: Weak States and Strong Spirits in China." In Meir Shahar and Robert P. Weller, eds., *Unruly Gods: Divinity and Society in China*, pp. 250–68. Honolulu: University of Hawaii Press, 1996.

Whaling, Frank. "The Hindu Tradition in Today's World." In Frank Whaling, ed., *Religion in Today's World*, pp. 128–73. Edinburgh: T. & T. Clark, 1987.

Whiting, Robert. *The Blind Devotion of the People: Popular Religion and the English Reformation*. Cambridge: Cambridge University Press, 1989.

Wiebe, D. "The Prelogical Mentality Revisited." *Religion* 17 (1987):26–61.

Willey, Gordon R. "Mesoamerian Civilization and the Idea of Transcendence." *Antiquity* 199/200 (1976):205–15.

Williams, Peter W. *Popular Religion in America: Symbolic Change and the Modernization Process in Historical Perspective.* Englewood Cliffs: Prentice-Hall, 1980.

Wilson, Bryan. *Magic and the Millennium.* London: Heinemann Educational Books, 1973.

———. *Religion in Sociological Perspective.* Oxford: Oxford University Press, 1982.

———. "Introduction." In Bryan Wilson and Jamie Cresswell, eds., *New Religious Movements: Challenge and Response,* pp. 1–11. London: Routledge, 1999.

Wilson, Steven. "Introduction." In Steven Wilson, ed., *Saints and Their Cults: Studies in Religious Sociology, Folklore, and History,* pp. 1–53. Cambridge: Cambridge University Press, 1983.

Wilson, Thomas A. *Genealogy of the Way: The Construction and Uses of the Confucian Tradition in Late Imperial China.* Stanford: Stanford University Press, 1995.

———. "The Ritual Formation of Confucian Orthodoxy and the Descendents of the Sage." *Journal of Asian Studies* 55 (1996):559–84.

Wolf, Arthur P. "Introduction." In Arthur P. Wolf, ed., *Religion and Ritual in Chinese Society,* pp. 1–18. Stanford: Stanford University Press, 1974.

———. "Gods, Ghosts, and Ancestors." In Arthur P. Wolf, ed., *Studies in Chinese Society,* pp. 131–82. Stanford: Stanford University Press, 1978.

Woodside, Alexander. "State, Scholars and Orthodoxy: The Ch'ing Academics 1736–1839." In Kwang-Ching Liu, ed., *Orthodoxy in Late Imperial China,* pp. 158–84. Berkeley: University of California Press, 1990.

Wright, Arthur F. *Buddhism in Chinese History.* Stanford: Stanford University Press, 1959.

Wrightson, Keith, and David Levine. *Poverty and Piety in an English Village, Terling, 1525–1700.* New York: Academic Press, 1979.

Yang, C. K. *Religion in Chinese Society.* Berkeley: University of California Press, 1967.

Yinger, J. Milton. *The Scientific Study of Religion.* London: Macmillan, 1970.

Yu, Anthony C. "Religion and Literature of China: The 'Obscure Way' of the Journey to the West." In Ching-I Tu, ed., *Tradition and Creativity: Essays on East Asian Civilization,* pp. 109–54. New Brunswick: Transaction Books, 1987.

Yu, Chun-Fang. "A Sutra Promoting the White-Robed Guanyin as Giver of Sons." In Donald S. Lopez Jr., ed., *Religions of China in Practice,* pp. 97–105. Princeton, N.J.: Princeton University Press, 1996.

Zaret, David. *The Heavenly Contract: Ideology and Organization in Pre-Revolutionary Puritanism.* Chicago: University of Chicago Press, 1985.

Zito, Angela R. "City Gods and Their Magistrates." In Donald S. Lopez Jr., ed., *Religions of China in Practice,* pp. 72–81. Princeton, N.J.: Princeton University Press, 1996.

———. "City Gods, Filiality, and Hegemony in Late Imperial China." *Modern China* 13 (1987):333–71.

Index

About the Author

Stephen Sharot is a Professor of Sociology and Chairperson of the Department of Behavioural Sciences, Ben-Gurion University of the Negev, Israel. He is author of *Judaism: A Sociology* (Holmes & Meier, 1976), the award-winning *Messianism, Mysticism, and Magic: A Sociological Analysis of Jewish Religious Movements* (University of North Carolina Press, 1982), and co-author of *Ethnicity, Religion, and Class in Israeli Society* (Cambridge University Press, 1991).

He has also published many articles in collective volumes and journals on religion and ethnicity, especially on Judaism and Jewish ethnicity in Europe, the United States, and Israel. The journals in which he has published include *Comparative Studies in Society and History, International Sociology, British Journal of Sociology, Ethnicity and Racial Studies, Ethnic Groups, Journal for the Scientific Study of Religion, Sociological Analysis* (now *Sociology of Religion*), *Review of Religious Research,* and *Religion.*